QANON+

THE#PIZZAGATES
OF HELL

UNREAL TALES OF OCCULT
CHILD ABUSE BY THE CIA

MICHAEL J. CAT

Published by:
Trine Day LLC
PO Box 577
Walterville, OR 97489
1-800-556-2012
www.TrineDay.com
trineday@icloud.com

Library of Congress Control Number: 2022936296

Cat, Michael J.
Qanon and the #Pizzagates of Hell: Unreal Tales of Occult Child Abuse by the
CIA—1st ed.
p. cm.

Epub (ISBN-13) 978-1-63424-405-3
Print (ISBN-13) 978-1-63424-404-6
1. QAnon conspiracy theory -- United States. 2. Conspiracy theories -- Political
aspects -- United States. 3. Conspiracy theories -- United States -- Psychological
aspects.. 4. Social media -- Political aspects -- United States. 5. Truthfulness and
falsehood -- Political aspects -- United States -- History -- 21st century. 6. Abused
children -- Mental health. 7. Secret societies. I. Cat, Michael J. II. Title

Cover Design by: "Cornbelt Media, LLC"

FIRST EDITION
10 9 8 7 6 5 4 3 2 1

Distribution to the Trade by:
Independent Publishers Group (IPG)
814 North Franklin Street
Chicago, Illinois 60610
312.337.0747
www.ipgbook.com

Show me that eye which shot immortal hate,
Blasting the despot's proudest bearing;
Show me that arm which, nerv'd with thundering fate,
Crush'd Usurpation's boldest daring!-

–Robert Burns

To my family, for all of the love, support, and putting up with me.

CONTENTS

INTRODUCTION

"Dear neighbor," went the missive, jotted in black ink on 8.5 x 11 print-er paper, folded neatly and slipped through the mail slot on my sister's front door. "I do not know if you are aware of the Democrats they are full of ½ humans from the bloodline of Cain. Some are <u>clones</u> like Joe Biden. They support full-term abortion, which is a murder ritual to their 'God' Moloch or Baal it's passing they fetus 'thru the fire.' They are by Luciferian/Satanists most of them are pedophiles and also they eat human flesh – 'cannibalism' Right in LA Cali + Washington DC they have their own private restaurants that Katy Perry and Lady Gaga get served 'food' there."

It was summer 2020 and the U.S. presidential elections were just around the corner, with drum beating from either side already reaching fever pitches. The delusions manifesting from members of both parties had always clearly been detached from reality, but, this time, those emanating from the Republican camp took on a new color. While the Democrats relied on Cold War tropes of painting the opponent as a Soviet mole, there was a growing contingent of Republicans that combined evangelical hysteria with almost science-fiction details of transmutating creatures involved in an elaborate scheme to conjure hell on Earth.

Even if you didn't really know anyone from this bizarre group, it was impossible not to be exposed to it. My sister had just put up a lawn sign declaring support for Democratic candidate Joe Biden. Her home was lo-cated in a middle class development with a Home Owners Agreement that adhered to some basic standards of American normalcy, but not too many. The fact that her house was in such an enclave meant that the note delivered to her doorstep probably came from a neighbor.

"Democrats are not who they say they are or who you Think they are. Please note how many people have recently switched parties due to Awakening Truths," the note continued, albeit in a new handwriting. "Gitmo in Cuba – called 'Camp Justice'

Military tribunals happening right NOW. Lies under the guise of social justice. You are being lied to. Queen of England not in her own castle as she has been moved + will NEVER Be able to Return. No more Kings/Queen of England ->"

What began as a letter from a concerned citizen had quickly devolved into a stream of consciousness struggle to convey the sheer immensity and horror of the conspiracy at hand.

"Bush family are Nazi. Clintons are witches high level. She kills children. B. OBama is gay. (it's okay, I just do not like being lied to.) Michael is Michelle. 'Big Mike' born a man. Still has his genitals. Presents or lies she's a she. Did not carry or give birth to the girls. Malia + Nasatsha (I am Satan spelled backwards).

"Dr. They friends who are a married couple let them 'have' the kids for $$$$, 'borrowing' Look that up because they look identical to the bioparents."

As page two began, the words were no longer placed in the standard top-to-bottom format of a letter, but scrawled in various locations on the paper like concrete poetry. Nevertheless, the author or authors seemed to still understand that they were indeed trying to communicate with another person, their neighbor.

Oprah Winfrey is a bad person
Ellen is a bad person
Jimmy Kimmel is a bad person
Tom Hanks and Rita – 'bad' bad

The old female Melinda Gates already dead 2013. SATANIC GENDER inversion. It's not just transgender."

This final claim was written in a new ink color beneath a printed out Facebook post filled with a handful of memes about the Gates family. It included comments below the post from fellow travelers in the world now known as Qanon.

On its face, Qanon was absurd to the extreme: former game show host, billionaire, suspected rapist and president of the United States Donald Trump, supported by a cadre of government rebels, had a plan to arrest a group of satanic pedophiles that secretly ran the U.S. government and world affairs as a whole. That alone was enough to write the entire thing off as Internet culture gone wrong, the collective insanity of lonely, right-wing American Christians who could only find solace for their suffering through online conspiracy theories. Those ramblings were simply those of a person, persons, or entire family made deranged by a post-truth world and concerned with my sister's political leanings. But dismissing these people could have been exactly what *They* wanted us to do. Rather than have a laugh about the strange note or perhaps consider calling the police, we could have decided to enter that world and determine if any of it was real.

The #Pizzagate phenomenon that then morphed into Qanon led to some rather terrifying consequences in more ways than one. One believer shot up a pizza shop while hopped up on #Pizzagate. Another murdered an Italian mobster on his doorstep. One more drove a train off the rails and toward a docked ship, believing that the conspiracy had since evolved to include the COVID-19 pandemic.

What would have made the Qanon phenomenon more disturbing, however, would have been if its believers were actually correct: a global pedo cabal had been sacrificing our children to conjure the devil and hell on earth. Would you rather have been smugly right in assuming that these people were lunatics or would you have preferred to sleep soundly at night knowing that you and your loved ones were safe from the satanic child snatchers?

It obviously seems like a silly question, but the fact of the matter is that there was a small kernel of truth embedded in the discussions of the Qanon community that fueled the fire in its early stages: the existence of Jeffrey Epstein, an actual pedophile who was connected to some of the world's most powerful people, including presidents Bill Clinton and Donald Trump, billionaires like Bill Gates and Leslie Wexner, Israeli Prime Ministers Ehud Barak and Shimon Peres, and the British Royal family.

Knowing that Epstein did have ties to these people in power, one should have naturally begun to look further and, if one looked far enough, one would have begun to wonder just what the real story was. Given the fact that that a small aspect of the #Pizzagate phenomenon was true – that some of the world's power elite may have been involved in the trafficking of minors – was there even a small possibility that others might have been?

It was with this in mind that I began researching about these strange ideas that bubbled through the Qanon community, trying to separate fact from fiction. Actually, if I'm being honest, this project wasn't so much about documenting an obscure subculture with growing importance. I already had one foot in #Pizzagate and one foot in what might generally be called consensus reality. Having stumbled upon one too many conspiracy theories with varying degrees of truth, I had to figure out what the hell was going on. I mean, what was real and what was some delusional dream world.

I embarked on a journey through not only the Epstein case, but the United States' own history with satanic panics, pedophile rings, mind control, and intelligence operations. Coming out of it, I came to a tenuous conclusion that not all that I had sorted through was true. Satanic rituals? Multiple personality trained assassins? International child trafficking by the CIA? What was Project Monarch and was it real? It was all a bit too much to believe and I didn't believe all of it.

Fortunately, providing me with advice along the way was a group of fellow travelers I came to refer to as the Lone Gundam. They were willing to question the consensus reality, at times inviting me deeper into the darkness of Qanon and, alternatively, presenting the skepticism necessary to bring me back to my senses.

Here, I'd like to document some of that journey and attempt to distinguish the real, the false and the in-between.

DEEP POLITICS VS CONSPIRACY THEORIES

As I begin, I think it might be worthwhile to distinguish between two slightly different concepts: deep politics and conspiracy theories. The latter is typically dismissed as unhinged, baseless fantasy. It is exactly how something like #Pizzagate is portrayed. It's *X-Files*, paranoid popcorn theater and speculation.

Deep politics is a concept developed by University of California, Berkeley professor Peter Dale Scott that refers to "the constant, everyday interaction between the constitutionally elected government and subterranean forces of violence – forces of crime – that appear to be the enemies of that government." As an example of "deep politics," Scott described what has come to be known as the "Susurluk incident":

> In 1996 the crash of a speeding Mercedes on a Turkish highway near Susurluk opened a window into the darker side of Turkish politics, and eventually the darker face of globalization as well. Any one of the victims would have made the local news, but the biggest news was that they were traveling together. Found in the wreckage were the bodies of a member of Parliament, a former deputy police chief, a beauty queen, and her lover, a politically connected hero-

in trafficker and murderer named Abdullah Çatli. The intrigue was heightened by the contents of the car: a cache of narcotics, thousands of U.S. dollars, pistols with silencers, machine guns, and six different sets of official identity documents for Çatli, including a special "Green Passport" (for public officials) signed by the Turkish minister of the interior. The more the press researched this so-called Susurluk incident, the more complex it became. The name in Çatli's passport, Mehmet Özbay, was an alias that, according to Lucy Komisar, was also in the passport of the Turkish shooter of Pope John Paul II, Mehmet Ali Ağca. But what raised eyebrows was the seemingly incongruous presence of ... Abdullah Çatli riding with the top police and government officials. Police had supposedly been hunting Çatli, a convicted international drug smuggler since 1978, for his part in the killing of scores of left-wing activists (Scott, 2014, 1-3).

Scott went on to describe how Çatli had headed the neo-fascist death squad, the Gray Wolves, which the Drug Enforcement Administration (DEA) suspected of being part of a group advised by CIA officers. This program overlapped with the CIA and NATO's Gladio operation that conducted terrorist campaigns in Turkey and throughout Europe. It was exposed in the 1990s that CIA liaison officer Colonel Türks frequently pulled from the Grey Wolves to fill the ranks of a secret army used to execute violence, torture, and assassinations on behalf of the Turkish army.

While Trump popularized a "deep state" concept in U.S. politics (Abramson, 2017), more or less referring to the long-standing government and intelligence officials that ran state bureaucracy for the satanic pedophile cabal, it actually had its roots in Turkish politics. Scott explained:

In the extended discussions of the Susurluk incident, the concept emerged in Turkey of a deep state (gizli devlet or derin devlet) underlying the public state, consisting of a parastatal alliance between the official police and the criminal death squads they were supposed to round up. But there were clearly international as well as national aspects to the grey alliance represented by the Turkish deep state. In 1982 Çatli had entered the United States at Miami together with Stefano delle Chiaie, an Italian neofascist and killer with whom he had much in common. Delle Chiaie had his own connections to post-Gladio terrorist activities in Italy, to the World Anti-Communist League (WACL), and more specifically to death squads working for Chile's Operation Condor in Argentina and Bolivia. (Scott, 2014, 1-3)

5

Already as I begin, it seems clear that legitimate political ideas like the notion of a "deep state" have been co-opted, flattened and exaggerated by the likes of political or media personalities such as Trump. Any serious study of the operations of intelligence agencies in the U.S. and abroad reveals evidence of a "state within a state" or "deep state" that operates outside of democratic control. Scott provides his own example for the U.S.:

> [T]he CIA for most of its existence operated under a secret exemption from legal review of its actions. Although this arrangement was formally terminated after Watergate, a new agreement under Reagan exempted the CIA from the need to report allegations of drug trafficking involving nonemployees. One can say that once again the public state had been encroached on and eventually weakened by a deeper force. Thanks to revelations in 2007 in Colombia of ongoing political collusion between public politicians and drug-financed paramilitary death squads, the preferred term for such collusion now appears to be parapolitica (in Spanish) or (in English) parapolitics.
>
> The absence of checks and balances to restrain the CIA's recourse to lawlessness has led, predictably, to the proliferation of that lawlessness. The House of Representatives Intelligence Committee reported in 1996 that, in the CIA's clandestine services:
>
> > "...hundreds of employees on a daily basis are directed to break extremely serious laws of countries around the world in the face of frequently sophisticated efforts by foreign governments to catch them.... A safe estimate is that several hundred times every day (easily 100,000 times a year) operations officers engage in highly illegal activities (according to foreign law) that not only risk political embarrassment to the United States but also endanger the freedom if not lives of the participating foreign nations and, more than occasionally, of the clandestine officer himself.
> >
> > "Thus, the Susurluk incident, with its ingredients of state authority, sanctioned violence, crime, and narcotics, can stand as a memorable synecdoche for parapolitics (or deep politics) – not just in Turkey but throughout the world. (Scott, 2014)"

In recording deep political events, "deep events" as Scott called them (Scott, 2014), one must find as much evidence as possible, documentation, witness interviews and anything tangible that can be used to prove the existence of these machinations. Where this becomes difficult is in the criminal underworld and halls of power, wherein unaccountable individuals and organizations don't document their actions or, if they do, they then destroy or manipulate that documentation. In these cases, it is sometimes possible to make tenuous arguments that certain groups and people are associated with different illicit activities.

Regardless of what I present here or how I present it, I know there are some people who won't separate deep politics and conspiracy theory. There may be no smoking gun in most of what I've come across, but I can hold in my mind the possibility that specific details may be true and what their implications are. For instance, I can't say for certain that celebrities and politicians were involved sexually with the minors that Jeffrey Epstein trafficked, but I can consider the possibility that they did and what it means if the leaders of the U.S. and other countries were the clients of a notorious trafficker of young girls.

PART 1

THE PEDO CABAL

Comet Pizza, Washington, DC.
Farragutful, Creative Commons

CHAPTER ONE

WHAT IS #PIZZAGATE?

What would your vision of hell look like? Would it be dead souls poked and prodded, tormented with methods specifically tailored to their sinful vices on Earth? Homer Simpson force fed donuts by cartoon devils in silly red costumes. Or would it look like continuous physical and psychological torture applied to the members of our society least equipped to fight back? Would it occur in the dank bowels of our planet, the magnum core generating scorching flames in which sinners toil eternally? Or the corridors of bureaucratic institutions, dented and stained linoleum, concrete floors, old fluorescent lights flickering overhead?

My vision of hell was our reality pulsating with blood and digestive fluids – a gelatinous blob that breathed in and out in and out. As I ventured the unstructured hallways, I might walk through an old Victorian home one minute, floorboards creaking with each step, and then into this sticky translucent mess the next, pink and purple lights shining dull from the other side of the thick goo. It was reality, the physical world along with the psychological one. The biosphere combined with the noosphere. As beautiful as it seemed to be for me most of the time, there was a permanent suffering that occurred – a suffering that didn't need to take place in a rational, loving existence. As beautiful as it was for me, it was a living hell.

I remember rocking our second, newborn son, Misha, to sleep around midnight. As I held him in my arms to slumber so my wife, Cindy, could get some rest between feedings, I found myself watching a bizarre video (Burners.Me, 2019). A writer and podcaster, Tracy Twyman, was saying that she was investigating the death of a very minor Hollywood actor named Isaac Kappy (Khalaj, 2019). Kappy, who'd been in the movies *Thor* and *Terminator Salvation*, had begun accusing Hollywood stars of pedophilia. Seth Green and his wife, in particular, had a secret dungeon for keeping children in their home, according to Kappy (Haney, 2019). He went on to say that Tom Hanks, Michael Jackson and Steven Spielberg were pedophiles akin to Jimmy Savile in Britain (TFPP Wire, 2019).

Then he fell from a bridge near Belmont, Arizona in May 2019. The death was ruled a suicide (Griffith, 2019).

Twyman said she'd discovered what she thought was a "creepy" campground in Williams, Arizona and that, when Kappy learned about the location, she believed he went to investigate it. He died soon after. Then, when Twyman posted a video on YouTube supposedly exposing child trafficking, she said she started receiving messages from the campground owner threatening her and her son. This same Arizona psycho took credit for hacking her computer, hijacking it and turning it into a mind control device tailored directly to her own psyche (Burners.Me, 2019).

The 27-minute video was the result of a "dead man's switch," that is it was meant to be published in the event of Twyman's own death, which reportedly occurred in July 2019. This was two months after Kappy's life ended and probably less than a month after my second son was born. And when it was the middle of the night and I was delirious from taking care of a newborn, it appeared so real. It wasn't, to use the term of people in Twyman's circle of conspiracy investigators, a "LARP" – some live action role play where the players actually dressed and acted out their characters' personas and lived out the plot of a game (Drachen, 2006).

While I tried to retain some skepticism, I half-believed the whole Kappy and Twyman story, even when no obituary for Twyman seemed to show up online for the next several months. The truth of the matter was that – borrowing another term from the #Pizzagate community, which took the phrase from the men's rights activists, who got it from the 1999 blockbuster film *The Matrix* – I was being "redpilled," seeing how the world "really" was, just as Keanu Reeves' character had (Sharlet, 2015).

How had I gotten to this point? Probably like most of the world, the 2016 election had thrown me for a loop. The preceding campaign season was a bizarre one, with the rhetoric from the Democratic and Republican camps dirtier than usual. It also featured strange interventions into the campaigns from outside forces, such as the director of the FBI (Apuzzo et al., 2016).

As candidate Hillary Clinton was attacked for her use of a private email server and what occurred in Benghazi, Libya while under her tenure as Secretary of State (Gass et al., 2016), real or imagined, a tape recording of a conversation between Donald Trump and Billy Bush released October 7, 2016 revealed that presidential candidate's attitude toward women and willingness to sexually assault them (David, 2016). This appeared to be the October surprise that would ruin his chances at winning the election – that was until Clinton had her own, stranger surprise.

On the message board site 4chan, where users posted using anonymous strings of letters, an account that called itself FBIAnon was clearly operating for the benefit of the Trump campaign. In October 2016:

> The task is this: unleash every meme, image, and horrible story about HRC that you can muster.... In order to be effective, you must proselytize.... For example: Start a website aggregating the images/facts and then try to get it linked to Drudge. Shove the images down every news anchor/journalists throat. Push out to people who you normally would have nothing to do with.... Why don't you invade their circles?... We should be spreading memes to subs on Reddit ... blitz Twitter, Tumblr, and all social media with memes on the Clinton Foundation tonight, the last night of the DNC.... We need TrumpGen with us, and the meme division blasting the Tumblr tags. Bring up the old methods that /b/ used to use during their Tumblr raids.... We're going to war tonight ... Repeat something often enough and it becomes the truth. Repeat after me: "Hillary is evil and will destroy the planet..."

The user also had some premonition about an event that was about to take place, saying, "More leaks will come. The time is not right yet. Expect an October Surprise." On October 17, 2016, 30 minutes after the Access Hollywood tape was published, WikiLeaks began publishing a trove of emails taken from the account of Clinton's campaign manager, John Podesta (Stein, 2016).

The emails included extensive information truly relevant to the problematic operations of the Clinton campaign, such as a possible quid pro quo between Clinton and the king of Morocco, her coziness with Wall Street that implied she may have been lying to the public about how the government deals with the finance industry, and the fact that Clinton was fed a question during her primary debates with Bernie Sanders (Stein, 2016).

However, more important than the actual incriminating evidence in the emails was something far more sinister. Once the emails were published, FBIAnon posted, "When you are reading Podesta's e-mails, remember that the Clintons deal in weapons, drugs, and people. Some terminology in use is far more nefarious than many of you suspect."

Meanwhile Internet sleuths were poring through Podesta emails for anything criminal. On November 2, 2016, a 4Chan post by anonymous user "qymNxRx3" was published with the thread title "PODESTA IS A FUCKING PEDO" (Silverman, 2016). It highlighted an August 8, 2009 email to John Podesta from Doug Band, chief advisor to Bill Clinton and involved in the Epstein scandal via Clinton. The email featured Band writing, "As John said, it doesn't get any better than this" along with a photo of two Asian women, Laura Ling and Euna Lee, eating pizza with Ling's six-year-old daughter (WikiLeaks, 2016). The women were arrested while investigating human trafficking in the Democratic People's Republic of Korea in March 2009 and released with the assistance of Bill Clinton August 5, 2009 when Clinton went to North Korea and flew them back to the United States (Lee, 2009).

qymNxRx3 instead interpreted the photo as women "showing off wares to Podesta and Hillary's high level staff." The term "cheese pizza" has at times been used as a reference for "child pornography" (both are abbreviated "CP"), but that alone wasn't enough to drive the theories that would emerge (OnSamander, 2017).

The next morning an anon with the ID "bU74pXJK" posted a thread titled 'Podesta/Pizza PAC Investigation Thread 15', mentioning James Alefantis and his Comet Ping Pong for the first time, which would come to play an important role in the #Pizzagate saga (Archiga, 2019). This thread was quickly updated with a picture of Wikileaks founder Julian Assange, and the following words:

> "Search for these possible doublespeak keywords in Wikileaks
> "hotdog" = boy
> "pizza" = girl
> "cheese" = little girl
> "pasta" = little boy
> "ice cream" = male prostitute "walnut" = person of colour
> "map" = semen
> "sauce" = orgy"

A Reddit thread posted by user tidus8922 played on hot dog references in the emails with the thread "Todd D. Stern dreams about John Podesta's 'Hotdog stand in Hawaii…'," with an email laid over a skinny person wearing a complete leather S&M suit (tidus8922, 2016).

The day after qymNxRx3's post, this coded list was spreading like wildfire across Internet forums, with agent provocateur and Trump supporter Mike Cernovich tweeting:

> ""I'm dreaming about your hotdog stand in Hawaii"
> This is code for something. Sex trafficking?
> https://wikileaks.org/podesta-emails/emailid/30231"

Meanwhile a separate development related to the spouse of Clinton aide Huma Abedin, Anthony Weiner, was unfolding that would greatly amplify the "discoveries" of web users. On August 28, 2016 the *New York Post*, run by Trump ally Rupert Murdoch, reported that Weiner had sent sexual text messages ("sexts") to another woman, which included a picture of himself with a semi-erect penis and lying in bed next to his toddler son. A month later, *The Daily Mail* ran a story saying that Weiner had sent sexts to a 15-year-old girl (Goodman, 2016). In turn, the New York Police Department confiscated a laptop that belonged to him and Abedin (Jarrett, 2016). This prompted FBI Director James Comey to reopen an investigation into Clinton's use of a personal email server with the belief that there may have been some of the emails deleted by Clinton on this laptop (Apuzzo et al., 2016).

On November 4, 2016, Erik Prince, founder of private mercenary firm Blackwater and an ally of Trump, told the Breitbart News Daily radio program that he had "well-placed sources" in the NYPD claiming that the police had found 650,000 missing emails that suggested extensive illegal activity by Clinton.

"They found State Department emails. They found a lot of other really damning criminal information, including money laundering, including the fact that Hillary went to this sex island with convicted pedophile Jeffrey Epstein. Bill Clinton went there more than 20 times. Hillary Clinton went there at least six times," Prince said.

He went on to claim, "There is all kinds of criminal culpability through all the emails they've seen of that 650,000, including money laundering, underage sex, pay-for-play, and, of course, plenty of proof of inappropriate handling, sending/receiving of classified information, up to SAP level Special Access Programs (Hayward, 2016)."

As researchers continued combing the emails for more allusions, they noticed strange exchanges. Podesta and his friends and colleagues seemed to discuss pizza in bizarre ways, sometimes in reference to children. One of the first emails these researchers were drawn to was addressed to Podesta with the subject "Did you leave a handkerchief" and read:

"Hi John,

The realtor found a handkerchief (I think it has a map that seems pizza-related. Is it yorus? They can send it if you want. I know you're busy, so feel free not to respond if it's not yours or you don't want it.
Susaner (WikiLeaks, 2016)"

15

A handkerchief with a pizza-related map on it? They then came across an email from Tamera Luzzatto, Chief of Staff to Hillary Clinton during her time as Senator from New York, that read, "With enormous gratitude to Advance Man Extraordinaire Haber, I am popping up again to share our excitement about the Reprise of Our Gang's visit to the farm in Lovettsville. And I thought I'd share a couple more notes: We plan to heat the pool, so a swim is a possibility. Bonnie will be Uber Service to transport Ruby, Emerson, and Maeve Luzzatto (11, 9, and almost 7) so you'll have some further entertainment, and they will be in that pool for sure. And with the forecast showing prospects of some sun, and a cooler temp of lower 60s, I suggest you bring sweaters of whatever attire will enable us to use our outdoor table with a pergola overhead so we dine al fresco (and ideally not al-CHILLo) (WikiLeaks, 2016)."

She appeared to be suggesting that some children would be brought as entertainment to the Podestas' heated pool party on a farm. Perhaps innocuous, but, at one point, Luzzato had a personal blog that noted:

> Evelyn is growing up, soon she will be the Queen of the entire U.S. of A, right now, for a limited time only, you can spend some time with her online, raw and uncut. Take advantage of this now, as in the future she will have the power of life and death over you (the-jazzcat, 2018).

Sure, it could have simply been a strange way for a grandma to talk or it could have been a reference to a product she was trafficking.

In total, there were 149 references to "pizza" and 78 to "pasta" with which they began interpreting using the food-based code. Emails scrutinized by #Pizzagaters included the following:

- January 6, 2014: from Tony Podesta to John: "Mary not free. Would love to get a pizza for an hour? Or come over."

- December 24, 2015: from John Podesta to Herb Sandler of the Sandler Foundation, Christmas Eve: "Ps. Do you think I'll do better playing dominos on cheese than on pasta?"

- March 1, 2015: Jennifer Palmieri to John Podesta: "Suffice to say we will not make it tonight, I am sad to say. Have to settle for the pasta John gave us at Christmas."

- September 29, 2015: Tony to John Podesta, cc'ing hkliegman@podestagroup: "The menu for Tuesday. Do you know what pasta you're doing? See you tonight?"

- April 11, 2015: Jim Steyer to John Podesta: "Walnut sauce for the pasta? ... was the sauce actually very tasty? (WikiLeaks, 2016)"

After reading into a variety of foods mentioned in Podesta's emails, web users began to explore beyond the leaks. Emails released by the elite intelligence firm Stratfor, for instance, contained their own odd references to pizza, including an Excel sheet about "pizza analysis," as well as an email discussing the division of a single slice of pizza (WikiLeaks, 2012).

It was in this investigation that #Pizzagaters also came across some odd practices on behalf of the Democratic elite. For instance, lobbyist Tony Podesta, John's brother, was a huge art collector, which was normal for the wealthy and powerful (Wainman, 2015). What was less normal was the type of art. For instance, it included the work of Biljana Djurdjevic, a painter known for depicting near-nude children being abused, including being hung from ropes or tied up.

A 2004 *Washington Post* described Tony Podesta's Margi Geerlinks collection as including "a boy seemingly born from a sewing machine ... a young girl knitting her own hair [and] a naked woman immersed in blood-red liquid." It also described "pictures of naked teenagers in their parents' suburban homes" from Guggenheim-hosted artist Katy Grannan that caused some guests of the Podestas to feel "horrified" (Dawson, 2004).

#Pizzagaters pointed to a "subterranean vault" meant for projecting multimedia works on massive white walls as an underground dungeon or perhaps tunnel complex for transporting children (Hooper, 2004).

John Podesta had at least one similarly creepy painting hanging at his office at Hillary Clinton's Brooklyn headquarters. Dubbed "We're Bringing An Old Friend Over For Dinner," the work showed a Podesta-looking figure in a suit laying on a dining room table beneath two men with knives and forks.

The Podestas were also friends with Dennis Hastert, an actual pedophile, former U.S. House Speaker during the presidency of Bill Clinton, for whom John Podesta was chief of staff. Due to the statute of limitations on some of his crimes, Hastert was sentenced to just 15 months in prison for being a "serial child molester" (Coen, 2016). The day the indictment was announced John Podesta was sent an email from Jake Siewert, a former Clinton and Obama official, noting, "Might be time for Denny to vanish to an undisclosed Japanese island (WikiLeaks, 2016)."

This seemed to be a reference to the island of Osaka, where, in 1965, Tony Podesta and Hastert attended the "People to People Student Ambassador Program" with future Japanese ambassador for global environmental affairs Masahiko Horie at something called Camp Nose (Hastert, 2004). In addition to the strange reference to the Japanese island, it was odd that the Podestas, Hastert, and Horie rose to such prominent positions, perhaps speaking to their important backgrounds or the role Camp Nose played in their future.

Other key details of the early #Pizzagate story included those related to James Alefantis, the owner of Comet Ping Pong Pizza in Washington D.C. and ex-boyfriend of David Brock, a key member of Hillary Clinton's campaign team. Named by *GQ* magazine in 2012 as one of the 50 most powerful people in Washington, D.C., Alefantis had an Instagram account of questionable taste.

- A young girl, arms taped to a table at Comet Ping Pong, a man standing behind her. Text along with the photo read, "New seating area / procedure for your youngest guests? Hilar."

- A photo of Kate Moss, possibly in her early 20s, topless.

- A picture of performance artist Marina Abramović carrying firewood, with the text, "#faggot Marina and Faggot."

- A baby's face and the text "#hotard"

- A man with a baby and the hashtag "#chickenlovers." "Chicken" had been used in the underground sex scene dating back to at least the 1960s to mean a young boy, often under age.

- At Tony Podesta's home, beneath a sculpture called "The Arch of Hysteria" by Louise Bourgeois. The piece was a human figure with their body in a painful arch, based on photos and drawings from two pages of a late 19th century book *Invention of Hysteria* by French neurologist Jean-Martin Charcot. The pose, however, was reminiscent of the victims of cannibal Jeffrey Dahmer, according to #Pizzagaters.

- Numerous pictures of children

- Alefantis at the Whitney Museum in front of an image from Jeff Koons' "Made In Heaven" series titled "Ilona's Asshole." It depicted Koons's penis being inserted into the vagina of his then-wife, Italian adult film actress Cicciolina. The pornogrpahic art was juxtaposed with a nearby sleeping guard (rebelskum, 2017).

What made this last image more notable was that Ilona Staller fled the U.S. with her two-year-old son, Ludwig, in violation of a U.S. court order.

During a custody battle with the artist, Staller claimed that Koons was physically and emotionally abusive. Moreover, she alleged that Koons had slept with Ludwig in the nude (Saxe, 1994).

Koons then went on to become a member of the Board of Directors of the International Centre for Missing & Exploited Children (ICMEC), dedicated to fighting child sexual exploitation, child pornography, and child abduction. The artist later established the ICMEC Koons Family Institute on International Law and Policy, the International Centre's research arm (ICMEC, n.d.). The ICMEC was the international version of the U.S.'s own National Center for Missing & Exploited Children (NC-MEC), a non-profit that was the de facto arm of the Department of Justice dedicated to tracking missing children (Office of Juvenile Justice and Delinquency Prevention, 2020).

Joshua Ryan Vogelsong, a DJ and bartender for Comet, had an even more questionable Instagram account, where he posted such explicit sexual content as:

- Pizza slices covering genitals with phrases like "Cum visit!"

- Two men sexually drooling over a pizza slice with the comment, "We're about to get pounded!"

- Artwork of a couple having sex on top of a slice of pizza (van der Reijden, 2017).

There was nothing overtly criminal about the Instagram of Alefantis or his employee, but it was definitely of questionable taste for him to post graphic nudity and slurs as the owner of a "family friendly" pizza place.

#Pizzagaters also drew attention to the musicians who performed at the restaurant. One band, psychedelic rock group Heavy Breathing, used artwork that featured a man flipping the bird with both hands and bent over naked, anus and penis on display, with the latter dripping a fluid. In one live video of a Heavy Breathing concert, the keyboardist was dressed up as the extraterrestrial "Majestic Ape" and had the following exchange with an audience member:

Majestic Ape: Jerry is known to hang out down here.

Audience member: Jerry!

Majestic Ape: He likes the world's sounds to [inaudible] …

Audience member 1: and little boys!

Audience member 2: and children!

Majestic Ape: I think that was his manager.

Audience member 1: Noooo!

(Audience laughs)

Majestic Ape: We all have preferences... (laughs in a sinister manner.)

(Audience laughs.)

Another video of the band at "a comedy roast for a friend on her 30th birthday, an event which happened to be held at the Comet" saw Majestic Ape tell the audience how obnoxious children were and said she had to "put a kid down: euthanasia! (van der Reijden, 2017)"

This all could be chalked up to the "edgy" aesthetic cultivated by/for Gen X, but a December 13, 2007 YouTube Christmas message from Majestic Ape was somewhat more explicitly disturbing. The clip began with faces morphing in between cuts of flickering images of bugs, torture, an occult ritual, the Earth surrounded by an esoteric language, a goblin holding a young girl, children, kids exhibited as pizza slices and candy ("hard candy" was another code word for child pornography), and continuous flashes of the billionaire new age guru Sathya Sai Baba, credibly accused of pedophilia (van der Reijden, 2017). Sai Baba's pedophillic acticities purportedly included participation by prominent Indian government officials, such as prime minister Atal Bihari Vajpayee. The FBI and U.S. State Department declined to investigate these accusations, claiming not to want to hurt diplomacy with India (van der Reijden, 2017).

Majestic Ape then relayed a story called "The Neutered Noel" about "a college turd with a Jewfro" who masturbated while watching "America in Peril," a 1995 speech by Mark Koernke about the New World Order (Koernke, 1995). Koernke was a far right conspiracy theorist associated with the extremely conservative John Birch Society and a frequent guest of Alex Jones' *InfoWars*. Majestic Ape explained that Neutered Noel could not produce semen and then followed with an announcement for the band's fourth album, Ghost Games.

As the #Pizzagate story evolved, the photos James Alefantis posted on Instagram came to be central in the narrative, as it was assumed that he was a pedophile serving "cheese pizza" to the elite of D.C. An FBI document containing a collection of symbols said to be calling signs for pedophiles was passed around the Internet and, like the word "pizza," was to become a decoder for interpreting the secret symbols of the child trafficking cabal (thejazzcat, 2018).

The Pizzagate community began seeing these signs everywhere in the physical world, including in the logos of several restaurants near to Comet Ping Pong (thejazzcat, 2018). The symbols were innocuous enough on their own, but when they began to fit into a grand narrative, they took on a new meaning. Used in isolation, a triangle could represent a slice from Besta Pizza, but when sat next to Comet and across from a bistro that featured one of these FBI symbols all within the same area of D.C. where Democratic elites operated, dots that would have otherwise remained unconnected took on a disturbing new picture.

What seemed like a collection of odd, sometimes even mildly suspicious paraphernalia was occasionally given some credence when real dirt was uncovered. For instance, the Pizzagate investigators discovered early on that the Clintons were linked to a woman named Laura Silsby-Gayler, who attempted to kidnap children from Haiti after the 2010 earthquake. While she and her organization, New Life Children's Refuge, claimed to be transporting orphans to a hotel for shelter, it was learned that most, if not all of the children, were not orphans (Katz, 2010).

Emails found in the leaked emails of Hillary Clinton showed that Secretary of State Clinton was regularly sent updates about Silsby-Gayler's story (WikiLeaks, 2016). Silsby-Gayler was let off the hook when former President Bill Clinton intervened on her behalf (Delva, 2010). She would go on to work for the Alertsense program, dedicated to the finding of missing children through an immediate notification system (AlertSense, 2016) . All of this naturally raised suspicions among an already suspicious online community.

Additionally, the acting head of U.N. peacekeeping in Haiti at the time, Edmund Mulet, had previously been accused of involvement in an "adoption ring" in Guatemala in the 1980s. Mulet was accused of generating paperwork, including tourist visas, for children purchased from biological parents so that adopting couples could take them back to their home country of Canada (Crespo, 2015).

Another story that had some more substantial evidence, but was not at all directly related to the Clintons, was that of João Teixeira de Faria, also known as "John of God," a Brazilian faith healer who received substantial media attention in the 2000s for the use of herbs and "spiritual surgery" to cure ailments. Faria was hosted on *The Oprah Winfrey Show* on two separate occasions (Oprah.com, 2010). During the various media programs focusing on the healer, his powers were provided with greater credibility than would have been scientifically acceptable. For instance,

21

professional skeptic James Randi criticized ABC News for cherry-picking his own comments on Faria to make the faith healer's abilities seem legitimate (Randi, 2005).

In 2019, Faria faced 600 accusations of sexual abuse and rape and was ultimately sentenced to 63 years and 4 months in prison (Nogueira 2019). Among the women who brought Faria's actions to light was Sabrina Bittencourt. The Brazilian activist additionally claimed that Faria ran farms dedicated to producing infants sold to childless couples around the world for £40,000 (Shakhnazarova 2019). Victims had reportedly said that Faria paid poor girls between 14 and 18 years old to live in his mineral mines or on his farms to produce children for sale on the black market. Bittencourt was found dead in April 2019 in what was ruled a suicide (Dias 2019).

Oprah Winfrey said in response to Faria's December 2018 arrest, "I empathize with the women now coming forward and I hope justice is served (Boadle 2019)." The Pizzagate community then latched onto details about the talk show host that ensnared her in a larger pedophile cabal including the likes of Jeffrey Epstein. The numerous photographs of Winfrey with jailed movie mogul and rapist Harvey Weinstein painted her in a poor light when juxtaposed with news clippings of a time when Winfrey hosted 72 young South African girls for a sleepover party (Daily Mail 2012). This was only made worse when Internet sleuths learned of the sexual abuse scandals occuring at the Oprah Winfrey Leadership Academy in South Africa (Whatley 2017).

Eventually, Pizzagate found itself moving off of the web and into the physical world. After failing to recruit several friends to come with him, on December 4, 2016, a 28-year-old man named Edgar Maddison Welch, traveled from a small city in North Carolina to Washington, D.C. and used an AR-15 rifle to shoot three bullets into Comet Ping Pong, striking the walls, a door and a desk. No one was harmed as Welch surrendered to police. Having read online that the pizza shop had imprisoned child sex slaves, Welch reported to police that his strategy was to "self-investigate" the #Pizzagate theory and see if there were children being kept there. According to an interview with the *New York Times*, Welch said he regretted the way he dealt with the situation but wasn't ready to reject #Pizzagate altogether. Welch pled guilty to a federal charge of interstate transportation of firearms and a local charge of assault with a dangerous weapon. Along with the payment of $5,744.33 in damages, Welch was sentenced with four years in prison (Hsu 2017). Just three days later, a 52-year-old man named Yusif Lee Jones from Shreveport, Louisiana called Besta pizza threatening employees that he would "save the kids" and "finish what the other guy didn't" (USAO – District of Columbia 2017).

Obviously, there wasn't enough there to actually pin anything on Oprah, but it would be hard not to conflate her with Harvey Weinstein, John of God, and Jeffrey Epstein, particularly when Ghislaine Maxwell was photographed with so many celebrities and power brokers that it became impossible not to agree with the George Carlin line that "It's a big club and you ain't in it."

It would, however, seem that one individual in particular – or the forces benefitting that individual – had managed to protect himself from the growing belief that the world's power elite was really a satanic cabal of pedophiles. Either by being involved in the initial rumor mill of Pizzagate itself or by getting assets into the conversation early, Donald Trump had somehow been positioned on the right side of the story.

By the time Trump was elected president in 2016, the narrative was such that Trump was going to expose the pedophile ring and bring Clinton and her accomplices to justice. This was driven in large part by one story that would become one of the most important in modern U.S. history. As baseless as much of the Pizzagate hysteria appeared to be, it did have one detail right: there was an actual wealthy pedophile who seemed to be supplying children to the world's elite, including Bill Clinton.

Epstein last Mugshot, July 2019

CHAPTER TWO

JEFFREY EPSTEIN:
INTERNATIONAL PEDOPHILE OF MYSTERY

Though I read through the Podesta emails with political interest, the Pizzagate narrative had mostly remained at the periphery of my attention at first. I saw bubblings of pizza-related emails on social media, but wasn't bothered to learn more. However, there was one story that did catch my eye. It was an investigative report published by Julie Brown in the *Miami Herald* in November 2018. As soon as I saw the name Jeffrey Epstein, I recalled a story I'd heard on a progressive radio show years earlier about his exploitation of young girls and his exploits with powerful people. The depth of depravity and corruption of the case had me agitated and unable to sleep. I had no idea that this would be the first of many nights in which I would find myself immersed in the horrific world of the deep state.

Jeffrey Epstein was described as a billionaire financier who purportedly managed the funds of only one publicly known client, Les Wexner. Before stepping down in the wake of Epstein's 2019 arrest, Wexner was best known as the CEO of L Brands, which owned such notable companies as lingerie maker Victoria's Secret, and clothing companies Abercrombie & Fitch and the Limited (Ward 2011). Their relationship was so close that Wexner gave his New York City mansion, the largest in Manhattan, to Epstein in exchange for nothing monetary (Steel, et al 2019).

In July 2019, Epstein was arrested on federal charges for sex trafficking of minors and was meant to be brought to tria (Chaitin 2019)l, but was found dead on August 10, 2019 of what was ruled a suicide (Sisak 2019) – one more victim of the "Clinton body count," according to #Pizzagaters (Stockler 2019). This came just about 11 years after Epstein pled guilty in Florida state court of procuring a child for prostitution and of soliciting a prostitute (Goldsmith 2008).

The original 2008 case was filled with irregularities. For instance, when police first raided Epstein's Palm Beach mansion in 2006, much of the evidence appeared to have been already removed. Epstein's friends, an interior decorator, and architect Douglas Schoettle, were there when the raid occurred, and seemed unperturbed. The materials the police managed to get their hands on weren't a slam dunk for conviction. Some of Epstein's recording devices and computers were gone, cords left hanging when cops arrived. Had Epstein been tipped off? "The place had been cleaned up," former detective Michael Reiter later told NBC News (Cronin & Robertson 2020).

While it was clear that Epstein had friends within the Palm Beach department, due to his large donation to the force, just how much sway Epstein had within the justice system was displayed when the case concluded. Alexander Acosta, U.S. Attorney for the Southern District of Florida at the time, agreed to a plea agreement with Epstein, referred to in the media as a "sweetheart deal" because he was sentenced to just 18 months in prison. The victims in the case were not given an opportunity to voice their issues with the trial in court. More disturbing was the fact that the non-prosecution agreement granted immunity from all federal criminal charges to Epstein and four named co-conspirators, as well as any *unnamed* "potential co-conspirators." In other words, anyone found involved in Epstein's trafficking of minors could avoid any consequences (Brown 2018).

Among the co-conspirators was Ghislaine Maxwell (Nanan-Sen, 2020). Described at times as a former girlfriend of Epstein (ABC 7 News, 2021), Maxwell was the youngest daughter of the late media baron Robert Maxwell. A British socialite who fled the U.K. for the States when her father died mysteriously, Ghislaine was also Epstein's pimp.

Epstein served just 13 months in a Florida prison, but was permitted to go on "work release" 12 hours a day, six days a week. While reporting to prison at 8 PM nightly, his jail cell was left unlocked and he was provided upscale food that other inmates were not (Brown 2018). Upon serving his time, Epstein was able to circumvent his probation, meant to limit his location solely to his residence in Palm Beach. He was actually able to travel globally, including to his private island, Little Saint James in the U.S. Virgin Islands (SPARGO, 2019).

These were just some of many indications that Epstein may have been receiving some form of protection from on high. Certainly based on the company that he kept, one would not be faulted for believing he was well-connected. In addition to his sole financial client, Les Wexner, Epstein was known to socialize and work with some of the most important and well-known individuals in the world. Photos of him and Ghislaine

Maxwell with celebrities and power brokers were so numerous that they became an Internet meme. A list of individuals he or Maxwell had been known to consort with included:

- The Clinton Family
- The Trump Family
- The British Royal Family
- Woody Allen
- Alan Dershowitz
- Lawrence Krauss
- Bill Gates
- The Rothschilds
- Steven Pinker
- Keven Spacey
- Chris Tucker
- Larry Summers
- Ken Starr
- Mort Zuckerman
- Deepak Chopra
- Saudi crown prince Mohammed bin Salman
- Jeff Bezos
- Elon Musk
- former U.S. Virgin Islands Gov. John P. de Jongh
- Barclays CEO Jes Staley
- Apollo Global Management CEO Leon Black
- New Mexico Governor Bill Richardson
- Former U.S. Senator George Mitchell
- Asset manager Glenn Dubin
- Nobel Prize–winning physicist Murray Gell-Mann
- bestselling author and theoretical physicist Leonard Mlodinow
- MIT professor and artificial intelligence researcher Gerald Jay Sussman
- neuroscientist Christof Koch
- Nobel Laureate Frances Arnold
- Silicon Valley wunderkind Paul Kirkaas
- Prince Bandar of Saudi Arabia
- Tony Blair
- former Utah governor and Republican presidential candidate Jon Huntsman
- The Kennedys
- Henry Kissinger
- David Koch

- Former Israeli Prime Ministers Ehud Barak and Shimon Peres (Feinberg 2019, Levenson 2019, TruthStamps 2020, ROGERS 2019, Colyar et al. 2019)

They were also affiliated with such prestigious institutions and organizations as:

- The Council on Foreign Relations
- The Trilateral Commission
- Harvard University
- MIT University
- The Clinton Foundation
- Deutsche Bank
- Hewitt School, an elite private girls school in Manhattan
- the Film Society of Lincoln Center
- MET Orchestra Musicians
- New York Academy of Science
- Rockefeller University
- the Santa Fe Institute
- the Theoretical Biology Initiative at the Institute for Advanced Study
- the Quantum Gravity Program at the University of Pennsylvania (Jeffrey Epstein VI Foundation 2013, Sgueglia 2019, Briquelet 2019, Stewart 2020, Zimmerman 2016)

There was substantial evidence to suggest that Epstein wasn't trafficking minors to powerful people just to cement his position among them, but also in order to obtain blackmail footage, ostensibly to control them or milk favors from them when necessary. It had been made clear that Epstein's various homes were outfitted with cameras and audio recording devices and the FBI removed numerous CDs from the pedophile's New York mansion that were labeled with names of girls he trafficked and the high profile clients with whom they were engaged in compromising behavior (Stanglin 2019).

A HISTORY OF HONEYPOTS

This type of operation was known in espionage parlance as a "honeypot," in which someone was drawn into a compromising situation, which was then used to blackmail that individual. Journalist Whitney Webb, who became an expert on the Epstein story, documented just how pervasive honeypots had been in recent political and underworld history. The way that Webb lined up these cases suggested that there may have even been a direct lineage connecting them through the present and Epstein. Her accounting began with a name now associated with both the Seagram's liquor empire and the NXIVM sex cult: Bronfman (Webb 2019).

The Bronfman family began selling liquor during the prohibition era, taking advantage of Canadian loopholes to sell alcohol in its family-owned hotels and stores (Yarhi Published Online, n.d.)

The liquor was transported and sold to the U.S. with the help of the American crimnal gangs, who ultimately purchased the booze in immense quantities. Members of the National Crime Syndicate included such well-known Italian- and Jewish-American mobsters as Lucky Luciano and Meyer Lansky (Faith 2008).

Samuel Bronfman, as well as his key middleman Lewis "Lew" Rosenstiel, who would later come to be a leading Seagram's competitor, were extremely close to Lansky in particular, throwing lavish dinners for the Jewish crime lord regularly (Entrepreneur.com 2008). He would return the kindness with protection of liquor shipments and tickets to boxing matches, among other gifts. New York State legislative investigations claimed that Rosenstiel "was part of a 'consortium' with underworld figures that bought liquor in Canada [from Samuel Bronfman]." The investigations asserted that other members of this consortium included "Meyer Lansky, the reputed organized crime leader; Joseph Fusco, an associate of late Chicago gangster Al Capone, and Joseph Linsey, a Boston man Mr. Kelly [the congressional investigator providing the testimony] identified as a convicted bootlegger (Gage 1971)."

The consortium was also linked to the U.S. federal government in a number of ways. Rosenstiel, for instance, made Louis Nichols, a career assistant at the FBI, the Vice President of Schenley Industries, one of the four largest liquor companies at the time alongside Seagram's (Mitenbuler 2015).

Lansky, in addition to Lucky Luciano and their respective crime families, became allies of the American intelligence toward the end of World War II. Through Operation Underworld, the mob was enlisted ostensibly to spy on docks on the east coast of the U.S. for fear of Axis sabotage, but also to quell labor unrest (Newark 2007). Lansky would later be tapped by the CIA in various attempts to oust Cuban leader Fidel Castro using the mobster's assets on the island (Colhoun 2013).

Rosenstiel, the mob, and the feds were all involved in honeypot operations, as well. Rosenstiel's fourth wife, Susan Kaufman, declared that her ex hosted extravagant parties at such venues as Manhattan's Plaza Hotel and brought "boy prostitutes" Rosenstiel hired "for the enjoyment" of specific attendees, such as key government officials and prominent criminals. Kaufman said that the parties were bugged with microphones kept for blackmail purposes. Her testimony was deemed credible and corroborated by two independent witnesses at New York's State Joint Legislative Committee on Crime in the early 1970s (Summers 2013).

Lansky too operated a blackmail operation through his mistress Virginia Hill. Journalist Ed Reid wrote in his book *The Mistress and the Mafia* that Lansky directed Hill to Mexico to seduce "top politicians, army officers, diplomats and police officials (Reid 1972)." In time, Lansky was said to have gotten his hands on compromising photos of FBI Director J. Edgar Hoover "in some kind of gay situation" with FBI Deputy Director Clyde Tolson, according to a Lansky associate (Summers 2021).

The FBI director, who had attended numerous parties held by Rosenstiel, had his own collection of blackmail material, as is well known. Journalist Burton Hersh, suggested that Hoover was linked to Sherman Kaminsky, who operated a honeypot with young male prostitutes in New York. Though the Manhattan District Attorney uncovered the operation in a 1966 raid, photos of Hoover and Kaminsky together went missing from the evidence collection once the FBI got involved (Hersh 2008).

For the CIA, Robert Keith Gray, former chairman and CEO of D.C.'s Hill and Knowlton PR firm, conducted honeypot operations (Webb 2019), sometimes with the prominent lawyer Roy Cohn (DeCamp 2005). Gray was also an associate of another compromising CIA agent, Edwin Wilson, sitting on the board of Wilson's CIA front company Consultants International. CIA agent Frank Terpil told investigative journalist Jim Hougan about the blackmail operations Wilson performed:

> Historically, one of Wilson's Agency jobs was to subvert members of both houses [of Congress] by any means necessary.... Certain people could be easily coerced by living out their sexual fantasy in the flesh.... A remembrance of these occasions [was] permanently recorded via selected cameras.... The technicians in charge of filming ... [were] TSD [Technical Services Division of the CIA]. The unwitting porno stars advanced in their political careers, some of [whom] may still be in office (Hougan 1984).

According to Nebraska Senator John DeCamp, Roy Cohn, once the chief counsel for Senator Joseph McCarthy during the Red Scare and later a close friend and mentor of Donald Trump, took over Wilson's operations. Cohn was close to Lew Rosenstiel and ultimately hosted his own blackmail parties at the Plaza Hotel (Newton 2012). In fact, he was made to abandon the McCarthy hearings when he tried to blackmail members of the Army. He rebounded thanks to a friend of former CIA director Allen Dulles, David Peck, who helped him get a job at the New York law firm Saxe, Bacon and O'Shea. Cohn brought with him a number of Mafia clients, such as the Gambino and Genovese families, as well as Lew Rosenstiel (Talbot 2016).

Rosenstiel's ex-wife Susan Kaufman stated that Cohn, Hoover and her ex-husband engaged in sexual activity with minors at one of these blackmail parties. New York attorney John Klotz, who investigated Cohn much later, uncovered some details that corroborated the honeypot story. Klotz told Burton Hersh:

> Roy Cohn was providing protection. There were a bunch of pedophiles involved. That's where Cohn got his power from – blackmail (Hersh 2008).

According to former NYPD detective James Rothstein, once head of the department's Human-Trafficking and Vice-Related Crimes Division, Cohn admitted executing a honeypot scheme that captured evidence of politicians with child prostitutes. Rothstein recounted to former Nebraska state Senator John DeCamp:

> Cohn's job was to run the little boys. Say you had an admiral, a general, a congressman, who did not want to go along with the program. Cohn's job was to set them up, then they would go along. Cohn told me that himself (DeCamp 2005).

When I traced the threads of these comprise activities, they were stitched from Lew Rosenstiel, Bronfman partner turned competitor, to Roy Cohn. Threads were further intertwined with the mob, in the form of Meyer Lansky, and the U.S. government, via J. Edgar Hoover and Edwin Wilson. They may have then tied to Jeffrey Epstein and Donald Trump.

By the time that Donald Trump bought the Plaza Hotel in 1988, it was said that "young women and girls were introduced to older, richer men" and "illegal drugs and young women were passed around and used (Gross 2016)."

Meanwhile, Epstein had been brought into the fold of a pro-Israeli group that also counted Cohn, the Bronfmans, Les Wexner, former CBS owner Laurence Tisch (who served in the Office of Strategic Services [OSS], the precursor to the CIA), director Steven Spielberg, and other prominent American Jewish businessmen among its members: the Mega Group (Webb 2019). The "philanthropy" organization, founded by Charles Bronfman and Wexner in 1991 (Skolnik & Berenbaum 2007), was made up of 20 of the richest and most powerful Jewish businessmen in the U.S. Its leaders branched across an array of Jewish, pro-Israel organizations such as the World Jewish Congress, B'nai B'rith, the Anti-Defamation League, the right-wing National Jewish Coalition, and the National Conference for Israeli and Jewish Rehabilitation (Webb 2019).

The Mega Group was not only firmly linked to the Israeli government, but also to Donald Trump. For instance, member Ronald Lauder, billionaire heir to the Estee Lauder cosmetics fortune, was a client of Roy Cohn and also a good friend of Trump (Haberman 2018).

Epstein's Intelligence Heritage

As news of Epstein's arrest erupted, I came across a handful of people online who had had a similar interest. In particular, I remembered a Canadian with the handle @ChalicothereX, who was engrossed in American deep politics, as among the first people I talked to about this. Soon, we connected with Theta, who seemed to have been immersed in Pizzagate since nearly the beginning. They also couldn't ignore the significance of a pedophile trafficking children to the world's elite.

As we embarked on our own separate explorations of the deep state, we began to exchange information about Epstein's connections. Sometimes, we came across strange coincidences. I think it was @housetrotter or @daveloach2 that discovered the fact that, while Trump acquired his yacht indirectly from Iran-Contra arms dealer Adnan Khashoggi (King 1991), Ghislaine's father Robert Maxwell bought his from Adnan's nephew, Emad Khashoggi (Maclean 2017). Sometimes, the information was more significant, like the fact that Adnan was also known to ply U.S. officials with young girls (Scott 2014). As our conversations continued, we called ourselves "the Lone Gundam" and my fellow Gundam would become invaluable in my personal investigation. I later learned that part of the reason any of these people had gotten into deep politics in the first place was Matt Kenner, the author of *Geohell: Imagining History in the Contemporary World*. They'd either befriended him online or read his book. In a way, he was the godfather to our clique. And, in fact, if I hadn't read *Geohell*, I might not have been open to parapolitics or even have met some of these people on the Internet. Though Matt had logged off Twitter years before, he had managed to bring us together. We all shared Webb's work and were impressed that anyone was covering this at all, even if it wasn't discussed in the mainstream.

However, the thread woven by Webb's research was not always the tightest. For instance, as much as I wanted to believe that the Bronfmans were executing compromise operations, her research more directly implicated Lew Rosenstiel. Moreover, Epstein's links to this lineage were also less clear. But there did seem to be a broader milieu that they all belonged to and members of this collective did operate honeypots.

With this milieu and its inclusion of Epstein in mind, it was possible for me to revisit Epstein's sweetheart deal with Alexander Acosta in a new light. According to Vicky Ward at *The Daily Beast,* when asked after Epstein's 2019 arrest what prompted his sweetheart deal, Acosta relayed to a former senior White House official, "I was told Epstein 'belonged to intelligence' and to leave it alone" (Ward 2019).

The *Miami Herald* reported that Epstein was an FBI informant, at the time that the bureau was under the control of Director Robert Mueller (Wieder & Hall 2020). It was believed that this may have had to do with Epstein's acting as a witness during the trial of two Bear Stearns executives in 2008. This, however, was not the intelligence that Acosta was referring to, as Epstein wasn't awarded this role until after agreeing to the plea deal.

Epstein was known to lie regularly about his life, but, according to a 2001 story by the *Evening Standard,* Epstein once claimed in the 1980s that he worked for the CIA, later changing his story and denying a CIA link (Rosser 2001). This wouldn't be altogether surprising, given charges that Epstein once handled some financial affairs for Adnan Khashoggi (Ward 2011).

I was hesitant to trust Epstein's own account, but he wasn't the only one calling him a spy. A former senior executive for Israel's Directorate of Military Intelligence, Ari Ben-Menashe, claimed that Epstein and Ghislaine Maxwell were working for Israeli intelligence as far back as the 1980s.

Ben-Menashe said in several interviews that he encountered Epstein while acting as the handler for Ghislaine's father, media mogul Robert Maxwell, on arms shipments from Israel to Iran as part of the Iran-Contra affair. According to Ben-Menashe, Epstein already had extensive connections in Israel. It was during that time that Epstein met Ghislaine, and Robert Maxwell had a paternal attitude toward Epstein as his daughter's relationship with him developed.

Ben-Menashe told James Robertson, one of the authors of *Epstein: Dead Men Tell No Tales*, "Maxwell introduced him to us, and he wanted us to accept him as part of our group.... Epstein was hanging around with Robert Maxwell and the daughter was hanging around there too, and that's how they met (Cronin & Robertson 2020, p. 45)."

In an interview with Zev Shalev, former CBS News executive producer and investigative journalist for the website *Narativ*, the Israeli spy said:

> Later on [Ghislaine] got involved with Israeli intelligence together with him. But not in this arms deal with Iran business.... These guys were seen as agents. They weren't really competent to do very much. And so they found a niche for themselves – blackmailing American and other political figures (Shalev 2020).

He also told Robertson:

> Mr. Epstein was the simple idiot who was going around providing girls to all kinds of politicians in the United States. See, fucking around is not a crime. It could be embarrassing, but it's not a crime. But fucking a fourteen-year-old girl is a crime. And he was taking photos of politicians fucking fourteen-year-old girls – if you want to get it straight. They would just blackmail people, they would just blackmail people like that (p. 45).

Philip Giraldi, a former CIA counterterrorism specialist, said that he had "little doubt" Epstein was managing an intelligence operation, which allowed him to evade justice. "There is no other viable explanation for his filming of prominent politicians and celebrities having sex with young girls," Giraldi put in an *American Herald Tribune* story in August 2019. "Epstein clearly had contact with former Israeli Prime Minister Shimon Peres and Ehud Barak and [Epstein's client Leslie] Wexner also had close ties to Israel and its government" (Cronin & Robertson 2020, p. 155).

I even went so far as to reach out to John Kiriakou, former CIA officer-turned-whistleblower who served time for revealing national security secrets while exposing the U.S. government's use of torture. I thought Kiriakou might have had interest in the story because he'd been inadvertently roped into the #Pizzagate narrative himself. According to a fringe website called Brighteon.com, he "blew the whistle" on elite child trafficking by the CIA (Ferkenhoff 2019). These sorts of sites mischaracterized his comments as the CIA "supplying children to elite pedophiles." In reality, the ex-spy provided a hypothetical situation during a panel at a peace conference. In the clip, Kiriakou noted:

"Your job as a CIA agent is to break the laws of the country you are serving. That's your job: Your job is to commit espionage, which in most countries is a death penalty crime.... Your job is to convince people to commit treason for you because they like you so much or they like the money that you're giving them so much. So, because it's the nature of your job to break the law, they're the rules that are written for you to carry out that job.... Now, the problem there is that most CIA officers would procure the child prostitute even if they felt funny about it. They would be told by headquarters, 'You have a job to do. Thi is a bona fide source here. Go and do your job.'"

The clip spread so quickly across #Pizzagate circles that the former CIA agent had to post comments on Facebook and Twitter, emphasizing, "Some fake news is circulating saying that I 'exposed an elite CIA pedophile ring.' This is simply not true. I know of no such ring, I never encountered pedophiles at the CIA, and I don't believe the CIA provides children to pedophile sources."

In an email to me, Kiriakou once again highlighted the fact that he'd never encountered any child trafficking in his line of work. Moreover, he believed blackmail was extremely rare and that the Agency educated its employees to stay away from it as a tactic:

"First, I'm *not* familiar with any procurement of children for anybody. Period. My point in that speech was that there was no rule against it. It was a matter of personal morality. I'm similarly unaware of this ever happening for the purpose of gathering blackmail material. To tell you the truth, we were always trained that blackmail was NOT the way to go in gathering information. The source would end up hating us for blackmailing him and the information would likely be unreliable," he wrote.

When presented with the example of J. Edgar Hoover, he replied, "I never, ever heard of anybody threatening a U.S. political figure in any way. Hoover had a monopoly on that. Remember, it's illegal for the CIA to collect information on Americans. Post-1975, there was no such collection. On the other hand, I did hear about the occasional officer using blackmail to threaten a source who was having second thoughts. Again, the Agency really didn't like doing that. They were always preaching to us that 'It's all about the relationship.' That's why we spent so much money on people. It was so much easier than blackmail."

"With that said, yes, I'm very familiar with CIA officers procuring women for sources," Kiriakou wrote. "Beyond that, many CIA officers accompany their targets and sources on sex trips to places like Bangkok and

Manila. One supervisor told me to take a source to Bangkok and to 'go ahead and get yourself a blowjob.' I told her 'Thanks, but I don't pay for pussy, and I'm not going to have the American taxpayer pay for it either.' Disgraceful. But that happens a lot."

As for Epstein, Kiriakou believed that he was most likely an Israeli spy. "I was convinced from the beginning of the Epstein saga that he was an agent of the Israelis. His entire life reads like an access agent operation. If you can't recruit a president of the United States or a former president, the next best thing is to recruit a friend of the president, like Epstein. Throw in underage girls and you force your target closer to your access agent. It was brilliant," he wrote.

When I asked if it would have been possible for an Israeli agent to run such an operation on prominent members of U.S. society, including presidents, without U.S. intelligence being aware of the situation, he replied in the affirmative, saying, "ABSOLUTELY. When I was first hired, the Director of Security told us that there were two 'declared' Israeli intelligence officers in the United States – one Mossad and one Shin Bet. But there were 189 'undeclared' officers that the FBI had been able to identify, all trying to collect intelligence on political figures, defense contractors, and scientists. The Israelis are on us like white on rice. They always have been" (Personal correspondence).

I was still hesitant to trust someone like Ben-Menashe, Giraldi, or even Kiriakou given the fact that, as spies, their jobs were to deceive. However, when I and the other Gundam turned to the history of Robert Maxwell, we found significant evidence of an intelligence connection, as well.

The patriarch of the Maxwell family was much more than a media giant who owned Pergamon Press, the British Printing Corporation, Mirror Group Newspapers and Macmillan Publishers, among others. He was also likely an asset of Israel's Mossad intelligence agency. He may have even worked for Britain's MI6, according to a strong collection of evidence put together by one Gundam who went by "@ElResisto" (@ElResisto 2019).

Born in Czechoslovakia, Robert Maxwell migrated to Britain in 1941, where he volunteered for the British Army, eventually making the rank of captain. His language skills having proven useful, Maxwell found himself "attached to an intelligence unit" in post-war Berlin in 1945, as reported by Anthony Delano and Peter Thompson in *Maxwell: A Portrait of Power*:

> Maxwell's first foray into intelligence – his questioning of German prisoners at the end of World War Two – was only brief. Acting

as a translator rather than interrogator did little to prepare him for his duties in Spandau Prison in Berlin. Held there were a number of leading Nazis including Rudolph Hess, Hitler's deputy; Hjalmar Schacht, the keeper of the Third Reich purse strings; and Friedrich Flick, the steel baron who had rivalled Krupp in Hitler's plan for world domination.

But here, in the cold grey granite fortress of Spandau, Maxwell showed an unexpected aptitude for asking shrewd questions based on long nights spent studying documents in his room. By the light of a naked bulb he would read and make copious notes, drinking endless cups of coffee from a pot on top of the room stove. He would memorise the questions he formed and then spend long hours putting them to a prisoner (Thompson & Delano 1991)."

Additionally, Maxwell was said to have been considering publishing as a business at the time and was able to secure a position as censor for the first English newspaper in the British sector of Berlin. After leaving the army, he secured a position with the Control Commission for Germany – British Element. He next hooked up with Ferdinand Springer and became the English agent for the biggest scientific publisher in Germany, Springer-Verlag. Springer had friends in spooky places, as well (@ElResisto 2019). As indicated in *Springer-Verlag: History of a Scientific Publishing House: Part 2*, author Heinz Götze suggested that Springer was able to extend the reach of his publications to the U.K. through his former scientific advisor, Paul Rosbaud (Götze 2008). Conveniently, Rosbaud had worked as a clandestine Aliied agent (XU) in Norway to provide details about German atomic research to Britain's MI6 and possibly the CIA's predecessor organization, the OSS (@ElResisto 2019).

In 1949, Springer and Rosbaud established Butterworth-Springer, with an existing company called Butterworth providing the financing and Springer the editorial capabilities. In just two years, the company had already collapsed, leaving Maxwell to take over and rename the business Pergamon Press. He couldn't do it alone, however.

The negotiation of the sale of Butterworth's shares to Maxwell was managed by none other than Frederick Vanden Heuvel. Heuvel was the MI6 station chief in Berne, Switzerland during the war, where he worked closely with OSS station chief and de facto founder of the CIA Allen Dulles. Because Maxwell didn't have the money to make the purchase, the funds came from an important figure in British intelligence, Sir Charles Hambro. A member of the Hambro family behind the long-established

Hambros Bank, Charles Hambro was the executive chief of the Special Operations Executive (SOE) during the war. This branch of British intelligence was responsible for everything from espionage to sabotage in occupied Europe.

In *MI6: Inside the Covert World of Her Majesty's Secret Intelligence Service*, Stephen Dorril explained the story behind Maxwell's purchase of Butterworth-Springer:

> ... There followed protracted negotiations organized by Vanden Heuvel and, in May 1951, Butterworth agreed to sell its interest to Maxwell for £13,000. Agreeing also to a change of name to Pergamon Press, Butterworth set aside a considerable debt of £10,000.
>
> As [Maxwell's] official biographer, Joe Haines, acknowledged, this was 'more money than Maxwell possessed at that moment, so he borrowed. He first went to Sir Charles Hambro. Who introduced Maxwell to Hambro varies with the different accounts. Haines says it was via the Board of Trade (BoT); Maxwell said it was Whitlock; Betty Maxwell claims it was Vanden Heuvel, Hambro's business "fixer." Whoever it was, the meeting gave rise to a City legend that Hambro had been so impressed by the forward-looking Maxwell and sufficiently persuaded of his business acumen that he ordered the chief cashier to give Maxwell a cheque book with authority to draw cheques up to a total of £25,000. In fact, the legend was no more than a cover story. The meeting certainly took place, but the matter of money had already been fixed by MI6 (Dorril 2002).

In *Robert Maxwell, Israel's Superspy*, Gordon Thomas and Martin Dillon made it sound as though Vanden Heuvel made an offer of support to Maxwell with the backing of MI6, but that Maxwell politely declined:

> By the end of the evening, [Vanden Heuvel] had proposed that Maxwell "could find a berth" with [MI6]. It would not be a full-time position, but one in which Maxwell would act as "a super contact man," Heuvel would recall telling the young officer.
>
> Maxwell had refilled his glass, saying nothing. Then he had smiled and said he would think about it. Heuvel had nodded. But he had sensed there was no point in raising the matter again, "Maxwell was not going to become one of our Jews," he said later.

@ElResisto pointed out that this dinner between Heuvel and Maxwell occurred in 1945, roughly six years before the deal to purchase Butterworth-Springer, raising questions about Thomas and Dillon's account:

Was Robert Maxwell's decision to get involved with scientific publishing in post-war Germany influenced by Heuvel? It certainly would explain how an army officer with no formal education or experience in publishing identified scientific publishing and distribution as a potentially lucrative business. It might explain how he thought to get involved with the British Control Commission for Germany and make use of the influence provided by this position, which Götze noted helped get around issues relating to internal German affairs, as mentioned earlier. It also might explain why, as Thompson and Delano write, "He also bought a huge number of prewar scientific journals from Springer that had been hidden away in Austria while the war raged."

@ElResisto considered the possibility that Maxwell was involved in a British strategy to "brain drain" Germany, just as the U.S. had with Operation Paperclip, in which over a thousand Nazi war criminals and scientists were brought to the States. @ElResisto noted that Risbaud provided the names of scientists in East Berlin to U.S. intelligence, as a possible lead. They further raised the question of whether or not this conversation between Heuven and Maxwell may have been concocted by Dillon and Thomas as a way to cover for Maxwell's British intelligence work, given the fact that Heuven suggested Maxwell did not take him up on his effort:

> It's been said that Maxwell had links to MI6, though as far as I can tell Heuvel is the only link. However, Heuvel is not listed by the authors Thomas and Dillon in their list of primary and secondary sources. This is complete speculation, but maybe someone wanted it explicitly published that Maxwell did not work for MI6 or for Heuvel. Note that Dorril's book mentioning the Heuvel connection came out 7 months before Thomas and Dillon's.
>
> One thing does seem certain though: Charles Hambro and Frederick Vanden Heuvel definitely provided Maxwell with the necessary funds to purchase a controlling share in Butterworth-Springer, which he then turned into Pergamon Press. This was Robert Maxwell's first highly successful foray into publishing, and it was funded by two men with deep ties to British intelligence.

Though Thomas and Dillon appeared to brush aside the possibility that Maxwell worked for MI6, the authors had no issues linking him to Israeli intelligence, which Seymour Hersh also claimed in *The Samson Option: Israel's Nuclear Arsenal and American Foreign Policy* (Hersh 1991).

According to Thomas and Dillon, while on the payroll of Israel's Mossad spy agency, Maxwell was provided with prostitutes from "the service maintained for blackmail purposes" while he was visiting Israel. Using a hotel decked out with cameras, Mossad was able to curate "a small library of video footage of Maxwell in sexually compromising positions."

As Ben-Menashe claimed, Maxwell was involved in the sale of arms during the Iran-Contra scandal, but that was just one major espionage operation in which the publishing magnate played an important role. He was also wrapped firmly in the arms of what journalist Danny Casolaro called the "Octopus," the PROMIS software story of the 1980s.

Considered a precursor to the NSA's PRISM software publicized by Edward Snowden (Ditlea 1997), PROMIS was a program originally developed by William Hamilton's Inslaw Corporation on behalf of the U.S. Department of Justice as a database management tool (Fricker 2013). It was when it fell into the hands of the NSA that it became a powerful weapon for electronic surveillance. The exact story behind how the tool's surveillance capabilities were created is murky, but may have involved top-secret development by the Wackenhut Corporation under the cover of a Native American reservation owned by the Cabazon Band of Mission Indians (Fricker 1993). There, software developers installed a backdoor into PROMIS that allowed Western and Israeli intelligence agencies to spy on the computers that hosted the program. Because Wackenhut went on to provide private security for Jeffrey Epstein (Redmond 2020), it was relevant that the security giant has long been deeply enmeshed in U.S. intelligence intrigues, including the maintenance of a database of over 4 million names of American dissidents that were likely fed to the FBI and CIA (Connolly 1992).

Western intelligence agencies, along with Israel's Mossad, determined that, to get PROMIS into the computer systems of their chief enemy, the USSR, they would need the right salesperson. Given his own Eastern European heritage and business connections, the chosen individual was Robert Maxwell. In addition to selling PROMIS to the Soviets, Maxwell worked with Republican Texas Senator John Tower to get the software onto the computers of Los Alamos National Laboratory (Thomas & Dillon 2003).

Before Maxwell would be found dead off the bow of his yacht, the *Lady Ghislaine*, in 1991, he would host a dazzling party on the boat in May 1989. The guest list included future president Donald Trump, Ghislaine Maxwell, journalist Mike Wallace, literary agent Mort Janklow, one-time Henry Kissinger staffer and secretary of the Navy Jon Lehman, who founded the right-wing Project for a New American Century, law partner of Roy Cohn Tom Bolan, and CEO of the future Time Warner, Steve Ross, who worked closely with New York criminals Manny Kimmel and Abner "Longy" Zwillman (*New York Daily News* 1989). Zwillman was a close associate of Meyer Lansky and Sam Bronfman (Webb 2019). Thomas Pickering, a Kissinger staffer involved in Iran-Contra (Pincus 1989), was also in attendance, as well as Senator John Tower, who worked with Maxwell on installing PROMIS at Los Alamos.

In just two years, Maxwell was discovered drowned. Some believed it was merely the result of one of the man's well-known midnight pisses off the edge of the ship. Others, such as Thomas and Dillon, suggested he was knocked off by the Mossad . Senator Tower died only two months earlier in a plane crash. @ElResisto reasoned Maxwell and Tower might have been involved in transferring U.S. nuclear secrets to Israel.

There were other details and unexplained circumstances of the Epstein story that seemed to suggest the possibility of intelligence connections, but weren't quite fleshed out enough to be considered evidence. For instance, how was it that Epstein, who had no college degree, came to teach mathematics at the prestigious Dalton School in New York? (Maeroff 1974). Could it have had anything to do with the fact that the director who hired him, Donald Barr, previously served in the OSS (Saxon 2004)? After all, I knew that the CIA recruited at the university level; could it have begun doing so even earlier? (Golden 2017).

How was it that Epstein climbed the ladder of Wall Street so quickly? Some, such as victim Maria Farmer, suggested that Epstein had a homosexual relationship with Les Wexner (Webb 2020). Could it have been that he used his blackmail skills to ensnare such men as Wexner?

It was probably a stretch to associate the Interlochen Center for the Arts (Lewis 2019), where Epstein attended summer camp at age 14, with his intelligence background, but he did build his own cabin at the Michigan-based academy (Briquelet 2019). Would #Pizzagaters have been reading too much into this connection by finding one of the FBI's pedophilia symbols on the Interlochen website?

How did it come about that Les Wexner acquired the CIA's Southern Air Transport airline company (Bello, n.d.), revealed to be a central component of the agency's drug and arms running operations during the Iran-Contra scandal (Block 2011)? And what did he use it for?

I reasoned that the significance of these details and more would surely be explored more fully by other researchers. For the purposes of my investigation, I had enough information to suggest with high probability that Epstein did have some sort of intelligence connections and/or an important role among the world's power elite.

Though the #Pizzagate community had explored some of these topics, such as Epstein's use of honeypot operations to compromise those in power, there was one figure that somehow seemed to escape that net. And when he was brought up, the community managed to twist his involvement into a positive. Was Donald Trump a deep-cover agent?

TRUMP AND EPSTEIN

By the time I was caught up with #Pizzagate, it had already morphed into Qanon. In fact, Qanon supporters had already been kicked off of their most mainstream platform, the message board site Reddit. Qanon boards had even been ejected from their original host, the even less politically correct message board site 4chan (Martineau 2017), as well as the even more problematic 8chan – possibly linked to a mass shooting in El Paso, Texas – and had moved to something called 8kun (Zadrozny & Collins 2018).

In other words, I was still trying to understand the legitimacy of the pedophilia component while most #Pizzagaters had moved on to worshipping someone or some group called Q.

The movement began on the /pol/ message board of 4chan, a forum where anonymous users mostly posted hate speech and crudely drawn cartoons of right-wing frogs named Pepe. While users were anonymous, it was possible to use the same string of numbers with which to identify an individual poster. "Q Clearance Patriot" claimed to have Q-level government clearance, meaning that they had the highest level security access within the Department of Energy, which included nuclear weapons.

Q posted enigmatic messages in a /pol/ thread called "Calm Before the Storm." Q was representative of a secret group within the government heading up a counter coup within the deep state. This of course presumed the existence of an initial coup, which Q said had previously been conducted by deep state players in support of Clinton and other Democratic Party officials – in other words, the pedo cabal. Q's job was to awaken the public to this counter coup by dropping "breadcrumbs," clues that they would have to decipher in order to understand the operation at work.

Q did have some minor and vague predictions fulfilled, such as the guess that Trump would tweet the word "small" on Small Business Saturday (LaFrance 2020). They also posted a picture from what was claimed to be Air Force One, though it was difficult to verify. These sorts of posts ("Q proofs," as they were called) lent credence to the possibility that Q truly was a government insider.

But posting on 4chan was only the tip of the iceberg. And the rest of the iceberg was indeed difficult to see below the dark, cold waters of the deep state. Q said that, behind the scenes, Trump and his deep state allies were unsealing a series of secret indictments and arresting members of the pedo cabal, such as Hillary Clinton, Barack Obama, Huma Abedin and the Podestas. As they were arrested, they were forced to wear ankle monitors (Reuters Fact Check 2021). And, soon, the Storm would come to take out the rest of their cadre, as Q said on November 2, 2017:

> My fellow Americans, over the course of the next several days you will undoubtedly realize that we are taking back our great country (the land of the free) from the evil tyrants that wish to do us harm and destroy the last remaining refuge of shining light. On POTUS' order, we have initiated certain fail-safes that shall safeguard the public from the primary fallout which is slated to occur 11.3 upon the arrest announcement of Mr. Podesta (actionable 11.4). Confirmation (to the public) of what is occurring will then be revealed and will not be openly accepted. Public riots are being organized in serious numbers in an effort to prevent the arrest and capture of more senior public officials. On POTUS' order, a state of temporary military control will be actioned and special ops carried out. False leaks have been made to retain several within the confines of the United States to prevent extradition and special operator necessity. Rest assured, the safety and well-being of every man, woman, and child of this country is being exhausted in full. However, the atmosphere within the country will unfortunately be divided as so many have fallen for the corrupt and evil narrative that has long been broadcast. We will be initiating the Emergency Broadcast System (EMS) during this time in an effort to provide a direct message (avoiding the fake news) to all citizens. Organizations and/or people that wish to do us harm during this time will be met with swift fury – certain laws have been pre-lifted to provide our great military the necessary authority to handle and conduct these operations (at home and abroad).
>
> POTUS will be well insulated/protected on AF1 and abroad (specific locations classified) while these operations are conducted due to the nature of the entrenchment. It is time to take back our country and make America great again. Let us salute and pray for the brave men and women in uniform who will undertake this assignment to bring forth peace, unity, and return power to the people.

It is our hope that this message reaches enough people to make a meaningful impact. We cannot yet telegraph this message through normal methods for reasons I'm sure everyone here can understand. Follow the questions from the previous thread(s) and remain calm, the primary targets are within DC and remain at the top (on both sides). The spill over in the streets will be quickly shut down. Look for more false flags – stay alert, be vigilant, and above all, please pray.

"For God so loved the world that he gave his one and only Son, that whoever believes in him shall not perish but have eternal life. Love is patient, love is kind."

God bless my fellow Americans.

4,10,20"

But I hadn't even gotten past the letter Q at that point, let alone figured out how 4chan or 8chan even worked. Because I was stuck at the word "Trump." Sure, in the past I had got sucked into placing heroes on pedestals. However, I learned that even the most well-meaning politician had faults. I was immediately disappointed when I learned that Bernie Sanders had supported the world's largest weapons manufacturer, Lockheed Martin, for bringing jobs to his state of Vermont. So, it would take a lot to convince me that a president, whether a former Secretary of State or the host of a game show, wasn't just as corrupt as every other weasel in the game. And, given his track record of swindling poor tenants out of money, brazen displays of racism, and likely acts of sexual assault, it would take even more for me to believe that Donald Trump was a deep-state savior.

"I've known Jeff for 15 years. Terrific guy," Trump said in a 2002 profile of Epstein for *New York* magazine (Karni & Haberman 2019). "He's a lot of fun to be with. It is even said that he likes beautiful women as much as I do, and many of them are on the younger side."

This and many other comments like it would come to be considered evidence that Trump was trying to alert the public to Epstein's abuse of minors, according to Qanoners. Given the fact that the comment was made several years before the official investigation into Epstein's affairs, he may have been ahead of the curve in terms of providing clues about his friend. If so, one wonders why he wouldn't have been more explicit about the enigmatic billionaire. Qanon would have responded by saying that Trump was in fact under deep cover, not wanting to compromise his long-term operation to expose the pedophilia that ran rampant throughout the halls of power until it was time to round them up and force them to face justice.

If that were the case, then Trump's cover was indeed deep. He permitted Epstein and Ghislaine to attend his Florida golf course Mar-a-Lago, numerous times (Unger 2021), including one instance in 2000, when they spent time there with Prince Andrew, who'd visited to use Trump's private jet (Reinhard 2019). Later that same year, the *Palm Beach Post* said all three – Epstein, Maxwell, and Prince Andrew – attended a tournament and celebrity event at the golf course (Smith 2000). Prince Andrew, the Duke of York and second son of Queen Elizabeth II of England, was named as one of the abusers of Epstein victim Virginia Roberts Giuffre (Graham 2019), who was recruited by Ghislaine Maxwell at Mar-a-Lago during this time (Crawley 2019).

Giuffre was already a sexual abuse victim by the time she met Maxwell at Trump's resort in the summer of 2000. She had been molested by a family friend from the age of seven (Crawley 2019) before living on the streets at 13 (Brown 2018), where she was picked up and abused by 65-year-old sex trafficker Ron Eppinger. Eppinger used his Miami modeling agency "Perfect 10" as a front for international sex trafficking until he was raided by the FBI (Dylan, et al. 2019). As investigators explored the Epstein scandal, they would learn that modeling agencies were often used as fronts for trafficking operations. This included MC2 Model Management, run by Epstein's friend and business partner Jean-Luc Brunel, which trafficked minors (Cobb 2019), and Trump Model Management, which trafficked undocumented workers (West 2016).

After six months of living with Eppinger, Giuffre returned to live with her father, a maintenance manager at Mar-a-Lago who was able to get her a job at the resort spa (Mansoor 2019). Upon meeting Maxwell at Trump's spa in 2000, she was groomed by Epstein and Maxwell while they promised her a future as a massage therapist. It was in March 2001 that she was allegedly trafficked to Andrew. According to one interview, Giuffre described it as a "wicked" and "really scary time," adding that she "couldn't comprehend how in the highest level of the government powerful people were allowing this to happen (Graham 2019). Not just allowing but participating in it."

According to court documents released in 2019, she said she was made to have sex with hedge fund manager Glenn Dubin, (Harvard-affiliated) attorney Alan Dershowitz, governor of New Mexico Bill Richardson, MIT scientist Marvin Minsky, lawyer and former Senator George J. Mitchell, and Jean-Luc Brunel (Sherman 2019). At age 19, Giuffre convinced her captors to allow her to go to Thailand to learn massage therapy, which she used as an opportunity to escape (Bicks 2019).

In addition to Giuffre, Trump had a connection to Epstein and Maxwell through another sex trafficking victim. Anouska De Georgiou, a one-time model who attended high school with future princess Kate Middleton, told *Dateline NBC* that she had been groomed by Epstein as a teen and then passed on to Trump by Ghislaine Maxwell when she was 20 years of age. Trump then put her up in an apartment he owned (grahamlester 2021).

The 2019 Dateline special described her situation with Epstein this way:

> Ms De Georgiou grew up in an affluent family and attended school with Kate Middleton at the illustrious Marlborough College.
>
> But telling of how billionaire Epstein bent her to his warped will, she told *Dateline*: "By the time I was being raped, it was too late."
>
> She added that the sick financier's cronies and enablers would turn a blind eye to his brazen abuse of *vulnerable young girls*.

A 1997 article in the *Sunday Mirror* explained how she was found by Trump:

> [Trump] met London model Anouska De Georgiou at a party in Manhattan. *Several American millionaires already had their eyes on Anouska. But she was there with Robert Maxwell's daughter Ghislaine, who has introduced several of her attractive friends to the property developer.* [Italics in the original] … Trump flew Madam Maxwell and the model south to the sunshine state where all three enjoyed a happy weekend together. When they returned to New York, Anouska was installed in one of Donald's many apartments there.

One claim that was sometimes made by Qanon supporters was that Trump had never been on Epstein's private jet, nicknamed the "Lolita Express." However, Epstein's brother Mark testified in 2009 that Trump had flown on the plane at least once (Mark 2019). Not only had Epstein been to Trump's residence in Florida, but Trump had been to Epstein's just three miles away.

In a 2003 *Vanity Fair* article, Trump was described as one of an intimate group of ultra-wealthy businessmen said to have had dinner at Epstein's mansion in Palm Beach (Ward 2003). Another 2003 article placed Trump at Epstein's New York mansion for a 30-person dinner that also included Google's Sergey Brin, Les Wexner, former British Cabinet minister Peter Mandelson, and Bill Clinton aide Doug Band (Bernard & Schoeneman 2003). Around the time that Giuffre was being recruited in 2000, Trump and Epstein attended the same small party hosted by Conrad Black, a media mogul convicted in 2007 for obstruction of justice and fraud (Clark 2007), the latter of which was ultimately overturned on appeal. Black would go on to support Trump in his bid for president.

Epstein testified in 2010 that he knew Trump, but pleaded the Fifth when asked if he'd ever socialized with him around minors:

> Q: Have you ever had a personal relationship with Donald Trump?
>
> A. What do you mean by "personal relationship," sir?
>
> Q. Have you socialized with him?
>
> A. Yes, sir.
>
> Q. Yes?
>
> A. Yes, sir.
>
> Q. Have you ever socialized with Donald Trump in the presence of females under the age of 18?
>
> A: Though I'd like to answer that question, at least today I'm going to have to assert my Fifth, Sixth, and 14th Amendment rights, sir (Hartmann 2019).

In fact, footage had since come out showing Trump and Epstein at a party in the company of a number of young women, ages unknown (Bohrer 2019).

Message pads confiscated from Epstein's property showed that Trump called Epstein twice in November 2004 (Feller 2021). Trump showed up under a special "Jeffrey" category in the pedophile's black book with 14 numbers, which included car mobiles, emergency numbers, the number for Trump's security guard and for his servant. Others in the Jeffrey category were David Rockefeller, Ehud Barak, Alan Dershowitz, then–Senator John Kerry, former senator and lobbyist George Mitchell, and lobbyist Thomas Quinn (Silverstein 2016).

Trump's daughter Ivanka and his brother Robert were also in Epstein's phone book, as was his former wife Ivana (Feller 2021). According to Epstein victim Maria Farmer, Ghislaine Maxwell and Ivana Trump would drive around New York City recruiting young girls as they exited school for the day (Webb 2020).

Just weeks after Epstein pled guilty to "knowingly and willfully conspiring with others known and unknown to … persuade, induce, or entice minor females to engage in prostitution" on September 27, 2007, it was reported that Mar-A-Lago finally banned Epstein from the resort. The reason stated in a *New York Post* story from the time was that Epstein had hit on a masseuse (DeGregory & Feis 2019); however, a lawyer for one of Epstein's victims claimed that Epstein attempted to seduce one of the resort members' underage daughters (Mangan 2020).

Brad Edwards, one of Giuffre's lawyers, served Trump a subpoena for a deposition in 2009. According to Edwards, it was "obvious" that Trump wasn't a part of Epstein's illegal operations (Silverstein 2016). That didn't preclude him from other improprieties. For instance, Trump had been accused by former Miss USA contestants of walking in on them naked, a fact that Trump himself admitted to on the Howard Stern show in 2005:

> Well, I'll tell you the funniest is that I'll go backstage before a show, and everyone's getting dressed, and ready and everything else, and you know, no men are anywhere, and I'm allowed to go in because I'm the owner of the pageant and therefore I'm inspecting it. You know, I'm inspecting because I want to make sure that everything is good.
>
> You know, the dresses. "Is everyone okay?" You know, they're standing there with no clothes. 'Is everybody okay?' And you see these incredible looking women, and so, I sort of get away with things like that. But no, I've been very good.

While Trump's quote was in reference to his behavior at Miss USA pageants, contestants at Miss Teen USA, where ages could have been as low as 15, made similar allegations (Stuart 2020).

Trump had also been credibly accused of sexual assault, sexual harassment and rape by at least 25 women (Relman 2019) . His own audio once again added credence to these allegations when he admitted to assaulting women in an infamous conversation with Billy Bush. Trump said that, in trying to seduce a woman, he might start kissing her, adding, "I don't even wait. And when you're a star, they let you do it. You can do anything. ... Grab 'em by the pussy. You can do anything" (Fahrenholdt 2016).

The most disturbing story by far, however, was brought to light in two 2016 lawsuits. The lawsuits alleged that, in 1994, Trump, along with Epstein, sodomized and raped a 12-year-old "Maria" and 13-year-old, Katie Johnson, at the midtown Manhattan mansion gifted to Epstein by Les Wexner (Kreig & Madsen, n.d.).

Johnson claimed that Trump knew she was 13 when he raped her, saying that he assaulted her at four separate parties held by Epstein in Manhattan. According to her lawsuit, while Johnson was at the New York-New

Jersey Port Authority Bus Terminal, she was invited into Epstein's party circle by a "recruiter," who claimed Johnson could become a model with introductions to the proper contacts at a party. When Trump encountered her for the fourth time at an Epstein party,

> Defendant Trump tied Plaintiff to a bed, exposed himself to Plaintiff, and then proceeded to forcibly rape Plaintiff. During the course of this savage sexual attack, Plaintiff loudly pleaded with Defendant Trump to stop but with no effect. Defendant Trump responded to Plaintiff's pleas by violently striking Plaintiff in the face with his open hand and screaming that he would do whatever he wanted. (DISTRICT COURT SOUTHERN DISTRICT OF NEW YORK 2016).

For the lawsuits, a classmate of Johnson signed an affidavit saying that Johnson told her of the assaults in the summer of 1994. A witness, "Tiffany Doe," that worked for Epstein when she was 22, signed an affidavit saying she'd witnessed Trump's assault and rape of Johnson on four occasions.

The second time Johnson interacted with Epstein, she said that Epstein raped her "anally and vaginally despite her loud pleas to stop." She claimed that he tried to punch her in the head while saying that he, not Trump, was the one who should have taken her virginity. The lawsuit included charges that Trump threatened Johnson by saying that her loved ones and she would be "physically harmed if not killed" if she told anyone. Epstein also reinforced this and threatened that, if Johnson "reveal[ed] any of the details of his sexual and physical abuse of her," her loved ones and she would be "seriously physically harmed, if not killed."

The threats from Trump at one point included that Johnson "shouldn't ever say anything if she didn't want to disappear like Maria, a 12-year-old female that was forced to be involved in the third incident" with Trump. Tiffany Doe claimed to have witnessed Johnson and Maria perform oral sex on Trump. Johnson said she hadn't seen Maria since they were forced to have a sexual encounter with Trump.

An investigation into the case of "Maria" by Wayne Madsen and Andrew Kreig found that the girl was abducted at 11-years-old in front of a pizza place in Waterbury, Connecticut. The reporters alleged that the Waterbury Police Department would not send them a copy of the police report about Maria's kidnapping. Locals suggested to the reporters that the circumstances around the girl's abduction were strange and believed that a pedophile ring in New York, just 77 miles away, had taken her.

Johnson said that, when she filed the complaint in April 2016, she began getting threats from blocked numbers on her phone. This led her to withdraw her complaints just ahead of the 2016 election (Kreig & Madsen, n.d.).

Needless to say, if I was going to hold Trump to the same standards as the rest of the names associated with Epstein, it would have been nearly impossible not to level the same accusations against him as I might have directed at Bill Clinton and the rest. Moreover, with Trump, there actual accusations made against him by a victim, which wasn't the case for all of the people in Epstein's black book or flight logs. If Trump were under deep cover, it seemed to me that he was more likely in Epstein's corner himself, aiding in the blackmail of powerful people.

Though people in the Qanon community were able to, at times, see beyond the two-party system and conclude that both Clinton and Bush Sr. were pedophiles, they were not always able to distinguish between the socioeconomic classes and come to the conclusion that the entire power elite was beyond accountability and had no interest in improving the lives of the rest of humanity. This came despite the fact that the Qanon community was able to see this trend both historically in the U.S. and internationally – specifically when it came to pedophile rings.

ARI BEN-MENASHE

In researching these topics, I continually ran into figures that would send my spidey senses tingling. There may have been nothing inherently wrong with them or their role in a specific story, but I just couldn't shake the sense that there was something beneath the surface there. In some cases, I'd look a little deeper and my suspicions would turn out to be warranted.

One individual I didn't entirely trust was the former agent of Israel's Military Intelligence Directorate, Ari Ben-Menashe. As they say, "once [a member of blank intelligence agency] always [a member of blank intelligence agency]." Along that line of thought, what made an ex-spy like Ben-Menashe want to go on record about a fellow asset, Jeffrey Epstein?

Ben-Menashe was most well-known for leaking to the press the existence of the Iranian side of the Iran-Contra affair (Boyle Mahle 2005). In 1986, he provided information about weapons being given to Iran by Richard Secord, Oliver North and Albert Hakim to *Time* magazine. When the publication couldn't corroborate the story, he passed it onto a Lebanese outlet that broke the earth-shattering news that would result in

Congressional investigations. Ben-Menashe claimed that he was instructed to do so by Yitzhak Shamir of the Likud party in order to bring down his rival in Labour, Shimon Peres (Hoffman & Silvers 1988). Notably, Peres was supposedly an associate of Epstein, so could Ben-Menashe still have been working on behalf of some political interests?

Ben-Menashe was arrested in the U.S. for violating the Arms Export Control Act (Hutchinson 2011). The spy said that he was told to plead guilty by the Israeli government as a means of avoiding prosecution in Israel (Ben-Menashe 2015). According to some sources, Ben-Menashe soured on his government when they didn't deliver on a deal to take care of him after his conviction, leading him to leak further stories to the press. This included the tale of Reagan's October Surprise against Jimmy Carter (Parry 2012). He said that he was involved in negotiations with the Iranian government to delay releasing American hostages to make Carter look bad ahead of the election.

In turn, Israel attempted to discredit him. For instance, an "authoritative source" told the *Jerusalem Post* "the Defence establishment 'never had any contacts with Ari Ben-Menashe and his activities" (March 7, 1990). The spy disproved these allegations when he handed over evidence of his employment to Robert Parry at *Newsweek* (Parry 2012).

Ben-Menashe was acquitted after nearly a year in prison (Hutchinson 2011). Even as a freed man, he continued spilling secrets. He revealed to Seymour Hersh the existence of Israel's nuclear weapons program, as well as Robert Maxwell's involvement with Israeli intelligence (Hersh 2013). This led to a suit against Hersh by Maxwell and his Mirror Group, which was settled in favor of the journalist.

The spy told congressional investigators that someone attempted to kidnap him and bring him to Israel to face justice. Before they could, a U.S. intelligence source told Robert Parry that, when Ben-Menashe was going to be brought to the U.S. for his testimony, he would be denied entry in Los Angeles and deported to Israel. Parry passed the information along to Ben-Menashe, who delayed his flight until he could be guaranteed a safe flight from the U.S. government (Parry 2012).

The spy faced further attempts to discredit him, including a *Newsweek* story saying that "inconsistencies may undermine Ben-Menashe's testimony in the British courtroom proceedings" (Barry et al. 1991). Parry suggested that the journalists involved in this campaign were linked to Israel and achieved their goal of "marginalizing Ben-Menashe by 1993, at least in the eyes of the Washington Establishment." He further claimed that, with the campaign complete, "the Israelis seemed to view him as a declining threat, best left alone. He was able to pick up the pieces of his life, creating a second act as an international political consultant and businessman arranging sales of grain" (Parry 2012).

Journalist Whitney Webb believed the spy continued to be marginalized, noting that Ben-Menashe's credibility and affiliations were still called into question, "with mainstream news outlets still referring to him as a 'self-described ex-Israeli spy' – despite the well-documented fact that Ben-Menashe worked for Israeli intelligence – as a means of downplaying his claims regarding his time in Israel's intelligence service" (Webb 2020).

Once the libel suit against Hersh was over, Ben-Menashe acted as a consultant, working with figures such as Robert Mugabe (Meldrum et al 2002), Venezuelan opposition leader Henri Falcón, and the military junta in Sudan (Nieberg 2019). Webb pointed out, "Ben-Menashe has also maintained ties to several different intelligence services and eventually became a controversial whistleblower whose information led to the arrest of the former head of Canada's Security Intelligence Review Committee, Arthur Porter."

While Robert Parry said that the Ari could be "his own worst enemy," he believed his information about Iran-Contra and the PROMIS software scandal to be reliable. Bill Hamilton, the ex-NSA agent who developed PROMIS, questioned Ben-Menashe's character, but believed his information about PROMIS. Hamilton told Whitney Webb: *"Ari Ben Menashe was the first source to tell us reliable information about the role of Rafi Eitan and Israeli intelligence vis-a-vis PROMIS but, in the end, of course, he was a clandestine services-type guy whose official duties include the ability and willingness to lie, cheat, and steal."*

Even as late as 2012, it appeared as though someone wanted to shut Ben-Menashe up. In 2012, he planned to meet Robert Parry to discuss further information about the covert activities of the 1980s. Before he could, a fire bomb destroyed his Montréal home. Parry's *Consortium News* noted that "the arson squad's initial assessment is said to be that the flammable agent was beyond the sort of accelerant used by common criminals" (Parry 2012).

Ben-Menashe had planned to bring a "senior Israeli intelligence figure" for the interview. When the attack occurred, the figure "concluded that the attack was meant as a message from Israeli authorities to stay silent about the historical events that he was expected to discuss." The event did result in "intimidating Ben-Menashe, shutting down possible new disclosures of Israeli misconduct from the other intelligence veteran, and destroying records that would have helped Ben-Menashe prove whatever statements he might make."

It at least appeared on the surface that Ben-Menashe had gone through a trial by fire to prove his credibility as a source for leaking sensitive information. Aside from being a real whistleblower, one of the few other possibilities would be that his allegiance laid less with Israeli intelligence and more with the U.S. As the Pentagon Papers focused attention on the military and not the CIA, Ben-Menashe's leaks at times focused on Israeli intelligence when alternative players could have been similarly highlighted.

For instance, there was evidence to suggest Robert Maxwell was affiliated with MI6, but Ben-Menashe tied him to the Mossad. He discussed the backdoor installed in PROMIS as an Israeli effort, when the CIA appeared to have been possibly culpable as well. In his latest interviews, he labeled Epstein and Ghislaine Maxwell as Israeli spies. However, the couple were operating on U.S. soil, interacting with and likely compromising powerful Americans, something that would seem to be difficult to achieve without the complicity of a U.S. agency.

Larry King, of the Franklin Credit Union singing the National Anthem at the 1984 Republican National Convention. Cspan.

CHAPTER THREE

THE FRANKLIN SCANDAL: A BLUEPRINT FOR EPSTEIN

When I first brought up Epstein to @housetrotter, a Gundam who had been researching deep politics for years, he pointed out that I should look into the Dutroux affair. What I found was a more brutal, more disturbing version of the Epstein story. And when I investigated Dutroux, this naturally led to Jimmy Savile, the Kincora Boys Homes, North Fox Island, and on and on. Each country in the world had its own Epstein. And not just one, but multiple. It seemed that, when I pulled aside the curtain of prestige that shaded the power elite, the whole operation was Epstein's. It was pedophiles all the way down. This was a non-exhaustive list of child trafficking networks around the world I came across in my research:

- South Africa: A South African police officer alleged that the country's defense minister at the height of apartheid, Magnus Malan, was involved in a pedophile ring in which mostly mixed race boys were sexually assaulted during "fishing excursions" on a local island. The officer, who co-wrote a book on the story with a journalist, was found with a bullet in the head shortly after the book's [*The Lost Boys of Bird Island*] publication (Chothia 2018).

- Belgium: One of the most notorious and horrific examples of child abuse networks bore the name "the Dutroux Affair," named for Marc Dutroux, one of the leading henchman in the group. While Dutroux received the blame for child trafficking, child pornography, torture and murder associated with this network, a club owner and Belgian businessman named Michel Nihoul was likely more important to managing its operations and high profile clientele (AP 2004). This clientele likely included a former Prime Minister and possibly even the Belgian royal family.

- Mexico: Hotel owner Jean Succar Kuri was accused by investigative reporter Lydia Cacho in 2003 of being involved in a child pornography and prostitution ring. Citing alleged victims and a hidden camera video of Kuri, others involved included Senator Emilio

Gamboa Patrón and Governor Miguel Ángel Yunes, as well as businessman Kamel Nacif Borge. Cacho was jailed for her work, with recorded telephone conversations of the governor of the Mexican state of Puebla discussing that the plan was to abuse and silence her (Cameron 2007).

• The UK: In 2012, reports of child sexual abuse by knighted celebrity Jimmy Savile were made public. The exact number of victims was difficult to pin down, but they numbered in the hundreds, as young as eight years old, over the course of 50 years. Many assaults took place within 5 to 75 different National Health Service (government-linked) hospitals (Sky News 2012). Separately, there was a suspected pedophile ring possibly operating out of the British House of Commons from 1981 to 1985 and involving former senior diplomat and MI6 operative Sir Peter Hayman (Stone 2015). Additionally, sexual abuse at the Kincora Boys Home in Northern Ireland in the 1970s was continually covered up for decades. In 2015, it was alleged that MI5, RUC special branch, and military intelligence used the the pedophile ring to blackmail and spy on hardline Irish loyalists (*Belfast Telegraph* 2016).

• The U.S.: As noted previously, Epstein was hardly the first high profile procurer of children for members of the power elite, though he may have attracted the most widespread attention. Millionaire Francis D. Sheldon, a descendent of Russell Alger, lumber baron, and later, war secretary for President William McKinley, acquired North Fox Island in Michigan where, in the 1970s, he would fly in children for abuse under cover of a summer nature camp charity. He fled the country before he could be held accountable (Cain 2019).

Meanwhile, in the 1970s and 80s, John Norman was operating a child trafficking and pornography ring that may have extended from Texas to Illinois and California and involved serial killers Dean Corll and John Wayne Gacy (Tron 2021). When authorities captured Norman, they found more than 30,000 index cards that were said to have included numerous names of clergy, politicians, and wealthy individuals as clients, which were turned over to the federal Department of Justice, who burned them without explanation.

More recently, there were the stories of USA Gymnastics, in which hundreds of minors were abused by coaches, gym owners and staff (Evans et al 2016). There were also the victims assaulted by Jerry Sandusky and possibly other assailants, who were then protected by Pennsylvania State University (Viera 2011).

In Hollywood, acclaimed director of *The Usual Suspects*, *X-Men*, and *Bohemian Rhapsody* Brian Singer and award winning actor Kevin

Spacey had been credibly accused of sexual assault against minors, perhaps linked to a larger network that included convicted pedophiles Brian Peck, a child acting coach, and Bob Villard, a child publicist (Berg 2015).

• Sweden: in 1976, Swedish police arrested a madam who supplied female prostitutes as young as 14 and 15 to high profile clients that included Justice Minister Lennart Geijer (The Local SE 2008).

• Iceland: In 2017, it was revealed that the father of the Prime Minister of Iceland, Bjarni Benediktsson, sought to clean the criminal record of a convicted pedophile. This resulted in the dissolution of the country's government and a new round of elections (Bilefsky 2017).

These are just a handful of accounts internationally that either alluded to or directly implicated powerful people in child sexual abuse networks. For instance, the Dutroux Affair appeared to extend beyond the borders of Belgium to France, Germany, the Czech Republic and even further. All of this indicated that pedophilia, sometimes associated with honeypot operations, was a recurring feature of elite circles that were not held accountable for their actions. Belgium and Iceland were particularly notable for the public responses that occurred. In the case of Belgium, over 300,000 people marched in the streets of Brussels to protest what they saw as a compromised investigation after magistrate Jean-Marc Connerotte, one of the few investigators thought to have integrity in the case, was removed from the investigation.

In Iceland, an entire parliamentary government dissolved as a result of public evidence of much less extensive ties to child abuse. The *father* of the country's prime minister wrote a letter arguing that a convicted pedophile should have his "honor restored." When the news was made public, an already fragile three-party coalition fell apart as one party decided to abandon the prime minister, resulting in snap elections.

Those two cases demonstrated that public outcry and even some form of consequences are possible in response to such abuses of power. However, fighting against forces so entrenched is an uphill battle fraught with danger, even death. This was evidenced best by one case that bore striking similarities to the Epstein saga.

THE FRANKLIN SCANDAL

Of course, I felt guilty. My mom was likely dying in there, but when I was in a hospital waiting room and swapping in and out with family members to visit a sick loved one, there was only so much I could do. Get a little work done on the computer. Chat with people I hadn't seen in awhile. Become fully absorbed in a book investigating a nationwide pedophilia ring in the United States in the 1980s.

And I wasn't the only one who took breaks from holding her hand and talking to her. My whole family would switch from being preoccupied with her pulmonary fibrosis to video-chatting with their spouses and kids back home or making work calls or doing spreadsheets. They even brought books and Kindles. So, which was worse? While some were reading the latest *Hunger Games*-style novel, I just so happened to be–

"What are you reading about?" my sister-in-law asked.

"The Franklin scandal," I answered, unsure of whether I should tell the truth.

"What's that?" she asked, genuinely curious. Where could I start?

In the 1980s, stories began to emerge in Omaha, Nebraska that would see a local credit union not only embroiled in allegations of financial corruption, but child and drug trafficking as well. During that decade, several sources independently began to report abuse of local youths by Lawrence E. King, Jr., a senior member of the state's Republican Party, as well as by prominent members of the Omaha community, including the owner of the state's largest newspaper, a Nebraska district court judge, the chief of Omaha police, and the owner of a large chain of department stores.

When a state senate committee was set up to investigate the matter, Committee Chair Senator Loren Schmit was told by an anonymous caller that, as a "good Republican," he should not pursue the investigation because it would "reach to the highest levels of the Republican Party" (Bryant, 2012, Ch. 1). In fact, it ultimately reached both the highest levels of the party and the U.S. government when it was learned that D.C. area "call boys" were given private midnight tours of the White House.

Upon returning from Thailand as an "information specialist" for the U.S. Air Force in the Vietnam War, Larry King established himself as a successful businessman in Omaha when he took over the failing Franklin Credit Union. By 1984, he had managed to turn the bank around and boost his own profile in the process, becoming an officer of the National Black Republican Council and singing the national anthem at the GOP national convention that year. He was invited to belt the Star Spangled Banner for the Grand Old Party once more in 1988 (Ibid., Ch. 1).

As King began seeking an ambassador position under the upcoming Bush Sr. administration, accusations against the way he handled the credit union had attracted enough attention that the state legislature initiated an investigation into the bank's financial affairs. While uncovering these financial crimes, it became impossible for the committee to separate the numerous reports of child sexual abuse and their ties to the credit union. The fact that there was a luxurious bedroom installed during the bank's latest renovation was just one among a number of strange details that also included King's mulitiple homes, extravagant lifestyle and extensive use of charter flights across the U.S.

One of the homes he maintained was a unit at the Twin Tower luxury apartments in Omaha leased to a photographer named Rusty Nelson. Nelson had a police report filed against him when a mother believed he was engaged in child pornography. She got this impression when he invited her and her daughter up for a photo shoot to create a commercial modeling portfolio and Nelson continuously attempted to lure the young girl into posing in erotic costumes and poses. Upon seeing photographs of scantily clad children in the apartment, she called some of his references, most of whom had never heard of him. There was one exception who warned to keep her daughter away from the photographer. As the Franklin investigation progressed, Nelson would be named by numerous victims of having photographed them in sexual acts with Larry King and his cohort (Ibid., Ch. 1).

The first victim to come forward in the Franklin case was a girl named Eulice Washington, a third grader, who had been placed with a foster family, along with her sisters Tracy and Tasha. Her new caretakers were Jarrett and Barbara Webb, who had a total of eight adopted and foster children, for all of whom they received state subsidies, including their adopted sons and daughters.

Physical abuse of the Washingtons began as soon as their first evening with the Webbs, when the youngest girl wet herself and Barbara Webb tied her to a doorknob, beat her and left her there for the duration of the night. The abuse would last eight more years while the girls were in the Webb home, corroborated by both the testimonies of the children themselves and Nebraska's Department of Social Services (DSS). The torture wasn't reserved for just the Washingtons, but all eight adopted and foster children (Ibid., Ch. 1).

Barbara Webb, who decked herself out in a mink coat, costly jewels and designer clothing, was the cousin of Larry King. The children were regularly taken to "Uncle Larry's" expensive home and parties. Eulice was also made to attend the North Omaha Girls Club, where Larry King was president. She told journalist Nick Bryant that the place was creepy with about fifteen "older men" who Bryant described as "[seeming] to salivate over the twenty or so teenage girls who were present" (Ibid., Ch. 1).

Eulice also told Bryant that, in one instance, Larry King removed a collection of videotapes from a locked cabinet at his house and handed it to his cousin, Barbara Webb. When the Webbs went out one night, the children went into their room and found the videos.

"[O]ne of the tapes explicitly showed 'teenagers' engaged in sex. The children also discovered pornographic pictures tucked away in the Webbs' dresser," Bryant wrote (Ibid., Ch. 1).

The children living with the Webbs finally grew the courage to leave, with pairs of them fleeing at various times only to be caught and returned to the Webbs. After lengthy battles between the foster parents and DSS, Eulice and Tracy Washington were finally able to escape their grasp and were placed in a foster home belonging to the Sorenson family. Once they began to feel comfortable with their foster mother, Kathleen Sorenson, they told her the extent of the abuse. Sorenson then brought in DSS and Nebraska State Patrol (NSP). Jarrett Webb had apparently begun molesting Eunice regularly about a year into her stay with the Webbs, at about nine or 10 years old. She was able to gain enough strength to threaten that she would tell Barbara about the abuse, saving her from sexual assault from the ages of 12 to 15, but he resumed when she turned 16 (Ibid., Ch. 1).

Eulice Washington claimed that she had been flown in a chartered plane to Chicago in fall 1984, where she was taken by limo to a hotel. There, Larry King made her wear a black negligee before taking her to a party where she was instructed to sit like a mannequin on a small "pedestal." Young men that had been on the plane with Washington were at the party as well, while two African-American adult males who had also traveled on the aircraft conducted security as older men arrived. As the party progressed, she saw the guests give money to King and leave with the young men. About forty-five minutes after the party started, she identified a national politician that entered the event with two white bodyguards. The politician left the party with a Boys Town student named "Brant," who never returned to the soirée or went on the flight back to Omaha. Boys Town would feature heavily in the Franklin story, as King sat on the board and the Catholic charity for troubled boys supplied residents for prostitution purposes. Washington recognized the politician from nationwide campaign ads and photos in Larry King's home (Ibid., Ch. 1). Though Nick Bryant didn't specify the politician, a separate news article, a book on the subject by John DeCamp (2005,

Ch. 13), and the descriptions of a victim named Paul Bonacci, suggested that it was George H.W. Bush.

Washington was also flown to New York in early 1985 on the same chartered plane used for Chicago, along with some of the same kids from Boys Town, two older female "hookers," two girls aged seven or younger, and Larry King's son. Again, they were picked up by a limo and taken to a hotel, where she was made to wear a different negligee and sit on a pedestal. She said that there was more open sexual activity compared to Chicago, where there was mostly only hugging and kissing on display. In New York, however, she was at one point surrounded by a group of men who masturbated in front of her. Washington was very consistent in her stories to various parties across the years, according to Bryant.

Nick Bryant noted just how absurd it was that the Webbs were able to maintain care of their foster children for so long, suggesting that some authorities may have even been intervening on their behalf. This included the FBI.

> If the authorities weren't cognizant of the Webbs' cruelty and malice, their failure to press child-abuse charges would be understandable, but they had pages and pages of documented corroboration regarding the abuse, and Eulice passed a polygraph on her repeated molestations by Jarrett Webb. ... According to documents I possess, a DSS social worker who made home visits to families renewing their foster care licenses had a very bad feeling about the Webbs, and she took it upon herself to make inquiries. She wrote a letter to her superiors explaining her suspicions about the Webbs; she also found that many of the DSS files pertaining to the Webb children were missing. The social worker said that FBI agents contacted her, and they told her it would be in her best interests to "forget this information" (Ibid., Ch 1)."

In June 1986, during intake procedures at Uta Halee, a residential psychiatric facility in Omaha for adolescent girls, 12-year-old Shawneta Moore hinted at some experience of abuse to a resident adviser named Kirstin Hallberg. Hallberg was a friend of Eulice Washington's foster mother, Kathleen Sorenson, and had been present during some of Eulice's disclosures. So, when Moore said she had attended North Omaha Girls Club, Hallberg asked Moore if she knew any of the Webb girls. She said she knew Eulice and Tracy. As Hallberg probed a little further, Moore became agitated and let out that she had participated in a prostitution and pornography "ring" (Ibid., Ch 1).

When she tried to flee the ring, Moore said her mother was raped as retaliation. Omaha police did have a report about the rape of Moore's mother, in which a man with a stocking over his head broke into their home around 3:00 AM and put a knife to her throat, asking, "Where's Shawneta?" before assaulting her. She called the Omaha Police Department (OPD), but the police appeared not to put much effort into solving the crime (Ibid., Ch 1).

When two other residents came to Hallberg hinting at involvement in a similar prostitution network to Moore's, Hallberg told her supervisor and proposed they call NSP. Her supervisor became distressed at the idea and, soon, Hallberg came to suspect that he was preventing her from helping the young girls. For instance, her supervisor expressed worry that the residents were confiding in her too easily. He suspended her for five days when he thought she was "over-involved" with the residents "beyond therapeutic level." Then, when she expressed her concern that Larry King's wife Alice was on the board of the facility, he became enraged and shouted at her. Soon after, her boss gave her the choice of whether to quit voluntarily or to stay and be fired. She chose the latter (Ibid., Ch. 1).

While at Uta Halee, Hallberg attempted to get Shawneta Moore to open up to her on several occasions, but the girl wouldn't budge. Finally, Moore left the facility and, over time, began to confide in her school counselor. In 1988, the counselor and Hallberg met together with the girl, who was on the verge of suicide because she preferred it to the suffering she would endure if "they" decided to kill her. "If they find out I've talked," Moore sobbed to Hallberg, "they will torture other kids in my name" (Ibid., Ch. 1).

Months later, while she began to feel safe and comfortable at Richard Young Hospital, Moore was able to open up about her story. In 1983, at the age of nine, she had begun going to the North Omaha Girls Club. There, she and four or five other girls became friends with a man named Ray that was about 45 years old. Ray would drive the girls to various locations to smoke marijuana, often abandoned buildings. But before he took them anywhere, he would blindfold them. After several weeks of this, Ray took them to a "party" after one of their weed-smoking sessions. There, Shawnetta found a group of men in their mid-thirties. After chatting with the girls for some time, they began to drink and do drugs. Once the children were "wasted," the men had sex with them, choosing whichever girl they wanted.

Both Shawneta and Eulice were brought to the attention of the Franklin Committee, charged with investigating the affairs of the credit union and

Larry King. Doing most of the legwork was former NSP officer-turned private investigator Gary Caradori and his assistant Karen Ormiston. Caradori found himself exploring the seedy corners of Omaha, trying to uncover the details of King's network. In his search, he found then-21-year-old Alisha Owen, in York Prison for writing six bad checks (Ibid., Ch. 2).

Owen reported to Caradori and his assistant that she met a group of residents at Boys Town in August 1983 when she was 14. One of the kids, named Jeff Hubbell, invited her to a party the following Friday, promising cocaine and alcohol. When the night arrived, Owen was taken by Hubbell and a "friend" to the Twin Towers where she was brought into a luxurious apartment filled with six adults and about 20 minors. Cocaine was sniffed off of a mirrored table while a pornographric movie featuring two adolescent boys was aired on a large tv. Owen didn't recognize the men in the room at first, but eventually learned two of them to be Larry King and Alan Baer, the founder of a large department store chain in Nebraska. There was also an older man named Rob that she would become all too close with. During the first party, she didn't participate in any sexual activity, but did watch as minors and adults went to bedrooms together and looked on as kids played the "501 game," unbuttoning each other's clothes with their teeth and feet. She was excited by the party, tried coke for the first time, and got to "play bartender" (Ibid., Ch. 2).

Her next party at the Twin Towers had similar themes, with the addition of World-Herald columnist Peter Citron in attendance. She became so inebriated that she accidentally walked into a bedroom and caught Larry King receiving oral sex from a pubescent boy. She later played the 501 game with Rob, undoing his zipper with her teeth. Afterward he invited her into his lap and groped her. She then lost her virginity to Troy Boner, another minor from the party (Ibid., Ch. 2).

At her third party, she was left alone with Rob, who placed her on his lap, groped her, and said inappropriate things to her about losing her virginity. When he unzipped her jumpsuit, she begged him to stop, at which point he twisted her wrist. He then disrobed her and made her perform oral sex on him. She followed the act by running to the bathroom and throwing up before crying. Rob apologized and told her to pick out a dress she liked at the department store owned by Alan Baer.

Soon, Owen learned that the man was the chief of the Omaha Police Department, Robert Wadman. After she picked out the dress, Wadman took her to a chic cafe in downtown Omaha, whose owner and hostess had been at King's parties. The cafe was typically closed during the afternoons, but the owner made an exception for Wadman. After eating, he led her down to the restaurant's wine cellar and made her put on the new dress while he masturbated. He tried to ejalucate on her, but she jumped back, incensing the police chief. At the next Twin Towers party, Owen tried to leave when Wadman showed up, but was blocked by a young security enforcer who went by "Larry the Kid."

From then on, Owen was unable to get herself out of the group, fearing for her life after hearing of kids who were murdered or sold by the gang. She was regularly threatened by Larry King and Larry the Kid, the latter of which sometimes beat and raped her. She was also financially rewarded for being a drug mule. Soon, Owen was meeting with Wadman, being forced into group sex, and flying to Los Angeles and Kansas City, with these out of state trips resulting in the worst abuse. Perhaps worse yet, Owen claimed that she eventually gave birth to Chief Wadman's child (Ibid., Ch.2).

The next victim Caradori found was Troy Boner, who was introduced to Alan Baer in August of 1983 at 16- or 17-years-old. Baer paid him for sex at a Twin Towers apartment multiple times and passed his photo along to Larry King. King too paid Boner for sex, eventually setting him up in a hotel where he would regularly stop by for sex, which Boner said included urinating on the Republican businessman. Boner corroborated a number of details related to Owen's story, as well, such as taking her virginity, her regular rendezvous with Chief Wadman, and her abuse by Larry the Kid. Boner also described the trips they took to other cities, such as Los Angeles, where they sometimes acted as drug couriers or were trafficked to sadistic clientele (Ibid., Ch. 2).

The accounts of Owens and Boner didn't always match exactly, which Caradori attributed in part to the trauma they endured, but may have also been a result of drug and alcohol abuse. Bryant recounted one such example:

> Boner, again corroborating Owen's allegations, discussed a private charter flight to California that included Larry King, Owen, Danny King (no relation to Larry King), two prepubescent boys, and himself. Boner and Owen remembered a stopover in Denver and then flying to Southern California. Owen, who admitted to being "bombed," recalled Larry King departing at a "small airport in California" with one of the prepubescent boys as the others proceeded to an airport near Pasadena – Owen speculated that the boy

had been either sold or murdered. Boner, who confessed he was "flying on coke," told a slightly different tale: Everyone departed the plane at the airport near Pasadena, and he said that Owen and Danny King [another trafficked youth] were picked up by a fat, older white male. He told Caradori and Ormiston that he then accompanied Larry King in a rental car as King dropped off each of the little boys at two different locations. As Caradori questioned Boner about the two little boys, he had great difficulty elaborating – he repeatedly turned his head to the right, sighed loudly, and made a number of nervous gestures. Boner ultimately said he believed the two younger kids had been "sold." In Southern California, Boner alleged, Larry King pandered Owen and Danny King to a pair of sadistic pedophiles, again corroborating Owen – she had said that she and Danny King had been served to a couple of sadistic pedophiles in Pasadena. Boner related that he and Larry King picked up Owen and Danny King following their nightmarish ordeal. According to Boner, Owen "looked and smelled" terrible and Danny King wanted to "go back and kill the guy."

Caradori next met Danny King (unrelated to Larry King), who seemed to be the most aloof of them all. Boner introduced a 14-year-old King to Baer in the fall of 1983, before going with Boner to Baer's apartment at the Twin Towers. It wasn't until their second meeting that Baer paid King for oral sex, which began a period of weekly sexual encounters. He then met Larry King at Baer's apartment in April 1984 and was made to have anal sex with him. When he begged him to stop, Larry King made Danny perform oral sex on him and then hit the boy when he spit out his semen. Independently, Boner and Danny King told of a time when Larry King made them have sex with each other. He also recalled the story about the two young boys on the private flight to Los Angeles and the abuse by the sadistic pedophiles (Ibid., Ch. 2).

Nick Bryant described just some of the many ways the various youths corroborated one another's stories as follows:

> Caradori videotaped Danny King for approximately six hours with periodic breaks, and then drove him to the apartment he rented for Boner. Caradori was a meticulous investigator, and he realized the importance of corroborating their videotaped statements. So he spent the next two days shuttling King to Omaha and Council Bluffs to identify the numerous locations he had mentioned throughout his statement. As Caradori and King navigated a major Omaha thoroughfare, King identified the Twin Towers and pin-

pointed Baer's apartment balcony. Caradori also had an associate shuttle Boner to Omaha and Council Bluffs for the same purpose – they subsequently photographed the locations named by Boner and Danny King. After accruing scores of photos, Caradori had Boner and King separately identify them, and they consistently corroborated each other on the photographed locations. Interestingly, the allegations of Owen and Danny King corroborated Shawneta Moore on one perpetrator, even though they had never met her. Moore had told Irl Carmean that an administrator for the Fort Calhoun school system accompanied Larry King to one of the child-sex parties she attended, and both Owen and Danny King identified the same individual as frequenting King's sex parties. Moreover, Owen, Boner, and Danny King corroborated Eulice Washington on the chartered flights. Owen and Boner also corroborated Washington on the entanglement of Boys Town's students in King's pandering network (Ibid., Ch. 2).

The last victim that Caradori identified that was willing to testify in court was Paul Bonacci. Bonacci claimed that he met the star reporter of the *Omaha World-Herald*, Peter Citron, at an amusement park in Omaha when he was 11. He was sexually abused by Citron from 1979 to 1987, which included group sex, with the reporter taking pictures. Citron also flew Bonacci out to California, where he maintained a home, and was present when the reporter molested other children, one of which Citron was charged with sexually assaulting. Bonacci was able to name the boy even though that name was never publicly released (Ibid., Ch. 2).

When he was 11, Bonacci also met Alan Baer. He was abused by Baer from 1979 to 1988, with Baer giving the boy drugs, money and jewelry during that time. Bonacci went to some one hundred parties at the Twin Towers luxury apartments, where he met other children named by victims in the ring, as well as photographer Rusty Nelson.

He also recounted to investigator Caradori and his assistant the numerous flights across the country he'd taken with Larry King. Bryant reported the boy's video recorded testimony to Cadori as follows:

> Larry King chartered a plane that departed from Eppley Airfield, near Omaha. The plane made a stop in Grand Island, Nebraska, where King picked up camera equipment, and then they stopped in Aurora, Colorado to pick up a boy named Nicholas, who was approximately thirteen years old. The plane refueled in Las Vegas, Nevada before landing at Sacramento. In Sacramento, Bonacci

said, they rendezvoused with a "little Italian guy" whom he identified as the "producer." The producer subsequently drove Bonacci, Nicholas, King and the pilot of the plane to a remote wooded area, where they met a few additional men, who comprised the "camera crew," and also a young boy named "Jeremy" – the producer said that Jeremy had been kidnapped. Jeremy was jostled into a small cage, and after he was let loose from the cage, Bonacci and Nicholas were ordered to run him down and drag him back to the older men. Bonacci stated that Jeremy divulged to him that he was from Idaho – he described Jeremy as roughly twelve years old, having braces on his teeth, with blond hair and brown eyes. Bonacci sobbed when he told Caradori and Ormiston that he and Nicholas were forced to have sex with Jeremy while members of the team – an adult male then kicked Jeremy in the face, molested him, and, as Jeremy screamed, shot him in the head with a handgun. Following the filming of Jeremy's murder, Bonacci said, he was transported to the hotel, where he had sex with the pilot. He described the pilot as having brownish blonde hair, a brown eye and a blue eye, a scar on his left arm, and an eagle tattoo on his chest. After having sex with the pilot, Bonacci slit his wrists in the hotel room (Ibid., Ch. 2).

His description of trips with King also included flights to D.C. where he said an operation was in place to compromise politicians and other powerful people. Key to this operation was Craig Spence, a flamboyant D.C. lobbyist known for hosting wild, cocaine-fueled parties for the political establishment of the nation. Friends said that his townhouse, located not far from King's own D.C residence, was outfitted with a sophisticated array of recording equipment and a two-way mirror. This fact was corroborated by "the D.C. madame," Henry Vinson, a business partner of Spence who supplied adult prostitutes for Spence's powerful clientele. Spence was reported to have said that the CIA installed the surveillance equipment for him, implying that it was intended for use in a honeypot scheme (Ibid., Ch. 5).

A 1982 *New York Times* article described the extravagant parties held by Spence as being "glitter[ed] with notables, from ambassadors to television stars, from senators to senior State Department officials." The story added, "Richard Nixon is a friend. So is [former Nixon Attorney General] John Mitchell. [*CBS* journalist] Eric Sevareid is termed 'an old, dear friend.' Senator John Glenn is 'a good friend' and Peter Ustinov [British actor and journalist] is 'an old, old friend'" (Gailey 1982).

Other guests included CIA Director William Casey, who Larry King described as a friend and role model, and Roy Cohn (Bryant 2012, Ch.

5). In fact, according to the *Washington Times* series that exposed Spence's compromise operation, Spence frequently mentioned Cohn to his friends and said that he hosted Cohn at his home on multiple occasions, including a birthday party hosted in Cohn's favor.

In addition to trafficking children, there were stories circulating that Spence and King were involved in the Iran-Contra affair. A May 1989 story for the *Omaha World-Herald* noted: "In the 6 ½ months since federal authorities closed Franklin, rumors have persisted that money from the credit union somehow found its way to the Nicaraguan contra rebels." This would fit into the larger pattern of the CIA using savings and loans businesses to secretly fund the Contras, including one that had the son of George H.W. Bush, Neil Bush, on its board. This bank in particular had done business with Franklin Credit Union. Also worth noting was the fact that King and individuals involved in Iran-Contra had established an organization called Citizens for America that funded a lecture tour for Oliver North and leaders of the Contras. King donated more than $25,000 to the group (Webb 2019).

Both Vinson and victim Paul Bonacci independently said that King and Spence were in business together. Vinson claimed that Spence attempted to force him into participating in the child trafficking business, but Vinson, the D.C. madame, refused to do so, which resulted in his ultimate arrest and imprisonment initiated by a raid on his apartment by the Secret Service (Bryant 2012, Ch. 5).

Aspects of the relationship Spence had with the child trafficking ring was made public in a 1989 exposé by *Washington Examiner* reporter Paul Rodriguez, which detailed midnight tours of the White House given to Spence's child prostitutes. Spence said that he was provided access to the White House by "top level" officials, including Donald Gregg, National Security Advisor for Bush at the time. Gregg worked at the CIA from 1951 to 1982, at which time he became National Security Advisor for Vice President Bush (Ibid., Ch. 5).

Bonacci's abuse in the Franklin scandal appeared to have been corroborated by a number of factors. Nick Bryant's interviews with child pornographer Rusty Nelson, as well as victims Alisha Owen and Danny King, confirmed that Bonacci was at child sex parties hosted at the Twin Towers. Troy Boner's 1993 affidavit corroborated it, as well. Nick Bryant adds, "Moreover, it would have been next to impossible for Bonacci to know about Larry King's DC activities if he wasn't thoroughly enmeshed with Larry King – Owen, Boner, and Danny King were unaware of Larry King's DC deeds."

In June, 1990, the Franklin Committee and Caradori had a closed-door meeting, during which Caradori expressed hesitation about turning over all of the evidence he'd collected over to law enforcement, specifically "various people in the FBI" and NSP, because he came to think they were hindering the investigation intentionally. The Franklin Committee struggled with the evidence it had amassed, not knowing where to turn for assistance given the authority figures involved. At first, the U.S. Attorney General's Office didn't respond to requests for help. Caradori tried to keep the names of the victims from the public (Ibid., Ch. 2).

Nevertheless, Owen was questioned by two NPS officers in prison, who apparently told her that the Franklin Committee didn't even exist. Owen feared that her being interviewed by the police in the Warden's office would give her a bad reputation and, indeed, she was beaten up by three inmates in the showers six weeks later. Though the State Ombudsman's Office found that the attack "was motivated, in part, because some of her fellow inmates thought that she might be an informant against the women at York" and that "We did not find, in our dealings with [Owen] in this matter, that she engaged in any exaggeration or magnification of the facts; nor did we detect any attempt on her part to stretch the truth or to falsely color the facts surrounding the assault upon her." Owen was placed on solitary confinement for her "protection" for almost two years (Ibid., Ch. 2).

Ultimately, the Franklin Committee handed Caradori's evidence over to the Attorney General, who then passed it onto the FBI. By November 1988, neither the FBI nor the U.S. Department of Justice interviewed Eunice Washington or Shawneta Moore. When the FBI did interview Moore, her close ally Kirstin Hallberg got an anonymous phone call the day before, warning her, "You and your friend … are doing the wrong thing, trying to bust up my boy Larry King. Now it's too late. Now I'm turning into a bloodhound." When she told NPS officer Chuck Phillips, aiding the feds in the investigation, about the threat, he asked if there was a link between Larry King and Moore's abuse, a naive response given the extent King was involved. Throughout the case, Hallberg noted how overbearing Phillips was, becoming "extremely angry" at "these kids being too scared to talk."

When Phillips went to interview Eulice Washington, he and his two accompanying FBI agents pushed themselves through the front door of the house of her grandmother, Opal, who said she wanted Senator Ernie Chambers, a prominent voice in the African American community, to speak with her grandchildren before any police interrogated her. Rather than give in to her request, Phillips and the feds tracked Eulice down the next day and subjected her to hours of grueling interviews. They then did the same with her sister Tracy at Omaha's FBI Field Office. A relative of the Washingtons' was quoted in the *Lincoln Journal* as saying, "The FBI has accomplished what it set out to accomplish – to make the girls seem as though all this were a fabrication (Ibid., Ch. 1)."

The Washington girls' one-time guardian ad litem, Patricia Flocken, was interviewed by the FBI in January 1989 and said that the agent questioning her "seemed pissed" and barked more than once that her testimony was simply "hearsay." A February 1989 article in the *World-Herald* quoted the FBI's Nick O'Hara as saying that there was no "substance to the initial allegations," a determination made before the FBI had even interviewed Larry King or the first two victims to come forward, Eulice Washington and Shawneta Moore. When they did interview him after the article's publication, he admitted to subletting a Twin Towers apartment to Rusty Nelson and said Nelson may have gone with him on a business trip to New York, but denied all of the other allegations.

Nick Bryant wrote, "King disclosed to FBI agents that he was a good friend of World-Herald publisher Harold Andersen, OPD Chief Wadman, and Nebraska Attorney General Spire – all three show up on King's party invitation lists. But, because of the unsavory rumors, nobody wanted to acknowledge their friendship with him or to admit that they attended his fabulous parties. He said that even FBI agents had frequented his parties in the past – he then looked at one of the FBI agents questioning him and contended that he had attended one of his parties. ... The FBI and NSP interviews documented in this chapter reveal that investigators approached all interviews with unbridled skepticism and hostility. Eulice and Tracy Washington and Shawneta Moore alleged that the investigators who interviewed them were extremely antagonistic, and Kirstin Hallberg and Patricia Flocken support their accounts" (Ibid., Ch. 1).

According to Shawnetta Moore, a Douglas County attorney and an individual on the hospital's staff said that, if she didn't speak to the FBI, the hospital wouldn't release her. She claimed that it felt like the agents were trying to trip her up. While she originally told staff at the hospital that she knew of five murders, she only told the FBI about three because she felt rushed by the FBI. Aside from that, her stories to staff and investigators were always consistent. She was additionally able to identify one of the buildings she was taken to at Fort Calhoun.

Pamela Vuchetich, the lawyer for Troy Boner, Danny King, and Alicia Owen, requested immunity agreements for her clients before she would allow FBI interviews. And while she was quoted in the *World-Herald* as saying she had negotiated such an agreement, neither Troy Boner nor Danny King actually had one by that point, though Owen did.

However, the FBI did speak to Danny King anyway. While Vuchetich said King "was not emotionally prepared to be interviewed," he agreed to it on an "informal basis in order to begin the interview process." An FBI debriefing by FBI Special Agent William Culver said that Culver and NSP officer Chuck Phillips "stressed to King that he should not feel that he must relate the exact same story to the criminal investigators that he told Caradori on the videotape." In his first session, about three-hours long, he recounted events just as he had to Caradori. He stuck to the story in his second five-hour session, as well. After being subjected to many hours of interviews across several days, Danny King finally recanted.

In March 1990, Troy Boner called Caradori terrified, begging him to come to the FBI office with him. He had signed a federal immunity agreement the day before and told Caradori that someone his friend recognized as a high-ranking official in the U.S. Attorney's Office threatened him with perjury. His friend knew the man from an adult bookstore and Boner claimed to Caradori that the man had a proclivity for "young kids." Carardori said he'd attend the meeting with the FBI if Boner's lawyer okayed it. However, Caradori received a call telling him he "would not be accepted at the FBI office in Omaha." A 1993 affidavit from Boner revealed the reason why the FBI likely didn't want Caradori present. According to the affidavit, Boner was threatened by the FBI agents that day, with Boner believing he had to either "lie or die" (Ibid., Ch. 2).

Eventually, Troy's brother was found dead of a gunshot wound made to look like a lost game of Russian roulette (Ibid., Ch. 6). He was one of 15 suspicious deaths between 1988 and 1991 (DeCamp 2005, Appendix A). These included Eulice Washington's foster mother, Kathleen Sorenson, and investigator Gary Caradori, who had had his vehicles tampered with on multiple occasions before finally paying the ultimate price in a mysterious plane crash.

In July 1990, Caradori flew his eight-year-old son AJ in his private plane to Chicago to see an All Star baseball game. While in the city, he took it upon himself to investigate the case, possibly meeting child pornographer Rusty Nelson for photographic evidence of King's abuse. Before making his return trip, Caradori called Senator Schmit to tell him that he'd made a break in the case. However, he never made it back to Nebraska. His plane exploded mid-flight, killing both Caradori and AJ (Bryant 2012, Ch. 2).

In the end, the grand jury issued a report – which members said was written with the help of the case's judge, Samuel Van Pelt – describing the Franklin scandal as "a carefully crafted hoax." Crafted by who? Journalist Michael Casey, a lead Caradori had relied on temporarily and early on in the investigation, and Gary Caradori himself, who had recently died in a mysterious plane crash. Crucial to the jury's determination was Troy Bonner's recantation, allegedly in the face of threats from the FBI. In the trial, Larry King had not even been subpoenaed because it was presumed he would plead the fifth amendment and, therefore, not be worth questioning. Rather than indict any of the perpetrators, the jury decided to indict the victims who refused to recant, Alisha Owen and Paul Bonacci, for perjury (Ibid., Ch. 4).

Despite the grand jury's conclusions, aspects of the story were vindicated after the case ended. One player in the ring, *Omaha World-Herald* columnist Peter Citron, pled guilty to sexual assault of two children in a separate trial (Ibid., Ch. 2). Father Hupp, former director of Boys Town, agreed to participate in a Discovery Channel documentary about the case, in which he validated the allegations about his institution (Ibid., Prologue). Former CIA Director William Colby, who served as committee investigator after Caradori's death, validated the story in the same film (Ibid., Ch. 2). Unfortunately, the documentary was never aired, but found new life on the Internet. For embezzling $40 million, Larry King was ultimately sentenced to 15 years in prison, 10 years fewer than Alisha Owens (Ibid., Ch. 1).

JOHN DeCAMP

Though he appeared to play the side of the victims in the Franklin Scandal, there was reason to look side-eye at former Senator and CIA officer John DeCamp. DeCamp's CIA career began under future CIA director William Colby as he formalized the Phoenix Program in Vietnam (DeCamp 2005, Introduction). Under Phoenix, the CIA worked with local authorities to divide rural villages into controlled hamlets and construct regional detention centers where any citizen suspected of having knowledge of Vietcong activities would be kidnapped and tortured. Once names of Vietcong collaborators were given up, assassination squads would enter the hamlets and murder not just the suspected collaborators but their entire families (Valentine 2016).

The atrocities committed under the Phoenix Program, countless My Lais altogether, were so horrendous that anyone involved at a high level would seem to lack the moral capability to go on to defend young people claiming to be abused at the hands of the CIA.

DeCamp was also involved in a CIA program that might have raised the eyebrows of #Pizzagaters. Under what was called Operation Babylift, the U.S. military executed the mass evacuation of about 3,300 South Vietnamese orphans to the U.S. and other countries in April 1975 (PBS, n.d.). As with the story of Laura Silsby, who attempted to "rescue" Haitian "orphans" and drew the attention of #Pizzagate sleuths, not all children taken by U.S. forces may have actually been orphans.

DeCamp would go on to find himself involved in a number of high profile cases that, if there were any deep state involvement, would require the services of someone on the inside to maintain control of the situation. This included the Columbine school shooting, child sexual abuse by the Catholic Church, and the Oklahoma City bombing (DeCamp 2005, Ch. 23).

Though he claimed not to have known what occurred at parties hosted by the Larry King, DeCamp admitted to having attended King's 1984 event thrown after the Republican National Convention in Dallas (Ibid., Ch. 7).

All of these would be minor starting points to begin exploring the possibility of controlled opposition in the Franklin scandal. However, there was at least one instance in which DeCamp did hamper the investigation. He recommended to Senator Schmit, who was heading the state investigation into financial and sexual abuse at Franklin Credit Union, to speak with the regional head of the FBI.

> In brutal language and with the most somber demeanor possible, Mr. O'Hara made it clear that probably his closest friend in the world was Police Chief Robert Wadman, and that anyone who would dare to accuse Robert Wadman of impropriety had better realize that in accusing Wadman, they were effectively taking on Nick O'Hara and the FBI."
>
> I realized instantly, that my advice to Senator Schmit may have been faulty. How could I have known in advance, that the head of the FBI and the former chief were so intimate in their business and personal relationships (Ibid., Ch. 9)?

I wondered if DeCamp performed other tasks to thwart the investigation. For instance, a memo from John DeCamp created a media firestorm about the case that may have had some negative impacts on how it proceeded.

DeCamp sent a letter suggesting that law enforcement had failed in its investigations into child sexual abuse, listing Larry King among four other well-known Nebraskans as "centerpieces in a coordinated program of child abuse." He went on to say that the information he had wasn't gained from the Committee or Caradori's tapes, but from word throughout town and that the media had covered it up. He then challenged the five people in the memo to sue him.

In reporting on the memo, the *World-Herald* and *Lincoln Journal* declined to print the names of the accused, but the names were announced by a caller on Omaha radio, causing the show's host to lose her job. Additionally, an individual running for office sent 10,000 copies of DeCamp's letter to voters in his district. Soon, there were reports on the story from the *Kansas City Star* and even in a small piece in *Newsweek* (Ibid., Ch. 9).

Author of *The Franklin Scandal*, Nick Bryant, said of the impact:

> Gary Caradori ... became increasingly agitated about the memo, because the media frenzy it incited created an unfavorable ripple effect for his investigation – he found it more and more difficult to coax victims and others who had information to come forward. The collective reverberations of DeCamp's memo, Caradori's investigation, and the impending Douglas County grand jury coincided with a pair of major 'surprises.'
>
> The first occurred when President George H.W. Bush rolled into town – Bush would speak at a February 7, 1990, fundraiser for Governor Orr, a fellow Republican. Larry King considered the president a personal 'friend' and proudly displayed a picture of himself and Bush, looking like the best of friends, at the Franklin Credit Union. You will recall that King hosted a $100,000 gala for the newly-nominated Bush at the 1988 Republican Convention in New Orleans.
>
> A source informed Caradori that King had purchased a ticket to attend the "$1,000-a-couple" fundraiser, even though the event's organizers later denied it. The source also disclosed to Caradori that when the Secret Service discovered King's plan to grace the fundraiser, they either ushered him to the federal courthouse or demanded that he make haste thereto.
>
> Either way, King made an impromptu appearance at the federal courthouse in the early afternoon of February 7, before U.S. Magistrate Richard Kopf ...
>
> Magistrate Kopf ordered King to undergo a "mental health evaluation" at the U.S. Medical Center for Federal Prisoners in Springfield, Missouri – "with no delay." King waived a hearing on Kopf's

ruling and immediately found himself en route to Springfield in the custody of two U.S. marshals. Kopf's preemptive decision on King's "mental health," made without a motion from anyone, was extremely odd, but the magistrate didn't feel inclined to defend his ruling (Ch. 2).

In addition to the memo and leaked names of the accused, the video-taped interviews with the victims by investigator Gary Caradori became public and may have played the biggest role in souring the public to the truth of the Franklin scandal. The tapes were turned over to the offices of Nebraska's Attorney General and the U.S. Attorney. From there, they somehow made it to the press. The release of Cadori's interviews allowed for the media to cut the footage in ways that could construct a narrative that the youths were lying, resulting in a key strategy for the defense in the case.

When the tapes were made public, DeCamp made the recommendation to Schmit not to protect the victims using committee funds:

> "You cannot and should not do anything to use committee funds or committee personnel to provide protection for these kids," I told Schmit. "Otherwise, you and the committee may be accused of impropriety and tampering with witnesses, and who knows what else. Painful as it is for me to tell you this, you have to find some other legal channel to provide protection for the kids. Whether that channel is the courts or a judge or whoever, it is something that either the lawyer for the kids should be doing, or some institution of government vested with the power and responsibility to do those things should be doing. But you, Senator Schmit, should not personally get involved in any way, shape or form in providing money or assistance or protection for these kids, nor should the committee, in my opinion" (DeCamp 2005, Ch. 9).

As I learned, without protection, the witnesses were bullied and, in the case of Kathleen Sorenson, killed. Otherwise, their loved ones, like Troy Boner's brother, were killed.

Absorbed by Pedophile Rings

Now, imagine that everything you just read was condensed into an even more jumbled and less coherent ball, held together with "ums" and "uhs," and then spit at you in a rambling monologue. And that that manic speech occurred in the cafeteria of a hospital. And you were my brother and/or his wife and could hardly breathe, let alone get a word in edgewise.

"Why do you know so much about this?" you would have asked.

"Lately, you could say I've become sort of a pedophile-phile."

That was what it was like to talk to me at the time. I did my best not to bring this sort of stuff up to Cindy, who was particularly uncomfortable with it for obvious reasons. But as strange as it seemed, it really felt like I was getting somewhere. Like there was a point or a center to this "research" and if I could find it, it might explain how the system at large worked and maybe even how to dismantle it.

Somewhere at the center or at least adjacent to the bull's eye was something called Monarch. I had come across the phrase while reading about Franklin. Something to do with Paul Bonacci, but it seemed like a Pandora's Box that I just wasn't ready to open.

One thing that was clear was just how unaccountable the power elite seemed to be. Just as the #MeToo movement demonstrated that sexual abuse of subordinates by superiors was a widespread problem throughout a variety of work environments – particularly by extremely wealthy and powerful individuals – the Epstein case and others like it suggested that child sexual abuse was also an issue in elite circles. The exact proportion of this problem, particularly when compared to "traditional" forms of child abuse in family settings, for instance, was difficult to determine. This was in large part because it was not recognized as a problem by society at large and those who performed these types of activities were generally free from consequences. There had been no public investigation into the extent to which the powerful people in Epstein's circle participated in sexual activities with minors. In the case of similar incidents, such as the Dutroux affair or the Franklin scandal, the cases were generally swept under the rug.

I also learned from these examples that they represented a pattern that seemed to be repeated throughout modern history, often by or in the service of intelligence organizations to perform blackmail on members of the ruling class. I made the tentative assumption that blackmail material could have been used as leverage to get those in power to execute their power in ways that benefitted specific ruling interests.

What I couldn't know was how interconnected such incidents as the Dutroux affair and Franklin scandal were exactly, but I did know that those social networks overlapped. Epstein, for instance, appeared to have had ties possibly to Mossad and U.S. intelligence. Ghislaine Maxwell was closely linked to the British royal family. Her father was said to be Mossad and possibly MI6. They were all linked to Adnan Khashoggi, who represented Saudi Arabia. So, it would not have been out of the question to think there may have been some, at least informal, ties between various child trafficking operations.

Did this mean there was a global pedophile cabal the way the #Pizzagate community described it? I couldn't say that everyone in the ruling class was a pedophile, but many of them may have been compromised with one form of blackmail material or another (with or without the abuse of children). They certainly weren't all Jewish or democrats, though, as I often found suggested by Qanon people.

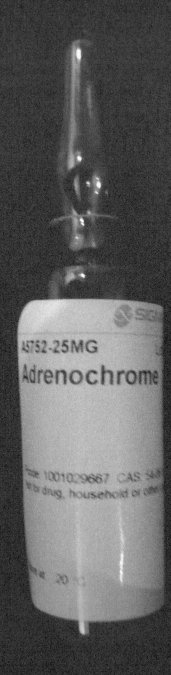

Vial of Adrenochrome
Eduardo Hidalgo Downing, Creative Commons.

CHAPTER FOUR

SATANISM ENTERS THE QNIVERSE

I hadn't realized it at the time, but I'd already crossed a threshold. I'd entered through the #Pizzagates of hell and I would never be the same again. Looking back behind me, I could barely make out the entryway. It was something like the foyer of an old colonial with wainscoting and walls papered with posts from forums, image sharing sites, and various forms of social media. Ahead of me stood a stairway ascending to the mansion's bedrooms. I knew I had to urinate, so I looked for what I thought was some sort of butler's half-bath beneath the stairs. Just as I suspected, there was a door there. I turned the ornate, iron handle, now oxidized to a green patina.

The half bath was, like the foyer, decorated with white wainscoting below blood-red paint. The toilet was one of those old timey johns with the tank mounted near the ceiling and a long chain hanging down, finished off with a small, teardrop wooden handle. I relieved myself into the porcelain fixture before yanking the chain. To my surprise, a panel behind the pot opened up to reveal steps descending below the home. From the abyss, I could see a faint light, the glow of a computer terminal I assumed. I'd come this far. I took my chances with the mystery hole.

It was hard to stay sane. I could admit it: there was a time when I messaged two of my best friends, still bleary eyed from lack of sleep with the new baby, and said, "Guys. I think #Pizzagate is real." My evidence was James Alefantis's Instagram. Honestly, it was disturbing. His goddaughter or whoever did have her hands taped to a table, though Alefantis claimed her sister had done it. And he joked about buying babies and used the hashtag #chickenlover. Or I think he did? Maybe it was someone commenting on his Instagram.

And the logo of Besta Pizza did have the FBI's pedo triangle symbol in it. Or maybe it didn't. Maybe someone had just photoshopped the symbol onto the logo to make a point? Things were blurry. For instance, at one point I thought Alefantis had posted nude photos of minors on his Instagram, but those were just the Jeff Koons *Made in Heaven* series in the background of a museum he was visiting.

Rightfully, my friends told me I was probably wrong and there weren't tunnels under the pizza places in D.C. As I regained my sanity upon regaining a reasonable sleep schedule, I became more clear-headed and decided to be more skeptical going forward. This meant not taking claims of satanic ritual abuse (SRA) at face value, especially those from #Pizzagate.

At some point, as Internet sleuths discovered the variety of actual pedophile rings in which the world's rich and powerful participated, the concept morphed. When Pizzagaters came across a message from performance artist Marina Abramović to Tony Podesta in the WikiLeaks email dump, the floodgates seemed to be let loose.

> Dear Tony,
>
> I am so looking forward to the Spirit Cooking dinner at my place.
> Do you think you will be able to let me know if your brother is joining?
> All my love,
> Marina (WikiLeaks 2016)

Right-wing blogger Cassandra Fairbanks may have been the first to pick up on the story on November 4th, 2016, just four days before the presidential election:

> In perhaps the most disturbing Wikileaks release to date, Tony Podesta (John Podesta's brother) is invited to a "Spirit Cooking" dinner with performance artist Marina Abramović.
>
> Dinner with a famous artist might sound deeply mundane, but there is far more to this story …
>
> While this seems like a completely normal and uninspiring email, a look at what 'spirit cooking' is, changes things immediately.
>
> In the video, Abramović is seen painting the recipe for these "spirit dinners," using what appears to be thickly congealed blood. The recipe read, at one point, "mix fresh breast milk with fresh sperm, drink on earthquake nights."
>
> So, we have to ask, did John Podesta's brother invite him to go drink semen mixed with breast milk? Yikes (Fairbanks 2016).

It was then picked up by Paul Joseph Watson at InfoWars (Watson 2016), published on the front page of the right-wing *Drudge Report* and at smaller outfits like *Danger and Play* and *Conservative Outfitters*, which referred to it as the "most disturbing email leaked from Hillary Clinton's inner circle" (Cush 2016).

Abramović had been known for her controversial art, particularly when she was younger, which featured self-mutilation, mutilation of others, the presence of a loaded gun and more. Spirit cooking was a concept devised by the artist with fellow performer Jacob Samuel in 1996 (Ohlheiser 2016). The idea was first published in the form of a cookbook filled with "recipes" for "evocative instructions for actions or for thoughts." One recipe called for chefs to "mix fresh breast milk with fresh sperm milk." Another required "13,000 grams of jealousy" (MoMA 1996).

In 1997, this was followed by a multimedia installation at the Zerynthia Associazione per l'Arte Contemporanea in Rome, Italy, where "enigmatically violent recipe instructions" were painted on white walls in pig's blood (Lacis 2014). Eventually, it evolved to become a form of dinner party entertainment for her friends, donors, and collectors (MIT Press 2017).

Posting a clip from a 90s performance of Spirit Cooking by Abramović, right-wing blogger Mike Cernovich wrote on social media:

> Those brainwashed by hoaxing media will find this outrageous, until they watch the video from a 1997 "performance." Occult symbolism, as I've reported on extensively, is done openly to taunt the public. It's a form of power and control. Secret Societies do not want to remain secret.

With a definition sourced from Everipedia, InfoWars described spirit cooking as "a sacrament in the religion of Thelema," founded by alleged "satanist Aleister Crowley (Watson 2016)." Crowley was not a satanist, but his occult teachings would lay the foundation for modern satanism, as I would soon learn. Some descriptions of her spirit cooking installation did bear a Thelemic resemblance. For instance, she was said to engage in a performance in which she made a painting from menstrual blood, breast milk, urine, and sperm, some of the ingredients in Crowley's "Body of Light," used as sacrament in his gnostic mass (Crowley 1904).

Once Abramović became associated with the satanism and Democratic power players, it wasn't hard to find more sinister elements in her work. In particular, a 2011 dinner that heavily featured cannibalism as a theme became the go-to for allegations that Clinton's inner circle ate people. The benefit gala saw a guest list of some 800 celebrities and socialites forced to don lab coats as they dined around long tables at the center of which were human heads. In actuality, hired models sat beneath tables, with their heads protruding through circular holes to give the appearance that they were being served on platters. Other tables featured models as decor, draping across the linens with fake skeletons on their nude torsos..

The "pies-de-resistance" were two cakes made to look like life-sized replicas of Debbie Harry and Abramović in the nude. Dining on their host's likeness were Gwen Stefani, Kirsten Dunst, Rosanna Arquette, Tilda Swinton and Will Ferrell (Trebay 2011).

While John Podesta did not attend the spirit cooking dinner at her home, according to Abramović, she did say that Tony was a "long-standing friend of mine" (Ohlheiser 2019). He was an important founder of the establishment of the artist's Marina Abramović Institute.

Stories of cannibalism among the rich were seemingly validated in the story of Arnie Hammer. In 2020, Hammer's ex-girlfriends shared supposed texts from the actor and heir to the Occidental Petroleum fortune in which he lustfully discussed his desire to rape them and remove pieces of their body to eat them (Sarkisian 2021). With these revelations, one could be forgiven for having some suspicions about the extent to which the wealthy might have eaten people.

Moreover, with liberal ideals already framed to be at odds with conservative Christianity, it wouldn't be hard for the narrative concocted by the likes of Cernovich to resonate with right-wing audience members. Whether or not any genuine satanism was ever discovered was hard to discern, in part because the evidence was often very fuzzy, metaphorically and literally. The most notable was the infamous temple on Epstein's island of Little St. James.

We didn't know what was in the Middle Eastern style edifice, striped blue and white and topped with a golden dome. In fact, we knew very little about the specifics of Epstein's affairs. That evidence remained firmly in the hands of government authorities, leaving plenty of room for wild speculation. For instance, what was Epstein doing with what appeared to be dental equipment in his bathroom? One could have the demons in their unconscious answer the question for them.

Internet sleuths also came across a bizarre sculpture from the home of Ghislaine Maxwell. It was a mask of a white man with blank eyes and Rapunzel-like braided locks hanging from his beard. The mask was mounted to a long brown cloth which appeared to have one of the FBI's pedophile symbols, a spiraled triangle, repeated along its length (Reddit user Tlee1641, n.d.)

Epstein victim Maria Farmer made it clear just how removed the lives of the wealthy were from ordinary citizens, though most of it didn't sound very occult. In an interview with Whitney Webb, she said that Robert Maxwell stole items from the British Museum.

> [Ghislaine] shows me [an artifact] on the mantle [of her apartment] and I'm like, "Oh, what's this?" And she said, "Well, these are things my father took from the British Museum." And she's like, "They're ancient relics." ... I'm like, "What do you mean he took them?" And she's like, "He took them. He liked them." And she's like, "This is an ancient, Peruvian Relic," you know? And she's showing me this stuff that was 22-carat gold that had been taken from graves.

Perhaps less surprising was the sexual paraphernalia Ghislaine showed her.

> And we went upstairs and she showed me this room and it was the weirdest thing I've ever seen in my life, Whitney. I walk in and there's like – how do I even explain this? It's like this place for your feet to hang on the wall and then these leather straps to put around your calves. So you hang upside down. And then there were all these like devices everywhere. Okay. So, I'm like, "What is that?" And I point to the wall and she said, "Well, that's for yoga. I can hang upside down for 45 minutes. Like a bat. Keeps me really young." I was like, "That's so weird." I said, "Well, what's this thing in the middle of the room?" She said, "Oh, that's a sex swing, honey."

Farmer claimed that she was held captive at the vast estate of Les Wexner in New Albany, Ohio. Calling Wexner the "head of the snake" for the Epstein operation, Farmer noted numerous strange features of the Wexner family lifestyle. Most overtly evil was the fact that the Wexners housed slaves from the Philippines and Thailand to perform manual labor.

> I said, "How long have you worked here?" And she said, "We were stolen." Like, what does that mean, they're stolen? They were trafficked ... they had women from the Philippines in Florida and then New York and in the house on ... and no one ever cares. Like I mentioned this and everybody goes, "Yeah, well they traffic people from the Philippines and Thailand as servants. It's like, so sick."

Less overtly evil, but venturing into bizarre territory was an underground tunnel connecting the guest house Farmer stayed in to the mansion where the Wexners lived.

> "It wasn't the basement, because they had a basement," Farmer told Webb. "It was like below that. And there was a sauna in that room [the basement], like a huge sauna. And then they had like a vault and then they had a door to an underground tunnel. And the only

way I knew it was an underground tunnel was because their maid told me, I said, 'What is this door?' Cause I used to keep everything down there [in the basement]. And she said, 'Oh, that's, that's the tunnel that leads to the main house.'"

The maid explained that the tunnel led to a 10,000-square-foot floor that raised into the main residence.

I'm like, 'Well, that's weird. Why would they do that?' And she said, 'Oh, you don't know?' And I said, 'No.' And she said, 'There's a giant 10,000-square-foot floor that raises up when someone goes through that tunnel and then they can enter the room secretly and then no one ever sees them. The floor raises up.' She said it's 10,000-square-feet. Now, this is just the maid telling me. And she cleans it. So, she really had no reason to not tell me the truth, you know? And she'd been working there a long time and I asked her, 'Have you ever met Les Wexner?' And she said, 'No , I've been working here about 20 years" (Webb 2020)

Farmer also claimed to see an occult looking statue about the various properties owned by Wexner and passed to Epstein. Years later she came to believe they were depictions of Moloch, a deity that appeared in the Leviticus book of the Old Testament to whom worshippers sacrificed children. There was some debate about the roots of this god and what type of sacrifices were performed. Some scholars believed that Moloch was a Canaanite deity, but others argued that the sacrifices referred to were offered to the Israelite god Yahweh. Beginning in the medieval era, Moloch had been depicted with a bull's head and arms stretching over a fire. The image appeared to combine the Minotaur legend with stories of child sacrifice by Catharginians (Wikipedia).

Other charges of satanism and the occult in the Qanon community were harder to decipher. Barely discernible videos that purported to depict abuse by Democratic leaders were circulated on the Internet. One video claimed to show John Podesta screaming at a child as he forced him into a scalding hot shower. It was too grainy and distorted to see anything actually occurring at all, but I could hear someone screaming. Who it was was impossible to tell, but convinced Internet users said that it was obviously the voice of John Podesta (Line 2020).

In 2018, it was claimed that an "extreme snuff film" called "Frazzledrip" was taken from the laptop of Anthony Weiner and showed Hillary Clinton and Huma Abedin raping and killing a young girl. Supposedly, the two women then drank her blood to absorb its adrenochrome before "tak[ing] turns wearing the little girl's face like a mask" (Emery 2018). Though I wasn't able to find the clip, there were images said to be from the video online, including one juxtaposed alongside photos of Comet Ping Pong. The collage created by an Internet user was meant to suggest the snuff film was shot at the pizza shop.

Adrenochrome was an important detail to understand, as it was featured heavily in Qanon lore. To be honest, I wouldn't have known about it if it weren't for Theta, who introduced the concept to me. A chemical compound derived when adrenaline was oxygenated, adrenochrome was thought to be extracted by members of the pedo cabal at the height of fear when a child was being sacrificed. It seemed to have a drug-like quality to the perpetrators, extending their lives; however, once the supply was interrupted, the youth of the addict quickly escaped. At least that's what the Q community believed.

The source of this urban legend dated back to the 1950s. In 1952, Abram Hoffer and Humphry F. Osmond conceived the adrenochrome hypothesis of schizophrenia, suggesting that the way the hormone was processed in schizophrenics resulted in disruption to the brain's chemical operations. In this article, the authors noted, "There are few who doubt that adrenochrome is active in animals or in man, and it is now included among the family of compounds known as hallucinogens – compounds like mescaline and LSD-25 capable of producing psychological changes in man" (Hoffer 1954).

The concept of adrenochrome as a drug in pop culture appeared to have first emerged in 1954 with Aldous Huxley's *Doors of Perception*, in which the author hypothesized that it would have a mescaline-like effect on the user (Adams 2020). In the 1962 novel *A Clockwork Orange,* the narrator discussed adrenochrome as one of the drugs that might have been used to lace milk (Friedberg 2020). Hunter S. Thompson's 1971 book *Fear and Loathing in Las Vegas,* and carried into its 1998 film adaptation, may have contributed most significantly to the current ideas about the compound: "There's only one source for this stuff ... the adrenaline glands from a living human body. It's no good if you get it out of a corpse" (Thompson 1971). By 2008, the first episode of the television show *Lewis* was depicting an adrenal gland being harvested from a live victim to extract adrenochrome as a drug.

The scientific literature suggested that the compound didn't require being extracted from a live mammal. The hormone was listed as an "essential medicine" by the World Health Organization for its ability to stop bleeding and could be purchased at a low price in most countries. Plenty of people had taken it and the effects seemed to range from uninteresting to uncomfortable (Ask Erowid : Id 3190). Only one user had made an entry about the drug on the website Erowid, dedicated to collecting information about psychoactive substances.

He purchased 250 mg of synthetic D, L-Adrenochrome with 99.98% purity for €70. Spaced out over the course of a few days between trials, he first placed 100mg under his tongue, then tried snorting 50 mg, and finally smoked 25 mg vaporized in a crack pipe, with each subsequent method increasing the speed of onset from five minutes to almost instant. The effects were "very light and really uninteresting (I wouldn't even call it a high)."

> First, it's wasn't hallucinogen nor psychedelic. I had a feeling of warmth through my body, I felt a numbness in my hands and my head (possibly linked to the haemostatic effect), there was some slight sedation, and a very slight short lived euphoria (the euphoria was a slightly more pronouced when smoked, but still very short lived)
>
> There's also some minor visual change (no visuals, just that I would see the room slightly differently than usual, but honestly that was some really minor change, a joint of hashish would have done the same, nothing really noticeable). There might be some slight myosis too (=little pupils), not really sure.
>
> To sum up, effects were extremely weak, absolutely not fun nor psychedelic in anyway, and short lived (I would say the slight initial euphoria is gone within 4-5 minutes, and the few strange feelings that I experience from the stuff are gone within about 1 hour (I couldn't say the exact duration as I didn't really checked my watch)
>
> Needless to say I was very disappointed by this uninteresting compound (genaro 2006).

From what I could tell, adrenochrome didn't have the effect that Qanon appeared to suggest. Then again, I hadn't come across documentation of someone who had extracted it from a live victim and used it immediately. However, as I would learn from Aleister Crowley, Hunter Thompson may not have been completely off base with his theory about obtaining adrenochrome via human sacrifice.

Widespread satanic rituals by the power elite was another story altogether, however. In fact, it was not even an entirely new story. The modern hysteria over occult child abuse had its roots in the 1980s, in what came to be referred to as the satanic panic.

CHAPTER FIVE

THE SATANIC PANIC
AND MCMARTIN PRESCHOOL

T he subterranean cavern below the stately home was strangely co-pacetic. It was a cave, no doubt, carved from the stone and earth of some geologically ancient land. But in that cavern was one of those moving walkways, like at the Denver airport. It stretched on for at least a decade at a slight downward angle and mounted on the rough, rocky surfaces of the passage with thick, aluminum brackets were large screens playing recent U.S. history back to me. Just when I thought a global pedo conspiracy was dark, dark stuff, it would only get more sinister as I moved deeper toward the center of hell. And it turned out hell looked a lot like grainy footage from a 1980s talk show.

The overall story was this: a secret underground network of satanists was taking over the planet, conducting occult rituals and killing kids. At least, that was the most exaggerated form of the story believed by some and broadcasted by such sensational outlets as the *Geraldo Rivera Show*. More accurately, accusations of child sexual abuse, and sometimes satanic ritual abuse (SRA), began to emerge at a string of daycares in the U.S. against a backdrop of a stronger cultural interest in satanism.

This backdrop had begun to be painted at the end of the 19th century, as occultism became popular among certain portions of society. By the 1960s, this morphed into explicit satanism as countercultural groups emerged, such as Anton LeVay's Church of Satan, that reacted to philosophies of love and kindness espoused by hippies. In the mix were the Manson Family and the Process Church of the Final Judgement, who didn't focus specifically on Satan, but included him as a part of more complex belief systems. Meanwhile, media forms exploring the occult and satanism also took root, such as *The Exorcist* and *Rosemary's Baby*.

One important artifact from this time was a book published in 1980 titled *Michelle Remembers*, a bestseller said to be based on the stories of Michelle Smith while hypnotized by her therapist (and later husband) Lawrence Pazder. Smith claimed to have undergone extensive SRA at the hands of members of the Church of Satan; however, it was a version of the church much older than LaVey's by many hundreds of years, Padzer believed. At five years old, Michelle was said to have been tortured, caged, sexually abused and made to participate in or witness a number of rituals that included human sacrifice (Beck 2015, Ch. 1).

The book began as a number of articles for *People* magazine and the *National Enquirer* before the co-authors were given substantial payment advances and royalty rights (de Young 2004). Almost 10 years after its publication, in 1989, Smith was invited onto the *Oprah Winfrey Show*, where she appeared with Laurel Rose Willson, the author of another SRA memoir, *Satan's Underground*. Winfrey presented their stories as fact without interrogating their validity (Shewan 2015).

A variety of researchers were unable to corroborate what was detailed in the book, such as a car crash described in the memoir that would likely have been reported on by a local newspaper that covered all major vehicle accidents at the time (Nathan & Snedeker 1995). Neighbors, teachers and friends of Michelle Smith did not recall her being missing for the 81-day satanic ritual that took place in the memoir (Culuhain 2002). Other details were impossible to verify, such as the summoning of Satan himself during said 81-day ritual before Jesus, the Virgin Mary, and Michael the Archangel interceded to rescue Michelle.

It was against this cultural backdrop that accusations of child sexual abuse began to emerge at daycare centers across the U.S. The case that seemed to set it off was the McMartin Preschool scandal. With the investigation beginning in 1983, McMartin would result in the longest and most expensive trial in California up to that point (Reinhold 1990). Some numbers revealed the breadth of the case: 400 children would be examined, 321 counts of child abuse against 41 children would be directed at seven staff members of McMartin, including its founder Virginia McMartin, her daughter Peggy and Peggy's husband, Ray Buckey (Eberle 1993). The investigation would last six years with a five-year trial.

The story began when a mother, Judy Johnson, noticed blood on the anus of her son, Matthew, a three-year old that attended a reputable daycare in the wealthy coastal neighborhood of Manhattan Beach in Los Angeles, California. At first, Johnson attempted to address the issue with Matthew's pediatrician, who thought it might have been pinworm. It wasn't until two months later, when once again seeing the blood, that Matthew indicated "Mr. Ray," McMartin's 22-year-old male teacher Ray Buckey, had put a thermometer in his rectum (Cheit 2016, Ch. 2).

Johnson then took her son to her pediatrician once more, who said that it may have been caused by sexual assault. The doctor suggested that she take him to the emergency room, where another physician also saw signs of abuse and, in turn, sent her to an expert at UCLA, who verified the allegations. It was then that the Manhattan Beach Police Department (MBPD) got involved (Ibid, Ch. 2).

The investigation began quietly at first, with the MBPD questioning a handful of parents in August 1983. They then made a decision that would cause the news of Matthew Johnson's story to percolate throughout the community. The day after arresting and then releasing Ray Buckey, the MBPD mailed a letter to the parents of almost 200 children who previously attended or were currently attending McMartin, recommending that they contact the police with any stories of abuse, possibly at the hands of Ray Buckey:

September 8, 1983

Dear Parent:

This Department is conducting a criminal investigation involving child molestation (288 P.C.). Ray Buckey, an employee of Virginia McMartin's Pre-School, was arrested September 7, 1983 by this department.

... Please question your child to see if he or she has been a witness to any crime or if he or she has been a victim. Our investigation indicates that possible criminal acts include: oral sex, fondling of genitals, buttock or chest area, and sodomy, possibly committed under the pretense of "taking the child's temperature." Also photos may have been taken of children without their clothing. Any information from your child regarding having ever observed Ray Buckey to leave a classroom alone with a child during any nap period, or if they have ever observed Ray Buckey tie up a child, is important.

Please complete the enclosed information form and return it to this Department in the enclosed stamped return envelope as soon as possible. We will contact you if circumstances dictate same.

We ask you to please keep this investigation strictly confidential because of the nature of the charges and the highly emotional effect it could have on our community. Please do not discuss this investigation with anyone outside your immediate family. Do not contact or discuss the investigation with Raymond Buckey, any member of the accused defendant's family, or employees connected with the McMartin Preschool.

THERE IS NO EVIDENCE TO INDICATE THAT THE MANAGEMENT OF VIRGINIA MCMARTIN'S PRE-

SCHOOL HAD ANY KNOWLEDGE OF THIS SITUATION
AND NO DETRIMENTAL INFORMATION CONCERNING
THE OPERATION OF THE SCHOOL HAS BEEN DISCOV-
ERED DURING THIS INVESTIGATION. ALSO, NO OTHER
EMPLOYEE IN THE SCHOOL IS UNDER INVESTIGATION
FOR ANY CRIMINAL ACT.

Your prompt attention to this matter and reply no later than
September 16, 1983 will be appreciated.

HARRY L. KUHLMEYER, JR.
Chief of Police
JOHN WEHNER, Captain (Ibid, Ch. 2)

Some reports began within a day of receiving the letter and, by October 1983, the police had identified eight families who had stories suggesting the possibility of sexual abuse related to the school. In a police log
noting responses, there were a series of mostly vague entries from this
time, with the most specific comment saying "victim, touched penis."
Most notes weren't elaborated upon, except to say they were "positive" for
the California Penal Code for child molestation ("288"). However, one
did include a comment that read, "strange behavior – pulls down pants
and fondles self. Kisses father in a way not like three-year-old." Another
read "older daughter says [Ray Buckey] wore no underwear, saw genitals."

In November, due to the difficulty of having gruff police officers interview children about such a sensitive topic, the MBPD outsourced their
interviews of potential victims to Children's Institute International (CII).
This ultimately played a crucial role in the defense of Buckey and other
defendants in the case. The questioning methods of CII were simple and
relatively objective at first, but, by January 1984, the interviewers became
much more confident in what they believed to be happening at the school
and their problematic methodology.

CII would come to use extensive badgering and leading questions
to get the answers their therapists wanted. CII interviewers would ask
children to divulge their "yucky secrets" to a "secret machine," an audio
recorder they had on hand. They would bring out anatomically correct
dolls for children to illustrate their abuse. And when leading questions
didn't produce answers, they sometimes resorted to name calling. In one
instance, CII Director Kee MacFarlane told five-year-old Mark Janes that
"other kids told her" he was at CII because of some "naked games." When
he couldn't remember any naked games, MacFarlane called him a "scaredy
cat" (Ibid., Ch. 2).

By January, not only had the questioning become more aggressive, but the media got wind of the story. Reporter Wayne Satz received a tip from a woman he had been dating at the time who just so happened to be "Kee" MacFarlane, Director of CII. When Satz broke the news for the Los Angeles ABC affiliate, the tale would begin to take on a life of its own and similar stories of abuse would emerge across the country, which various media figures would describe as byproducts of the McMartin scandal.

CII's investigation grew such that its therapists believed more than 300 children had been abused by seven caretakers at the school. But the allegations of abuse that were often made carried with them details that stretched the credulity of police, therapists, parents and the public at large. Children were claiming that teachers were involved in elaborate trafficking networks involving celebrities, such as 80s action film star Chuck Norris (*Los Angeles Times* 1985). In some cases it was claimed that they killed animals to scare the children. As extreme as that may have sounded, the stories became even more surreal: perpetrators flying and trips through toilets into underground tunnels. One boy told interviewers, "Mr. Ray pushed the button and the trap door opened into the alligator pit (Ibid., Ch. 2)."

Among the details that were clung to by parents in the McMartin trial was the possible existence of tunnels beneath the school, within which some children claimed to be transported to graveyards, churches and other locations for occult rituals and torture. In large part, this fixture of the story had been debunked ... to an extent.

In 1990, some parents were able to obtain permission from the new owner of the McMartin Preschool lot to perform a more extensive investigation of the site and they gathered what could be considered an expert team. Leading the charge was former FBI Special Agent in Charge of Los Angeles Ted Gunderson. Professional miner Gerald Hoobs was there to ensure safety and aid in the identification of underground elements. E. Gary Stickel, PhD., director of Environmental Research Archaeologists, was recommended to conduct the dig by Rainer Berger, Ph.D., Professor and Chair of the Interdisciplinary Program of the Archaeology Department at UCLA (Churm 1990).

Stickel defined a tunnel as "an underground feature that would connect to the surface of the site and extend underground for some distance ... (with) dimensions large enough to accomodate adult human movement through it." Based on this definition, he determined the following:

> The project unearthed not one but two tunnel complexes as well
> as previously unrecognized structural features which defied logi-

cal explanation. Both tunnel complexes conformed to locations and functional descriptions established by children's reports. One had been described as providing undetected access to an adjacent building on the east. The other provided outside access under the west wall of the building and contained within it an enlarged, cavernous artifact corresponding to children's descriptions of a 'secret room'. Both the contour signature of the walls and the nature of recovered artifacts indicated that the tunnels had been dug by hand under the concrete slab floor after the construction building.

He said the area had been filled in with "fill dirt" mixed with "historic debris, as if to mimic the surrounding terrain. Not only did the discovered features fulfill the research prequalifications as tunnels designed for human traffic, there was also no alternative or natural explanation for the presence of such features." Among the debris was a sandwich bag with a Disney character that Stickel believed, based on the copyright, could not have been from before 1983, suggesting that one of the students or teachers had brought it down to the tunnels. He also found bones belonging to cow, pig, dog, rabbit, rodent, reptile and other animals and a plate on which three stars/pentagrams were drawn. Stickel additionally had a geologist confirm a report by the builder of the preschool that the soil was compacted when the preschool was built, so any openings would have dated after its construction in 1966. The tunnel's roof was so shallow that if it had been made before the preschool was built, it would have collapsed had anyone walked on it (Stickel 1990).

A "critical analysis" by W. Joseph Wyatt, professor of psychology at Marshall University and board certified forensic psychologist, suggested that what Stickel found was the "filled-in remains of a rural family's trash pit that pre-dated construction of the school." He based this on the fact that the home was likely rural in its early history, so that city trash pick up was probably not available. This meant that the owners would have had to dig holes in which to dispose of their garbage and when one hole filled up, a new one would be dug, resulting in a string of trash pits.

Much of the debris Stickel found would fit the description of trash from the 1920s to 1960s, until the time the school was built in 1966. Wyatt listed the debris as "sections of boards, wood fragments, a variety of metal objects, an inner tube, numerous bottles, TV antenna wire, tin cans, scissors, eye glasses, exposed film, cinder blocks, plywood, tar paper, roofing nails, four trash-filled pots (three of metal, one of crockery, the largest about fourteen inches tall, all in disrepair), a one-gallon glass food jar, 35 to 40 rusted tin can fragments, a crockery lid, an old medicine bottle, various glass fragments from a large jar, a small 'pestle-like stone,' a rusted metal rod, and 60 to 70 rusted metal can fragments." South Bay Antique Bottles and Collectibles estimated that the bottles dated from the 1920s up to 1960, with the majority dating to the 1930s and 40s.

Dr. Charles Schwartz performed a zooarchaeological analysis of the animal bones on behalf of Stickel and determined that they came from standard cuts of butcher meat made with a bone saw, lending more credence to the trash pit theory. As for the three items that ended up underground after the school was built, Wyatt also had alternative explanations. He suggested the Disney sandwich bag was "carried underground by a squirrel, gopher or other burrowing rodent. This activity, known as bioturbation, is common and was noted by Stickel."

The other two items were two metal plumbing pipe fastener clips about two feet below the ground (and, therefore, into the "tunnel" area) installed on a pipe connecting to a toilet in classroom #3. Because Stickel could not find an opening in the above bathroom's concrete floor through which to install the clips, Stickel assumed that they must have been installed from within the tunnel.

Wyatt's alternative explanation was this:

> Evidently Stickel did not consider the possibility that a plumber might have dug inward from outside the building and down just enough to repair malfunctioning plumbing. Given that the classroom floor was concrete, a plumber (and the building's owner) likely would have preferred an outside route, rather than use of a jackhammer to tear through the classroom's concrete floor.

Critics pointed to the myth of underground tunnels and the children's exaggerated stories as evidence that the McMartin parents had gotten whipped up into a moral panic.

Most of the Gundam didn't know what to believe about the satanic panic, then or now. @Gumby4Christ, in particular, was skeptical. Others, like Theta and @KetracelBlack, were more willing to believe it. I remember Theta specifically sharing a map of all of the underground tunnels in the U.S. @KetracelBlack had studied theology and theorized that ritual abuse, satanic or otherwise, had long been used by the elite throughout history. I tried to maintain a middle ground, allowing myself to at least imagine the extreme possibilities offered by Theta and @KetracelBlack and then rely on @Gumby4Christ's lawerly rationality to keep me from floating off into space – because I couldn't begin to imagine the horrors of SRA in another galaxy, let alone our own.

Devil Worship: The Rise of Satanism
Jeremiah Films, 1989.

DEVIL WORSHIP
THE RISE OF SATANISM

Chapter Six

LITTLE MCMARTINS:
A 20TH CENTURY WITCH HUNT?

S imilar to how I tried to maintain an even keel mentally, it turned out that stories of SRA probably had a middle ground, as well.

Tom Charlier and Shirley Downing, a pair of reporters from a Tennessee newspaper, were responsible for a list of thirty-six cases thought to fit a pattern of satanic panic daycare cases. Published as a six-part series for *Commercial Appeal* in January 1988 titled "Justice Abused: A 1980's Witch-Hunt," the chronicle of stories would come to represent a sort of authoritative list used by other writers to inform the satanic panic narrative. For instance, Debbie Nathan and Michael Snedeker relied on the series heavily to describe the "junior McMartins" in their popular book *Satan's Silence: Ritual Abuse and the Making of an American Witch Hunt* (Cheit 2014, Ch. 1). David Shaw, who won a Pulitzer Prize for his criticism of media coverage of McMartin for the *Los Angeles Times*, highlighted the Charlier and Downing series for indicating "among many other things, the large number of child molestation cases that had resulted in dismissals, acquittals and dropped charges and the startling number of similarities among many of the cases" (Shaw 1990).

These were just a few of the cases I came across that provided a picture for the wave of abuse allegations that spread across the country in the early 1980s.

Kern County: Though McMartin was often credited as starting the string of child abuse accusations against daycare staff in the 1980s, another story in Kern County, California predated it by at least a year. In 1982, the two daughters of Alvin and Debbie McCuan accused their parents of sexually abusing them as a part of a ring that included the Kniffen family, whose two sons also alleged abuse. The case grew to include 60 children testifying abuse and 36 people convicted, 34 of whom had their convictions overturned on appeal. The McCuans and Kniffens were given a combined sentence of over 1,000 years in their 1984 conviction and all four were released from prison in 1996, when their convictions were overturned.

John Stoll received 40 years for 17 counts of lewd and lascivious conduct and served the longest amount of time in prison, 19 years, before having his conviction overturned. One accuser, Ed Sampley, told the *New York Times*, "It never happened (Ibid., Conclusion I)."

Jordan, Minnesota: in Minnesota, 24 defendants were categorized into two child abuse rings in a trial that began in August 1984 and ended just two months later, quite quickly compared to the protracted McMartin trial. The story began at the Valley Green Mobile Home Park when a mother told the police that a neighbor had molested her teenage daughter. The daughter told police of other young victims who named other abusers. Soon, one out of about every 110 adults in a town of 2,700 people were defendants in the case, including police officer Greg A. Myers, his wife Jane, and their neighbors, deputy sheriff Donald J. Buchan and his wife, Cindy. Adults were accused of hosting ritualistic sex parties that included sadism, bestiality, and a game of hide-and-seek where children who were found were taken to bedrooms to be abused (Ibid., Conclusion I).

Country Walk: The Country Walk Case took place in a Miami suburb where recently married couple 34-year-old Frank and 16-year-old Ileana Fuster were accused of molesting eight children while operating a babysitting service in 1984. Frank had been convicted for manslaughter in 1969 and fondling a 9-year-old child in 1981. Nevertheless, his probation officer approved his working at a daycare. Children accused him of sexual abuse, sometimes game-like in nature, and said that he would sometimes wear a terrifying green mask and also mutilate birds as a warning not to tell anyone about the abuse. Frank's son from a previous marriage, Noel, tested positive for gonorrhea. While Ileana originally testified to her husband's innocence, she later recanted and then recanted her recantation (Ibid., Ch. 6).

Fells Acres Day Care Center: In 1984, a four-year-old at Fells Acres Day School was said to have wet his pants while napping, at which point his teacher, Gerald Amirault changed his diaper. When the boy was found playing sexual games with his cousin later that year, his mother and uncle, the latter of which was molested when he was young, interrogated the boy, who suggested that Amirault had sexually abused him. Police were called in and, in turn, asked all parents from the school to look for signs of abuse, which included minor behaviors such as bedwetting and changes in appetite. Ultimately, Amirault was accused of abusing more children, as were his mother, Violet Amirault, and sister, Cheryl Amirault LeFave. The trial included children testifying with their backs to the defendants and facing the jury and resulted in all three defendants being sent to prison (Ibid., Conclusion I).

These were just a handful of the 36 included in the Charlier and Downing series. By far the most extreme and well-known were the Kern County and Jordan, Minnesota cases. Beyond the reporting of the Tennessee journalists, there came to be other stories that were later included under the umbrella of the satanic panic and/or day care abuse scandal narrative, including cases that occurred in Canada, Australia, the United Kingdom, New Zealand, the Netherlands, and Scandinavia.

When it came to the claims of SRA, evidence of the ritual murder of children was typically never found, despite otherwise zealous investigations by police and district attorneys. This phenomenon, in which children were thought to be victims of SRA, was attributed to social hysteria manifested by a collision of forces: social workers, therapists, teachers, police, district attorney's offices, parents and media, all of whom became driven by extreme care for society's children and the evangelical movement that was rising in prominence at the time. While concerned parents began to see abuse, therapists and the like fed questions to would-be victims, and the authorities simply investigated where necessary. The media, thirsty for exciting stories, did what it does best and broadcasted the most titillating tales across television, newspapers and magazines. What resulted was what some referred to as a modern day "witch-hunt" or "McCarthy era," in which these forces sought to believe the children and pin allegations on innocent members of society. Such a narrative was presented in Nathan and Snedeker's *Satan's Silence: Ritual Abuse and the Making of a Modern American Witch Hunt*, for example, which was often considered one of the definitive texts on the case.

Only, as Ross Cheit, Brown University professor of Political Science and International and Public Affairs, pointed out, the witch-hunt narrative that came to be accepted as common sense actually oversimplified the events of that time period considerably. Exactly what was real and what was not from the satanic panic was still difficult to determine, but I tried to find some clarity when researching the phenomenon.

In the case of McMartin, there were serious details that appeared to have been glossed over in the media accounts that came in the wake of the trial. There were anomalous occurrences that one might have used to paint the image of a dark conspiracy. For instance, two crucial witnesses died during the trial, including a private investigator who was said to have committed suicide the day before testifying and Judy Johnson, who died of liver disease from excessive drinking brought on by the stress of the trial and increased paranoia. Additionally, a disillusioned assistant DA fed details of the trial to a pair of screenwriters who would go on to win an Emmy for their depiction of the case in an HBO movie. But the story didn't require a dark conspiracy to discredit the witch hunt narrative. No, the details were as ordinary as the children's testimony and the medical evidence of abuse by Ray Buckey. Before the problematic Children's Institute International (CII) became involved, parents had already presented relevant accounts to the MBPD.

Early on in the investigation, police noted that Tanya Mergili "willingly responded with details of her abuse" and "mentioned being tied up by Ray Buckey, shut in closets, and playing something called the horsey game." According to Tanya's mother, Tanya told her that "Buckey had tickled her in the area of her vagina beneath her clothing." Further, Mrs. Mergili said her daughter had been exhibiting oversexualized behavior, such as "[b]ending over, spreading her cheeks and saying 'is my hole cute?' Ray-Ray used to like me to do this." The doctor who examined Tanya at UCLA transcribed in her medical report – six weeks before CII became involved – that "Tanya described Ray touching penis to rectum, vagina, mouth. Also masturbating himself and touching her (Cheit 2014, Ch. 2)."

Also questioned by police before CII entered the picture was Sara Barton, who attended the preschool from September 1981 until August 11, 1983. Sometimes Barton was the only child in the class during afternoon sessions when Ray Buckey was the only adult present. Her parents went to the MBPD when they received the letter, writing on the form sent to the police that Sara said she "had seen Ray Buckey's penis and touched same."

Further, Sara's mother, Gloria Barton, told the grand jury in March 1984 that her daughter got vaginitis in spring 1983. Despite using over-the-counter medication repeatedly, the problem resurfaced – until Sara started a new preschool that September. When they were using the medication earlier in the year, Sara asked her parents to apply some to her anus, but would not explain why when asked (Ibid., Ch. 2).

Gloria Barton would eventually be described as maintaining a "fanatical belief that enveloped their children and demanded their participation." However, Cheit noted, "Even though she was positive there had been some kind of sexual contact between Ray Buckey and her daughter, she was 'concerned about stressing her daughter' … we see clearly that the earliest responses from this child provided relevant evidence for the investigation. The significance of the evidence is unclear, and her parents, though concerned, certainly did not overreact at the time. All of those facts are omitted entirely from Nathan and Snedeker's detailed critique of this child, which relies entirely on later events to discredit the child. Gloria Barton became an outspoken, activist parent who saw a widespread conspiracy behind the McMartin case" (Ibid., Ch. 2).

Another student considered a "possible" victim by the MBPD was Sally Gregg, who was also in a class where Buckey was often the only adult. Her parents responded to the MBPD letter by writing, "preliminary discussion with Sally, she said 'Ray Ray does not wear underpants.' Sally has been overly interested in touching my genital area."

Though the Greggs never went down to the station for an interview, Sally was mentioned by another girl, Kathy Wilcox, who said "that Ray would take girls into the bathroom at school and put his finger in their vagina" and referenced Sally as possibly being present. This drove them to participate in a CII interview in late November (Ibid., Ch. 2).

Five years old at the time of initial interviews, Mary Gordon was an important character in the case because she was not in contact with other families, her parents said that they wanted to limit how many interviews their daughter experienced, and her comments were made earlier than others in the investigation. In response to the MBPD letter, Mary's parents asked their daughter if anything bad had occurred at school. Apparently, Mary said that Buckey had "put his finger down her throat and asked her to pretend that her mouth was a house" and also inserted his fingers into her vagina. In an interview with the police, Mary said that "the suspect has not fondled her genitals but put his finger inside her pussy" and "that the suspect called her a bad name, i.e. fucking ass and then spit down her throat." She had also required antibiotics for a throat infection in the spring of 1983. Police notes added:

> The victim was very anxious when asked if she had told her mother that Ray had put his fingers here, while pointing to her vaginal area. Mary responded yes, then no, and yes again. Mary then stated that Ray smelled her pussy with his finger and that he put his head down there, referring to her genital area (Ibid., Ch. 2).

Mary went on to become the first child interviewed by CII that became a complainant in the case. The interviews earlier on in November

1983, when CII was brought in, were non-leading and patient. The defense complained about Mary's behavior in the videotaped session, but made no comments about her being badgered. Instead they concluded: "This child is wild; she runs around the room, screams and yells her answers, hits Kee [MacFarlane, of CII] and is the most vulgar child I've ever seen." Unlike the defense critique of many later interviews, there was no claim that the child was badgered or coerced, just that she was "vulgar."

Mary began to discuss Buckey unprompted sixteen minutes into the CII interview, saying, "We're going to talk about him, aren't we?" The interview continued as follows:

> Interviewer: Yea, why not? Want to draw a picture of Ray Ray or what did you say? You want to draw a picture of his dick?
>
> Child: This is what his dick is.
>
> I: That's what his dick looks like?
>
> C: No. It's a very long one. Know what it has? See that's him and there is his long dick.
>
> I: Did anything come out of his long dick?
>
> C: Yea.
>
> I: What comes out?
>
> C: Poo."

Mary's answers were conflicting, indicating she may have seen Buckey's penis, but saying that "poo" came out of it, raising skepticism. Later on, Mary said that she had not seen Buckey naked. However, she contradicted herself once again in a later exchange:

> I: What happened? Did anybody ever touch you?
>
> C: No response.
>
> I: You can tell me.
>
> C: Ray Ray being mean to me.
>
> I: Show us. Has Ray Ray ever taken his clothes off at school?
>
> C: Yes he has and you know what, they're been bad to me (Ibid., Ch. 2)

Mary then shouted into the microphone: "We had been bad ladies and gentlemen! He has been mean to this little girl! He touched her in the pussy!"

Of Mary's interview at CII, Cheit concluded:

Though some responses could be read as evidence of sexual abuse, it would make sense to characterize this interview as raising the possibility of sexual abuse more than proving it. The statements from Mary that were obtained before November seem much stronger as evidence than the CII interview. Moreover, the CII interview was summarized in a one-page log that appears far more definitive than the actual interview. The defense summary does the opposite, however, making far too strong a claim that the interview contained nothing more than some 'vulgar' words. In these varying interpretations, one can see two competing views of the case, neither loyal to its complicated facts (Ibid., Ch. 2).

Other students were tracked down by the police during this time period, including one parent who said "that her daughter Nina had been tied up in a closet and played a horsey game at the school with Raymond Buckey." In total, Cheit said, "at least eight families with children who attended the McMartin Preschool in 1982 or 1983 reported what they viewed as incriminating statements or highly suspicious behavior suggesting sexual abuse at the preschool in response to the MBPD's letter."

This all occurred before any media coverage or CII was involved. Even when CII was brought in, early recorded interviews with some children introduced potentially relevant details that did not seem to be the result of leading questions or aggressive tactics on the part of therapists. It was only by the end of the first month of questioning that the problematic methods of CII began to occur, as interviewers became more rigid and confident about their narrative. However, only three children from early on went on to be included as the case moved forward.

Cheit noted:

> [A] full-text search of the CII interviews with all the children who ended up in the criminal trial reveals that the following words do not appear even once in any of the interviews: Satan, devil, tunnel, candle, grave, chant, cemetery, robe. Several of those children eventually made claims that involved such words, but none of those statements originated with the CII interviews.

In December, there were no new complainants in the case, but the list of suspects grew beyond Ray Buckey to include five female teachers and the school's wheelchair-bound founder Virginia McMartin. Cheit said that, before the ABC story broke, it began to create controversy within the Manhattan Beach community.

A parents' meeting at UCLA Medical Center in late October drew parents from about a dozen families; scores more attended the community meeting in Manhattan Beach on January 24. Those developments made it more likely that a child generating specific claims in January might have heard that information from someone else, rather than actually having experienced it. Most likely, the child's parent heard it from someone else's parent.

Over the course of the next three months, the number of interviews grew along with the number of complainants, with CII interviews indiscriminately determining that all children interviewed had been abused. Cheit noted:

> Most significantly, the interviewers had clearly reached the conclusion that there had been massive abuse at the preschool; they could not possibly be said to have an open mind about the interviews during these months. I have reviewed the videotapes of two interviews in February, one in March, and two in April. All involved children who became complainants in the case. None of the interviews had the feeling of open-ended inquiry that characterized some of those from November (Ibid., Ch. 2).

Another key factor in driving the seriousness with which the parents took the abuse allegations in their community was the medical findings by the doctors involved. Dr. Astrid Heger and Bruce Woodling conducted their examinations at CII and, while they contributed significantly to the research related to sexual abuse in children (e.g., the application of the newly invented "colposcope" to sexual abuse cases), the general medical understanding about this topic at the time was severely lacking. With Drs. Heger and Woodling seeing signs of abuse where there were none (e.g., "microcontusions" only visible with a colposcope), parents had authority figures validating the tales of their children.

Cheit said:

> Yet, these shortcomings do not mean their evaluations should be rejected out of hand. The changes in medical knowledge that occurred between 1984 and the late 1980s, particularly two well-known studies by Dr. John McCann, discredited some 'findings' from the early 1980s, but they did not dismiss all relevant medical knowledge from that era.
>
> The significance of evolving medical knowledge in the McMartin case cannot be ascertained without case-by-case analysis of the

constellation of findings reported for each child. The first original effort at such analysis – given here – reveals that a considerable amount of the evidence presented in the McMartin case would still be considered strong today (Ibid., Ch. 2).

In the end, even the juries were not able to throw out all of the charges against all of the defendants. When the case finally went to trial, all but two of the defendants were dropped, Peggy McMartin and her husband Ray Buckey. The former had all charges against her cleared, but 13 of 65 charges were maintained against Buckey (McNally 2003). According to the *Los Angeles Times*, "Nine of the 11 jurors who agreed to be interviewed said they believed that some children were abused, but that the prosecution, for the most part, had failed to prove beyond reasonable doubt that the Buckeys were responsible (Wilkinson & Rainey 1990)."

Buckey was then retried for six of the remaining 13 counts of which he wasn't acquitted, which resulted in a hung jury. Rather than push on, the prosecution refrained from pursuing the case further and all charges were dropped.

Though McMartin stood out as the most widely remembered case from the Satanic Panic, Cheit went on to examine the other stories of widespread child sexual abuse at the time and how they were viewed through the lens of the national media. Cheit provided an extremely thorough analysis of the authors responsible for the portrait of a country-wide satanic panic, determining that many of the 36 cases that the authors claimed to be miscarriages of justice generated by the satanic panic were poorly categorized.

Among the cases were some that not only didn't involve prosecutions but didn't even result in any arrests. 16 of the cases did not get to the trial stage. Some had charges dropped and others never had charges brought to begin with (Cheit 2014, Conclusion I).

The majority of the stories included in the list of 36 did not fulfill the proper criteria for representing widespread satanic abuse allegations. For instance, just a few, such as Jordan, McMartin, and Kern County, had charges of large-scale abuse. Only four had a large number of supposed perpetrators, including Jordan, Kern County, and McMartin. Many only had one or two perpetrators.

Another criteria designated by Downing and Charlier for inclusion in the list was that they occurred at daycares, which was not true for 10 cases. More importantly, satanic or ritualistic elements were not present in a majority of the cases. Cheit wrote:

One problem that becomes clear on researching secondary sources is what I call satanic exaggeration. As it turns out, fewer than one-quarter of the thirty-six cases actually fit the primary theme of the series, which combined the idea of witch-hunts over child sexual abuse with claims of ritualistic or satanic overtones. Some of the cases Charlier and Downing discuss had nothing to do with satanic or ritualistic abuse. Moreover, several that did involve such elements were clearly based in reality (Cheit 2014, Conclusion I).

Some of the ritual or satanic elements used as criteria by Charlier and Downing included items that weren't inherently ritualistic or satanic, such as "activities in the basement," "activities during naptime or trips to rest room," or "Barbie dolls." Others were common to sexual abuse as a whole, including "oral sex."

Another issue with their list and categorization was the fact that some seemingly bizarre elements actually made sense in the context of the case. In an investigation in Richmond, the sole "ritualistic" element was "stabbed, or murdered babies or children," yet Charlier and Downing noted that the case began with the discovery of the dead body of a girl.

Cheit wrote:

> [E]ven by Charlier and Downing's inflated accounting, many of the thirty-six cases involve only one or two of these elements – and many more apparently didn't involve any. Eleven of the cases included in this table have only one or two of the forty-one listed "elements." In short, a handful of the thirty-six cases account for the vast majority of the entries – and several of those cases are never discussed in the article (Ibid., Conclusion I).

Also crucial was how many cases actually featured substantial evidence of abuse. Cheit noted two instances, neither of which took place in daycares, where the cases were clearly baseless. In contrast, three cases did not feature unjustified charges, with strong evidence against the defendants in each. Others were a mix of justified and unjustified charges with credible evidence of abuse. Cheit discussed nine of the 36, such as Jordan and Kern County, that included substantial evidence of abuse, six of which contained "more evidence of abuse than has ever been recognized in the witch-hunt narrative."

Jordan, Minnesota and Kern County, California were the two largest and most extreme, after McMartin. Minnesota state attorney general, Hubert Humphrey III, decided that, in the Jordan investigation, there wasn't evidence of child murders and determined that the investigation was problematic. However, he also concluded that there was abuse of children, just that he could not determine the exact number of victims.

A commission was created to investigate the county attorney who oversaw the arrests in the case. The Olson Commission determined that even after removing the testimony of ten children who underwent over 12 interviews, there was enough evidence to proceed against nine defendants (Ibid., Conclusion I).

In Kern County, the story began with two young girls, Bobbie and Darla McCuan, whose step grandmother (that is, married to their biological grandfather, Gene Barbour) Mary Ann Barbour suspected that the girls were being abused by their step grandfather (married to their biological grandmother, Linda), Rod Phelps. Mary Ann had apparently raised her concerns well before the case was brought to authorities. In 1979, she told the girls' mother, Deborah McCuan, that Bobbie had visible vaginal bruises that she attributed to Phelps. Deborah claimed that it came from a fall. Later, she supposedly told Mary Ann what Phelps had done was "no big deal." Deborah had actually brought Bobbie to the doctor months before the confrontation with her stepmother, with medical records from before 1980 indicating injury to the girl's "pubic area." A pediatrician who saw Bobbie months later said that the injuries could not have been caused by the fall described by Deborah because there were no skin lacerations. Instead, the doctor said Bobbie had signs of sexual abuse.

In an interview with Kern County Sheriff's Office in October 1981, Bobbie said Phelps had molested her two years prior and that her own father, Deborah's husband Alvin McCuan, had been molesting her approximately once a week since then. Worth noting was the fact that the girls' mother, Deborah, had accused Phelps of molesting her when she was young, but later recanted. As an adult, she seemed determined to minimize the abuse of her own children (Ibid., Conclusion I).

The judge reviewing the case years later concluded that the "earliest stages of the investigation" were well founded. It appeared that it was in April 1982 that the case exploded from two victims and perpetrators to nine victims, nine named perpetrators, and many unnamed perpetrators. It was at this time that the girls were moved to live with another family, who became ensnared in the case.

The judge determined that the boys of the family with whom the girls had moved in, the Kniffens, had been questioned using extremely leading techniques. Judge Stuebbe reviewed the tapes and said, "the questions themselves were almost always suggestive of the answer" and "questions that were answered 'wrong' were asked again (Ibid., Conclusion I)."

One piece of evidence in several of these cases, including McMartin, proved to be problematic. Dr. Bruce Woodling, a pioneer in the use of the colposcope, conceived of a concept called the "wink response," in which the anus of an unabused patient would "wink" if stimulated, while an abused victim would not exhibit this response because they'd been conditioned to abuse in the area. Eventually, Woodling's theory of a wink response was determined by the medical community to be unproven and unfounded. In turn, advocates of the witch hunt narrative often highlighted this concept as evidence of poor medical evidence in many of the cases considered a part of the satanic panic.

However, with one of the Kniffen boys, Dr. Woodling observed anal dilation over 20 mm without stool present, significantly different from a wink response and better described as gaping. His observation was corroborated by another doctor in the case, who said "it appears to be a learned response to the body to avoid injury from repeated sodomy." The judge involved in overturning the Kern County convictions concurred that it was "clear that even under the most recent medical studies" that the dilation described by Woodling was "a very strong indication" of sexual abuse (Ibid., Conclusion I).

The pediatrician that saw the girls in 1980 said in 1982 that she considered what she found to be abnormal, including the fact that Bobbie's "hymen had been transected," which was to say that there were cuts on the edges. While those determinations would still have been relevant today, others wouldn't, such as the doctor's testimony that sexual activity resulted in vaginal "rounding," which was no longer an accurate medical finding. However, the doctor also noted anal gaping in Bobbie that she hadn't seen in 1980 and had never seen an anal lining like that of the pictures presented of Bobbie in court.

Though Nathan and Snedecker admitted that such medical evidence strengthened the case against Alvin and Debbie McCuan, they didn't explain why they included both of the McCuans in the dedication page of their book anyway if Alvin seemed to be guilty of sexual abuse. In fact, they included a number of questionable people on that page, such as Grant Self, also convicted in this Kern County case.

Cheit wrote:

> Nathan and Snedeker dedicated their book, in part, to Self – a man
> who is unquestionably a serial child molester (two of his convic-

tions rested, separately, on photographic evidence and on an adult eyewitness) ... had no explanation for 115 disciplinary charges in prison, including possession of 'full frontal nude photographs of children.' Self succeeded in getting one of his 1984 convictions set aside – the one connected to John Stoll. The boys in the case, except Stoll's own son, had recanted their testimony (Ibid., Conclusion I).

Cheit did not deny that the Kern County and Jordan cases spun out of control, but argued that a witch-hunt narrative overshadowed, oversimplified, and misinterpreted the facts of many of those cases. There were issues in the 1980s related to poor training of therapists and police in questioning children, as well as some poor standards in the underdeveloped field of medical examination of child sexual abuse. But that alone wasn't enough to generate an entire satanic panic.

So, as much as I would have liked to believe that the whole thing was unsubstantiated, there was truth there. Some parents, though probably not all, had reason to suspect their children were being abused. Whether or not all of the stories that came out were true, was another story.

Though the various day care abuse cases may not have fit into the witch hunt narrative constructed in the media, I had a hard time denying that a satanic panic was created at the cultural level to some extent.

For instance, it was during this period that FBI agent Kenneth Lanning rose to prominence as an expert on occult crime. Joining the Bureau's Behavioral Science Unit (BSU) in 1981, where he and his coworkers conducted research and taught new recruits in a unit dedicated to profiling serial killers and the like. Additionally, the unit would be called in to consult with police forces about specific crimes. In 1983, Lanning said he received his first phone call about ritual abuse. The cop on the line told Lanning that he'd spoken with a woman who said she'd been abused as a child by her parents along with other adults. The story included murder, mutilation, and blood drinking. The next week, he received a call with virtually the same details. Several weeks passed and the FBI agent took another call, this time about bizarre abuse at a daycare. Nine months later and the list of calls about SRA had ratcheted up to 20 or 30 (Beck 2015, Ch. 5).

Though Lanning claimed he was skeptical at first that a large group of people could commit such brazen acts of violence on a large number of victims, he said he decided to rely on the interdisciplinary approach of the BSU by calling in experts, such as psychologists, social workers, and other researchers. According to the fed, these specialists appeared to believe wholeheartedly in the SRA phenomenon and thought it was an urgent matter to be dealt with immediately.

Lanning went on to host a four-day Day Care Center and Satanic Cult Sexual Exploitation of Children seminar in 1985. The event took in police, FBI agents, lawyers, social workers and other professionals from around the country to educate them about SRA. Pamphlets described the over 400 "occult organizations" in the U.S., without listing their size or activities or distinguishing between violent groups and minor countercultural organizations. Sandi Gallant, an intelligence officer from the San Francisco police department, provided a brochure aiding police in uncovering SRA (Ibid., Ch. 5).

A checklist included "Were victims forced to devour mutilated parts?" Important occult dates were listed, such as "February 2nd, Candlemas or Ormelc." "Ritualistic indicators" were broken up into "Ritual Items/Signs" (chalices, robes, pentagrams, key of Solomon, masks, swastikas, inverted cross, cameras, jewelry), "Restraints/Weapons" (chains, knives, drugs, ropes, firearms, swords), "Ritualistic Activities" (bloodletting, crying, screaming, nudity, screaming, sacrifices, invoking satan, singing). Sandi Gallant described Satanists during her lecture as "normal, intelligent, working class men and women" that would "traditionally be underachievers (Ibid., Ch. 5)."

Meanwhile, there was a growing Christian home video movement that both took advantage of the ability of American consumers to watch movies in their living rooms and the momentum of the Satanic Panic. Among the most prominent producers of right-wing, Christian VHS tapes was Jeremiah Films, which began associating Mormonism and Hinduism with the threat of paganism in the early 1980s. At the end of the decade, it released *Devil Worship: The Rise of Satanism*, which played on the typical themes of Luciferian influence on U.S. culture, such as occult symbols in children's toys and human sacrifices in film.

What made Jeremiah Films and others like it so interesting was the increasing blend of the political with these so-called Christian ideas. As Robert Skvarla explained, the head of that Jeremiah Films, Patrick Matrisciana, and evangelist Jerry Falwell both used VHS to disseminate their messages, ultimately combining their efforts to take on the Democratic Party, specifically the Clintons.

Concurrent to the release of Satanic Panic-inspired material, Matrisciana began producing videos that focused on America's then developing culture war. In rapid succession, Jeremiah Films released *AIDS: What You*

Haven't Been Told (1989) and co-produced *Gay Rights, Special Rights: Inside the Homosexual Agenda* (1993) with Matrisciana-run front group Citizens United for the Preservation of Civil Rights. The documentaries attack the LGTBQ community, drawing on the same kind of tenuous logic as Devil Worship and Trick or Treat, but substituting gay and trans activists for Satanists.

Matrisciana soon found spiritual allies in other evangelicals. Jerry Falwell had ascended to the highest levels of political power through the Moral Majority and the Liberty Alliance, groups that engaged in grassroots organizing and propaganda campaigns around many of the same issues (Matrisciana ally at CCAP Tim LaHaye also sat on the board of the Moral Majority). One of Falwell's primary methods, like Matrisciana, was the home video market. Productions like *The National Endowment for the Arts Exposed* (1993), a video produced by the Liberty Alliance, excoriated the government for funding art by openly gay artists. So, in 1994, Matrisciana and Falwell set their sights on a common target: Bill Clinton. The 1992 Democratic primary saw Democrats adopting LGBTQ issues into their platform and primetime speeches by gay activists at the Democratic National Convention. This new progressive agenda provided Falwell-affiliated groups an opportunity. Martin Mawyer, founder of the Christian Action Network and one-time editor of Falwell's Moral Majority Report newsletter, was quoted as saying, "We hope to educate the American public on what Bill Clinton has promised the homosexual community."

Matrisciana and Falwell began pooling resources to develop documentaries attacking Clinton on multiple fronts. Matrisciana created another innocuously-named front, Citizens for Honest Government, and put together a documentary titled *Bill & Hillary Clinton's Circle of Power* (1994), which Falwell promoted through his Liberty Alliance (Skvarla 2021).

With the subsequent release of *The Clinton Chronicles,* Citizens for Honest Government began to accuse the Clintons of involvement in Arkansas prostitution operations, as well as drug trafficking at Mena Intermountain Municipal Airport, and the death of Deputy White House Counsel Vince Foster. While there was strong evidence that Mena was an important part of the domestic component of Iran-Contra (Hopsicker, 2004), it was this last element that would end up fueling right-wing theories about the Clintons decades later. The implication that the Clintons had murdered Vince Foster became just one in a list of assassinations executed by the political dynasty. Skvarla wrote:

Matrisciana's reporting on Foster's suicide and the other deaths contributed to what became known as the Clinton Body Count, a list of names of people who were alleged to have been killed by the Clintons, though neither Matrisciana nor Falwell were responsible for its creation. The conspiracy theory had already been circulating as early as 1993. Linda Thompson, an Indianapolis lawyer, quit her job after Randy Weaver's arrest following a shoot-out with federal agents at Ruby Ridge and founded the American Justice Federation so she could produce media exposing, what she called, the New World Order. Her work included the Branch Davidian apologia *Waco, the Big Lie* (1993) before moving into the Clinton Body Count. She compiled a list of alleged Clinton victims titled 'The Clinton Body Count: Coincidence or Kiss of Death?' around the same time as Foster's death but did not identify him as a victim. The list made its rounds among far-right activists over the course of the next year, ending up in the hands of William Dannemeyer who attempted to pass it along as a legitimate document certifying crimes committed by the Clintons before himself ending up in *The Clinton Chronicles*.

Matrisciana would edit a second version, now dubbed *The New Clinton Chronicles* (1996), to account for the mainstreaming of the body count conspiracy theory. It added Thompson's list onto the end of the new video along with contributions from conservative journalist Christopher Ruddy, who had kept Foster's death in the news through funding supplied by right-wing megadonor Richard Mellon Scaife and his pet projects The Western Journalism Center and the *Pittsburgh Tribune-Review*. (Scaife also backed the Clinton-obsessed *American Spectator* and its Arkansas Project.) Witnesses sourced in *The Clinton Chronicles* and Ruddy's writing would go on to appear in mainstream coverage of the case, often identified as experts, until journalist Murray Waas discovered that Matrisciana had paid them with funds from a bank account jointly held with Ruddy (2021)."

As the Epstein story flooded the news in 2019, the "Clinton Body Count" would be resurrected. Seth Rich, the deceased Democratic staffer who some suggested, including Julian Assange, supplied WikiLeaks with Podesta's emails, was added to the list. As was Epstein, whose "suicide" in prison became such a large meme that it wound up on national television in the form of the phrase "Epstein did not kill himself." Not only did that sentence grow to be so widespread that it was rendered meaningless, but the pedophile's death was included as yet another in the Clinton Body Count.

In the end, the FBI's Ken Lanning claimed that he realized that both sides of the SRA debate were becoming extreme in their views, with SRA activists conducting a "witch hunt" and the cynics representing a "backlash," and neither able to meet the other side.

"Each side," Lanning wrote, "tends to take an all-or-nothing approach to complex issues … relies heavily on raw emotion … [and] conveniently fails to define its terminology."

This made me wonder: was the truth behind today's satanic panic also somewhere in the middle?

Paul Bonacci

CHAPTER SEVEN

ACTUAL INSTANCES OF SATANIC ABUSE?

The extent of SRA was nearly impossible to determine, but even skeptical researchers found examples of the phenomenon.

University of California psychologist Gail Goodman, for example, conducted a study for the National Center on Child Abuse and Neglect analyzing 12,000 accusations of SRA. While she found no evidence for "a well-organized intergenerational satanic cult, who sexually molested and tortured children," she did collect "convincing evidence of lone perpetrators or couples who say they are involved with Satan or use the claim to intimidate victims." This included "grandparents [who] had black robes, candles, and Christ on an inverted crucifix – and the children had chlamydia, a sexually transmitted disease, in their throats (Goldman 1994)."

In a 1996 study conducted in the UK, 62 cases of ritual abuse from between 1988 and 1991 were provided to the research team by the police and social welfare agencies (Hughes & Parker in Bibby 1996). At the behest of the British government, anthropologist Jean LaFontaine determined that SRA was performed not for religious worship but sexual gratification. Her later research suggested that rituals were also invented to scare victims or justify sexual abuse, with sexual abuse taking place outside of the rituals (Kitzinger 1995).

In the U.S., David Finkelhor published a 1988 report investigating 270 cases of sexual abuse in daycares in the country, concluding that 36 were substantiated as SRA (Finkelhor et al 1988), but the definition of "substantiated" SRA was considered loose by critics as only a single agency out of possibly many working on the case only needed to decide SRA occurred, even if there were no consequences for a daycare or arrests made (de Young 2004).

With that in mind, I thought I'd revisit the Franklin scandal. The descriptions from Franklin victims Shawneta Moore and Paul Bonacci were made up of the most disturbing content imaginable. Though they were young at the time of their abuse, they recalled the events later on, outside of the context of leading questions.

Shawneta Moore, for instance, was reluctant to even share any details of her abuse. It wasn't until she was checked into a hospital where she didn't believe the staff was linked to the King family and its cohort that she was able to go into detail. She told Richard Young Hospital caretakers that, after six months of attending parties in which older men would have sex with young girls, Moore was brought to her first "power meeting" in an empty shack adorned with "candles and other weird stuff." Men who went by the nicknames Ace, King's Horses, Jerry Lucifer, and Mike attended the sessions wearing robes with inverted crosses. The head of the group donned a black cape and wore rings featuring gold skulls. After being warned that the room would begin to spin, it did in fact begin to spin and Moore understood that she'd been drugged. Nick Bryant described what happened next:

> At approximately 7:00 P.M. Moore was locked in a small room with a Caucasian baby girl – Moore and the infant were alone in the room for about five hours. At around midnight, she said, the men opened the door to find Moore holding the little girl. They took the infant from Moore, and told her that she would achieve 'power' by killing someone she really loved. Moore then detailed a series of inconceivably gory and horrific events that entailed the men ritualistically murdering the infant. Though the events that Moore described are incomprehensible, she provided hospital staff with the unflinching, meticulous specifics of the events as she said they unfolded. After the infant was murdered, Moore divulged to hospital personnel that she became hysterical and one of the men had to hold her down. Moore then disclosed that she was forced to remain locked in the small room for approximately twenty-four hours. While Moore sat in the dark, locked room, she said she heard the men whipping and beating one of the girls. Moore told hospital personnel that as she sat in the locked room, she felt that the girl who was whipped and beaten had it much easier than she did. Shortly after the men stopped assaulting girl, they unlocked the door of the small room and informed Moore she passed the test. The men then drove Moore to a park near her house and dropped her off. Moore said she felt dazed as she wandered home, and, upon entering the house, her mother gave her a beating for having been missing for two days. Moore said the next time she saw the men was at a party, where the girls were again forced to 'sleep around.' She identified Larry King as attending this party. Moore also told Richard Young staff about four additional 'sacrifices.' She said that

a little boy was ritualistically murdered because he threatened to notify authorities of the sacrifices. She also named one of the girls who had been slaughtered (Bryant 2012, Ch. 1).

Bonacci's tales were even more difficult to wrap my head around. Bryant provided less information about the allegations of SRA in his book, saying that they were difficult to verify and likely knowing just how absurd they may have sounded. However, Senator John DeCamp, who acted as Bonacci's lawyer, was much more willing to include those details.

> Dr. Densen-Gerber testified [to the Senate Franklin committee]: "I've been in this field for an awfully long time. I should have realized that's what these three patients were telling me. It was so horrific for me to contemplate. Taking a two-year-old child and placing it in an open uterus, in a dying woman. To have this child covered with blood. I used denial myself after all these years. ... [This] has occurred, according to Sorenson, in Nebraska, and now she's dead. And the same thing that is described, this ceremony, was described by Bonacci as occurring in Nebraska (DeCamp 2005, Ch. 15)."

A former Boys Town student named Nikolai Cayman was not involved in the Franklin grand jury case and was only tracked down by Nick Bryant decades later. Cayman corroborated some of the less graphic charges of satanism.

"A lot of the parties were outrageous – it was like one big orgy, but some of these parties weren't always nice. You'd get tortured, handcuffed, beaten, and videotaped. To this day, I have scars all over my body from flying with King. Doctors have asked me where I got all these scars," Cayman told Bryant. "They would have these weird rituals, but I didn't realize what they were. At first I thought whatever, but, as I got older, I started to realize that these were satanic rituals. There was cutting, blood drinking, chants, and dancing (Bryant 2015, Ch. 3)."

I honestly couldn't make a clear conclusion about the extent of SRA in the U.S. in the 1980s. Given what I knew about Epstein's ties to celebrities, the idea that children at a Los Angeles daycare would be the victims of celebrity pedophiles didn't actually seem all that surprising. And even children's visions of flying witches and alligator pits could have been explained by their abusers dosing them with hallucinatory drugs.

From the stories I heard about sadistic and powerful people, even satanic rituals didn't seem like much of a stretch. Ed Buck was one individual in particular that exposed the more sinister side of the elite. A wealthy democratic donor, Buck had been accused of giving African American men lethal doses of crystal meth for his own sexual gratification, killing at least two men in the process. It wasn't until a coalition of 50 civil rights groups demanded an investigation in 2019 that the murderer was charged with nine felonies (U.S. Department of Justice 2020). Would it really have been much of a leap if Buck had worn a black cloak and murmured some Latin while he did those sorts of things?

The whole concept had me wondering what it was exactly that made rich people want to be rich. There was obviously the ease and comfort of being able to get anything you wanted whenever you wanted. But why the desire to hurt people? I figured that it must have been that, after being able to achieve a god-like status in the physical world, ordinary activities lost their zeal. A game of frisbee with the kids or a quiet, romantic dinner was no longer releasing the dopamine and serotonin necessary for contentment. Was it some form of exhilaration that they sought? Maybe to fully realize their omnipotence?

Or what if there really was something you could obtain from human sacrifice, adrenochrome or otherwise, that accomplished something for these monsters that ordinary mortals like me couldn't even fathom?

PART 2

THE ILLUMINATI

Merovech, the supposed founder of the Frankish Dynasty, the Merovingians were said to claim that their lineage included the blood of Christ and the seed of Satan.

CHAPTER EIGHT

THE REAL STORY OF THE ILLUMINATI

Not only were my two young boys and wife beautiful reminders of how magical the world could be, but I was living in a remote town where cool, crisp breezes regularly circulated throughout the valley between two immense mountain ranges. My life was a very real embodiment of what the romantics called the "sublime." But I couldn't feel the sublime, allow it to permeate my being. I was instead watching it locked behind a pair of glass eyes as the homunculus of my being ventured onward.

I hadn't realized it, but the moving walkway had ended. Unconsciously, I watched my step as the track was eaten by the metal teeth of the conveyor's terminal point, a green light emitting from its deep, electric throat. I was guided forward into the dank cavern ahead by the sounds of low droning, punctuated by rattling sounds and ghostly whistles. There was a dull flame in the center of the room, surrounded by occluded figures dancing, their shadows cast on the walls of the cave. A couple of blindfolded youth were being harangued, prodded and pierced.

Suddenly, the covers were removed from the kids' faces, exposing only the whites of their eyes as they threw themselves about the space snarling wildly. One of the boys tackled a drum player, wearing the head of some monstrous beast, and sank his teeth deeply into the drummer's bicep, tearing out a piece of flesh. Catching me wince behind the rock, he lunged toward me.

Falling backward, I felt a dull thud against my skull. It all went black. As my conscious perception gave way to delirium, I wondered, "Who is in charge here? Who is causing this suffering to occur?"

Did our rulers simply fit into C. Wright Mills' conception of the power elite? To him, the rulers were "the political, economic, and military circles which as an intricate set of overlapping cliques share decisions having at least national consequences. In so far as national events are decided, the power elite are those who decide them." Or was it even more conspiratorial? Were there actual secret societies that made decisions in smoky board rooms or secluded castles? Was there really an illuminati?

For Qanon, the Illuminati was more or less interchangeable with "the cabal," the global satanic pedophile elite that ran the world. In drop 299, Q used [P] for the first time to possibly represent the top of a pyramid, the heads of the cabal, with those in the Qanon community debating on its meaning. One writer, who went by the pseudonym NeonRevolt, noted:

> We all know that a pyramid has three sides, and these three sides were Soros, the House of Saud, and the Rothschilds...
>
> But honestly – what bugged me at the time was that this wasn't really a complete pyramid.
>
> /_\ – leaves a big gap at the top.
>
> And as someone who has been on the chans for a long time – I had long thought that Q could have easily triforced a top to that pyramid (NeonRevolt 2020)."

The author wondered who was represented by [P], possibly the Pope, the Pinay Cercle or the Payseurs, a French banking family.

Q !!TPb.qbhqo **ID: 913bb1** No.51984 🔗 📑   299
Dec 7 2017 22:05:16 (EST)

Rothschilds (cult leaders)(church)(P)
Banks / Financial Institutions
WW Gov Control
Gov Controls People
SA
Oil Tech Sex/Children
SA Controls (assigned) US / UK Politicians / Tech Co's (primary)
Soros
Controls organizations of people (create division / brainwash) +
management / operator of slush funds (personal net worth never
reduces think DOJ settlements Consumer Iran Enviro pacts etc etc)
/_\ - Rock (past)(auth over followers)
_\ (present)
(Future)
Order is critical.
Strings cut to US/UK.
Expand your thinking.
Swamp drain.
1 - sexual harassment exit + future
....
[R] - No.
Bomb away.
Q

Q was asked whether or not the letter referred to the Pope and appeared to suggest that the Pope worked for P or something along those lines.

Q !xowAT4Z3VQ **ID: 3474d4** No.884858 ⬚ ▮   998
Apr 3 2018 19:49:59 (EST)

> Anonymous **ID: 65a39c** No.884833 ⬚ ▮
> Apr 3 2018 19:48:54 (EST)
>
> llesofldlkes.png   ⬇
>
>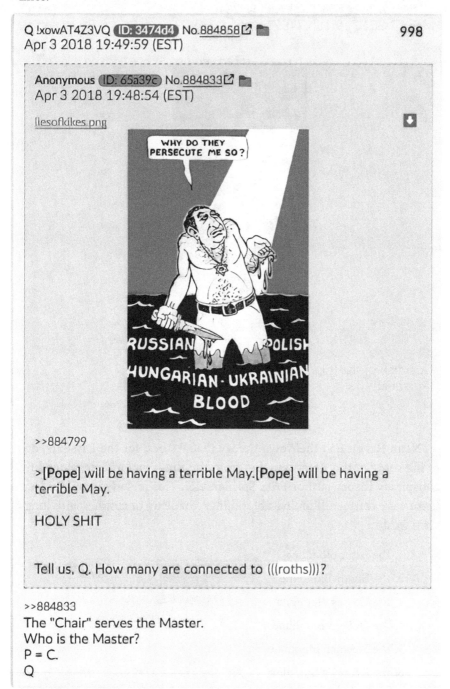
>
> >>884799
>
> >[Pope] will be having a terrible May.[Pope] will be having a terrible May.
>
> HOLY SHIT
>
> Tell us, Q. How many are connected to (((roths)))?

>>884833
The "Chair" serves the Master.
Who is the Master?
P = C.
Q

There was also some sort of implication that the Freemasons, often represented by an owl, were the guardians of the Pope?

Q !4pRcUAOIBE **ID: 610b24** No.1449784 ☑ ▣   **1413**
May 17 2018 19:15:27 (EST)

Guardian_P.png

Guardian of the Pope.
[Personal]
Q

Neon Revolt had their own theory that P stood for the Payseurs, deriving some of this determination from the Illuminati lore developed by conspiracy theory author Fritz Springmeier. This included the idea that there were thirteen Illuminati bloodlines, made up of families with long-term wealth:

1. The Astor Bloodline

2. The Bundy Bloodline

3. The Collins Bloodline

4. The DuPont Bloodline

5. The Freeman Bloodline

6. The Kennedy Bloodline

7. The Li Bloodline

8. The Onassis Bloodline

9. The Rockefeller Bloodline

10. The Rothschild Bloodline

11. The Russell Bloodline

12. The Van Duyn Bloodline

13. The Merovingian Bloodline

Named for Merovech, the supposed founder of the Frankish Dynasty, the Merovingians were said to claim that their lineage included the blood of Christ and the seed of Satan. They maintained the goal of bringing about the Anti-Christ, possibly through a Babalon Working-style bit of sex magick that I would come to learn more about. They considered themselves the rulers of all of the Illuminati, descended from Egyptian pharaohs. According to some Illuminati lore, the Payseurs were descendants of Marie Antoinette said to belong to the Merovingian line. The Payseurs were claimed by some to have established the Federal Reserve and to own Exxon, Heinz, and Quaker Oats among others. Conspiracy personality David Icke, described the family this way:

> In 1872, a Payseur company, the Charleston, Cincinnati and Chicago Railroad, established a telegraph company called Western Union. It formed a subsidiary called AT and T in 1875 and today it is one of America's biggest telephone and communication companies.
>
> The Charleston, Cincinnati and Chicago Railroad company is the parent company for the Federal Reserve, the privately owned "central bank" of the United States. The Payseur empire became heavily involved in banking. Their Bank of Lancaster became the North Carolina Bank and then Nationsbank. The biggest bank in Texas, Interfirst, of which George Bush is a director, merged in 1987 with Republic Bank to form First Republic. This was later absorbed by Nationsbank which then merged with the Bank of America.
>
> These two launder CIA drug money and that's appropriate because the forerunner to the CIA, the OSS or Office of Strategic Services, was created from the Payseurs' own security network which was formed by the Selma, Rome and Dalton Railroad to protect the Military Railroad System. It's all wheels within wheels, family within family, and Americans have not a clue who really runs their

lives and their country.... The Payseur family have now lost control of their empire, but the same reptilian tribe are still at the helm (Icke *2001*)."

Altogether, the Illuminati were supposedly striving for a one-world government, carried out through large think tanks and international advisory bodies.

It seemed absurd on its face, but could there truly have been a secret society of powerful elites ruling global affairs, perhaps enacting a New World Order?

What began as an 18th century Bavarian secret society dedicated to enlightenment ideals became a pop culture phenomenon and fixture in conspiracy culture in part thanks to a hippy-era movement called Discordianism. A satirical pseudo-religion, Discordianism was established by Kerry Thornley, Greg Hill, and their prankster friends as a means of spreading confusion, pushing people to question their assumptions in an amusing way.

Among the ideas meant to generate this effect was that the real Illuminati had never ceased to operate and continued to control our lives today. This concept in particular was developed by Thornley, as well as Discordians Robert Anton Wilson and Bob Shea, editors of *Playboy* magazine at the time, who wrote *The Illuminatus! Trilogy*. The books leveraged an experimental writing style that jumped from first to third person and wavered between hallucinations and thoughts of a cast of characters that included a squirrel, a pinup model, a New York City detective and an artificial intelligence. The main narrative began with an investigation into the murders of JFK, Martin Luther King, Jr., and RFK and became enmeshed in a web of conspiracies controlled by a ruling elite called the Illuminati (Wallis & Duguid, n.d.).

"Shea and I were finished with *Illuminatus!* when we read *Gravity's Rainbow* and then on the rewrite we deliberately threw in a couple of references to it, but we had worked out the structure on our own, mostly on the basis of the nut mail that *Playboy* gets," Wilson said in an interview. "Shea and I were working on the Playboy Forum, that being a discussion between the editors – that being Shea and me at that time – about the basic ideas of civil liberties and the limitations of government and the general libertarian philosophy. And since we were attacking the Government for attacking the rights of the individual on all sorts of issues like drugs and abortion, consensual sex between adults, we were getting an awful lot of nut mail from people who thought they were being persecuted by the Government, imagining the most baroque paranoid fantasies. And we started thinking of how all these people had different theories about what was wrong with the world, and suppose they were all right? Suppose all these conspiracy theories were going on at once? (laughs) So we bounced that around for a few drinking parties and then suddenly Shea said 'You know, we could turn this into a novel.' We should really have dedicated the book to all the paranoids, from whom we learned so much."

The letters referenced by Wilson urged *Playboy* to investigate such topics as police spying on U.S. civilians, Nazis still active in important positions in society, and the Pope, mafia and military colluding, along with more absurd ideas of Atlantis, gnomes and the like. Rather than investigate the various tips sent in, the editors' way of dealing with all of this information was to treat them all as true and create a single story encompassing all of them. *Illuminatus!* was written between 1969 and 1971, giving the authors at least five years to explore some of the tips they received, such as COINTELPRO and MKULTRA, more seriously before they were ultimately disclosed to the public (cuttlefish_btc 2016).

As a satirical piece of literature, *The Illuminatus!* series had the effect of making all of the conspiracy theories, such as government manufactured anthrax and secret Nazi battalions, seem as ridiculous as the idea of Atlantis. By instead treating them as a joke, Wilson and Shea served the ends of actual conspirators, such as the FBI and CIA. We would learn that the "paranoia" mocked by the satirists would actually be well placed when these deep state programs were revealed.

But even the idea that secret societies didn't exist or play an important role in global affairs was not as silly as it appeared on its surface. Exclusive social organizations had existed and shaped communities since prehistoric civilization first took root.

Kwakwa̱ka̱á̱wakw canoe welcoming with masks and traditional dug out cedar canoes. On bow is dancer in Bear regalia.

CHAPTER NINE

ANCIENT SECRET SOCIETIES

I don't know how I came across it – maybe it was just a reference at the bottom of a Wikipedia article – but in trying to understand the validity of the Illuminati theory, I found *The Power of Ritual in Prehistory: Secret Societies and Origins of Social Complexity* by Brian Hayden, Research Associate in the Department of Anthropology at the University of British Columbia and Professor Emeritus at Simon Fraser University. The book suggested that secret societies were not only real and potentially influential but that they had been around since the dawn of humanity (Hayden 2020).

At its most basic, a secret society was a non-kinship organization, usually hierarchical, with selective membership. Specialized knowledge was not only kept from the public, but also guarded within the group so that those with higher rankings were privy to information that lower members were not.

Secret societies had existed since prehistory, often including among their members community leaders. Until recently, archeologists and anthropologists believed that these groups among hunters and gatherers served to benefit the community, making decisions to serve the best interests of the clan at large. However, recent research from the likes of Hayden suggested that these organizations were in fact mostly used to benefit the members of prehistoric secret societies themselves, particularly those of higher rank.

Using excavation sites across three continents, as well as anthropological evidence, Hayden showed that far from working for the welfare of their communities, traditional secret societies emerged as predatory organizations that operated for the benefit of their own members. Among the tools at their disposal were rituals, the manipulation of cultural myths, and threats of violence. Leaders of these groups claimed to have the secrets of life and the universe, the ability to control spirits, raise the dead, exorcise demons, and more. To demonstrate these powers, they performed ancient forms of stage magic in which members ate or spit burning coals and initiates emerged from smoke or descended from the sky. These tricks had real consequences as anyone who trespassed on secret society turf was beaten or killed.

To enter or advance in societies, it was often required that initiates come from important families and pay dues, frequently in the form of large feasts. Not only were they put through harrowing physical trials to promote loyalty, but they might have had to make their wives available to leaders for sex or give their wives away. In some cases, "they had to provide human sacrifices, engage in cannibalism, or even eat their own sons."

Hayden cited Johansen as saying "that the underlying motivation of the organizers of secret societies was to promote their own self-interests by creating a hegemonic control over rituals and experiences that they claimed gave them supernatural powers or influence."

The exploitation of supernatural powers would provide leaders with an aura of cosmological power that demanded obedience. While not everyone in a community would believe in this power, there was enough of a threat and social adherence that it would be difficult to express skepticism without fear of reprisal from the secret society. Additionally, gifts of food, debts, or threats of force could ensure acquiescence from the members of the public.

Central to the power that a secret society held over a community were the rituals they performed in order to showcase the power, both arcane and material, their members had. Exuding these elements were the ritual objects and strange costumes from distant, exotic locations, as well as the provision of foreign meals including meat from power animals. These rituals also involved public, often very disruptive components. Hayden wrote:

> In order to persuade community members of the power of the supernatural forces that secret societies claimed to control, they periodically put on dances, displays, and processions of some of those powers for everyone to see. Society members impersonated spirits by the use of masks, costumes, and unusual noise-making devices. They also developed highly sophisticated stage magic techniques, all of which provided fascination and entertainment for non-initiated spectators, as well as instilling terror. Thus, spectators witnessed dancers becoming crazy and possessed, going around biting bits of flesh from people, or tearing dogs apart and eating them. Some of those who were possessed destroyed house walls and furniture. Some could handle fire, keep burning coals in their mouths, make rattles dance by themselves, change water to blood, bring dead salmon to life, have arrows thrust through their bodies. Some

initiates even cut off their own heads only to be brought back to life. The material power (derived from spirit power) of the society was also manifested in the form of lavish feasts, spirit costumes and masks, and the destruction of property such as the burning of fish oil and killing of slaves.

Hayden noted that this public havoc was meant to drive the community to these secret societies for protection over unruly forces:

> A major benefit that secret societies claimed to provide to their communities was protection from dangerous supernatural powers which secret societies themselves periodically unleashed in communities to demonstrate how much danger the community might face without their protection. McIlwraith (1948b :58,71– 90) observed that the Cannibal Societies of the Bella Coola not only commanded the most awe, but instilled fear and terror in non- members. Manifestations of non- human behavior inherited from ancestors and evoked by Kwakwakawakw possession dances included the raw uncontrolled power of supernatural entities that wreaked havoc in the material and social world via their possessed human agents. Demonstrations of this raw power involved the possessed person destroying property, tearing off people's clothes, biting people, and cannibalism . Cannibal-possessed people ran through all the houses of the village biting various individuals, even those of high rank (Boas 1897:437,440– 3,528,531,635,651– 6; Drucker 1941:202,213,216) or took "pieces of flesh out of the arms and chest of the people" (Boas 1897:437). It was said that if the Hamatsa (cannibal) spirits could not be pacified (by dances and songs), then there would always be trouble (Boas 1897:573,616). People who suffered injuries from such acts had to be compensated. The cannibals could become excited at any time if provoked by any perceived slight, the mention of certain topics, mistakes in rituals, or improper actions (Boas 1897:214,557; Olson 1954 :242; Garfield and Wingert 1977:41), thus posing a constant threat to individuals and the community. Members of other secret societies like the Fire Throwers and Destroyers could similarly wreak havoc (typically destroying almost anything in their frenzies and biting off pieces of flesh from women's arms – all of whom had to be compensated), and they regularly did so when they contacted sacred powers, only to be brought under control by the higher ranking members with the secret knowledge to control supernatural forces (Halpin 1984 :283– 4,286,289– 90). This was similar to the Panther dancers among the Nuuchahnulth described by Boas (1891:603) who

knocked everything to pieces, poured water on fires, tore dogs apart and devoured them. McIlwraith (1948b :58,71– 90,107,118,127) repeatedly mentions the terror that such events created through- out the entire village, especially for the uninitiated who often cow- ered in their houses or rooms while destruction rained down on their houses or persons from "Cannibals," "Breakers," "Scratchers," "Bears," "Wolves," and other supernatural impersonators. As previ- ously noted, other dancers claimed to capture or steal the souls of spectators (Boas 1897:561,577; McIlwraith 1948b :5,63).

Also important to the power of secret societies was the induction of sa- cred ecstatic experiences in initiates at various levels of advancement to val- idate their claims of supernatural powers. This could have been based on the use of psychotropics or sensory deprivation and musical tools. They might have also involved the violation of taboos, such as eating human flesh.

> Comparative studies have identified a wide range of well-known techniques for inducing altered states of consciousness and sacred ecstatic experiences (SEEs) (B. Hayden 2003 :63– 73). Some of the more common techniques include severe physical trials such as fasting, sensory deprivation, prolonged dancing or drumming, use of psychotropics, auditory or visual driving, strong emotional perturbations including being "shot" or "killed" or forced to con- sume human flesh. Except for the use of psychotropic substances, all these techniques were used on the Northwest Coast. As Loeb (1929 :249) observed, death and resurrection constituted one of the leitmotifs of most secret societies. Typically, the possess- ing spirit took the initiates away, killed them, and returned them initiated and reborn, as with the Nuuchahnulth Lokoala (Wolf) Society and Kwakwakawakw societies, which had to remove a piece of quartz from a 'dead' initiate in order to revive him (Boas 1897:585–6,590,633,636). Nuuchahnulth initiates were described as entering into states of 'mesmerism,' while Coast Salish novices went to the woods for 'inspiration' (Boas 1897:639,646). Tsim- shian, Wikeno, and Xaihais initiates into the Heavenly or Canni- bal series of dances were supposed to have been taken up into the sky during their periods of seclusion, and were subsequently to be found on the beach (see Fig. 2.3) when they fell back to earth (Drucker 1941:206,214,220,221; Halpin 1984 :283– 4). For the Kwakwakawakw, the primary goal of the winter ceremonies was to bring back youths who were in ecstatic, wild states while they re- sided with the supernatural protector of their secret society.

At times, a piece of flesh from a slave or an animal would be eaten either as an act of real or simulated cannibalism during initiation ceremonies.

> While the sacrifice of slaves during potlatches and secret society performances seems to be generally accepted as an aspect of some Northwest Coast ceremonialism, the issue of cannibalism is strongly debated. There are numerous claims of first-hand accounts, and there appear to have been desiccated corpses involved in ceremonies, but it cannot be known whether human flesh was actually consumed, or perhaps only touched to the mouth, or whether stage illusions were used to make it seem as though cannibalism was occurring in order to intimidate spectators or to establish fearsome reputations. In other parts of the world such as Melanesia and Africa, secret societies were more certainly using cannibalism as a means to intimidate any who opposed them. Thus, this may have been a tactic used by a range of secret societies both ethnographically and prehistorically, including on the Northwest Coast.

Many of these acts were not real, but simulations. Much that Hayden described and referenced were early acts of stage magic. That didn't mean that people weren't actually hurt. Slaves were regularly killed to make the magic more believable:

> [I]nitiates in the Cannibal Society took human flesh with them to eat on their celestial journeys, for which a slave was killed, half of which was eaten by members (Boas 1900:118). However, McIlwraith (1948b :107) felt that this was done with stage props rather than real consumption of human flesh, except that he acknowledged that slaves were sometimes killed, possibly to make such claims more believable (108). He also reported that chiefs belonging to secret societies killed slaves and buried them in their houses in order to give more power to their Kusiut paraphernalia. The sacrifice of slaves was also recorded as a regular part of the Wolf ceremonies of the Nuuchahnulth (Boas 1897:636) and was reported by Kane (1996:121–2,148–9) a half century earlier. Members of the Quinault Klokwalle (Wolf) Society also had a reputation for killing and eating people during their secret rites (Olson 1936:121).

Hayden described the length that one Chief went to execute a believable trick:

> One of the most remarkable accounts is of Chief Legaic who found a look-alike slave and had him act as Legaic in a performance. The

slave impersonating Legaic was then killed and cremated as part of the performance, after which the real Legaic rose miraculously from the burial box containing the slave's ashes (Halpin 1984 :283– 6).

To ensure loyalty, secret societies also used spies, disinformation agents, and members dedicated to dealing out punishments, threats, violence and summoning supernatural powers. Naturally, the secret society would need to use its ritual knowledge to contain these forces.

> Those who did not accept secret society claims or dictates were targeted and frequently eliminated one way or another. Some groups employed spies to identify such individuals. Thus, as tends to be true of many secret societies, anyone disclosing or discovering that the appearances of the spirits were really humans in masks, or anyone disclosing the tricks behind stage magic performances, was either inducted into the society (if deemed desirable) or killed outright.

CHAPTER TEN

MODERN SECRET SOCIETIES

I learned that secret societies continued on from prehistoric times into antiquity, including the Greek mystery cults, and the medieval era. One of the most important for understanding modern secret societies was the Knights Templar, a Catholic military order that protected Christian pilgrims traveling to Jerusalem in the 12th through 14th centuries (Spence 2020).

Over time, the Templars became a major economic force in Christendom with almost 1,000 forts across Europe and the Middle East, many of which operated as prototypical banks. Among its debtors was France's King Philip IV, who arrested members and pushed Pope Clement V to disband the order in 1312. In addition to rumors about what went on during Templar rituals, the gruesome murder of the group's leaders gave rise to legends long after their fall.

There were stories that Templar initiation ceremonies included such sacrilegious acts as spitting on the cross and denying Christ, as well as kissing inappropriately. Outside of the initiation rituals, members were also accused of homosexuality and worshipping idols like the goat figure Baphomet or the mummified head of John the Baptist. Arrested by King Phillip, many Templars, including Grand Master Jacques de Molay and Geoffroi de Charney, Preceptor of Normandy, were tortured until they confessed to a variety of crimes. They were then burned at the stake for heresy in Paris in 1314.

It was claimed that De Molay shouted as he went up in flames that he would see King Philip and Pope Clement soon before God. His true words were transcribed on parchment to be: "Dieu sait qui a tort et a péché. Il va bientot arriver malheur à ceux qui nous ont condamnés à mort" ("God knows who is wrong and has sinned. Soon a calamity will occur to those who have condemned us to death"). Just a month later, Pope Clement died. King Philip was killed in a hunting accident within the year.

The group crumbled as other members were arrested, folded into a variety of Catholic orders or sent into retirement. The Pope ordered Templar property to be given to the Knights Hospitaller, with the exclusion of any property in Aragon, Castile or Portugal, the last of which became a home for many remaining Templars (Spence 2020).

Since then, a number of modern organizations claimed to be the rightful continuation of the society. The Templars were also the basis for many legends about the fates of religious relics such as the Holy Grail and the Ark of the Covenant. Their symbols made their way into both Freemasonry and witchcraft. Baphomet, for instance, became an idol associated with satanism. There is a contested theory that Freemasonry was a direct descendent of the Templars and, if that was not the case, perhaps they became the spiritual heirs in terms of power and influence (Spence 2019).

The Freemasons grew out of stonemason guilds from the Middle Ages. As European cathedral building waned, stonemason lodges began to allow members who were not stonemasons. By 1717, the first Grand Lodge, linking together many other lodges, was established in England. By 1730, the first lodge in the American colonies was created in Philadelphia with Benjamin Franklin as a founder.

Decades later, on December 16, 1773, nearly 200 people dressed like Mohawk tribesmen nabbed 342 chests of about 45 tons of tea belonging to the East India Company. They dumped the goods into Griffin's Wharf in Boston as a symbolic act against British rule. This, in turn, would help ignite the American Revolution.

While the Boston Tea Party wasn't the work of Freemasons themselves, the Sons of Liberty was a spin-off of Freemasonry. In response to British taxes, the group emerged in Boston in 1765, generating resistance against royal control, and, later, operating as a shadow government within British-held territories during the war. The act at Griffin's Wharf was a form of retaliation against the damage done by the East India Company against American smugglers, who had been raking in huge sums of money by evading royal duties. When the British corporate giant cut tea costs in the colonies so low, smugglers were put out of business, including Sons of Liberty members Samuel Adams and John Hancock.

Though Adams and Hancock were masons, fellow masons Benjamin Franklin and George Washington disagreed with the tactics of their brothers, evidence that Freemasonry wasn't exactly a grand conspiracy, but, like all organizations, fraught with disagreements. In fact, there were Freemasons on either side of the war, with Freemason Washington receiving aid from French and Prussian Freemasons Marquis de Lafayette and Baron von Steuben during the Battle of Yorktown. On the other side was British Freemason Lord Cornwallis. In addition to the fact that there were a number of Freemasons among the revolutionary leadership, the war's greatest turncoat was Freemason Benedict Arnold.

American Freemasons played pivotal roles in their revolution, as did French Freemasons in the revolution across the pond. In France, on July 14, 1789, a mob of a thousand people stormed the old fortress of the Bastille, an armory and prison, and demanded entrance. The commander of the facility and his army of 100 guards stood their ground until the mob took control, releasing seven prisoners and killing the commander and some of his men.

The revolution was prefaced by the bankruptcy experienced by France as King Louis XVI poured funds into the revolution in America. This resulted in the summoning of the Estates-General, meant to provide council to the king. While the estates of the clergy and nobility represented just two percent of the country's population, it took up over 50% of the council's seats, which contrasted dramatically with the third estate, representative of the rest of the French populace. The inequality was blatant to the third estate and set the stage for revolution.

Another event that pushed the animosity of the people even further was the dismissal of the King's liberal finance minister. On the streets of the bustling Palais-Royal area, where coffee houses and shops were frequented by Freemasons, the firing was framed in such a way as to generate further animosity toward the king. The leading Freemason in France at the time, the Duke of Orleans Louis-Philippe, happened to be the owner of the Palais, as well as the master of the largest Masonic lodge in the country, the Grand Orient Lodge, and was a brother of the Nine Sisters Lodge (Neufs Soeurs). Though he was the cousin of King Louis, Louis-Philippe was a champion of the revolution and changed his name to Philippe Égalité, Phillip the Equal. In fact, when the Bastille was stormed just days after the firing of the finance minister, the mob hauled a bust of the duke around the fortress as Nine Sisters member Camille Desmoulins stoked the flames of anger among the crowd.

The Duke of Orleans, Camille Desmoulins and Desmoulins's mentor, Freemason Count Mirabeau, ultimately joined the Jacobins, the most powerful of the political clubs during the revolution. The Nine Sisters was a key link between Masons in France and those in the colonies. Benjamin Franklin and John Paul Jones became members in 1778 and brought three other American revolutionaries along: Thomas Paine, Thomas Jefferson, and John Adams. The Marquis de Lafayette, was also a member.

135

So, while the Freemasons didn't have omnipotent or even cohesive control over the revolutions, they certainly represented a powerful influence. And their influence continued into the modern era.

The Great Seal of the U.S. was a Masonic symbol approved by Washington that was then placed on the one-dollar bill during the presidency of Mason Franklin D. Roosevelt. At least 15 presidents, five Supreme Court chief justices, and a variety of congress members had been masons. Other famous and powerful masons included:

- J Edgar Hoover
- Earl Warren
- Jesse Jackson
- John Jacob Astor,
- Andrew Jackson,
- William "Bud" Abbott,
- Salvador Allende,
- Nat King Cole,
- Samuel Colt,
- Duke Ellington,
- James Naismith,
- Scottie Pippen,
- Michael Richards,
- The Ringling brothers,
- Strom Thurmond,
- Shaquille O'Neal,
- Oscar Wilde
- Denton T. "Cy" Young
- John Wayne (Freeman 2019)

It wasn't the only secret society with influence either. The Knights of Malta, a Catholic secret society that also represented a sovereign nation without borders, boasted four CIA directors as members: William "Wild Bill" Donovan, John McCone, William Casey, William Colby, and George Tenet (Heimbichner 2020).

Founded by the father of President William Howard Taft, one of Yale's secret society, the Skull and Bones, was known for grooming its members to become future leaders. In fact, it even served as a recruiting ground for CIA assets. Famous members included:

- William Howard Taft
- William and McGeorge Bundy
- George H.W. Bush

- George W. Bush
- John Kerry
- William F. Buckley, Jr.
- Frederick Wallace Smith, founder of FedEx
- Stephen Schwartzman, founder of the Blackstone Group
- Henry Stimson, secretary of war under FDR
- Supreme Court Justice Potter Stewart
- Averell Harriman
- Time magazine founder and CIA asset Henry Luce
- J. Richardson Dilworth, the Bonesman who went on to manage the Rockefeller fortune (McEnery 2011)

THE PROPAGANDA DUE MASONIC LODGE

Perhaps one of the most obvious modern uses of secret societies as means of influencing social affairs took place in Italy in the 1960s, 70s and 80s. The Propaganda Due (P2) lodge was a "black" Freemason lodge, meaning that it was not officially recognized by the national order of Freemasonry in Italy. Nevertheless, its members included some of the most prominent and right-wing members of Italian society. This included the heads of all three Italian intelligence services; Prince Vittorio Emanuele of Savoy, the son of the last king of Italy; and future prime minister Silvio Berlusconi (Report of the Parliamentary Commission 1984).

The P2 lodge served as one important node in a network of right-wing structures throughout Europe that was leveraged by the CIA and NATO to prevent a leftward shift by national governments on the continent. This network was the result of a post-World War II CIA program in Italy called Operation Gladio, which had counterparts and nodes in Belgium, Switzerland, Portugal, France, Norway, Greece, Austria, West Germany, The Netherlands, Finland, Spain, Sweden, Denmark and Turkey (Ganser 2005). Though the program had different names in each country, "Gladio" came to be a catch-all term for the CIA- and NATO-backed network as a whole.

The ostensible purpose for Gladio was the establishment of a "stay-behind" network of operatives within Europe to fend off a Soviet invasion. To fill the ranks of the network, Nazi and Italian fascist soldiers were recruited as World War II came to a close. As a part of the program, these troops were secretly trained for clandestine operations (Haberman 1990). Weapons caches were hidden throughout the countries where Gladio took root. In Italy, this occurred with the help of Italian intelligence and military, fascist elements, and leading businessmen under the cover of the P2 lodge (Francovich 1992).

Rather than solely prepare for a Soviet invasion, the Gladio network attempted to prevent any leftist control over the affairs of the country. As the Communist party rose in popularity, the Gladio network carried out a series of terrorist attacks, "false flags" that were then pinned on leftists (Ganser 2004). These "Years of Lead," as they were called, saw numerous atrocities committed. The 1969 Piazza Fontana bombing resulted in the death of 17 people and wounding of 88 more. The 1974 Piazza della Loggia bombing ended the lives of eight people and injured 102. The 1980 Bologna bombing saw 85 people killed and over 200 wounded. There was additional evidence to suggest that the Gladio program played a role in the kidnapping and murder of Italian Prime Minister Aldo Moro, for allying too closely with the Communist party (Flamigni 2003).

In addition to turning public opinion against leftist movements in Europe, Gladio was meant to execute what had been called a "strategy of tension," in which the overall atmosphere of terror would drive the general population to turn to the state for security purposes (Ganser 2004).

Of the many countries linked to the stay-behind network, only Italy, Belgium and Switzerland conducted parliamentary inquiries into Gladio (Belgian parliamentary report concerning the stay-behind network 1991).

The existence of the program was first made public by right-wing terrorist Vincenzo Vinciguerra during his 1984 trial (Scott & Hughes 2008), but became much more widely known and validated by Italian Prime Minister Giulio Andreotti in 1990, when he brought the subject to the floor of the Chamber of Deputies (Vulliamy 1990). In the 80s and 90s, Andreotti was likely the political ally of Licio Gelli, the fascist Master Mason of the P2 lodge, according to Italian Ministry of Grace and Justice Claudio Martelli (D'Angelo 2015).

In Switzerland, the investigation turned up evidence that British intelligence had trained Swiss soldiers to resist not just a possible Soviet takeover, but also a leftist majority in parliament. In Belgium, no concrete conclusions were drawn, as the Belgian secret services refused to cooperate in the investigation.

Ten years after Andreotti's bombshell, a report from a parliamentary investigation in Italy stated that U.S. intelligence had driven the terrorist attacks and promoted a strategy of tension (Willan 2000). Six years later, the U.S. State Department released a message dismissing all of these accusations and said that allegations of its support for false flag attacks were derived from documents forged by the Soviets (U.S. State Department) . Outside of these official inquiries, there was evidence linking the attempted assassination of Pope John Paul II in Turkey by the Gladio-linked fascist group, the Grey Wolves (Head 2010).

BILDERBERG, LE CERCLE AND OTHER GROUPS

As far as I could tell, the Freemasons were no longer planning revolutions and the Propaganda Due lodge in Italy was an aberration, but there were still contemporary secret societies that may have affected undue influence on global affairs. In the 20th century, there were a variety of sometimes overlapping organizations that served as exclusive meeting venues for some of the world's most powerful people. In the U.S., this included the Council on Foreign Relations and the Trilateral Commission, among others. Abroad there was the Bilderberg Group, The Pinay Cercle, the Roundtable Group, and, later on, the World Economic Forum.

These clubs didn't have the same mystique and symbology as the secret societies that typically came to mind, such as the Freemasons, but they retained extreme exclusivity and, though their members may have only met once or twice a year, made collective decisions on behalf of their respective nations.

An American foreign policy think tank, the Council on Foreign Relations (CFR), was "dedicated to increasing America's understanding of the world and contributing ideas to U.S. foreign policy" (CFR website) through closed discussions, conducting research, and publishing the journal *Foreign Affairs* (Shoup & Minter 1977). Established in 1921, CFR had about 4,000 members, ranging from prominent media figures and academics to politicians and intelligence and military officers. Members had included such individuals as CIA Director Allen Dulles, Nelson Rockefeller, George H. W. Bush, Gerald Ford, Henry Luce (Publisher Time/Life), Arthur Ochs Sulzberger (Publisher *NY Times*), William Paley (Owner CBS), Walter Cronkite (CBS), Dan Rather (CBS), Bob Schieffer (CBS), Peter Jennings (ABC), James Reston (*NY Times*), Anthony Lewis (*NY Times*), Harrison Salisbury (*NY Times*), Rupert Murdoch, Michael Eisner, Bill Clinton, George Stephanopoulos, and Brian Williams.

Though the CFR was not a formal policy making institution, the influence of its members was such that its policy goals aligned closely with those of the U.S. State Department (Shoup 2004). Exclusivity was in part established by the cost of corporate membership, ranging between over $25,000 for "Basic" and "Premium" and over $50,000 for "President's Circle" (Council on Foreign Relations Annual Report 2006). Additionally, all members were U.S. citizens. Members had access to hear speakers, including foreign prime ministers, CEOs, and U.S. officials.

In 1974, Zbigniew Brzezinski and David Rockefeller founded the Trilateral Commission (TLC). Members were selected by the Chairman of the Executive Committee, who was David Rockefeller for most of the organization's existence (Rockefeller Archives). It essentially acted as a private circle for U.S. leaders and the interests of the Rockefeller family. For instance, President Jimmy Carter and Vice President Walter Mondale were Trilaterals in 1977, as were 18 others from the Carter administration, out of a total of 77 American members (Sutton 1995). In 1993 President Bill Clinton and Vice President Al Gore were Trilaterals, along with 20 of their cabinet members. 10 days after Barack Obama was sworn in, he appointed 11 Trilaterals (12% of the TLC's total U.S. membership (Wood 2013)) to top positions in his administration.

The Bilderberg Group meetings, founded in 1954 by Prince Bernhard of the Netherlands with funding and assistance from CIA Director Allen Dulles (Molitch-Hou 2020), was a series of secretive annual meetings attended by about 120 leaders in finance, military and government. They discussed projects such as the creation of the "Euro" (Rettman 2009) and executing the 1973 oil crisis (Engdahl 2004).

Though the existence of the group was denied for some time, it was exposed in part by a 1977 report by journalist Dominique Bromberger (Bromberger 1977) and publicly acknowledged itself (Bilderberg website), but became described as a place for world leaders to meet and relax away from paparazzi. With about 100-150 guests in recent years, attendees included Henry Kissinger, David Rockefeller, Prince Charles, Peter Mandelson, Lord Carrington, David Cameron, Queen Beatrix of Holland and the chairman of Barclays Bank (Midgley 2018). The first Chinese guest was welcomed in 2011. New invitees were expected to speak so that they could be analyzed by the steering committee. Speakers presented for 10 minutes before a report was drawn up about their comments and provided to attendees. The exact location of the meetings was not released publicly and the site featured armed guards during the meeting (Ronson 2001). The report from the first Bilderberg noted ominously: "When the time is ripe our present concepts of world affairs should be extended to the whole world (Bilderberg Conference 1954)."

According to Secretary General of NATO Willy Claes, who was at a Bilderberg meeting in 1994, everyone in attendance was provided with a report and were "considered to use this report in setting their policies in the environments in which they affect." He said that the same two guests were not allowed to sit adjacent to one another more than once to increase networking related to discussing important topics (Skelton 2010).

The Steering Committee typically had about 28 members, recently including Étienne Davignon, journalist Bill Moyers, diplomat George W. Ball, perennial Bilderberger Victor Halberstadt, BBC Senior Independent Director Marcus Agius, Gabriel Hauge, Richard C. Holbrooke, Winston Lord and Paul Wolfowitz.

According to minutes from the 1973 meeting, which included CEOs from Royal Dutch Shell, British Petroleum, Total S.A., ENI, and Exxon, discussions included increasing the price of oil by 400% and a "plan [on] how to manage the about-to-be-created flood of oil dollars" (Engdahl 2004). In 2009, former chairman Étienne Davignon said the conference "helped create the euro in the 1990s," corroborated by leaked documents (Rettman 2009). Two of three Presidents of the European Central Bank had been Steering Committee members. The third attended Bilderberg just before he became president. The predecessor to the Bank, the European Monetary Institute was also headed by Bilderberg attendees.

After attending his first meeting in 1991, Bill Clinton was elected U.S. president the following year. Tony Blair attended in 1991 and became Prime Minister of the UK in 1997. Emmanuel Macron attended in 2014 before becoming Prime Minister of France in 2017 (Bridge 2017). In 1966, the top agenda item was to reorganize NATO. Since then, no permanent Secretary General of NATO had been selected unless they'd attended a Bilderberg conference (Bilderberg Conference Report 1966).

Honorary President of the Supreme Court of Italy and former Senior Investigative Judge Ferdinando Imposimato, claimed that the Bilderberg Group was involved in the false flag attacks that were part of the Gladio program (Reinvestigate 911 n.d.). This was not surprising, given that a related group, the Pinay Cercle, was closely linked to the Gladio operation.

Beginning as a solely European organization for its first 15 years, it began hosting annual conferences in Europe and Washington D.C. starting in 1968. While Bilderberg enjoyed the pretense of legitimate business negotiations and networking, leaked documents from Le Cercle indicated the open discussion of political subversion, fraud, and arms trafficking.

Organized in 1952 by Jean Violet, a close associate of French Prime Minister, Le Cercle began as a Franco-German alliance with anti-communist and catholic Christian tendencies. The reach extended across the

Atlantic when CIA officer Ted Shackley became involved (McCormack 2002). Former chairs Kwasi Kwarteng and Nadhim Zahawi "denied they had any knowledge of how Le Cercle funds its operations" (Johnston 2019). Corporate sponsors had included Philips, Standard Elektrik Lorenz, Shell, and the Ford Foundation (Teacher 2015).

David Teacher claimed that "throughout the 1970s the Cercle Pinay complex was active [influencing elections in the UK,] France, Germany, Spain, Portugal, Italy and Belgium." He wrote that "the Cercle complex can be seen to be an international coalition of right-wing intelligence veterans, working internationally to promote top conservative politicians who would shape the world in the 1970s and 1980s (Teacher 2015)."

The first investigation into the group came in 1979, with the Langemann Papers quoting a planning paper by Brian Crozier about a project by the group "to affect a change of government in the United Kingdom" (accomplished). This was likely a reference to aiding in the election of Margaret Thatcher, the year after she was invited to attend Bilderberg.

Four members of Le Cercle presented at the Jerusalem Conference on International Terrorism in 1979, with other speakers well connected to the Pinay group, which led to the establishment of "terrorism research" organisations, suggesting that it may have aided in the shaping of the "anti-terror" narrative that would soon emerge. Visitors to the event had been associated with international controversies, such as Al-Yamamah arms deal which involved attendee John Carbaugh among others, and the oil deals in the Middle East, which included the participation of Ted Shackley after he left the CIA in 1979 (Teacher 2015).

MODERN RITUALS

Okay, so even if secret societies continued to exert influence, did they still involve cannibalism and the sacrifice of slaves? It would have been difficult to confirm, as their rituals didn't appear to have the same aspect of public display that they did in prehistory. As with ancient orders, modern rituals differed from group to group, even within specific societies. Moreover, many organizations cultivated an intentional aura of mystery and grandiosity mixed with disinformation so that outsiders could not determine the true nature of what occured during ceremonies.

Though no Freemason lodge was identical, there was a general initiation ritual that had been made public. The blindfolded, bare chested initiate was said to enter the lodge from the west and toward the worshipful master on the East, representing the myth that the wisdom of light sprang from the East, with the blindfold signifying ignorance and the exposed chest demonstrating that he was not a woman. The left pant leg of the candidate was rolled up as a means of showcasing his health and strength.

The initiate then knelt at the altar in the center of the lodge, where he placed his hands on a religious text of his choice and took a binding oath pledging to execute certain secret actions and not to execute certain actions related to his membership in the lodge, obligations known only to members. He was then sworn to secrecy, taught lessons about Free-masonry and its symbols, with each degree up to 33 building upon the knowledge of the previous degrees. The lessons were meant to educate the initiate about the virtues of Freemasonry. Finally, he was told the se-cret symbols of the lodge, how to recognize other members and how to be admitted as a visitor to other lodges (Spence 2020).

Perhaps more intriguing was the supposed initiation ritual for the Skull and Bones society, with specific details unclear or unverifiable due to the nature of the club. On the night in which 15 Yale seniors "tapped" 15 juniors to enter the secret clan, the initiates were slapped on the shoul-der and asked, "Skull and Bones: Do you accept?" Upon acceptance, they were handed a message entwined with black ribbon and the seal of the group. Written on the note were the time and location for the would-be member to meet on initiation night, as well as an instruction to wear no metal.

On that night, the candidate could be taken to the basement of a Bones house, where two members dressed in skeleton suits made them swear a solemn oath of secrecy for the events that would take place later in the evening. Then, the new member headed to the grand door of the club's crypt on campus. The door opened and a gun might be pointed at them as they were guided inside. The candidate might have been entombed in a coffin and brought to the center, Room 322, of Skull and Bones headquar-ters. The Bonesmen chanted as the new member was removed from the coffin and provided with robes with symbols on it, reborn into society. A bone with the initiate's name was thrown into a pile and the new members were sunken into mud. One story had it that room 322 was filled with skulls of notable Americans with the head of the Native American Coch-ise or Geronimo kept in a jar filled with jade in the center of the quarters.

Once the ceremony ended, the initiate received a check for $15,000 as a gift from the exclusive group. They may even have gotten an annual stipend of $20,000. Another grand gesture was a trip to Deer Island in the St. Lawrence River. There, the new class of Bonesmen would meet the leaders of society, active Bones alumni that led banks, businesses and the U.S. itself.

In their senior year, Bonesmen were required to participate in a confessional that took place on two separate days in the Skull and Bones tomb. The first night was an autobiography of everything that had happened to the members in their lives, including the most heartbreaking tales of trauma and shame, as well as their life's ambitions. The second night involved divulging everything sexual that the member had engaged in, from first masturbation stories to tales of intercourse. This seemed to be a confessional process that surely could have been recorded for blackmail purposes.

The ties between Bonesmen was meant to continue throughout the lives of members, with George H.W. Bush convening a meeting of his brothers while running for President. If one mentioned the phrase "Skull and Bones" in front of a member, that member was supposed to immediately leave the room without saying a word. At death, some Bonesmen were thought to leave a small portion of their estate to the club (Rosenbaum 1977).

OLD FORMS, NEW GUISES

So, it appeared as though the relative secrecy and influence of these organizations varied significantly, with the heydays of some long gone and the others remaining to some extent or another. But secret societies didn't seem to be a modern invention. They existed in nearly all civilizations since the dawn of humanity. And many of their practices didn't appear vastly different from those today, though the superstitions and specifics obviously differed considerably.

It was difficult to sift lore from fact when examining the details of ancient secret societies but it appeared that both simulated and real human sacrifice and cannibalism occurred in some cultures. This was never a widespread practice, but a ritual demonstration of power by the society on the surrounding community and the members themselves. It was often a form of terrorism to elicit complicity.

I had a hard time determining the extent to which any real violence occurred in more contemporary organizations, in part due to their secrecy as well as the general mystique generated by these groups. So, I reasoned that, though secret societies, cults and the like had become the bogeymen in any number of conspiracy theories, I couldn't rule out their influence in world affairs. But did they really sacrifice children in some occult rituals?

While not central to the case, there were elements of the Franklin scandal that stretched credulity in ways echoed by Pizzagate. At least three victims claimed to be subjected to abuse at the hands of people in robes during occult rituals. They described such horrific acts as child torture and sacrifice. Could the Qanon people have been onto something? Were the power elite really dealing with the devil?

PART 3

SATANISM AND THE OCCULT

Aleister Crowley, Golden Dawn,
The Rites of Eleusis in 1910.
Public Domain

CHAPTER ELEVEN

A BRIEF HISTORY
OF THE SATANIC MASS

W hen I came to, the dancers were gone, as was the cave. My body looked to be intact. Where I found myself was actually quite picturesque. If I had to guess, it was somewhere near Nag Hammadi in ancient Egypt. There was a smattering of green flora within a desert of beige before a vast sea, wavering lines of heat haze dancing at the horizon. I walked down the dune toward the settlement ahead, sand flowing into my sneakers and anchoring my feet every step of the way.

To understand why Q people thought the elite were sacrificing children to the devil, I knew it was necessary to have some knowledge of where the concept of satanic rituals came from.

Hugh Urban, professor of religious studies at Ohio State University, argued that the idea of black masses was mostly a twisted fantasy that fearful Christians projected onto their enemies. Two divergent sects of Christianity, the Gnostics and the Cathars, were important examples of oppression by the dominant strains of the religion. They were described as participating in pagan-style rituals in which children were murdered, human flesh was eaten, and homosexual sex and incest were performed. In large part, this was because these sects were challenging church authority (Urban 2008, Ch. 7).

In the fourth century AD, the widely egalitarian Gnostic groups stood in stark contrast to the hierarchical Christian churches of the mainstream. In addition to leveling the playing field between priests and congregations, many Gnostics allowed women to become religious leaders. Perhaps more importantly, they believed that it was possible for people to discover the spark of divinity within themselves, potentially challenging the authority of Christ and the church altogether. And, though, many Gnostics had a negative attitude toward the body and sex, they were framed as debauched heathens (Ibid., Ch. 1).

Epiphanius, who would go on to be bishop of Salamis, claimed he came upon a Gnostic group in Egypt and saw their "love rites" (agape) in which they ingested sexual emissions from men and women as the sacrament in their version of a Christian mass. And if a woman became pregnant as a result of an agape orgy, Epiphanius described the horror that would occur:

> They serve up lavish helpings of wine and meat even if they are poor. When they have had their drink and filled their veins, as it were, to bursting point, they give themselves over to passion. The husband withdraws from his wife and says to her: "Rise up, make love with your brother." The miserable wretches then indulge in promiscuous intercourse. And, though it truly shames me for the disgraceful things they did ... nevertheless I shall not recoil from saying what they did not recoil from doing, so as to arouse in my readers a shuddering horror of their scandalous behavior. After copulating, as if the crime of their whoredom were not enough, they offer up their shame to heaven. The man and woman take the man's sperm in their hands and stand looking up to heaven. With this impurity in their hands, they pray ... offering to the natural Father of the universe what is in their hands, saying "We offer you this gift, the body of Christ." And so they eat it, partaking of their own shame and saying, "This is the body of Christ, and this is the Passover."
>
> ... Similarly with the woman's emission at her period: they collect the menstrual blood which is unclean, take it and eat it together and say "Behold the Blood of Christ..." They practice the shameful act not to beget children but for mere pleasure.... If one of them happens to allow the sperm to penetrate the woman and make her pregnant, listen to the outrage that they dare to perform. At the right moment they extract the embryo with their fingers and take the aborted infant and crush it with pestle and mortar; when they have mixed in honey, pepper and other spices and perfumed oils to lessen their nausea, they all assemble to the feast, every member of this troop of swine and dogs, each taking a piece of the aborted child in their fingers.... And this they consider the perfect Passover (Ibid. Ch. 1).

Between the 11th and 14th centuries, a Gnostic movement in northern Italy and southern France faced similar persecution. The Cathars were even more extreme in their attitude toward the body, essentially embracing dualism and rejecting the physical world as a "source of pain and an alien imposition on true nature that are pure spirit." In turn, sex and even marriage and producing children were thought to reproduce the suffering of the physical world. This resulted in a more equal attitude toward the sexes. More importantly, they attacked the Catholic Church as corrupt and greedy, driving the Cathars to pick up followers around Europe and become a potentially powerful force on the continent.

They were subjected to the inquisition and the Albigensian Crusade, which essentially wiped the sect out by the end of the 13th century. On the propaganda front, they were attacked as secret sex-fiends and satanists. Pope Gregory IX, in particular, said in 1233 that they worshipped the Devil, believing that God had sinned by ejecting Lucifer from heaven. According to the Pope, their ceremonies included a "banquet and the appearance of a black cat, whose hind quarters were kissed by most of those present," and peaked with the "extinguishing of the lights followed by a promiscuous and sometimes homosexual orgy."

Throughout the Middle Ages, similar accusations would be thrown at such groups as the Brethren of the Free Spirit and the Knights Templar. Though Pope Urban argued that most of these allegations were baseless, there was some evidence that aspects of the Catholic Mass were used for magical purposes. For instance, the Eucharist may have been used "to cause disease or to obtain love, or even to procure abortion or death." Some suggested that, in the 16th century, Catherine de' Medici, Queen of France, may have conducted a Black Mass that included human sacrifice to aid the health of her ill son, Philip. The 13th century Pope Honorius III was thought to have written the *Grimoire of Honorius*, a text that discussed how to use Mass for occult purposes, such as summoning spirits to execute one's will (Ibid., Ch. 1).

In the 15th century, a figure arose that became firmly associated with the origins of SRA. French baron Gilles de Rais was not only one of the richest men in France, but also a compatriot of Joan of Arc, serving as her protector and a military chief. When he was arrested in 1440, however, he became known as the world's first serial-killer, with allegations that he had murdered hundreds of children, at times employing the use of alchemy and sorcery. It was still debated whether the accusations were true or if this was a politically motivated arrest. Urban claimed that he may have only sacrificed one child in a magical ritual and then became so wracked with guilt that he gave the victim a Christian burial (Ibid., Ch. 7).

In the 17th century, another high profile account of the occult occurred, this time in the court of Louis XIV. Apparently preoccupied with losing the king's affection, Louis' mistress, Madame de Montespan, took part in a black mass in which a naked woman was used as an altar and a chalice filled with wine and the blood of three to four infants was passed around to celebrate communion. According to interrogator Nicolas de la

Reynie, the priest in the ceremony "has cut the throats and sacrificed un-counted numbers of children on his infernal altar. … It is no ordinary man who thinks it a natural thing to sacrifice infants by slitting their throats and to say the Mass upon the bodies of naked women. (Ibid., Ch. 7).

The Marquis de Sade further drove the perversion of the Mass into the collective imagination in his pornographic writing. In such books as *Justine, Juliette,* and *Lusts of the Libertines,* he used the Mass as the back-drop for extreme sexual acts, sometimes including the Pope himself. In the *Lusts of the Libertines,* he wrote:

> [The libertine] fucks a whore throughout a Mass being held in his private chapel, and ejaculates furiously at the moment the host is raised aloft …. He fucks whores on the holy altar while Mass is proclaimed, their naked arses spread apart on the sacred stone.… He farts and has a whore fart into the holy chalice, they both piss into it, they both shit in it, and finally he splurts his spunk into the mess. He makes a small boy shit onto the plate of the Eucharist, then devours the turd while the boy sucks his cock.… He takes holy communion then, while the wafer is still in his mouth, has four whores shit upon it.… He rubs the whore's clitoris with the Host until she drenches it with cuntcream, then shoves it up her cunt and fucks her, ejaculating over it in turn (Ibid., Ch. 7).

Written depictions of Black Masses in literature would come to inform real world manifestations of the ritual by the likes of Anton LaVey in the decades to follow. The most notable description came from J. K. Huysmans' *Là bas* ("Down There"), which the author claimed was inspired by his own search for a Black Mass. Whether or not he ever actually witnessed one was never determined. French occultist Joséphin Péladan argued that *Là bas* demonstrated an "absolute and definitive ignorance of the laws of satanism."

Huysmans claimed that he had met the defrocked priest, Abbé Boul-lan, who established a religious group dubbed the Society of the Repara-tion of Souls that some believed to be a front for illicit violent and sexual behavior. One account claimed, "whenever a nun fell sick or complained of being tormented by the devil, Boullan would apply remedies com-pounded of consecrated hosts and faecal matter; and on 8 December 1860, at the end of his Mass, he sacrificed upon the altar a child which Adèle Chevalier had born him at the moment of Consecration."

Boullan told Huysmans when they met in 1889 that he was not a sa-tanist but an expert on sex demons. The priest then appeared in Huys-mans's book as the character Canon Docre. The figure conducted a Black

Mass in an old convent, beneath a crucifix in which Christ's sorrowful face had been distorted into "a bestial one twisted into a mean laugh. He was naked, and where the loincloth should have been, there was virile member projecting from a bush of horsehair."

Docre was decked out in a red hood with Buffalo horns and called Christ the "Artisan of Hoaxes, Bandit of Homage," responsible for the "Chicanery of thy ... commercial representatives, thy Popes, to answer by dilatory excuses and evasive promises." In contrast, the devil was described as the "King of the Disinherited, Son who art to overthrow the inexorable father," and was celebrated his various sins: "Master of slanders, Dispenser of the benefits of crime, Administrator of sumptuous sins and great vices, Satan, thee we adore, reasonable God, just God! Superadmirable legate of false trances ... thou savest the honour of families by aborting wombs impregnated in the forgetfulness of the good orgasm ... and thine obstetric spares the still-born children the anguish of maturity, the contamination of original sin.... Hope of Virility, Anguish of the Empty Womb, thou dost not demand the bootless offering of chaste loins ... thou alone receivest the carnal supplications and petitions of poor and avaricious families. Thou determinist the mother to sell her daughter, to give her son; thou aidest sterile and reprobate loves; Guardian of strident Neuroses, Leaden Tower of Hysteria, bloody Vase of Rape!"

Docre then shoved the host into his mouth, broke it apart and spit it out, with Huysmans writing:

> In a solemn but jerky voice he said "Hoc est enim corpus meum," then instead of kneeling ... before the precious Body, he faced the congregation and appeared tumified, haggard, dripping with sweat. He staggered between the two choir boys who, raising the chausible, displayed his naked belly. Docre made a few passes and the host sailed, tainted and soiled, over the steps.... A whirlwind of hysteria shook the room.... Women rushed upon the Eucharist and, groveling in front of the altar, clawed from the bread humid particles and divine ordure.... Docre ... frothing with rage, was chewing up sacramental wafers, taking them out of his mouth, wiping himself with them and distributing them to the women, who ground them underfoot, howling, or fell over each other struggling to get hold of them and violate them. The place was simply a madhouse, a monstrous pandemonium of prostitutes and maniacs" (Urban 2008, Ch. 7).

In researching the satanic panic and Qanon, I came across early Christian attacks against fringe sects framed as legitimate depictions of Satanic

153

worship. Specifically the passage from Epiphanius was framed as depicting as actual practices by Gnostics, laying the foundation for satanic rituals. However, it wasn't the Gnostics that introduced blasphemy to their ceremonies. It was a man named Aleister Crowley, who realized the depictions of Gnostic masses conceived by the ancient Christian mainstream. Though his Gnostic Mass was said not to include sexual penetration, it was sexual in nature, with the priest using his "lance" to part the veil of a priestess before taking off her clothes. She, in turn, proclaimed:

> I love you! I yearn to you! Pale or purple, veiled or voluptuous, I who am all pleasure and purple, and drunkenness of the innermost sense, desire you. Put on the wings, and arouse the coiled splendour within you: come unto me! To me! To me! Sing the rapturous love-song unto me! Burn to me perfumes! Wear to me jewels! Drink to me, for I love you! I love you (Ibid., Ch. 4).

In place of a typical wafer, the host was what Crowley called a "cake of light," made from "meal & honey & thick leavings of red wine: then oil of Abramelin and olive oil" and softened with fresh blood. As for this last ingredient, menstrual blood was the preferred form, ranked above even a child's blood: "The best blood is of the moon, monthly: then the fresh blood of a child … then of enemies; then of the priest or of the worshippers: last of some beast (Crowley 1909)." The recipe wasn't entirely different from what Marina Abramović relied on in her spirit cooking rituals.

As I changed Misha's diaper, a crisp zephyr floating through the open window of his room, I pondered the phrase "fresh blood of a child." This was Aleister Crowley? Number 73 on the BBC's 2002 list of 100 Greatest Britons, according to a television poll (Spence 2008). I began to wonder if there was some truth to the possibility of satanic sacrifice.

CHAPTER TWELVE

ALEISTER CROWLEY,
THE WICKEDEST SPY IN THE WORLD

The Godfather of modern Satanism – whether he'd call himself that or not – was Aleister Crowley. The Beast 666. The Wickedest Man in the World. Known for inventing the gnostic mass, magick sex rituals for converting the forces of the aether into physical power. Crowley did not explicitly worship Satan, but did offer alternative interpretations of religious icons, such as the devil, that would work their way into Satanism and other new age religions.

As I soon learned, Crowley was more than just an infamous practitioner of the dark arts, but also a spy, serving as an agent of British, and possibly U.S., intelligence during and after the First World War. Crowley's development in the world of the occult seemed to have occurred simultaneously with his journey in espionage. Richard B. Spence, University of Idaho professor and author of *Secret Agent 666: Aleister Crowley, British Intelligence and the Occult*, reasoned that he was likely already involved in espionage while a student at Cambridge University. Though Spence made many educated deductions about what the magician was up to in terms of spy operations, he also provided concrete evidence that confirmed Crowley's involvement with British Naval Intelligence. The Beast's expertise appeared to be in infiltrating subversive groups for the purposes of gathering information and sabotaging their activities as an agent provocateur.

In England, this meant joining the Hermetic Order of the Golden Dawn, an occult organization that combined elements of Freemasonry and Rosicrucianism with other esoteric movements from the time, such as Theosophy. Membership happened to include several individuals prominent in the Legitimist/Jacobite movement, such as Golden Dawn founder Samuel MacGregor Mathers. These activists sought to overthrow the British government and establish sovereignty for the British islands, Scotland, Wales, Ireland and Cornwall. For this reason, the Golden Dawn included Irish separatists like the poet William Butler Yeats (Spence 2008, Ch. 1).

As a part of a larger Legitimist movement that aimed to restore various European rulers to their thrones, Crowley participated in a gun running operation with Mathers and the Fifth Earl of Ashburnham, among others, to arm Carlists in Spain. On their third trip supplying weapons to those who dubbed Don Carlos the rightful heir to the Spanish throne, their boat was seized by French customs on behalf of the Spanish consul (Ibid., Ch. 1).

After this affair, Crowley's next task may have involved dissolving the Golden Dawn altogether. He rose the ranks of the group quickly, ultimately earning the ire of senior members angered by his rapid ascent. As retaliation, they refused to allow Crowley to be given the cult's "Adeptus Minor" degree. In turn, Crowley convinced Golden Dawn founder Mathers to initiate him anyway, creating disunity among the leadership. Mathers ordered Crowley to take the club back physically, such that the upstart occultist made his way into the lodge wearing a black mask and ceremonial attire waving a ritual dagger around and threatening the members. This led to the expulsion of both Crowley and Mathers from the Golden Dawn, which in turn resulted in the disintegration of the order altogether (Ibid., Ch. 1).

During all of this time, the Beast engaged in travels to far-flung places, from Mexico to Russia and China, potentially performing covert intelligence gathering activities while there, according to Spence. In 1907, he founded his own occult group, the A∴A∴. Shortly after, the beast attracted the attention of a separate occult organization, the Ordo Templi Orientis (OTO), when he featured supposed Rosicrucian secret sex rituals in his publication, *The Equinox*.

The OTO was established by German intelligence agent Theodor Reuss with the goal of uniting disparate Masonic groups and other esoteric orders under a single organization. The story went that when Reuss learned in 1912 that Crowley had somehow independently learned the basis for sex magic without being in the OTO, he was initiated to join its ranks. He became the chief of the OTO branch in the British Isles, the Ordo Mysteria Mystica Maxima (MMM), and would go on to become the leader of the OTO for the English speaking world (Ibid., Ch. 2).

When Crowley joined the OTO, he had already developed a significant reputation and managed to concoct a philosophy that would influence occult religions, including branches of satanism, going forward. Crowley's *The Book of the Law* – supposedly dictated to the mage in Egypt in 1904 by Aiwass, messenger for the god Horus – would serve as the foundation for his new religion of Thelema. The driving principle of this religion could be boiled down to the phrase "do what thou wilt shall be the whole of the Law," a principle that would see Crowley experiment with any drug or sexual act he possibly could. Both were generally meant to fuel the magick rituals Crowley performed in his attempts to achieve a godlike existence.

Among the key practices for the OTO that would trickle into some future movements was the idea that sex could produce powerful forces, with a variety of acts correlating with different manifestations in the physical world. This idea of sex magick was, according to Hugh Urban, mostly derived from orientalist, Western understandings of Tantra practices from India. Though they twisted many of these ideas around, western notions of sex magick helped to normalize Tantric ceremonies as Victorian attitudes toward sex began to loosen (Urban 2008, Ch. 4).

In particular, Crowley believed that it was possible to create a "magical child" with the right ritual and concentration. Urban wrote:

> As Peter Koenig summarizes the upper degrees, Crowley's VIIIth degree unveiled ... that masturbating on a sigil of a demon or meditating upon the image of a phallus would bring power or communication with a divine being.... The IXth degree was labeled heterosexual intercourse where the sexual secrets were sucked out of the vagina and when not consumed ... put on a sigil to attract this or that demon to fulfill the pertinent wish.... In the XIth degree, the mostly homosexual degree, one identifies oneself with an ejaculating penis. The blood (or excrements) from anal intercourse attract the spirits/demons while the sperm keeps them alive (Ibid. Ch. 4)."

According to the Beast's diary, *Rex de Arte Regia*, he performed 309 acts of sex magick between 1914 and 1918. These were conducted for both spiritual purposes, like obtaining new powers, and material ones, like obtaining a mistress. He even believed it possible to achieve wealth by imagining a shower of gold coins at climax. Urban counted 48 acts of financial sex magick to represent the majority of the total during this time.

Soon after joining the OTO, Crowley landed in New York City and connected himself to a British spy posing as an Irish nationalist, John Quinn, to monitor German espionage agents as well as the Irish separatists who aimed to unite the cause of Ireland with that of the Germans during World War I. To do so, he began writing for multiple American vehicles of the German propaganda department called *The Fatherland*

and *The International,* both run by George Sylvester Viereck and aimed at influencing American opinion in favor of German interests. Crowley described his task in the following way:

> I knew that the only way I could combat the influence of German propaganda in the States was to identify myself with it in every way, and by making it abhorrent to any sane being, gradually get the minds of the American public to react against its insidious appeal.... My real scheme was to ingratiate myself with the other side that I should obtain their full confidence, and so be able to betray their plans to England (Spence 2008, Ch. 4).

Though he claimed that he was "playing a lone hand" without "authority from London," according to a U.S. Military Intelligence Division dossier on Crowley's activities during WWI, "Aleister Crowley was an employee of the British Government ... in this country on official business of which the British Consul, New York City has full cognizance (Ibid., Introduction)."

At one point, Crowley even claimed to have aided the U.S. Department of Justice, writing, "my services are contained in the records [of the Department of Justice] to this day." He said that the U.S. was more willing "to take advantage of my help" than the U.K., saying that it "helped me to the fullest possible extent" (Ibid., Ch. 7).

Among his tasks, Crowley wrote propaganda for Viereck, saying this about his German-American employer, "I worked upon the mind of Viereck to such an extent that from relatively reasonable attacks on England, he went to the most stupid extravagances, with the result that he published the most futile rubbish from my pen" (Ibid., Ch. 4). However, Spence suggested that Viereck may have been a double agent, with Crowley attempting to hide that fact or being unaware of it.

The Beast also may have played a role in sniffing out one of the fathers of psychology, Harvard professor Hugo Muensterberg, as a German spy (Ibid., Ch. 4). Other tasks potentially included bugging the offices of *The Fatherland* and even coaxing the U.S. into the war via a plot to sink the Lusitania (Ibid., Ch. 5). These were all hypotheses Spence made based on a variety of sources, including the writings of Crowley and others from this nexus of German assets.

Another detail worth noting was the fact that Crowley was known to experiment with drugs, which Spence suggested could have been precursor work to British intelligence exploration of psychotropics for interrogation and other purposes. Spence wrote:

Crowley, circumstantial evidence suggests, was a pioneer in this bizarre field, and his groundbreaking work may have informed some of those later experiments. He once boasted, "I have myself made extensive and elaborate studies of the effects of indulgence in stimulants and narcotics," and produced "a vast quantity of un-published data" on the subject. Throughout his American stay, the Beast routinely administered mescaline or other drugs to willing and unsuspecting subjects (spicy curries were a favorite means), methodically cataloging the results. These observations ended up in another of his journals, Liber CMXXXIV, The Cactus, which he described as an "elaborate study of the psychological effects pro-duced by Anhalonium Lewinii … compiled from the actual re-cords of some hundreds of experiments." The Cactus vanished after the war (Ch. 7)."

Spence suggested that possible evidence of Crowley's application of psychotropics could have been found in an incident involving a U.S. col-laborator with a German government named Louis Smith:

Smith and his wife started to suffer from chronic paranoia and hallu-cinations. They believed that they were being watched and followed (they were), and even thought that C.C. Crowley [another German collaborator unrelated to Aleister], or someone who looked like him, was spying on them. Smith, driven over the edge, finally went to the police. Once in custody he talked nonstop and by 28 October had confessed to his work with C.C. Crowley for Bopp. Oddly, the Feds kept all this under wraps for the next month (Ch. 7).

Whether or not Crowley's research did make it into the hands of intel-ligence, I did learn that the precursor to the CIA's MKULTRA program admitted to at least a cursory interest in Crowley's research into psycho-active substances for potential use as a "truth drug," but supposedly aban-doned it because they found the writing of Crowley "simply too difficult to fathom" (Albarelli 2011).

Spence offered the possibility that Crowley also kept tabs on the Indi-an nationalist movement. For instance, by supplying Anglo-Indian critic Ananda Coomaraswamy with a mistress while also wooing Coomaras-wamy's wife, Crowley was able to gain information from the author and his social circles in New York (Spence 2008, Ch. 8).

When Crowley returned to Europe in 1919, he likely continued to spy on leftists, fascists and others that may have posed a threat to the British state. An asset for the French Army's intelligence arm (the Service de renseignements), named Pierre Mariel, asserted that Crowley was involved in espionage in Italy, but that the British labeled him "rather inept" and said his "moral corruption" and poor money management required "the very greatest caution" if he were to be used (Ibid., Ch 11).

All the while, the Wickedest Man in the World continued his magical work, establishing a school for his teachings on the island of Cefalu in Sicily, Italy. The location would become the stuff of lore for decades to come, as Crowley conducted magickal workings and indulged in the sins of the flesh. The Abbey was shut down by Mussolini in April 1923, purportedly due the debauched reputation it had gained, including an incident that became highly publicized in the U.K. by a woman named Betty May. May's husband, Raoul Loveday, died at the Abbey earlier that February after he was made to drink the blood of a sacrificed cat. Crowley claimed that the liver infection Loveday suffered was caused by a local polluted stream. For a taste of what life was like at the church, Burgo Partridge summarized Betty May's account as follows:

> Inside the abbey, the Beast ruled with a rod of iron. His women had to dye their hair alternately crimson and black. The verbal use of the first person singular was prohibited, and punished by self-inflicted wounds. Drugs lay about the house. Even Crowley's son, aged five, was an addict. This child remarked to the outraged Betty: "You must leave me alone! I am beast number two, and can shatter you!" (Horsley 2019, Ch. 21)

However, it may have actually been Crowley's involvement with British intelligence that saw him booted from the country. After the Beast was driven out, the Italians found papers evidencing the Abbey of Thelema's use as an anti-fascist, anti-Italian propaganda center. The OVRA secret police also uncovered material from the "special espionage service (servizio speciale di spionnagio) of the British Foreign Office" (Spence 2008, Ch. 11).

He wasn't only forced to leave Italy, but was separately forced out of the OTO. In 1921, Reuss expelled Crowley from the group, to which the magician replied by declaring himself Frater Superior and "Outer Head" (OHO) of the Order. Because Reuss was too ill to respond, Crowley continued to maintain the position after Reuss's death in 1923. Soon after, the group splintered around Crowley, with a group led by Karl Germer following the Beast, another rejecting him altogether and a third that claimed to believe in Crowley's spiritual guidance but not his management of their affairs (Ibid., Ch. 11).

Crowley continued his espionage work, using his "magick" as a cover. There were rumors that he could have been involved in the capture or interrogation of Nazi Deputy Führer Rudolph Hess, who abandoned the Reich in the hopes of a backdoor peace deal with the British. While there didn't seem to be much evidence that Crowley concocted the astrological symbols used to convince Hess to travel to the U.K. or that the mage engaged in applying his expertise in psychotropics to interrogating the Nazi leader, he at least tried. In a letter to Bond author and British spy Ian Fleming, dated four days after Hess was captured, Crowley wrote: "If it is true that Herr Hess is much influenced by astrology and magick, my services might be of use to the department in case he should not be willing to do what you wish (Ibid., Ch. 14)."

However, Fleming noted that one of his big regrets was never having had the Beast interview Hess. While he wasn't used as an interrogator, British intelligence may have entertained some of the beast's proposals for espionage operations. Fleming said, for instance, that Crowley "put forward some madcap ideas to the intelligence authorities ... one being dropping occult information [on the enemy] by leaflet (Ibid., Ch. 14)."

It was difficult to separate Crowley's reputation and the reality, in part because of the mystical and joking nature of his texts as well as the show he put on for the public, walking a fine line between dispensing with social mores and committing illegal acts. And all of this was made more complicated knowing his history in espionage. Nowhere was this more problematic than in his apparent advocacy of human sacrifice, "apparent" being the operative word.

The recipe for Cakes of Light wasn't the only time he referenced using children in magickal workings. In Crowley's most widely read text, *Magick in Theory and Practice*, the mage wrote: "For the highest spiritual working one must accordingly choose that victim which contains the greatest and purest force. A male child of perfect innocence and high intelligence is the most satisfactory and suitable victim (Horsley 2019, Ch. 20)."

A footnote on the page added, "It appears from the Magical Records of Frater Perdurabo that He made this particular sacrifice on an average about 150 times every year between 1912 e.v. and 1928." Crowley later suggested that the note was a joke about masturbation, claiming that discussing masturbation was not allowed in publishing at the time, but that describing the murder of a child was acceptable. Author Jasun Horsley pointed out, however, that the rest of the text surrounding the mention of child sacrifice did not seem satirical. That text read as follows:

It would be unwise to condemn as irrational the practice of those savages who tear the heart and liver from an adversary, and devour them while yet warm. In any case it was the theory of the ancient Magicians, that any living being is a storehouse of energy varying in quantity according to the size and health of the animal, and in quality according to its mental and moral character. At the death of the animal this energy is liberated suddenly. [F]or nearly all purposes human sacrifice is the best.... Experience here as elsewhere is the best teacher. In the Sacrifice during Invocation, however, it may be said without fear of contradiction that the death of the victim should coincide with the supreme invocation (Ibid., Ch. 20).

There was no mention of adrenochrome, but the energy released upon death seemed to be a principal feature of the ritual. What made this reference all the more disturbing, satirical or poetic or not, was an entry in Crowley's diary from August 12, 1920 and reprinted in *The Magickal Record of the Beast 666*, about his "Scarlet woman," one of his lovers at the time and the mother of two of his children:

Her breasts itch with lust of Incest. She hath given Her two-year bastard boy to Her lewd lover's whim of sodomy, hath taught him speech and act, things infinitely abhorred, with Her own beastly carcass. She hath tongued Her five-month girl, and asked its father to deflower it. She hath wished Her Beast to rape Her rotten old mother – so far is woman clean of Her! Then Her blood is grown icy hard and cold with hate; and her eyes gleam as Her ears ring with a chime of wedding bells, dirty words, or vibrate, cat-gut fashion, to the thin shrieks of a young child that Her Beast-God-Slave-Mate is torturing for Her pleasure – ay! and his own, since of Her Cup he drank, and of Her soul he breathed.

Horsley pointed out that the above passage "describes the sodomizing of a two-year-old boy; the oral abuse of a five-month baby girl; the invitation to rape the same infant; and the sadistic torture of at least one of these children" by Crowley (Ch. 21).

At the Abbey of Thelema, children were exposed to the libertine lifestyle of the cult. This meant that adults participated in sexual activities without regard for who might witness them. About this situation, Horsley wrote:

Crowley's credo included satisfying all sexual desires, combined with an insistence that any kind of sexual repression distorts the essential (sexual) nature of children. So how exactly did Crowley draw the line, once these 'instincts' were in play, between allowing children to watch adults engaging in sex acts and allowing, or encouraging, them to participate? The only way to prevent this from happening would be to make that line both very clear and very firm. There is nothing of the sort, either in Crowley's prescriptions (and proscriptions), or in the accounts of what occurred during his time at the Abbey." (Ch. 21)

While I would have preferred concrete evidence as to whether or not Crowley was engaged in child sexual abuse or performed human sacrifice, these writings opened up that possibility. After all, his stated philosophy was one that appeared to open up that possibility. Crowley noted, "*The Book of the Law* solves the sexual problem completely. Each individual has an absolute right to satisfy his sexual instinct as is physiologically proper for him (Ibid., Ch. 21)."

Given what I knew about other intelligence honey pots, his possible participation in black mail operations also presented that possibility. A Soviet mole named Kim Philby sent a report to Moscow in 1942 saying that the U.K.'s Secret Intelligence Service was looking into a "complicated racket" tying Royal Air Force officers and members of British high society to drug smuggling, orgies, and black masses. The ring was being operated, supposedly, by the German Embassy in Dublin, which used Welsh fishermen and nightclub owners to move drugs into England. All of this was a means of blackmailing officers to gain information. In the mix of activities was "the notorious occultist Aleister Crowley (Spence 2008, Ch. 14)."

Similarly, George Makgill, who operated a private intelligence organization called Section D for the British Empire Union and the Economic League, suggested that Crowley was involved in "international traffic in drugs and the traffic in women and children." One agent in Section D, code named "H," had supposedly "uncovered a blackmail plot, involving two well-known politicians, connected to Crowley's activities in the island of Cefalu [sic] (Ibid., Ch. 14)."

Occult rituals and orgies would certainly have been blackmail-worthy, as would homosexual acts with Crowley himself. Could Crowley have been a more esoteric version of Epstein? It probably didn't mean anything but, when Crowley sued author Nina Hamnett for defamation, as well as for the following decade, he employed a notable lawyer named Isidore Kerman, who just so happened to be an adviser to Robert Maxwell, the father of the notorious Ghislaine (Ibid., Ch. 13).

Though I didn't know it at the time, there was one operation, referred to as "Plan 241," proposed by the mage in 1942 that would foreshadow CIA operations to come. To friend, student and spook Robert Cecil, who labeled the strategy as "black propaganda" that was "as black as black could be." The idea was to recruit individuals "whom despair had rendered not only murderous, but suicidal" and have them kill two Germans before killing themselves with the number "241" somewhere on the murderers' dead bodies. Then, it was hoped that some copycat killers would follow suit. According to Cecil, the strategy "did not find favor (Ibid., Ch. 14)."

That may have been the case, but as I moved closer to the center of the nebulous glob of deep state evil, I found that there were similarities between Crowley's Plan 241 and other operations possibly executed by U.S. intelligence.

Chapter Thirteen

SCIENTOLOGY, CROWLEY'S STRANGE BEDFELLOW

C rowley's influence would go on to permeate many facets of pop culture, from The Beatles to Led Zeppelin, from New Age bookshops to mass paperbacks like *The Secret*. But it was his influence in intelligence and esoteric groups that concerned me because it was there that I believed any hints of occult child sacrifice by the power elite would lay. And, as I researched the intersection between the two, I found myself traversing two parallel paths toward Satan.

The first I went down didn't involve so much satanism per se but Devil-friendly ideologies and it was a route that was covered in blood, murder and the fingerprints of deep state agencies. The second was one paved by an earthly incarnation of Beezlebub himself and, depending on what you believed, suggested the possibility of child abuse of which #pizzagate investigators so desperately sought proof.

The first winding path began at the U.S. branch of the OTO, the Agape Lodge in Pasadena, California. Founded in the 1930s by Crowley acolyte Wilfred T. Smith, the group boasted at least one future intelligence agent, Army officer Grady Louis McMurtry, who would later work for U.S. Army intelligence (G-2), during the Korean Wa . By the 1940s, the lodge was led by CalTech rocket scientist John Whiteside "Jack" Parsons, who worked on top secret military projects while at Aerojet Engineering Corporation. In 1950, Parsons admitted to stealing classified documents from his then-employer Hughes Aircraft, a firm heavily linked to U.S. intelligence and the mob. Parsons claimed that he wanted to copy the papers when applying for a job with an Israeli program linked to the Mossad called the American Technicon Society (Urban 2012).

But before that, this "James Dean of the Occult" was engaged in a much more notorious act. He performed a bit of sex magick called the "Babalon Working," meant to generate a moonchild who could bring about the New Aeon of Horus based on Crowley's teachings. He wasn't alone in this project, but was accompanied by a young Naval officer named Lafayette Ronald Hubbard, better known as L. Ron Hubbard.

Parsons believed that, despite the seaman's lack of training, Hubbard was already quite attuned to the work at hand. This was due in part to Hubbard already claiming to have a Guardian Angel, something the Thelmites sought to achieve through their magickal workings. His was called "The Empress," a winged beauty with red hair. Parsons determined that, due to Hubbard's ability to view the astral plane, he would act as the "Scribe" for the ritual. He became the "voice" for Babalon, as she spoke through him and Parsons wrote down her words.

To begin, Parsons performed the OTO VIII degree ritual, an act of masturbation that would summon the elemental world in order to draw a female partner, his Scarlet Woman, to him for the subsequent steps. Parsons believed that the procedure worked, as he'd met a redhead named Marjorie Cameron soon after, who was willing to engage in magickal rituals with him. Between February and March 1946, the pair, with Hubbard present, conducted IX degree sex magick, to bring about the moonchild. He wrote to Crowley to say that he was successful in the endeavor, that he had impregnated Cameron and would be her guardian for nine months.

Outside of their magickal project, Hubbard, Parsons, and his sister-in-law and former girlfriend Sara "Betty" Northrop established Allied Enterprises. The plan was to buy yachts on the East Coast and sell them for a profit on the West. While Parsons threw down nearly his entire life savings at $20,970.80 on the endeavor, Hubbard put in just $1,183.91. Crowley had his own misgivings about Hubbard, noting, "Suspect Ron playing confidence trick – Jack Parsons weak fool – obvious victim prowling swindlers."

When Parsons realized that Hubbard had run off with not just his money but his ex-girlfriend, he pursued him to Miami, where Hubbard and Northrop were making their escape on a yacht. Parsons invoked Bartzabel, the spirit of Mars, as a means of cursing the pair. Related or not, a strong wind did come in and cause the yacht to return to port before Hubbard ultimately made off with the money and the woman. Crowley wrote in response that he was enraged at the "idiocy of these goats."

Parsons was left without a moonchild or his funds. He continued to struggle financially and, years later in 1952, he was killed in what was thought to be an accidental chemical explosion. Meanwhile, Hubbard had gone on to establish one of the most lucrative cults in modern history, the Church of Scientology. And when Hubbard left Parsons high and dry, he took some of Crowley's ideas with him.

Church critic and son of Hubbard, L. Ron Hubbard Jr., said that his father was "deeply involved in the occult." Jon Atack also suggested that

Crowley's ideas were at the center of Scientology, though the Church denied any connection. Instead, it argued that Hubbard was acting as an agent of the Office of Naval Intelligence to shut down the powerful and evil OTO cult. It was true that Hubbard was a part of ONI, but generally had a very bad reputation. In a fitness report about Hubbard, Rear Admiral Frank A. Braisted wrote that he "consider[ed] this officer lacking in the essential qualities of judgment, leadership and cooperation. He acts without forethought as to probable results. He is believed to have been sincere in his efforts to make his ship efficient and ready. Not considered qualified for command or promotion at this time. Recommend duty on a large vessel where he can be properly supervised."

In an essay titled "Occult Roots of Scientology? L. Ron Hubbard, Aleister Crowley, and the Origins of a Controversial New Religion," Hugh Urban suggested that, in his method of blending concepts from a variety of sources, Hubbard did appropriate some of Crowley's ideas, alongside pop psychology, eastern religions and science fiction.

One concept that found its way into Dianetics was the idea that self-actualization, the highest of goals, would be represented by the ability to speak to one's Guardian Angel. Crowley's was Aiwass, who communicated to him the *Book of the Law* in Egypt in 1904. Of this concept, Crowley wrote, "the Single Supreme Ritual is the attainment of the Knowledge and Conversation of the Holy Guardian Angel."

Shortly after fleeing with Parson's lover and money, Hubbard recorded an obscure work, titled *Affirmations*. The only portions of the text made public were available as the result of a lawsuit on behalf of the Church of Scientology against former church member Gerald Armstrong. In this suit, the Church seemed to have confirmed its ownership over the text and its authorship by Hubbard.

Written in 1946 or 1947, *Affirmations* was supposed to have been read into an audio recorder and played for Hubbard himself to listen to. It suggested that Hubbard was participating in a ritual as he recorded it, repeatedly stating that his "magical work is powerful and effective." The incantations were meant to be integrated into the listener's mind, convincing them that they had psychic abilities. The recording also continuously referenced a female guardian, the key guide to the listener's spiritual affairs. According to Urban, "much like Crowley's Magick, the *Affirmations* also assert that one who is in contact with the Guardian is virtually invincible and all-powerful."

Urban also saw similarities related to astral projection in both Dianetics and Crowley's beliefs. In Thelema, it was said to be possible to detach one's spiritual body to make long journeys across space and time. The ability to cultivate this Body of Light along with communicating with one's Guardian Angel could render a magician omnipotent.

Hubbard even engaged in sex magick. Though it was referenced in the lawsuit, a document discussing "The Blood Ritual" was "so sensitive that no part of it was read into the record." Those who saw it said that it "consisted of Ron and his then wife mingling their blood to become One," and was dedicated to the Egyptian goddess Hathor, while also referring to Nuit, Re, Mammon, and Osiris. Crowley was also heavily influenced by Egyptian religion, referencing Nuit and Osiris, among others, and describing how to invoke Hathor, the Goddess of Love, in his book *Magick in Theory and Practice.*

Beyond these rare documents, there were similarities between the two religions in terms of an overarching philosophy. While Thelema was meant to grant mages with superhuman powers via a "cycle of action" achieved in magick rituals, Scientology relied on the process of auditing to liberate one's spiritual self, or "thetan," from our physical dimension. In turn, they could become telepathic, psychic, and telekinetic. Hubbard used Crowley's term "cycle of action" to say "Scientology 8–8008 is a design for a new cycle of action.... It tells what the cycle of action goes to – an unapplied infinity of potential."

Urban wrote:

> One of the central themes in Hubbard's lectures from roughly 1952 to 1958 is that the thetan is not only an immortal entity of infinite potential but can also be trained to "exteriorize" or separate itself from the physical body. Hubbard himself, it is true, rejects the use of the specific phrase astral projection as a kind of mystical delusion. However, his account of exteriorization – the exact same term used by Muldoon, we might note – is almost identical to Crowley's account of projecting the Body of Light. As in Crowley's magical practice, exteriorization is one of the most important techniques in Hubbard's early Scientology practice and is described in detail in numerous lectures gathered in publications such as The Philadelphia Doctorate Course (1952), Scientology 8–8008 (1952), The Creation of Human Ability (1954), and The Phoenix Lectures (1954).

Other crossovers included the fact that theta (Θ) was both key to Scientology and was the first letter in the core law of Crowley's Thelema, as well as the first letter in his pseudonym Therion. It was one of the most important symbols for the Beast as the sigil of Babalon, present in a number of his works. Outside of Thelema, the sign was also a central symbol in religions such as Hinduism.

Hubbard also started spreading the Church of Scientology as a religion in 1954 in a newsletter called "The Golden Dawn," the same name of the occult society to which Crowley once belonged. The symbol Hubbard chose for his church bore a resemblance to both the figures used by the original Golden Dawn and by Crowley for his church: an eight-pointed cross. The Golden Dawn cross appeared on the back of the cards in Crowley's famous "Thoth" Tarot deck.

Urban also highlighted "most of the early followers of Dianetics and Scientology had already been involved in various forms of occult, esoteric, magical, and other alternative traditions long before joining Hubbard's movement. In his sociological study of the early membership of the church, Wallis found that 'over half of them had prior ment in marginal religions, Rosicrucianism, Theosophy, Christian Science, Baha'i ... hypnosis or Jungian analysis (Urban 2012).'"

I'd heard that Scientology's auditing process had been used to obtain blackmail information on initiates. The new members provided extensive personal and private information that was then stored in a "preclear folder" that the church could then use to harass members if they wished to flee the group. As a result, the church seemed to have held a number of Hollywood celebrities, such as John Travolta and Tom Cruise, hostage, for fear that their secrets might be leaked to the public. In a way, Scientology seemed to operate like a giant compromise operation.

I wondered if the entire world of power worked like this, with various bodies blackmailing individuals to do their bidding. There were the intelligence agencies compromising politicians, religions compromising members – what if the Catholic Church used its confessionals in a similar manner?

It would certainly explain a lot, like why the Vatican couldn't throw out its pedophilic members so easily and why the elite couldn't be held accountable. These were thoughts that would hover in the back of my mind as I continued my investigation. And, soon, I found the growth from OTO to Scientology sprouted a strange new flower when two of its members decided to start their own cult.

It's Mary olde England as MTM turns o

her winning smile

A N ever-perky Mary Ty-
er Moore turns on a
London street peddler
with her smile.

Around the time this pho-
to was shot in 1967, the actress discovered that she
had diabetes.

Devastated by the diagno-
sis, the 30-year-old Mary
feared the worst. "The pic-

ture in my mind was that of
a reclining, semi-invalid,
draped in a comforter," she
recalls in her 1950 autobiography.

But she didn't let it stop
her. The sometime Emmy

winner learned to live with
the disease and forged
ahead to have the biggest
success of her career: The
Mary Tyler Moore Show.

Since then, Mary has
braved other tragedies in-

cluding alcoholism and
death of her only child
chis. But with the hel
her third husband, Dr
ert Levine, she remain
best.

"Nature gives you
ability to accept what yo
got to accept," she say
osophically. "And learn
it honestly."

CHAPTER FOURTEEN

THE PROCESS CHURCH
OF THE FINAL JUDGEMENT

O ut of Scientology came another religious organization that would achieve its own lesser fame, the Process Church of the Final Judgement. In London, two Scientology members, Mary Ann MacLean and Robert Moore, believed they could improve on Scientology's notorious auditing process, including the use of the E-meter which they called the P-scope, and began their own group in 1965 (Wylie & Parfey 2009).

Moore was an architect, studying at Regent Street Polytechnic in London when he joined the Church of Scientology. MacLean's background was more obscure. She was from Scotland and worked as a prostitute in the U.K.; however, there were widely spread, but difficult to validate rumors that she was once married to U.S. boxer Sugar Ray Robinson, a story she herself promoted, and played a role in England's Profumo Affair. According to longtime friend of Moore and fellow Process Church founder Tim Wylie, neither of these rumors was true:

> It's been suggested in some recent articles that Mary Ann might have had some involvement with the Profumo affair, the sex scandal that brought down a cabinet minister and the conservative government. Before I joined The Process I'd bumped into Christine Keeler, one of the two call girls called as witnesses, who had heard nothing of a Mary Ann. Besides, I'm perfectly certain that had she played a part in the scandal she'd have been only too ready to tell us all about it.
>
> It was often difficult to know whether Mary Ann was exaggerating about the people and the events in her life, or indeed plain old making it all up. I certainly believed her in the moment. Yet there's no record, for example, of her ever marrying (as the story went) Sugar Ray, and his son assures us that to his knowledge there was never a Mary Ann in his father's life."

From early on, the duo appeared to have a unique ability to speak to people and understand their inner workings. In odd sessions of Compulsions

Analysis, the pair's improved form of auditing, a member of the group would sit across from a newcomer and ask them questions, to which the newcomer was only meant to answer silently in their own heads. The auditor would then tell the newcomer what their unconscious was saying, a technique that seemed to actually work according to new Processans. So, by the time that Robert and Mary Ann had ditched the name Compulsions Analysis in favor of "the Process" and their own surnames in favor of the more gothic sounding "De Grimston," they had cultivated a following of somewhere around 25 dedicated members. These included wealthy, middle class Londoners whose parents were concerned about the fates of their children.

With these parents attempting to sue the group, The Process decided to flee to the Bahamas in 1966, where it evolved from a mere Scientology spin-off into something more gnostic. With the group of 30 followers meditating on the barren beach of Nassau, lacking food or shelter, all members began to feel they were speaking to "The Beings," some otherworldly, perhaps godly force. It was a true religious experience, according to the Processans. The Beings instructed them where to head next, which was a very remote town in Mexico called Xtul. There, they began to take on a new religious vocabulary, worshipping four gods: Jehovah, Lucifer, Satan and Christ (Wylie & Parfey 2009).

The Church determined, "Jehovah is strength. Lucifer is light. Satan is separation. Christ is unification (Baddeley 2010)." None of these religious figures was considered good or evil, but just aspects of human nature, with every individual embodying two of these deities. Members were meant to follow the god or gods that they most identified with (Wylie & Parfey 2009). For Processans, the real "devil" was represented by the "Grey Forces," the conforming and mediocre masses (van Luijk 2016, p. 304). They also believed that the end of life on Earth was imminent, brought about by the unification of the four gods and the reconciliation of opposites (Lewis 2001, p. 215).

As Hurricane Inez approached their austere sanctuary in Xtul, the cult returned to London, where their status began to climb. Donning black robes with purple lining and wearing silver crosses, they presented a stark contrast to the flower children that had otherwise taken root in 1960s England. Publishing magazines with themes like "Sex" and "Fear" and playing music in a coffeeshop located in a posh part of the city, they ultimately began to connect with celebrities, including Marianne Faithfull, a singer and actress who posed for an issue of their publication, as well as Mick Jagger (Wylie & Parfey 2009).

By 1968, the Process had moved to the United States, where achieving the status of a legal religion did not require the same hurdles as it did in the United Kingdom (Introvigne 2016, p. 332). Spreading out across the country, the group now known as The Process Church of the Final Judgement established chapters in New Orleans, New York, San Francisco and Los Angeles. They began to interact with a growing number of celebrities there, too. George Clinton's Parliament took inspiration from the Process for its *Maggot Brain* album, for example (Taylor 2008). In San Francisco, the Process made friends with John Phillips of the Mamas and the Papas (Sanders 2002). According to Ed Sanders, author of *The Family* and a member of the Fugs rock group, Phillips contributed an unknown but large sum to the Process Church (Sanders 2016).

It was here that rumors about the cult began to take on lives of their own, as Phillips was also a good friend of Sharon Tate and Roman Polanski, as was Mama Cass. All of the above were heavily involved in a party scene in Los Angeles that featured some questionable guests, including Charles Manson and the purported assassin of Robert F. Kennedy, Sirhan Sirhan.

A Processan minister inducts two acolytes into the Church, at which time they become initiates of the Covenant of Christ and Satan.

Chapter Fifteen

THE PROCESS MEETS CHARLES MANSON

When I requested a used copy of the first edition of *The Family* by Ed Sanders for Christmas, I had to explain to Cindy that my interest in the Manson cult was purely academic. I had very little interest in the murders themselves, but wanted to know if the egomaniacal leader, who considered himself an earthly incarnation of both Christ and Satan, had any ties to a different devil-worshipping cult, the Process, which actually only revered Satan as one of four gods. Luckily, she shrugged off her concern and was relieved to hear that it had to do more with our shared interest in New Age cults than a macabre obsession with serial killers.

Exactly what Manson's connection to the Process was was difficult to determine. There were many overlaps between his Family and the Process cult. That they may have shared the same social circles and geolocations appeared to have been clear. In San Francisco in 1967, Manson's headquarters was located just two blocks from the Process on Cole Street (Sanders 1971, p. 88). When the Family moved to Los Angeles, there were details suggesting they met the Process there, as well, at a house referred to by the in-crowd as "the Spiral Staircase." Manson member Robert Beausoleil told Ed Sanders that the Manson Family met the Process at the Spiral Staircase, a detail confirmed to Ed Sanders by Family member Patricia Krenwinkel (Sanders 2016, Afterword).

Dianne Lake also claimed to have joined the Manson Family when she met them at the Spiral Staircase at the age of 14. She reportedly told Inyo County district attorney investigator Jack Gardiner and his wife, to whom she became a ward during the trial, that she had memories of the Process and that the Family received money from them. She said the Family's unusual sex acts and drug use came from the English cult. Gardiner also reported that other Family members, specifically Leslie Van Houten and Christopher Zero, discussed the English cult while in Inyo County jail (Ibid., Afterword).

When Manson and his followers were arrested for the murders of Sharon Tate and the rest, the Process made the decision to request an essay from Manson for publication in the new "Death" issue of the church's magazine (Wylie & Parfey 2009). Meanwhile, the female defendants charged with the Tate-LaBianca killings were embroidering the logo of the Process while in jail (Sanders 2002).

Other parallels included the fact that Manson set up a similar hierarchy with similar terminology in his cult, with members dubbed as fathers and mothers, sisters and brothers. He purportedly borrowed their belief that the end times would be brought about by the reconciliation of Christ and Satan, though Manson added the element of a race war to the mix.

The overlap between the two were significant enough that ties between Manson and the Process were investigated by multiple U.S. agencies. Immigration and Naturalization Service (INS) criminal investigator Richard Smith wrote a report stating that Sirhan Sirhan "had attended some parties given by television personalities on behalf of [the Process], where rites took place usually dealing with sexual deviations and heavy drug use. One of these parties took place at Sharon Tate's home (Ibid., Afterword)."

The report was written on the basis of information from an FBI investigation into the Robert Kennedy assassination. Ed Sanders wrote that a heavily redacted version of this FBI report was provided to the Yonkers police department as it explored the Son of Sam murders. Sanders corroborated these details by relaying that CBS television reporter Carl George, claimed that a sheriff's office homicide detective tied Sirhan Sirhan to the Process (Ibid., Afterword).

The INS report suggested that the Process hired Manson to kill Tate. According to Sanders, INS investigator Robert Smith told LA private investigator Larry Larsen that the murder involved "something that [Tate] unfortunately overheard that she was not supposed to overhear either in regards to Sirhan Sirhan or about Sirhan Sirhan." Larsen claimed to Sanders that, after an extensive interview in which Smith answered all of his questions, the interview concluded as follows: "And then I asked the obvious question, 'What did Sharon Tate allegedly overhear?' and he said, 'I cannot discuss that. It's a matter of national security'" (Ibid., Afterword).

Smith reportedly wanted to launch a full investigation into this nexus of connections but was told by his employers not to push further because the daughter of a prominent New York congressman was a member of the Process. According to Sanders, INS investigator Robert Smith stuck to his story when Sanders questioned him directly in 2000 and 2004.

A musician Sanders interviewed separately told him that he saw someone that looked like Sirhan Sirhan at a party thrown by a friend of Sharon

Tate in the same hotel in which Tate lived at the time, the Chateau Marmont. The musician said that Tate was in attendance and that no strange sexual activities took place (Ibid., Afterword).

Private investigator Larsen also reportedly told Sanders that IRS intelligence agent John Daley had claimed to have learned from a couple in Los Angeles that the head of the Process had contracted Manson to kill Tate.

Paul Whiteley, a former LA County sheriff department homicide detective who played a role in Manson's arrest, apparently told Ed Sanders that Manson follower Bruce Davis was sent by Manson to England, possibly to visit the Process. Sanders said Davis "was associated over in England with the head honcho of the satanic cult, an Englishman who cofounded the cult." The LAPD also claimed to have tracked Davis traveling to London to spend time not just with the Process but local Scientologists as well. This was said to have occurred in November 1968, just after the Family was thought to have possibly murdered Clida Delaney and eight-month-pregnant Nancy Warren near Ukiah, California, beating them and then strangling them "with thirty-six leathers thongs." Upon returning from London in April 1969, he headed back to London in November once more after the murder of two Scientologists, of which he was considered a suspect. He arrived in the right time span to have been in the city for the murder of Manson family friend Joel Pugh. The British Immigration office said Davis gave Scientology headquarters as his address (Ibid., Afterword).

Peter Levenda wrote in Part Two of his *Sinister Forces* series:

> Since Davis was regarded by California investigators as "Manson's second-in-command," this constant traveling back and forth between California and London – Specifically to either Scientology or Process headquarters, or both – is evidence of a larger plot. Davis was later convicted for his role in the murders of Gary Hinman and Donny Shea, the two "bookend" murders that took place before (Hinman) and after (Shea) the seven Tate/LaBianca killings, during the period July 26-August 26, 1969. He reappeared in February 1970 at the Spahn Ranch and then disappeared again when he was convicted for the Gary Hinman murder, only to reappear in Los Angeles in December 1970, when he turned himself in to authorities..." (Levenda 2011)

Church documents from a 1977 U.S. government raid of Scientology headquarters evidenced significant concern with its perceived links to Manson. They sent members out to track down Family member Steve Gorgon, later convicted for the murder of Donny Shea, who was thought to have information about Manson's relationship to the church (Cooper). Someone then came forward saying that Manson had audited 150 hours of Scientology in prison (Levenda 2011).

"The picture painted is frightening, for it shows a Manson at turns extremely enthusiastic about his training … and terrified to the point of demanding to be put into solitary confinement so that he could escape his auditor," Levanda wrote. "It was after the Scientology cell broken up at the prison by the warden that another inmate after his release began sending Manson books on hypnotism and ' black magic.'"

Separately, *New York Daily News* reporters William Federici and Michael McGovern wrote an article at the time of the murders titled "Believe Cultist Hired Sharon Killer." The authors claimed an agent from the Bureau of Narcotics and Dangerous Drugs (the precursor to the DEA) was investigating the drug angle to the killings. The story went: "Beautiful Sharon Tate and four others are believed to have been the victims of an assassin hired by a member of a cult which met regularly for sex-drug rituals in her posh Bel Air home, authorities disclosed today." Other details from the article included the fact that famous people and business executives were members of the cult and that, at the Tate house, "an assortment of the cult's tools – including black leather masks, whips, ropes, and chains" was found (Ibid., Afterword).

Another story from another author at the paper claimed: "a source close to the investigation declared that here had been a 'wild party' attended by some of 'the biggest freaks and weirdos' in Hollywood.' What's more, probers said Sharon and the other four might have been victims of an assassin hired by a member of the cult that met regularly in the Polanski home for sex-drug rituals" (Ibid., Afterword).

Actor Steve McQueen, longtime friend and ex-boyfriend of Sharon Tate, gave an interview in which he discussed the occult activities of his social circle, "I was on the ring of it. Jay Sebring was my best friend. Sharon Tate was a girlfriend of mine. I dated Sharon for a while. I was sure taken care of; my name never got drawn into that mess. [Sebring] was having an affair with the girlfriend of a warlock. It may be for the worse, but I was always against it. I was one of the ones who always felt that I was one of the good guys, but boy I tell you, they did a number on me. I'm against that whole thing."

McQueen said he "didn't know it was the occult. It's bullshit is what it is. No, I really didn't know what it was, and by the time I did, I had never gone to any of the meetings. Never knew anything about it, and was always against it. It was never for me."

This implied that Sebring and possibly Tate were involved in the sinister rituals. Three Tate friends, Joanna Pettet, Sheilah Wells, and Shahrokh Hatami, however, told Ed Sanders that Tate had not been involved in the occult (Ibid., Afterword).

Along with tales of Satanism, there were also rumors of sadomasochism and strange videos. Record producer Terry Melcher, son of Doris Day, previous owner of the house where the Tate murders took place, and a good friend of Polanski, was quoted in *Doris Day: Her Own Story* as saying:

> [The] murders had something to do with the weird film Polanski had made, and the equally weird people who were hanging around the house. I knew they had been making a lot of homemade sado-masochistic-porno movies there with quite a few recognizable Hollywood faces in them. The reason I knew was that I had gone out with a girl named Michelle Phillips, one of the Mamas and Papas, whose ex-husband, John Phillips, was the leader of the group. Michelle told me she and John had dinner one night, to discuss maybe getting back together, and afterwards he had taken her up to visit the Polanskis in my old house. Michelle said that when they arrived there, everyone in the house was busy filming an orgy and that Sharon Tate was part of it. That was just one of the stories I had heard about what went on in my former house. (Day & Hotchner 2006)

Detectives who investigated the scene of the Tate murders told author Tom O'Neill that they had uncovered a video of Sharon Tate having sex with two men against her will. At a party some time before the killings, guests were said to have sodomized a drug dealer who had burned them with a bad sale (O'Neill 2020). Manson even claimed in an interview with the tabloid *Hollywood Star*, "Don't you think those people deserved to die? … They were involved in kiddie porn" (Terry 1989). This was before Polanski was accused of raping a minor in 1977, providing new context for that case.

According to *The Shadow Over Santa Susana* by Adam Gorightly, Manson also told a Hollywood tabloid, "Dennis Wilson gave me a $5,000 videotape, TV thing for tapes that fit only to an elite bunch (porno ring) that was worldwide" (2009).

PROCESS

Four

UK 5

USA 2

SEX

LUCIFER   JEHOVAH

SATAN
& THE GREY FORCES

Three Paths and
a Quagmire

Chapter Sixteen

The Process Meets Son of Sam

J ust as I had to justify my interest in Manson as being part of some abstract research, I had to tell my wife that I was only reading about the Son of Sam as it related to the Process Church and Manson. I just wanted to know if the Process was really evil or just some new age subculture. I left talk of Satanism out of the conversation, once again, so as not to bog her down in the details or raise suspicions that I was going full Q. However, it was hard not to let the crazy out when I was drunk and around strangers.

"Oh you're from New York?" I asked Darlene, the 70-year-old mother of one of our friends. "Were you in the city during the Son of Sam killings?"

It was the first time I'd met her, but I had had a cocktail or two. It was the third birthday of Prez, our oldest son, after all. "Do you remember them at all? Like, was the city in a panic?"

"You know, I don't remember that well. But, yeah, we were all terrified. Me and my girlfriends – we wouldn't go out late and we'd always make sure we weren't alone. Wear our hair up, you know, because we heard he killed girls with long hair."

"Oh, wow. Did you know they might have been linked to a satanic cult?"

"Huh? They?"

"Oh yeah. Berkowitz didn't act alo – "

"Hey, honey," Cindy called to me. "Can you grab Prez? I think he's about to eat some rocks."

As I continued along the tenuous thread connecting Manson and the Process Church of the Final Judgement, I found myself in the Bronx, Queens, and Brooklynof 1976, where the Son of Sam murders took six lives and wounded 10 others. One of his most famous contributions to serial killer culture was coded letter writing. Son of Sam sent a letter to Jim Breslin at the *New York Daily News* that read:

> "Hello from the gutters of N.Y.C., which are filled with dog manure, vomit, stale wine, urine, and blood. Hello from the sewers of N.Y.C.

which swallow up the delicacies when they are washed away by the sweeper trucks. Hello from the cracks in the sidewalks of N.Y.C. and from the ants that dwell in these cracks and feed on the dried blood of the dead that has seeped into these cracks.

"J.B., I'm just dropping you a line to let you know that I appreciate your interest in those recent and horrendous .44 killings. I also want to tell you that I read your column daily and I find it quite informative.

"Tell me Jim, what will you have for July twenty-ninth? You can forget about me if you like because I don't care for publicity. However you must not foget Donna Lauria and you cannot let the people forget her either. She was a very, very sweet girl but Sam's a thirsty lad and he won't let me stop killing until he gets his fill of blood.

"Mr. Breslin, sir, don't think that because you haven't heard from me for a while that I went to sleep. No, rather, I am still here. Like a spirit roaming the night. Thirsty, hungry, seldom stopping to rest; anxious to please Sam. I love my work. Now, the void has been filled.

"Perhaps we shall meet face to face someday or perhaps I will blown away by cops with smoking .38's. Whatever, if I shall be fortunate enough to meet you,I will tell you all about Sam if you like and I will introduce you to him. His name is 'Sam the Terrible'.

"Not knowing what the future holds I shall say farewell and I will see you at the next job. Or should I say you will see my handiwork at the next job? Remember Ms. Lauria. Thank you. In their blood and from the gutter 'Sam's Creation'.44

"Here are some names to help you along. Forward them to the inspector for use by N.C.I.C: 'The Duke of Death' 'The Wicked King Wicker' 'The Twenty Two Disciples of Hell' 'John "Wheaties"-Rapist and Suffocator of Young Girls'

"PS: J.B. Please inform all the detectives working on the slaying to remain.

"P.S: J.B., please inform all the detectives working the case that I wish them the best of luck. 'Keep 'em digging, drive on, think positive, get off your butts, knock on coffins, etc.'

"Upon my capture I promise to buy all the guys working on the case a new pair of shoes if I can get up the money."

("Written on envelope) Blood and Family Darkness and Death Absolute Depravity .44" (Terry 1989, Ch. 3)

The story of how those killings, said to be performed by a sole perpetrator with a .44 caliber Bulldog revolver, could be linked to the butchering of a movie star seven years earlier was a muddy one. The key artifact making this connection was a book called *The Ultimate Evil* first published by U.S. author and investigative reporter Maury Terry in 1987. Terry was actively engaged with police in the immediate wake of the Son of Sam killings, producing stories for the *New York Post* and other media. Through his work, he was able to get the case reopened by Queens District Attorney John Santucci.

Santucci was not responsible for the larger case by the state against Berkowitz, due to the fact that the killer's arrest occurred in the Bronx. However, half of the shootings occurred in Queens, and Santucci attempted to push forward the theory that Berkowitz had accomplices. Assistant District Attorney Herb Leifer reportedly told Terry, "We're confident David didn't act alone, but we need an insider – either Berkowitz or someone else – so we can put this entire package in front of a grand jury (Ibid., Introduction)."

Maury Terry and some of his associates at the *New York Post* and other outlets were able to communicate with Berkowitz at various times from his arrest in 1978 into the 90s. *Post* writer Steve Dunleavy received a letter from the killer about a month after his arrest, with handwriting that didn't match the Breslin message, lending credence to the possibility of multiple perpetrators. It read in part, "When I killed, I really saved many lives. You will understand later. People want my blood but they don't want to listen to what I have to say.… There are other Sons out there – God help the world." This resulted in the headline in the paper: "BERKOWITZ WARNS OF MORE 'SONS.' LETTER TO POST SUGGESTS ACCOMPLICE" (Ibid., Ch. 8).

Berkowitz himself ultimately came forward saying that he did not work alone. The earliest account of this was from an interview with Berkowitz in 1978, a detailed account of which was published by Terry in *The Ultimate Evil*.

Terry got his first chance to meet Berkowitz in person while the admitted killer was being held at Central New York Psychiatric Center in Utica just two months after his arrest. Terry went to the facility along with Felix Gilroy, the lawyer of Jim Mitteager, a *Post*-related journalist who'd secretly gotten photos of Berkowitz in the hospital. Gilroy had planned to speak to the Son of Sam in preparing for a trial against Mitteager related to possibly bribing hospital staff. As a friend of Mitteager, Terry provided Gilroy with some questions about possible accomplices.

By examining the letters sent by the Son of Sam to the *New York Daily News* and Berkowitz's background, Terry and other investigators traced potential perpetrators to Berkowitz's neighbors, the Carr family. Terry had decoded the Son of Sam messages to implicate a pair of brothers in particular, John "Wheaties" and Michael Carr, the sons of one Sam Carr. By the time of their meeting with Berkowitz, John Carr had died of a suspected suicide in Minot, North Dakota, where he previously served at a nearby Air Force base, though he was known to travel between there and New York. Terry described the questioning of Berkowitz about the Carrs this way:

> Gilroy asked, 'Do you know a person named John Carr?
>
> Yes.
>
> How did you know John Carr?
>
> I don't want to talk about it.
>
> This was a major confirmation of my suspicions, and I swallowed hard at the disclosure. Gilroy began pressing, and Berkowitz began sidestepping. Finally, Felix asked: "Are you intentionally not answering my questions?"
>
> Yes.
>
> When did you meet John Carr for the first time?
>
> I don't remember.
>
> When did you meet Michael Carr for the first time?
>
> I don't remember.
>
> You remember now that you have met them?
>
> Yes.
>
> You just don't remember when; is that correct?
>
> Yes.
>
> What is your present attitude? Do you think you will ever get out of jail?
>
> No.
>
> Do you think if you gave me the answers to these questions that other people might end up in jail?
>
> There is a good possibility, and I wouldn't want that to happen.
>
> You are protecting somebody, then; is that what you are telling me?
>
> I don't know, but I don't want to see anyone else in jail. (Ibid., Ch. 12)

At a later point, Gilroy followed up to get a specific number of people involved in the murders.

> Q. How many people are you protecting by not disclosing everything?
>
> A. I don't know.
>
> Q. Would it be fair to say it is at least eight or ten people?
>
> A. Well, I don't know.
>
> Q. Can you give me an approximate number?
>
> A. *I think it is in the hundreds.*
>
> Q. *Did you meet all these people or did they just operate among themselves?*
>
> A. *I'd rather not say* (Ibid., Ch. 12)."

Still further on, Berkowitz admitted that other accomplices could still have been on the loose.

> "Q. Is there any chance these other people may be hurting people like you did?
>
> "A. There is a possibility (Ibid., Ch. 12)."

Gilroy then told Berkowitz that his refusal to answer left him with a feeling that he was part of a larger group. "I will give you an example," Gilroy said. "For instance, the question about whether or not somebody called the Elephas disco and detoured the cops away that night – whether you did that or somebody else did that. If you could answer that question for me, we would know. That would be one example. Can you answer that question?"

"It wasn't me," Berkowitz replied.

John Carr's drug counselor Lee Slaghter confirmed the relationship between Berkowitz and Carr, implicating Carr in the murders as well:

> John told me he looked up to Berkowitz because Berkowitz wasn't afraid to do anti-establishment things. He told me they used to bum around together in Yonkers. But something happened between them. There was bad blood between them after a while.

He also said that John Carr "had a tremendous amount of detailed knowledge of the [.44] shootings, like the kinds of cars the victims were in and things like that. He said he knew more about the Son of Sam case than the police did. He also alluded to being at crime scenes, but his inference was subtle. He didn't actually say he was." Slaghter then said: "I told all this to a New York detective who called me and asked me about John shortly after his death. I don't remember [the detective's] name." (Ibid., Ch. 14)

As hard as they might have been for me to believe, these details were corroborated in a variety of ways by Berkowitz, witnesses at the various crime scenes, investigators, prison informants, and Maury Terry. Multiple vehicles were also seen at the murders, sometimes interacting with the killer. NYPD officer Richard Johnson, said that he and the other officers originally investigating the case found unresolved discrepancies in statements from witnesses and surviving victims. Among the issues with the sole perpetrator story was the fact that witnesses saw people of differing heights, sizes and other features at the crime scenes, resulting in a variety of eye-witness sketches. Johnson said, "Why are there three [suspect] cars, five different [suspect] descriptions, different heights, different shapes, different sizes of the perpetrator? Somebody else was there." (Kurtis 29:35)

The group that executed the murders wasn't just made up of ordinary psychopaths. In the 1978 interview with Gilroy, Berkowitz admitted that he and his accomplices were in a "witches' coven."

> Q. Do the words "witches' coven" mean anything to you?
>
> A. I have heard it before.
>
> Q. Were some of these people [suspected conspirators] involved in the witches' coven?
>
> A. I believe they were. Yes.
>
> Q. Were you in that same coven?
>
> A. Yes.
>
> Q. Did you meet regularly?
>
> A. Well, I can't really say. I don't want to say…
>
> Berkowitz then said some people had dual natures and were part "spirit," making it difficult to bring them to justice…

The witches' coven, seemed to hold a special place for the Prince of Darkness, as Berkowitz admitted the Carrs worshiped satan:

> Q. Can you distinguish between a person who is – as you would say Michael Carr is – not a nice fellow and an ordinary person?
>
> A. I'd say anybody who worships the devil is not a nice person.

THE PROCESS MEETS SON OF SAM

Q. Are you telling me that Michael Carr worshipped the devil?

A. I believe he did. I believe [John] Carr did (Terry 1989, Ch. 12).

John Carr's affinity for Satanism was confirmed by associates in Minot, North Dakota, where he was previously stationed at the local Air Force base. This included Phil Falcon, who ran a coffee shop that catered to occult customers and hosted rituals that included the murder of German Shepherds. Falcon told Terry and local sheriffs that Carr was "very much" into satanism, adding that "John read my entire collection of occult books, [from] how to make amulets to the 'third eye.' "

He recalled one time when John Carr and an associate named Donny Boone tried to conduct a ritual at his residence.

"I came to my house and here were Donny and John," Falcon said. "When I walked in the door, they were in the kitchen, and Donny had this animal, whatever it was. He had cut its throat and it was bleeding all over the kitchen. He was going to take it into the other room there. There was a [magic] circle drawn and they were sacrificing it. Old Donny Boone was drinking the animal's blood. It was running down his chin." He threw the guys out, saying, "It was an unbelievable mess to clean up" (Ibid., Ch. 14).

Berkowitz also acknowledged to Gilroy that there was significance behind the occult symbol included on the Son of Sam letters, which Terry traced to nineteenth-century occultist Eliphas Levi. Terry further believed the name of the occultist was part of the reason one of the .44 caliber shootings took place outside the Elephas discotheque in Queens (Ibid., Ch. 12).

Aside from the letter sent to the *Daily News*, Berkowitz sent a letter to the patriarch of the Carr family, Sam Carr, to complain about his dog's barking. He additionally mailed a get-well card to his former landlord, Jack Cassara, using Sam Carr's home as his return address. Berkowitz also sent a threatening letter with Cassara house as his return address to volunteer sheriff's deputy Craig Glassman. Berkowitz admitted to Gilroy that this strategy was meant to get him caught, telling the lawyer, "Well, I wanted the police to come and find me."

Terry believed that Berkowitz was trying to avoid becoming the scapegoat for the cult. "As detailed earlier, he hoped he would be arrested for these relatively minor crimes and off the streets in the event the cult decided, as was discussed, to offer the police a scapegoat for the Son of Sam shootings. Berkowitz didn't want it to be him," Terry wrote. Berkowitz further stated that he hoped he would be turned in sooner:

Q. You knew that Sam Carr had gone to Queens, to the task force, to turn you in; didn't you?

A. Yes.

Q. Did you think that the fact Sam Carr went to turn you in would cause the police to come and catch you sooner than they did?

A. Yes. [This was another major admission. Berkowitz was saying that before his arrest he knew that Sam Carr had turned him in as a Son of Sam suspect.]"

In a moment outside of the interview cell, Gilroy told Terry he didn't think Berkowitz was lying.

"No, he knows too much and he didn't want to give it up. It slipped out of him," Felix said. "If he just wanted to lie he'd weave some tale about barking dogs and demons, like he did when he got picked up. Or else he'd laugh at us and say we were full of crap and goodbye. Besides," Felix added, "all this information was dug up first – he's not said anything we can't back up. Hell, the only reason we're even asking him these things is because the evidence was uncovered first." (Ibid., Ch. 12)

In his exchanges with Terry and Gilroy, Berkowitz hinted that he was worried about the safety of undisclosed people. In 1993, 17 years after his arrest, he clarified that he copped to being the sole murderer because other members of the cult said they would kill his father and half-sister if he didn't (Terry 1993).

In the 1980s until his conversion to Christianity in the 1990s, Berkowitz cut off contact with outside investigators, but a pair of prison informants named Vinny and Danny supposedly continued to provide information from the .44 Magnum Killer about the operations of his cult. Vinny said that the letter mailed to the *Daily News* was written by a group, not by Berkowitz alone. He described a core group of 22 members with an expansive fringe and an inner circle of 12, called the "Children" that planned the murders.

Vinny reportedly told Terry:

Drugs are involved. I feel the real key to exposing the Group is through drug and porn connections. Illegal weapons are also, but not as good 'cause that's sporadic. And they already have arsenals. But they need steady supplies of drugs for their own "parties" and to make money. And remember, those who head this may not believe this crap about Satan. They believe in how people can be led and used. Used in a very effective way. Sickeningly effective... And when you touch drugs and porn and call girl type operations and daughters of middle-class people at school, things get hot. 'cause politicians may be involved. Or influential persons... Look – whoever heads this isn't from the City. At least, he lives outside. I think Jersey or Long Island. At least, he has some sort of big place. A regular Hugh Hefner place for parties, kinky sex... This group has strong holds in a lot of ways. Besides "dedication" is "intimidation" or "guilt" – but fear is strongest.... Blackmail exists, also. Or people won't talk because they're co-conspirators. Now listen, you know that coven book where they write their crimes? ... But that book is "insurance." The members figure it's occult but that book is insurance against rats... I have things which lead me to suspect they may have filmed (or videotaped) many of these crimes. I have more than a suspicion. They have certain killings on film... They not only ransacked Berkowitz' place to make him look 'mad,' but he was supposed to 'get caught' in a final act. (Terry 1989 Ch. 20)

In one letter, Vinny provided clues to several people that were going to be murdered by the cult, hoping that the journalist would warn the Brooklyn DA and prevent the crimes:

> I went to see my fortune story behind the brownstone in Brooklyn Heights, 'cause I went to NYU [New York University] at that time. That night, I met my date in Washington Square Park. Tom, and Ronald, and David were there, too. We had some coke [cocaine] and a hamburger. We then saw a movie: *Frankenstein Meets Mickey Mouse* and *Rodan the Flying Monster*. Narcoee and Ebee and Sissy Spacek and Rudi Kazooti were there. Roy Rogers and Dale Evans are my favorite stars. Next to James Camaro who is white but dresses like an Indian. We were a regular jet set of the occult. Kennedy assassination taught that conspiracy theories are thought of as fairy tales. The insane act solo.... On October 31, look for a kinky or bizarre assassination. Male(s) and female(s). Their heads shot off.... And they'll remove the evidence like when they ransacked Berkowitz' place. Or leave misleading clues like in 1977. Just keep this in mind if you stumble on something. A Halloween shooting. That will convince me."

There ultimately was a murder of two people on Halloween, a photographer named Ronald Sisman and a young college student named Elizabeth Platzman. The two had gunshot wounds to the backs of their heads. Platzman had her hands tied behind her with cord. The apartment looked burglarized, with police theorizing it was based on a drug deal gone wrong, as Sisman had a large amount of cocaine. Terry believed that Sisman had been alluded to in the coded message:

> The dead man was, logically enough, a photographer. He was re-ferred to twice in the coded Vinny letter. First as 'Ronald.' Next as 'Sissy Spacek.' His name: Ronald Sisman, and Vinny had written down his name two weeks before the murder, which occurred on the night of October 30, or shortly after midnight on Halloween, in Sisman's Manhattan brownstone… (Ibid., Ch. 20)

After Sisman's death, Vinny claimed that the photographer owned the snuff films produced by the cult, including footage of one of the Son of Sam murders. The inmate apparently got the name of Sisman, who he re-ferred to as Sisseck, from another prisoner, as Berkowitz wouldn't give it up. The message from Vinny also apparently included corroborating information, such as the fact that Sisman's brownstone had a chandelier:

> Berkowitz had told me about Sisseck, and he told me an inside job was in the works for Halloween. But he didn't say that Sisseck was the planned victim. I don't think he knew it. He was getting info from out-side, but there was a lag sometimes. But he knew Sisseck before. He'd been to his brown-stone with Michael Carr. … He told me Sisseck was dealing, and that there was a party going on when they got there. He saw the chandelier. Berkowitz waited while Michael Carr got the stuff.

Vinny had also provided clues from Berkowitz as to who may have been near the top of the pyramid, using both "Roy Rogers" and "Rodan the Flying Monster" as nicknames for who that might have been. In 1982, a year after Vinny wrote the letter, Terry visited him in prison to see if he could be more specific.

> I can't remember if the key word is 'dale' or 'Evans' in that one. Whichever, him and Roy Rogers are the biggies.
>
> "Then what about Roy Rogers – Rodan? Who the hell is he?" Zuckerman asked.
>
> "His first name is Roy," Vinny replied.
>
> "And he lives in a big mansion in a town with two names on Long Island. Shit, I can't quite come up with the damn town, but it be-gins with an S.

"Sands Point?" Zuckerman tried. Vinny looked thoughtful.

"That may be it. But he's into all sorts of weird shit with whips and chains and kinky crap."

"What's his last name?" I asked quietly. The visiting room wasn't crowded, and Zuckerman and I were dressed as downbeat as possible to resemble nothing more than street friends of Vinny. Still, we didn't want to call any attention to ourselves by appearing to interrogate him. Serious questions were asked with relaxed smiles.

"Damn, it's something like Rodan, or Rudin, or Rodin," Vinny said, pressing his thumb and forefinger to his forehead. He was under a strain, and it occasionally showed.

"I'm sorry, but I'm a little nervous here. But this guy beat the shit out of some actress and took videotapes of it. At the mansion. Berkowitz was at his place once – and in Minot, too." (Ibid., Ch. 21)

It was while leaving this meeting that Terry realized who was near the top of the cult hierarchy. In 1980, a young actress named Melonie Haller was discovered unconscious and covered in blood on a commuter train from Long Island to Manhattan. She claimed to have been beaten and raped while being filmed at a party. One guest, businessman Robert McKeage, admitted in court to assaulting her and was given 30 days in prison. But the host of the party had remained untouched. His name was Roy Radin, a famous Broadway producer with a mansion on Long Island.

If Vinny was reporting the truth, as he heard it in coded form from Berkowitz, the producer was involved in satanic rituals, S&M, drug dealing and more. After going missing for several weeks in May 1983, the body of 33-year-old Roy Radin was found dead in the desert about 60 miles north of Los Angeles. With the help of former FBI Special Agent in Charge of Los Angeles Ted Gunderson, Terry traced the grisly murder to who he thought to be one of the satanic cult's members. This member, according to Berkowitz, went by the nickname "Manson II," a satanic assassin who had been a member of the Manson Family and was called in to perform hits on behalf of the larger cult. Berkowitz knew Manson II because the hitman had participated in at least one of the Son of Sam murders. One of the four people sentenced for the killing of the Broadway producer was a man named William Mentzer, a contract killer and former security guard for *Hustler* publisher Larry Flynt. This was Terry's Manson II (Ibid., Ch. 23).

Radin had been killed for financing issues related to a film he was working on with producer Robert Evans called *The Cotton Club*. Karen Greenberger, who had been speaking to Evans regularly at the time leading up to the murder, had had her producer role stripped by Radin, preventing any chance at profiting from the film. She was ultimately convicted of second-degree murder and kidnapping and, while multiple witnesses believed Evans was involved in the murder, Greenberger testified that he had no part in killing Radin.

If Radin really was linked to the Son of Sam, he could have been the last loose end for the cult to tie up, though the film financing motive appeared more likely. In addition to Sisman the photographer and John Carr, other suspicious deaths related to the cult included Michael Carr, who was killed in a car accident in New York soon after being questioned by police. Jerry Berg, a friend of John Carr's in Minot, died in a freak timber accident while with another possible cult member (Ibid., Ch. 17). There was also a Minot satanist named Donny Boone, but he was killed in a car crash in Arizona in 1976. The Carrs' brother-in-law, a police officer suspected of being involved in the cult, had his squad car shot up. A friend of Berkowtiz's named Howard Weiss was shot to death in his apartment, supposedly at the hands of an ex-lover (Ibid., Ch. 13). Berkowitz himself had his throat slashed in prison around the time he was writing outside investigators.

Additionally, witnesses and investigators close to the case were harassed and, in one case, possibly murdered. Sheriff's Lt. Terry Gardner in Minot had his car shot at. A pair of John Carr's friends, Darlene Christiansen and Tom Taylor, who had talked to police about Carr and his satanic activities, had their vehicle run off the road (Ibid., Ch. 17). Minot *Daily News* reporter Jack Graham had had a confrontation with the satanist suspected of killing Berg and died in an accident with an 18-wheeler on the road in Michigan two weeks later (Ibid. Ch. 19).

And all of this, Terry believed, was tied to a cult from England.

> According to Danny and Vinny, the cult originated in England. They didn't know the names 'Process,' 'Chingon' or 'OTO,' but the English-origin information was enough to put it over the top. Both the Process and Aleister Crowley's OTO were rooted in England. The group had a main headquarters near Los Angeles, and both confirmed that Manson II was from L.A… (Ibid., Ch. 20).

When I looked at the Process, it was difficult to see anything directly harmful or violent about its members, who seemed too tame to perform anything more than theatrics. Their ideology was one that was far too convoluted to attract many members and the cult was known for abstaining from both alcohol and sex.

However, there were elements that did overlap between the Process, Manson and the Son of Sam cult. In addition to worshipping Satan, all three had neo-Nazi features. Mary Ann DeGrimston considered herself the reincarnation of Hitler's Minister of Propaganda, Joseph Goebbels (Levenda 2011). They actively courted George Lincoln Rockwell, the founder of the American Nazi Party (Wylie & Parfey 2009). Manson linked up with Nazi groups in Southern California, which may have been where he conceived of his race war ideology. David Berkowitz "possessed and wore Nazi insignia (Ch. 13)," while John Carr was an avowed Nazi and befriended Fred Cowan, a Neo-Nazi and possible member of the cult who would go on to shoot up Neptune Moving Company while on a rampage to take out his Jewish employer (Ch. 7).

Then, of course, there were the dogs. While the Process maintained a pack of German Shepherds, caring for them better than they cared for their own members or the children of their members, Terry linked the supposed Son of Sam cult to a string of murdered canines in Untermyer Park near Berkowitz's apartment. During the Gilroy questioning, Berkowitz admitted as much:

> Q. When you were living there, were people killing dogs and putting them on the aqueduct?
>
> A. Yes.
>
> Q. Did you know who was killing the dogs then?
>
> A. I had an idea.
>
> Q. Would it mean anything to you if I told you they were still killing dogs in that area?
>
> A. I'm not surprised.
>
> Q. You have some idea [who was killing the dogs], is that it?
>
> A. Yes.
>
> Q. Would it be possible that the same people who are killing the dogs could also kill people?
>
> A. It is possible (Ibid., Ch. 17)."

Later on, Berkowitz even claimed that cult members would attempt to secure jobs at a local animal shelter in order to obtain German shepherds for sacrifice.

There were also links to Scientology across the Son of Sam saga, the Process and the Manson Family. Michael Carr, who Berkowitz claimed was in the satanic cult with him, was a high-ranking Scientologist in Clearwater, Florida (Ibid., Ch. 13).

According to information Maury Terry published after 1997, Berkowitz confirmed the details of a 1977 police report about a witness that supposedly saw him with a "Father Lars" at the Manhattan Headquarters of the Process. Terry described the response of Berkowitz:

> "It's true. I was there with him," Berkowitz said of the report, which was ignored by the NYPD. Berkowitz said he had a reason to visit the group's headquarters: "They had a big role in all of it." Specifically, he charged that the overall plan for a series of shootings was brainstormed during a surreal meeting at Moloch's White Plains-area home in the spring of 1976. Present at the meeting, Berkowitz said, were at least eight Process leaders and members, along with "some friends of theirs" and "at least two" lower-ranked members of the Westchester cult – including himself. "They tossed different ideas around," Berkowitz said. "One of them was to kidnap young girls and kill them in cemeteries. Another was to copy the Manson thing in rich neighborhoods. But the goal was to paralyze New York, and they eventually decided on the .44 shootings." "Did they ever say they were involved in the Manson killings?" I asked. "Yes, they did," he replied. (Ibid., Epilogue.)

Founding member of the Process Tim Wylie did corroborate that the group had "a large, single-story house with a lake on 26 acres of prime Westchester County real estate," but that didn't mean that that was information only members and associates like Berkowitz might have had. Given how well-known the Process was, that information may have been available to anyone who looked into it (Wylie & Parfey 2009).

The intrigue behind the Process deepened when I considered the role of its leaders, Mary Ann and Robert, who secluded themselves from the rest of the organization and only appeared occasionally to great awe on behalf of the rest of the Process. Mary Ann, known to be as controlling as she was captivating, did sometimes dictate orgies among select Processans. She also arranged marriages between disparate members and, in the chance that children were born into the cult, saw to it that they were raised in a collective, albeit neglectful fashion.

While living with the New York City Chapter, Process member Kathe McCaffrey, who went by "Sister Beth," oversaw eight children ages five and under from nine in the morning to midnight. She left the chapter when she gave birth to her own son and, upon her return, learned that some older kids were moved to a "farm" outside of the city, presumably the location in Westchester. Those younger than four were "being housed in a windowless basement room measuring about 10'x10'. They weren't receiving regular medical care, their shoes were too small and cramping their feet, and they were bathed in a dank boiler room in which a kind of shower hose was rigged up (McCaffrey in Wylie & Parfey 2009)."

She also noted, "When I first got to the city, I was asked to go to the kitchen to help prepare a meal. I heard little kids' voices from a room off the kitchen. The room turned out to be a pantry. When I opened the door I found two approximately 18-month-old babies in nothing but dirty diapers, in a 3'x8' room with a couple of windows placed near the ceiling of the room. This was where they spent their whole days." (Wylie & Parfey 2009)

This neglect led to injuries and possible sexual abuse, according to Sister Beth: "In Chicago the children were cared for during the day by a woman with a heroin problem and an ex-con who used to wash paper diapers for reuse. There were unconfirmed allegations of sexual abuse of the children. They were left alone at night in their first-floor apartment. One child, Daniel (aged eight or nine), leapt from the roof and fell on his back and was refused medical care."

Sister Beth noted she was shunned by the cult "for insisting on medical care for my son (he ended up in hospital) and then again for coming to his aid after a traumatic event." They also minimized the amount of medical care expecting mothers could receive. She "was allowed to receive prenatal care only one month prior to giving birth. I was not permitted to go to the hospital once I'd entered labor until the higher-ups said I could, and I was in labor for 36 hours. At the time I was living in a room with one other woman (I had the bottom bunk bed, she the top), and about seven children."

Sister Beth relayed stories of children being removed from their parents, as well: "One Processean confided in me that her child was taken in the middle of the night, that she had no idea where the child was living, and that she was not to speak of it." She recounted another similar instance: "Mother Diana had her second child (Lucius was the father) taken away from her immediately after she gave birth. I don't know if she knew where the child was."

Both Ed Sanders and Maury Terry claimed that there was an offshoot of the Process called the Four P or Four Pi movement, whose leader was the Grand Chingon, a sobriquet that Manson had for himself as well. That the Four P existed and was a descendent of the Process I could not verify. The only evidence that it did exist aside from Sanders and Terry's accounts was a strange news story from 1970, in which a hitchhiker carrying Anton LaVey's *The Satanic Bible* and a human finger in his pocket was arrested after a hit-and-run near Big Sur. The man was Stanley Dean Baker and he quickly confessed to the crime, telling police, "I have a problem. I'm a cannibal (Blanco n.d.)."

Baker was not alone. His accomplice, Harry Allen Stroup, also maintained a severed finger in his possession. The cops then uncovered the mutilated body of victim James Schlosser in the Yellowstone River with his heart and fingers missing.

Baker claimed he was a part of a Satanic cult called Four Pi that had recruited him from his home state of Wyoming. He said the cult, led by the Grand Chingon, had committed other human sacrifices in the Santa Ana Mountains south of Los Angeles (Terry 1989, Ch. 9).

In an interview with private investigator and alt-media personality Ed Opperman, former NYPD detective James Rothstein said that he believed there was a connection between the Process and Son of Sam, but was not clear on how direct that link was. Rothstein was one of the earliest police investigators of the Son of Sam cult, uncovering evidence of child and animal sacrifices in the boroughs of New York in 1965, long before the first Son of Sam murders. He appeared to attribute any ties between the Process and Son of Sam to be related to an overlap in occult subcultural groups and not necessarily through a formal organization, calling them "birds of a feather." Rothstein further suggested that the Smiley Face murders that moved from the eastern region of the U.S. and westward were linked similarly to the Son of Sam murders he was investigating. He believed that Jeffrey Dahmer was even tied to the same milieu, again refraining from suggesting a formal organizational connection (Opperman 2013).

The whole web was very difficult to navigate. While reading *The Ultimate Evil*, I was a near-believer in Terry's theory that there was a nationwide satanic cult running drugs, pornography, people and weapons. I told the Lone Gundam about the possibility and they thought it was an interesting theory but argued that there wasn't quite enough evidence there to establish a link between the three semi-satanic groups. @Gumby4Christ, in particular, was skeptical of the whole thing. He pointed out that Terry's conception of the Process seemed pretty uninformed. He threw out the idea that the Process was a red herring, possibly to distract from the real murderers.

Was there such a thing as a patsy cult? Could the Manson Family have deliberately associated itself with the Process in order to throw people off of the trail of some other satanic group? Thanks to Ed Sanders and Maury Terry, as well as the Manson Family, the Process came to be associated with the Manson and Son of Sam murders for years after.

There appeared to be plenty to suggest that Berkowitz didn't act alone and that his possible compatriots were involved in cult worship. The story felt less believable when Terry began to get his information from inmates other than Berkowitz, who described a large satanic cult involved in drugs, weapons, snuff films and pornography with Broadway producer Roy Radin involved in leading the whole thing. I couldn't rule all of this out, including the possible participation of the Process, but the case didn't seem strong enough to be convincing.

Interestingly, when Robert de Grimston was forced out of the church, the Process gave up a public attachment to satanism, becoming an evangelical Christian group called the Foundation Church of the Millennium under Mary Ann DeGrimston in 1975. This would have been a year before the planned Son of Sam murders, suggesting that one or the other leaders of the Process was not a party to the planning. Then, after disappearing for many years, the Process re-emerged once again in 1993 as the Best Friends Animal Society, one of the largest animal-focused non-profits in the world. This led to theories that the cult had merely mutated and continued to conduct sacrificial rituals under the guise of animal care, despite the cult's long-standing stance against animal cruelty (Wylie & Parfey 2009).

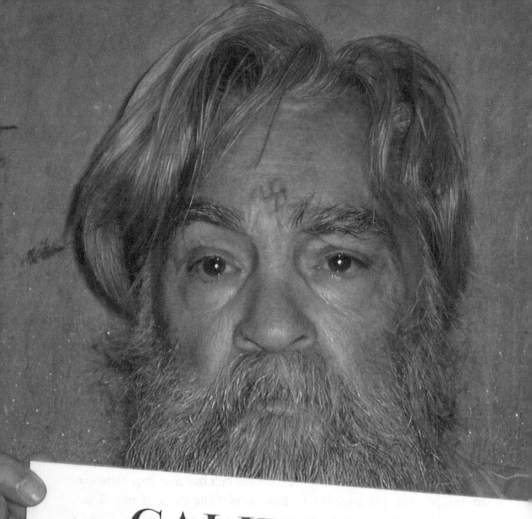

CALIFORNIA
STATE PRISON
MANSON, C
B-33920
06/16/2011

CHAPTER SEVENTEEN

SECRET AGENT CHARLES MANSON

As I sunk lower into some imagined, unfathomable sphere of parapolitical horror, I realized that there was not enough information to concretely link Manson to the Process cult. However, a couple of Gundam had been talking about an intensive book on the Manson murders titled *Chaos: Charles Manson, the CIA, and the Secret History of the Sixties*, by Tom O'Neill. From their conversations, I gleaned that what Manson *did* have were some interesting connections to U.S. law enforcement and intelligence agencies. This included the special treatment Manson was afforded by the police.

When Manson was released from Terminal Island prison in Los Angeles County on March 21, 1967, he almost immediately violated his parole by heading to Berkeley, California. Rather than having his parole revoked, as might typically have occurred and had even happened to Manson years earlier for failing to report to his supervisor, he was allowed to live in the new city, under the watch of Roger Smith, a probation officer and student at UC Berkeley's School of Criminology.

Smith and Manson had an almost familial relationship, with Manson referring to his PO as "Jubal Harshaw," a key character from the convict's favorite book, *Stranger in a Strange Land*. As a part of the National Institute of Mental Health-funded San Francisco Project, Manson became Smith's only client, a stark contrast to the other probation officers in the program who maintained caseloads of between 20 and 100 individuals. The experimental initiative sought to understand how federal supervision impacted recidivism, with six total POs receiving "normal" workloads of 100 cases, "ideal" numbering 40 clients, and "intensive" loads of 20 cases. While Smith began in the middle group, he eventually had only Manson as a client by the end of 1967.

Smith would later go on to serve as the godfather for Manson's cult-born child, Valentine Michael aka "Pooh Bear," and provide Manson with surprising latitude, allowing him to move to Los Angeles and even take a trip to Mexico, which would seem to be far outside of his parole vicinity.

O'Neill interviewed Roger Smith's assistant at the time he oversaw Manson, Gail Sadalla. Apparently, Smith told Sadalla in 1968 that he had already been the convict's probation officer in the early sixties at the Joliet Federal Prison in Illinois. However, O'Neill noted that Manson had never been in the Illinois parole system, only held in jail there for a few days in 1956. When O'Neill told Sadalla that Smith had no recollection of meeting Manson before March 1967, she replied, "He didn't remember that? I'm surprised… It was always my understanding. That's why there was this connection" (O'Neill 2020, p. 285-288).

Despite his close relationship with Manson and the freedom he granted him, Smith wrote in an essay for *Life* magazine, "Charlie was the most hostile parolee I've ever come across. He told me right off there was no way he could keep the terms of his parole. He was headed back to the joint and there was no way out of it" (Ibid., p. 301).

Manson's ability to skirt the law was not limited to his treatment by Roger Smith. It seemed that the Los Angeles Police Department (LAPD), Sheriff's Office (LASO), and District Attorney's office all opted not to pursue the convict's many illegalities before the 1969 killing spree. Between his March 1967 release and his 1969 capture for the Tate-La Bianca murders, Manson was at various times arrested for driving under the influence, possession of marijuana, and corrupting a minor, among other crimes. But the charges never appeared to stick.

The Family's residence at the Spahn Ranch outside of LA was under constant heavy surveillance by LASO and LAPD during the summer of 1969. This was no ordinary stakeout from a hidden unmarked cop car. LAPD relied on aircraft to surveil the ranch and LASO had an informant within the camp. A 16-page warrant drawn up by LASO described Manson as the "leader" of the criminal operation there, noting that he was "on Federal Parole for Grand Theft Auto." This meant that the department was aware of his parole status, but didn't put him behind bars.

The LAPD was also regularly taunted by the reckless parolee. According to the warrant, around July 29, 1969, the LAPD's Ted Leigh discovered loaded ammunition clips for a carbine that "fell from a dune buggy while on the highway." The LAPD was then contacted by Manson, who claimed the ammunition as his own and said he would pick it up (Ibid. 161-166).

About two months before the murders, on June 4, 1969, Manson was arrested and charged with operating a vehicle without a license, driving under the influence, and using illicit substances. After apparently telling the booking officers that he was on federal parole, he was still released with no charges. This wasn't without effort on the part of some law enforcement officials. The chief of the San Francisco probation office, Albert Wahl, communicated to the head of probation in Los Angeles, Angus McEachen, in an attempt to get Manson back to San Francisco to face consequences. Wahl acknowledged that not only was his file on Manson "incomplete," but Manson had been moving "freely between San Francisco and Los Angeles" for quite some time and Wahl was unaware if the con had permission to do so. He also pointed out that Manson had been arrested two other times in McEachen's jurisdiction. Wahl then sent a letter to the head of the national office in Washington. When McEachen went to nab Manson in the Los Angeles County jail while awaiting arraignment for the drug charge, he found that Manson had been released the previous day and the DA decided not to file charges (Ibid., p. 297-300).

The LASO ultimately launched one of the biggest raids in state history on Spahn Ranch, uncovering multiple stolen vehicles, underage girls, drugs, and weapons. When Manson was arrested, a collection of stolen credit cards fell out of his possession. All of this would have been enough to at least send Manson back to prison for parole violation, let alone possibly convict him of new charges. Nevertheless, the DA chose not to prosecute and Manson was released.

A week later, LASO picked him up once again for different charges and let him go. Then, on August 24, he was arrested for possession of marijuana and contributing to the delinquency of a minor when he was caught with some joints after having sex with 17-year-old girl in an abandoned cabin (ibid., p. 164-166). According to a LASO detective from the time, Preston Guillory, there was a mandate from his superiors: "Make no arrests, take no police action toward Manson or his followers" (ibid., p. 154).

Family member Susan Atkins, later convicted for the Tate-LiBianca murders, was afforded a similar level of latitude. After Manson's June 4, 1969 arrest for driving while high, Atkins was the only passenger taken into custody that day who wasn't released immediately. When Atkins was held for two weeks, her probation officer suggested, "The best thing is to revoke the defendant's probation as it appears she has no intentions of abiding by it." Instead, Judge Wayne Burke of Mendocino County Superior Court actually terminated her probation two years early, saying that "the defendant has not violated probation. She has complied with the terms. Probation is reinstated and modified to terminate forewith. She is released" (Ibid. 153-154).

The most egregious error of all may have been when LA Deputy Sheriff William Gleason spoke with Manson follower Kitty Lutesinger less than a day after the Cielo Drive murders. The cult member told Gleason, before the killings had made the news, she had been "programmed [by Manson] to believe" that the Black Panthers killed Tate and the rest, meaning that she was aware of the murders before it had been publicized. This should have raised serious scrutiny from the LASO deputy, but rather than bring her in for further questioning, Gleason quietly left on his merry way (ibid., p. 169).

In trying to understand how an obviously criminal parolee could be kept free long enough to establish a cult and orchestrate high profile murders, O'Neill came across numerous people close to the case that suggested Manson was an informant of some kind. Lewis Watnick, the former head deputy DA of Van Nuys, who did not work on the Manson case but worked in that office at the time, made the suggestion that, given the pattern of catch and release, "It dovetails right in. Manson was an informant."

Apparently, a LASO officer suggested something similar to O'Neill, wondering if Manson "had his finger in a bigger pie." Robert Schirn, the DA who both approved the LASO raid of the Spahn Ranch and dismissed the charges, said, "Another possibility, sheer speculation, is that [Manson] may have been an informant for somebody" (ibid. 173-174).

Though O'Neill didn't consider it, as I read about Manson's special treatment, I couldn't help but think of the compromise operation run by Epstein. Manson was known to travel with young girls, often minors, that would give themselves over physically at Manson's command. Two celebrities that accepted their offers were record producer and son of Doris Day, Terry Melcher, and Beach Boy Dennis Wilson. The Family stayed with Wilson for an entire summer, until they became too much for him to handle. O'Neill wrote:

> The Family spent their days smoking dope and listening to Charlie strum the guitar. The girls made the meals, did the laundry, and slept with the men on command. Manson prescribed sex seven times a day: before and after all three meals and once in the middle of the night. 'It was as if we were kings, just because we were men,' [Family member Tex] Watson later wrote. Soon Wilson was bragging so much that he landed a headline in Record Mirror: 'I Live with 17 Girls.'"

With their friend Gregg Jackson, Wilson and Melcher called themselves the "Golden Penetrators," a trio dedicated to laying with as many women as possible. This relationship, O'Neill implied, likely resulted in Melcher becoming involved with the girls, as well:

> Sometime in that summer of '68, at one of Wilson's marathon parties, he crossed paths with Manson for the first time. After another such party, Melcher rode back to Cielo Drive with Wilson, and Manson came along in the back seat. As Melcher later testified, Manson got a good look at the house from the driveway. (ibid., p. 89-91)

Could it have been that Manson had compromising material on powerful people throughout California?

Other details from the story suggested that something even more complex may have been at work. These included the work that Roger Smith was engaged in before, during and after his position as Manson's parole officer. While a doctoral student at the Berkeley School of Criminology, Smith relied on a "participant-observer" approach to study the connection between violence and drug use in Oakland gang members. Immersing himself, along with other researchers, at "outposts" in Oakland, he observed the drug culture near churches and community centers, where he came to the conclusion that substance abuse often correlated with the onset of violent behavior. This background suggested that Smith's interest in Manson may have been partially scientific in nature.

When Manson was released from prison, Smith was the one to send Manson into the Haight to "soak up" the "vibes." After one LSD trip, Manson "seemed to accept the world," according to Smith. This was at the same time that Manson wound up in jail once more for interfering with a police officer's arrest of a new underage Family recruit. Manson was released after only a few days.

Smith was then chosen to lead research into the influence of amphetamines on violence in Haight-Ashbury, funded again by the National Institute of Mental Health (NIMH) who had paid for the San Francisco Project, in which Smith served as Manson's parole officer. The NIMH admitted in 1976 that it had acted as a funding front for the CIA in the sixties. Though Smith's work wasn't explicitly singled out by the NIMH, it at least raised the possibility that Smith was engaging in work for the intelligence agency.

Smith's Amphetamine Research Project (ARP), sought to examine three phenomena in the region. These included, the "individual" experience, "collective or group experience," and how "violence is generated within the speed marketplace." He deployed his typical participant-observer role, watching hippy groups and encouraging his research team to join them. Of the experience, Smith said, "[I] took off my gray-flannel suit and my wing-tip shoes and grew a moustache. Soon the kids on Haight Street were calling me the Friendly Fed and asking me to help them with the law."

The results of the ARP were never made public, despite the fact that two reports on the topic were scheduled to be published in the *Journal of Psychedelic Drugs*. While those papers never saw the light of day, a paper by Smith called "The Marketplace of Speed: Violence and Compulsive Methamphetamine Abuse" included information about participant-observation, such as the fact that the research had led a social scientist to be involved in illegal activities. Smith wrote that, in order to blend in with a "deviant group," it was necessary to lead them to believe "that they can trust him with information which, in other hands, would place them in jeopardy, and perhaps most important, he must resolve the moral dilemma of being part of something which he may find morally objectionable (at best), probably by association he could himself be arrested... in a very real sense, he becomes a co-conspirator... with information and insight which under normal conditions the average citizen would be obliged to share with law enforcement... he must try to understand what individuals within the group feel, how they view the 'straight' world, how they avoid arrest or detection..."

Smith operated the ARP out of the Haight-Ashbury Free Medical Clinic (HAFMC), where he also saw Manson and the Family frequently. It was difficult to determine where the lines between parole officer, researcher and friend were. Smith claimed to Tom O'Neill that the Family visited him there for no particular reason, saying that he didn't see Charlie at the clinic until after Smith ended his term as parole officer. However, the ARP apparently began as Smith was still overseeing Manson for the San Francisco Project. Former staff at the HAFMC told O'Neill that Manson attended many mandatory parole meetings with Smith there (ibid., p. 289-301).

The work of Roger Smith dovetailed with the work of another researcher with similar subjects of interest and a similar name. David Smith created the HAFMC the year before Roger joined, though David Smith never completed his PhD in pharmacology. In exchange for the ability to observe them, the clinic gave the hippies free treatment of sexually transmitted infections, unwanted pregnancies, and other issues associated with the summer of love. This included Manson and "Charlie's girls," as they were referred to at the clinic (ibid., p. 304-308).

According to Emmett Grogan, the founder of the Diggers, an anarchist collective that also helped hippies in the area, David Smith wasn't necessarily in the scene purely out of the kindness of his heart. In his autobiography, *Ringolevio*, Grogan wrote that Smith was "more concerned with the pharmacology of the situation than with treating the ailing people who came to him for help." He also said, "[T]he patients were treated as 'research subjects' and the facility was used to support whatever medical innovations were new and appropriate to the agency." (ibid., p. 321)

Among these "subjects" was the Family. David Smith described the cult in his book *Love Needs Care*, saying that Manson started to "reprogram" his followers through the application of mind games and acid. This would include pop psychology and mystical practices that ultimately caused them to perform "unconventional sexual practices." While they were under the influence of LSD, Manson would tell them, "You have to negate your ego." Smith said that Manson would objectify them to erase their self-control until they became "self-acknowledged 'computers,' empty vessels that would accept almost anything he poured in."

David Smith said that Charlie's girls "swarmed over [Roger] Smith and often filled the [clinic] reception room, bringing operations to a standstill." David suggested that "Charlie frequently offered [Roger] the services of his harem." Tom O'Neill claimed that Roger never accepted the offer (ibid., p. 308-311).

The Smiths weren't the only ones from HAFMC studying the Family. If Roger Smith was a participant-observer, Alan Rose was a member-participant. Rose helped establish Roger Smith's ARP and, according to David Smith, "was like my disciple and I was like his father." Rose was the head administrator of the clinic and acted as a research assistant to both Smiths. When the Family visited HAFMC, he fell in love with the girls and became a follower of Manson such that, when the cult split for Los Angeles in June 1968, taking some Family members with him, Rose asked the girls that weren't hand-chosen by Manson to live in his home. When they later joined Manson at Spahn Ranch, Rose went as well and stayed with the Family for four months.

About Rose's motivations, David Smith told Tom O'Neill, "Al became enraptured with their philosophy and he traveled with them." Smith said that Rose took LSD, "and then six of the girls just fucked his brains out and he saw God … He borrowed some money from me and he didn't pay it back and it turned out he gave it to Charlie. … So it was, like, very weird."

Rose and David Smith wrote a paper somewhat based on the experiences of Rose's life with the Family titled "The Group Marriage Commune: A Case Study" published in the HAFMC's *Journal of Psychedelic Drugs* about a year after the murders, in September 1970. It attempted to distance the clinic from the Family, never mentioning Manson's last name, claiming he lived in the Haight for just three months instead of an entire year. The paper didn't even mention the murders that would occur after the period of observation (ibid., p. 323-325).

Both Smiths studied amphetamines and LSD, giving them a keen insight into the dynamics of the Haight and the Family. According to a 1969 article published by the HAFMC, David Smith took two groups of eight albino mice, put them into confined settings to simulate crowding, and observed their behaviors after the mice received injections of amphetamines. Within 24 hours, the creatures went from calm and innocuous to breaking into "frenzied attacks of unrelenting rage," fighting one another and injuring themselves with frantic self-grooming. It was determined that the negative impacts of confinement had been exacerbated by the toxicity of the drugs by 400%. Another experiment saw mice dosed with mescaline, chlorpromazine, or reseperine before they were injected with amphetamine, sometimes causing the mice to divide themselves into disparate groups, with the murderous mice splitting off from the less violent ones. Or the drugs might calm the rodents and completely reduce their desire to attack each other, depending on the right combination of psychotropics.

David Smith apparently claimed to O'Neill that he accurately predicted a flood of amphetamine users into the Bay, which coincided with his 1967 opening of the clinic. In turn, there was a split between acid heads and speed freaks in the Haight, with the former choosing pacifism and the latter supposedly associated with violence. David Smith's research on mice mirrored what occurred in the area. The rodents on amphetamines, he said, "become inordinately aggressive and assaultive… [turning] upon one another with unexpected savagery. Their violent behavior is probably intensified by confinement for it is strikingly similar to that observed in amphetamine abusers who consume the drugs in crowded atmospheres."

Meanwhile, the "speed freaks" in the area around the clinic "lashed out with murderous rage at any real or imagined intrusion," committing rape, assault and torture in response to their paranoia. He wrote, "Cut off from the straight world, crammed together in inhuman conditions, and controlled by chemicals, they behaved, quite naturally, like rats in a cage."

206

O'Neill suggested that David Smith's NIMH-funded studies necessarily built upon the previous work of NIMH psychologist, John B. Calhoun, who noted in his research with rats that the animals became aggressive when in confinement, raping, killing, eating each other and murdering their young. Using a term that David Smith would go on to deploy frequently, Calhoun said that a dominant male rat would become a "behavioral sink," which he defined as "the outcome of any behavioral process that collects animals together in unusually great numbers… aggravating all forms of pathology that can be found within [the] group."

This male would dominate the other males and create a "harem" out of the females. Calhoun also described a group of "probers": males that were "hypersexualized" and sexually assaulted males and females, eating their young. He said probers would engage in "berserk," "frenzied" assaults on sleeping rodent families. The only authority the probers would cow to was the dominant male, running away when he emerged.

David Smith built upon Calhoun's work both in experiments with rats and his observations of people in the Haight. In papers Smith published for the clinic journal, he explored "whether a dramatic drug-induced experience" could generate "a lasting impact on the individual's personality." A separate report noted "frustrated anger" caused some individuals to test out acid, saying, "The soil from which the 'flower children' arise is filled more with anger and aggression, thorns and thistles, rather than passion and petunias." He said that "emotional pressure" applied during an acid trip could cause "images and sensations of anger or hate magnified into nightmarish proportions."

Smith also conceived of an idea he dubbed "the psychedelic syndrome," in which a collective of people with similar attitudes would succumb to a "chronic LSD state" that led to a shared "interpretation of psychedelic reality." As they took LSD more and more, this shared sense of the world would become more reinforced. Continual dropping of acid could lead to "the emergence of a dramatic orientation to mysticism." Those already suffering from "prepsychotic personalities," would experience "a long-term psychological disorder, usually a depressive reaction or a schizophrenic process."

Much of what David Smith researched could readily be applied to Manson. Whereas in the Haight, Manson supposedly convinced his followers to give up amphetamines in favor of LSD, with which Manson could indoctrinate them, it wasn't until the Family moved to LA to ultimately embark on a killing spree that it began to experiment with speed it got from the Hell's Angels. David Smith relayed to Tom O'Neill that he was told as much by Susan Atkins. "When they went to the south, they got very deeply involved in speed," Smith told O'Neill. "They were trading sex for speed, and [Atkins] thinks that Helter Skelter and the ultimate crime was a paranoid speed delusion."

Family member and convicted murderer Linda Kasabian suggested in a 2009 documentary that they took amphetamines on the night of the murder. Susan Atkins corroborated this in parole hearings and books. Tex Watson, also convicted of murder and a member of the Family, said that he snorted speed with the cult and used it each night of the Tate and La-Bianca killings (ibid., p. 309-321).

During the trial, lead prosecuting attorney Vincent Bugliosi declined to call any of these researchers affiliated with the clinic as eyewitnesses, despite how close they were to Manson and the extent to which they observed the Family. As suspect as Manson's relationship to the clinic staff was, there was one individual that appeared to elucidate the true nature of the Family's purpose. His name was Louis Jolyon "Jolly" West and he took an office at the HAFMC to find subjects for his own LSD research.

West was an expert on LSD, since he began researching the topic as a part of the larger subject of controlling human behavior. This included "deprogramming" U.S. prisoners of war returning from Korea. By 1967, he'd written a chapter called "Hallucinogens" for a psychiatry textbook, in which he described the spread of acid on college campuses, saying that it caused people to become "unusually susceptible and emotionally labile" due to a "loosening of ego structure." He warned that "LSD cults" were emerging that would attract young people "with a pathological desire to withdraw from reality" and wanted a "shared forbidden activity in a group setting to provide a sense of belonging." He also predicted in a 1965 paper titled "Dangers of Hypnosis" that hypnosis would be used by cult leaders to cause followers to violate their moral codes to perform violent acts and be unable to remember it.

In the Haight, he opened up a lab dressed to look like a "hippie crash pad" and called it the Haight-Ashbury Project (HAP). The HAP seemed to be directionless, allowing anyone to come use the locale for anything as long as research students were allowed to observe and take notes. One such assistant came to write about the project, "I feel like no one is being honest and straight and the whole thing is a gigantic put on... What is [West] trying to prove? He is interested in drugs, that is clear. What else? (Ibid., p. 341-350)"

O'Neill, who uncovered an immense amount of information with his book, perhaps revealed the most with his research on West. Not only did he learn that the HAP was funded by a CIA front, the Foundations Fund for Research in Psychiatry, Inc., but he learned that West was directly involved in the CIA's mind control program, MKULTRA.

Despite the fact that West denied being involved with the CIA for his entire life, O'Neill found correspondences between the scientist and the chief of the MKULTRA program, Sidney Gottlieb, in West's archive at UCLA discussing his research for the agency. O'Neill wrote:

> Addressing Gottlieb as "S.G.," he outlined the experiments he proposed to perform using a combination of psychotropic drugs and hypnosis. Enumerating short- and long-term goals, he offered a nine-point list, beginning with a plan to discover "the degree to which information can be extracted from presumably unwilling subjects (through hypnosis alone or in combination with certain drugs), possibly with subsequent amnesia for the interrogation and/or alteration of the subject's recollection of the information he formerly knew." Another item proposed honing "techniques for implanting false information into particular subjects … or for inducing in them specific mental disorders." West wanted to reverse someone's belief system without his knowledge, and make it stick. He hoped to create "couriers" who would carry "a long and complex message" embedded secretly in their minds, and to study "the induction of trance-states by drugs." All of these were the goals of MKULTRA, and they bore a striking resemblance to Manson's accomplishments with his followers more than a decade later. "Needless to say," West added, the experiments "must eventually be put to test in practical trials in the field."

A classified report for the CIA called "The Psychophysiological Studies of Hypnosis and Suggestibility" suggested that West had been able to go so far as to swap the "true memories" of individuals with "false ones" without their knowing. To do so, he had to use "new drugs" capable of "speeding the induction of the hypnotic state and in deepening the trance that can be produced in given subjects."

He elaborated:

> It has been found to be feasible to take the memory of a definite event in the life of an individual and, through hypnotic suggestion, bring about the subsequent conscious recall to the effect that this event never actually took place, but that a different (fictional) event actually did occur.

West conducted these experiments on patients suffering from mental health problems, lamenting that "[t]he necessity to obtain most of the subject material from a population of psychiatry patients made standardized observations very difficult." To achieve the standardization necessary, West envisioned "a special chamber [where] various hypnotic, pharmacologic, and sensory-environmental variables will be manipulated."

Though West believed that LSD alone was not enough to manipulate an individual's behavior, he did think that a combination of hypnosis along with extended periods of isolation and sleep deprivation was more effective. Hypnosis made it so that "a person can be told that it is now a year later and during the course of this year many changes have taken place ... so that it is now acceptable for him to discuss matters that he previously felt he should not discuss. ... An individual who insists he desires to do one thing will reveal that secretly he wishes just the opposite (ibid., p. 360-364)."

When O'Neill approached David Smith with what he'd uncovered about West, Smith said, "[T]he military experiments are added proof that my hypothesis is correct – that it can be done." O'Neill confirmed that Smith was referring to the ability to brainwash someone using acid, even though the CIA had always maintained that it was never able to actually execute mind control. The reason for this so-called failure in brainwashing on the part of the CIA was explained "in part because they were basically taking normal subjects, not susceptible girls in a reinforcing environment," according to Smith.

O'Neill asked Alan Scheflin, a forensic psychologist and law professor who'd written an extensive book on the MKULTRA program based on CIA documents, if it were possible that "the Manson murders were an MKULTRA experiment gone wrong?" Scheflin apparently replied, "No, an MKULTRA experiment gone right (ibid., 368-369)."

Manson's CIA links continued to follow him all the way up to the night of the murders in Cielo Drive. The first sight of the dead bodies came not from Polanski's maid, who would come to the house hours later and report them to the police, but from a man named Reeve Whitson, a friend of Polanski. Though it was never reported, Whitson was at the murder scene at least 90 minutes before the maid arrived when he called Tate's friend, photographer Shahrokh Hatami, to alert him to the news.

Whitson would go on to be a sort of "amateur" detective that helped prosecutor Vincent Bugliosi manage the case behind the scenes. This included putting pressure on Hatami as a witness on the stand, apparently threatening him with deportation to his native Iran if he didn't corroborate seeing Manson at the house on Cielo Drive in the past, before the murders took place.

In looking into Whitson's contacts, Tom O'Neill heard two assertions more than once. One was that the mystery man had said to multiple friends, including Hatami, "[I]f they had listened to [Whitson] that a lot of people may have not been killed (ibid., p. 186)."

The other claim was that Whitson was CIA. This was told to O'Neill by Neil Cummings, a lawyer that knew Whitson since 1984; his ex-wife, Ellen Josefson; and his daughter, Liza.

Cummings claimed that Whitson was in a specialty, highly-secretive branch of the agency and that he discussed how he'd been trained to kill, executing those skills in multiple instances. Cummings said Whitson "was closer to [the Manson case] than anybody."

Whitson's daughter reported to O'Neill, "He told me that he worked within the Central Intelligence Agency. And he was in a part of the agency that was absolutely nonexistent. He did not exist."

John Irvin, an MI5-affiliated British film director, said Whitson was able to obtain meetings at "the highest levels of the defense industry" … "within minutes" and that he was "on the fringes of very far-out research… not discussed openly because it verges on the occult" (ibid., p. 194-203). What I gathered from all of these details about the Manson murders at the very surface level was that there was definitely something going on beneath that surface and beyond Manson's race war philosophy. Given Manson's special relationship with the law, it appeared that, at the very least, he may have been an informant, maybe for the FBI. However, it appeared even more likely to me that he was a CIA asset, or even an experiment in mind control. The Gundam couldn't argue with the evidence and seemed to agree with the conclusion O'Neill alluded to and I was convinced by.

To what end? I could see at least one of the useful applications of a Manson experiment when I considered a criminology paper published by Roger Smith titled "Status Politics and the Image of the Addict." In it, Smith explored how the image of Chinese opium smokers was negatively impacted in early 20th century San Francisco. Law enforcement posed as addicts to infiltrate the opium smoking community with an aim to "characterize the addict as a dangerous individual likely to rob, rape, or plunder in his crazed state." In turn, the image was extrapolated to the general Chinese population, giving the police the ability to crack down on them with public support. Smith said, "The Orientals were viewed as a threat to the existing structure of life in this country." He further noted that, after the stigma was developed, the Chinese population was "differentiated and degraded to the satisfaction of society (ibid., p. 320)."

A similar approach were applied to the countercultur movement of the 1960s to make them look drug-addled, sex obsessed, and violent. In turn, this group – which threatened the war machine, patriarchy, white supremacy, and capitalism as a whole – could be dealt with however necessary to ring in a new rightward push. A decade later and the emergence of an underground network of child-nabbing Devil worshippers could drive the culture even further to the right. It was a sort of domestic Gladio of a very American flavor.

From time to time, I found myself so trapped in the hall of mirrors that I considered that even Manson's crew might not have committed the murders. After all, Manson was only found to be guilty of brainwashing his Family into performing them and didn't actually kill anyone himself. Looking at the sham of a trial that sent the Family to jail, it didn't take much of a leap of cynicism to assume that they weren't involved at all.

Perhaps it was an even more professional hit job led by Reece Whitson, with satanists as useful cover. Maybe even both the Manson Family and the Process were patsies. A smokescreen to shield some professional crew conducting hits across Los Angeles for reasons still unknown. If that were the case, that left rumors about Tate and Sebring dabbling with the occult. Those could have been accoutrements to add to the smokescreen or there could have been a different satanic group altogether. The Four P?

I was tangling my mind in knots based on hearsay and questionable sources. I decided to run back across the Crowley-Scientology-Process-Manson-Son-of-Sam trail and start again, this time with another left hand path in mind that I knew would lead to undiluted Satanism and a name I had heard here and there in my investigation: Lt. Col. Michael Aquino.

CHAPTER EIGHTEEN

THE CHURCH OF SATAN
AND THE TEMPLE OF SET

O nce again, I was in a liminal zone. Unlike the typical goop I had often found myself sludging through, this was something more like a gas. A haze. A purplish one. A purple haze. It reeked of incense. What I'd always imagined an opium den to smell like, except there was nowhere comfortable to sit. The Nazi regalia on the walls had also never been in my opium conceptions before.

Stumbling through the fog, I found myself in a medieval study surrounded by wooden shelves lined with occult texts. At the center, beneath a glass case rested a book, most likely bound with human skin and written in blood. Notes in the margins were probably scrawled in shit and/or semen. Lifting the enclosure, I delicately opened the text to find a human tongue bookmarking a page.

I had honestly never cared about Satanism before. It appeared edgy for the sake of edginess. Like what you'd buy at a Hot Topic in a mall in 2000. But, now, I was finding myself reading about it to the point of occasional fear. Satanism was no longer that cool semi-joke religion that challenged evangelicals who posted the Ten Commandments in courthouses with their own statues of Baphomet to make a point about separation of church and state. I was starting to worry that, maybe the Qanon people were right and elite pedophiles were sacrificing children in the name of Satan.

From what I could tell, the Church of Satan wasn't actually that threatening, but I did worry about one of its offshoots. The Church of Satan started innocuously enough. It was founded in 1966 by Anton Szandor LaVey, a one-time circus performer and later a San Francisco police photographer (Urban 2008).

Just as Crowley invented a form of Gnostic mass, LaVey was one of the modern inventors of an actual Black Mass, performed in his all-black Victorian home in San Francisco. These ceremonies were said to be elaborate forms of theater, as was the church as a whole. An unholy inversion of the Catholic mass, the black mass saw a nude woman lying upon the altar beneath the Sigil of Baphomet, the goat-headed god said to be worshipped by the Knights Templar. LaVey emerged with horns and a cape to an audience wearing black robes. He then pointed a sword in the four cardinal directions, invoking Satan, Lucifer, Belial, and Leviathan before a chalice filled with some chosen drink, such as whisky, was handed around to attendees. The ritual also included the desecration of the ritual itself and the host, such as placing the wafer, made of coarse black bread or turnip, between the breasts of the altar and then putting it to her vagina before dropping it to the floor and stomping on it. Other sacrilegious acts included the nun raising her habit and urinating into it, with the urine then being flung into the four directions. Throughout, LaVey would utter a combination of Latin parody of the Catholic Mass and French and English prayers to Satan. This included extensive excerpts from Huysmans's *Là bas* (Urban 2012).

Altogether, the black mass actually seemed less extreme than Crowley's Gnostic version. However, there was no doubt that he was influenced by the mage. Though LaVey claimed that he had "extended [the philosophy of Crowley] onehundred fold," he did believe, like Crowley, that humans ought to discover their will and act in accordance (Dyrendal 2012).

Asbjørn Dyrendal, author of *Satan and the Beast: The Influence of Aleister Crowley on Modern Satanism,* argued, "LaVey also kept a balanced interest for those aspects of Crowley's ideas about magic that he found useful, borrowing important elements of his understanding of magic from Crowley. More broadly, LaVey shared a similar purpose with Crowley: to create a structure and propagate a vision of freedom from the restrictions of Christianity. (Dyrendal 2012)"

While LaVey did not focus as exclusively on sex magic as Crowley did, he did believe sex as one of many methods for channeling energy using one's passion. Dyrendal wrote, "Much of LaVey's recipe for ritual magic involves stimulating the senses and exhorting the appropriate emotions for the ritual working. This is to concentrate both attention and will, and should work to 'isolate the otherwise dissipated adrenal and other emotionally induced energy.' This 'adrenal energy' is what supposedly fuels the magic." In this case, LaVey had added a distinctly adrenal component to Crowley's sexual workings, perhaps another indication of where the power of adrenochrome might have entered the picture.

A direct descendent of LaVey's Church of Satan was Lt. Col. Michael Aquino's Temple of Set. In 1975, LaVey began to sell access to higher titles in the church, causing high-ranking temple member Aquino and other leaders to break off and form their own satanic religion. In addition to the commercialization of satanism performed by LaVey, Aquino took issue with the less scholarly approach of his former leader.

According to Dyrendal, Aquino "acknowledges Crowley not only as Magus of the Aeon of HarWer but also as an Ipsissimus. Aquino's cited works refer to a vast number of Crowley's writings, and he appeared to know them in some detail. The reading list of the [Temple of Set] also contains Crowley's complete works, as well as further examples of writings about Crowley and later developments of Thelema. A knowledge of Thelema is considered to be a very important part of a [Temple of Set] member's studies."

Though Crowley believed in a role for both white and black magic, Aquino rejected the concept of white magic as consisting of "efforts to deceive the consciousness into believing that it has been accepted into the objective universe." White magic could be used temporarily when appropriate, according to Aquino, but the practitioner should have understood that it involved lying to oneself. Dyrendal noted:

> This is a critique that runs through much of Aquino's treatment of him: by expressing a wish to align with the natural, "objective" universe, Crowley is deceiving himself with regard to the way the world, the self, the will, and magic works.

Also unlike Crowley, the Temple of Set claimed not to have engaged in sex magic rituals. Dyrendal wrote:

> According to Zeena Schreck, a onetime High Priestess of the Temple of Set, the practice of sex magic is not specified within the curriculum of the Temple and no emphasis is placed upon it, thus differentiating the approach of Aquino and his associates from the sex magic of Thelema and the Typhonian O.T.O.

Because the Temple of Set may not have seen sex as a method for summoning magical power, it may have been for other reasons that Aquino found himself at the center of a case of satanic ritual abuse in the 1980s.

In 1987, the FBI and U.S. Army began investigating accusations of child sexual abuse at Presidio Child Development Center, run by the U.S. Army in San Francisco, which looked after an average of over 250 children per day. Allegations began the previous winter when Mike and Joyce Tobin brought their three-year-old son home from the center and the boy said he had been hurt. A doctor verified that he had been sexually abused. The culprit, according to their son, was his teacher, "Mr. Gary" Hambright (Maclay 1987).

Initially, Gary Hambright was charged with "sodomy, oral copulation and lewd and lascivious conduct." The charges were dropped, however, after a federal judge said that the child couldn't testify competently at his age and his remarks to adults would be considered hearsay. The case next widened when authorities identified 37 children as possible victims. In the fall of 1987, Hambright was charged on 10 counts of lewd and lascivious conduct with children and two counts of sexual acts with children, with 10 victims identified (*New York Times* 1987).

The medical evidence was less ambiguous than other cases associated with the satanic panic, as four children contracted chlamydia and some had evidence of anal and genital trauma. A 1992 article by Diane Ehrensaft, Ph.D., in the *American Journal of Orthopsychiatry* said that the "severity of the trauma for children at the Presidio was immediately manifest in clear cut symptoms. Before the abuse was exposed, parents had already noticed the following changes in their children: vaginal discharge, genital soreness, rashes, fear of the dark, sleep disturbances, nightmares, sexually provocative language, and sexually inappropriate behavior. In addition, the children were exhibiting other radical changes in behavior, including temper outbursts, sudden mood shifts, and poor impulse control. All these behavioral symptoms are to be expected in preschool children who have been molested" (Ehrensaft 1992).

Stories from the children had many of the tell-tale signs of potentially poor interview techniques in that the children relayed stories of multiple abusers, being taken to off-site locations, participation in "games" like "poopoo baseball" and the "googoo" game in which they were made to eat feces and urine and were urinated and defecated on. The children also claimed that they had weapons directed at them and were threatened with death or the murder of their loved ones (Goldston 1988). Unlike some of the cases included in the witch-hunt narrative, however, three houses had been positively identified by children, including that of Michael Aquino.

In August 1987, Presidio student Kinsey Adams-Thompson, the three-year-old daughter of Army Captain Larry Adams-Thompson, had, according to court documents, "become visibly frightened upon seeing LTC Aquino and his wife at the Army's post-exchange that day and called them 'Mikey' and 'Shamby.'" In an interview with the FBI, Kinsey said that she and others had been molested by "Mikey," "Shamby," and "Mr. Gary" at "Mr. Gary's house." At that point, the Presidio investigation grew to encompass more suspected perpetrators, Aquino and his wife, Lilith (U.S. Court of Appeals for the Fourth Circuit 1992).

Army CID records further indicated, "[Kinsey's] earlier statements to the child psychiatrist and her mother about 'Mikey' and 'Shamby,' persons until then unidentified, support the validity of the identification." She then matched her description of Aquino with "identification from a photo and video line-up" which "also corroborate the identification at the PX." Perhaps most importantly, "Kinsey identified plaintiff's house as the place where 'Mr. Gary' took her from the Child Development Center, and where she saw 'Mikey' in 'Army clothes' like her father's" (Army CID report).

What lent further credence to the children's testimony of satanic rituals was the fact that Aquino was an avowed satanist, formerly functioning as a leading member of the Church of Satan before founding the Temple of Set. Though High Priest Aquino denied the latter was associated with Satan, as it worshipped the Egyptian god Set, he did describe himself as the "Anti-Christ" in the religion's texts and the church was a splinter group from the Church of Satan. Temple priest Don Webb said that a believer of the Setian religion "chooses as role model a 'god against the gods.' We choose an archetype that corresponds the disharmonizing part of our own psyches.... This role model is the 'Lord of this World,' who is rejected by the Right Hand Path as the Prince of Darkness" (*San Francisco Chronicle* 1994). The church's website at one point featured a white pentagram and its answering machine once declared the Temple of Set as "the only international Satanic religious institution" recognized by the U.S. government (Lyons).

Michael Aquino wasn't an ordinary lieutenant colonel, but a former member of the Army's 306th Psychological Operations (PSYOPS) Battalion. He once worked as a Green Beret, as well as a liaison officer in NATO countries, and also as consulting faculty for the U.S. Army Command and General Staff.

Aquino joined the Church of Satan in 1969 and became a priest in Kentucky while on leave from the Vietnam War. In 1970, Aquino was stationed in Bén Cát in South Vietnam where he was involved with such psyops as deploying helicopters featuring sets of ultra-high-decibel loudspeakers. Psyop pilot Dale Seago said the group would "take them up above the cloud layer where they couldn't be seen, where the rotor blades couldn't be heard, but you could very clearly hear the broadcasts on the ground." One tape Aquino created "began with this wailing Vietnamese funeral music and then phased into screaming, gradually getting louder." The idea was to take advantage of local beliefs about "the necessity of burying the body of the deceased because if they didn't do that the souls would be condemned to wander eternally tormented by demons." Once the screaming on Aquino's tape ended, the sounds of a Viet-Minh soldier dying would emerge. Seago said, "It was chilling and then finally you hear him being dragged away screaming by the demons" (Constantine 2007).

According to Seago, the psyop team would "wait for a really severe thunderstorm and they would take the choppers up, go over the cloud layer, and through these buckets of rain and jagged lightening and thunder, you'd hear this stuff coming out of the sky. Apparently it was quite effective. He won a lot of notoriety for that in Vietnam."

Major Jack Downing, a consultant for the CIA's infamous MKULTRA program, said Aquino took over his position in "human ecology." Downing said, "At the time of my leaving, my role ... as human ecology expert was taken up by another officer, a Michael Aquino, who was trying out these [mind control] principles in the context of Anton LaVey's church" (Constantine 2007).

Downing's role represented the darkest aspects of MKULTRA. "I was working alongside the CIA as a consultant in psyops and as a specialist in 'human ecology.' That's a phrase that connotes different things, depending on the context, from the wholesome to the not-so-wholesome. In the capacity for which I was employed, it was a way of pinning down the psyche and behaviors of human beings in differing environments or under various circumstances. It employed the observational principles of anthropologists and psychologists alongside the more manipulative techniques of advertisers, social engineers and 'golden age' brainwashers. It was, in retrospect, a very unorthodox and ethically questionable thing." Downing said "we brought the MK [mind control] projects into the war. The extreme circumstances of warfare gave us excellent opportunities to observe the ways certain mind control technologies might work."

As an intelligence officer and high priest, Aquino participated in a practice familiar to both some organized religions and espionage agents: blackmail. Temple defector Kevin Filan said, "Aquino uses embarrassing information obtained while people are members of their cult to attempt to discredit or harass them later. This is among the most odious of their tactics. I was 'outed' and my workplace posted to the nets with the suggestion that people 'pay me a visit' in an attempt to silence my criticisms of their cult" (Constantine 2007).

One member, Lillian Rosoff, was harassed by Aquino for two months after leaving. He would call her early in the morning and one time came to her door and banged on it at 3 AM, demanding she come back to the church. According to an affidavit, Aquino shouted he "was tired of playing games with her," and that she'd "better watch out for his next move." She said she had "an intense fear" of the priest and did "not know how far the defendant [would] go" "due to past experiences" with Aquino. She was granted a restraining order against him in 1999 (Constantine 2007).

Aquino also had a keen interest in Nazism, specifically the occult aspects, which he described as "a very powerful area of magic … unrealized by the profane?" (Rashke 1990). He highlighted the "uncanny attraction of the Third Reich" and said that "techniques perfected by the Nazis continue to be used/abused – generally in an ignorant and superficial fashion – by every country of the world in one guise or another" (Newton 1993).

In 1985, a group of defectors that included a high level member and Aquino's brother-in-law founded their own church, the Temple of Nepthys, citing Aquino's "obsession" with Nazism as one of the reasons for leaving (Newton 1993). In fact, it was discovered that Aquino had an SS uniform in his home. He'd also paid a visit to Nazi occultist Heinrich Himmler's Wewelsberg castle in Germany to perform the Stifling Air rituals in 1982. According to a November 3, 1987 article in the *San Francisco Chronicle*, "In his book Crystal Tablet of Set,' [Aquino] writes that he performed the rituals to recreate an order of knighthood for followers of Satan."

The *San Francisco Examiner* noted that, despite his public occult identity, Aquino "claims to have reported directly to the Joint Chiefs of Staff…. Expert of psychological warfare, Aquino wanted to use satellites for brainwashing the U.S. public."

Seago said that, as a part of the 306th Psychological Operations Battalion with Aquino in 1976, the force "dealt with psyop on a national policy level." Aquino and Seago weren't the only military personnel in the Temple of Set, nor the only ones with intelligence backgrounds. Dennis K. Mann and Captain Willie Browning were described in an Army CID investigative report filed with the San Francisco Police Department as "Captains, Military Intelligence." Member Bruce Bibee was a former captain in Aquino's psyop unit in San Pedro, California. Also worth noting was that Aquino's brother-in-law, a former Pittsburgh police officer named William Butch, was a naval reservist (Constantine 2007).

As for his attitude toward children, Dale Seago said that Aquino had a great deal of antipathy toward the son he had with his first wife, Janet.

"Regarding children. I don't know how he feels about them in general. I do know that he virtually hates his son, Dorien," Seago said. "If he felt he could get away with it – and he probably didn't mean this literally – he would happily go into [Dorien's] room at night and smother him with pillows." Seago said that Aquino did not kill many people in the war, but that he had done so "once or twice" and "he found he had no particular emotional reaction to it." Seago also said that Vietnamese houseboys, "would have nothing to do with Aquino's quarters. He had a Baphomet plaque up on the wall, candles and a makeshift altar. He had a bit of a reputation as a magic man among the locals and nobody would go near him."

A month after Aquino's home was searched in relation to the Presidio case, there was a fire at the Army Community Services Building next to the childcare facility. The *Mercury News* pointed out that "the fire occurred on the autumnal equinox, a major event on the satanic calendar." It destroyed the Army Community Services Building, as well as some of the records from the Child Development Center. Another fire broke out three weeks later, completely destroying a building that housed four classrooms, including Gary Hambright's. The Bureau of Alcohol, Tobacco and Firearms concluded "both fires, contrary to the Army's finding, had been arson (Goldston 1988)."

According to the *Mercury News*, evidence of a satanic cult had emerged on the Presidio base. Though the exact details were unclear, graffiti, an altar and other artifacts indicated some sort of ritual on the base, with a former MP saying, "we've got a cult on the Presidio of San Francisco and nobody cares about it…. We were told by the provost marshal to just forget about it."

Though the legal case against Aquino was ultimately dropped, the Army CID continued to investigate him and, in August 1989, he was accused by Army investigators of "Conspiracy, Kidnapping, Sodomy, Indecent Acts or Liberties With a Child, False Swearing, Intentional Noncompliance With Article 30 Uniform Code of Military Justice, Maltreatment of a Subordinate and Conduct Unbecoming an Officer (Army CID report)." As a result, the high priest of Set was "titled," meaning that he became the subject of a criminal investigation report. No judicial or legal action was taken, including arrest or conviction of a crime. Essentially, titling was simply a blotch on one's military career. Aquino sued to have the title removed without luck. Commanding General of the Army CID made the decision in September 1990: "Plaintiff remains titled for Conspiracy, Kidnapping, Sodomy, Indecent Acts and False Swearing" (United States District Court For the Eastern District of Virginia).

Aquino tried to argue that the Army's behavior toward him was discriminatory based on his religion. The Army's response was this:

> This investigation was not a "witchhunt." Plaintiff was not targeted because of his religious beliefs. In fact, as plaintiff repeatedly points out ... the Army has been aware of [Aquino's] religious beliefs throughout his career and has not interfered with his religious practices. The sole reasons for this investigation and the CID decision ... are the facts that point to plaintiff's sexual abuse. This included the evidence that Kinsey Adams-Thompson, "in a completely public setting, identifies ... a man who sodomized her" and forced her to "place her mouth on his penis." (Constantine 2007)

Aquino additionally tried to argue that he was not in the area during the time of the assaults at Presidio. The Army denied this too, allowing that he had traveled to D.C. and St. Louis, but was "back in the Presidio in San Francisco during that summer."

The Army even validated evidence of the bizarre paraphernalia seen by the victims, noting photos of Aquino's home "show masks, guns, toy animals and ceremonial items that are similar to things described by Kinsey and other children. A notebook from plaintiff's apartment contained the name 'Mike Todo,' and 'Todo' was one of the persons present at 'Mr. Gary's' house" (Constantine 2007).

The Army ultimately terminated the satanic priest's service in 1990 and he was processed out of the Army Active Reserves. In 1988, all charges against Hambright were dropped. U.S. Attorney Joseph Russionello concluded that there was evidence of child molestation but "insufficient evidence" to tie it to those charged. Some parents sued the Army, with settlements reached in some cases (Constantine 2007).

The story didn't end there, however. Aquino was interrogated in May 1989 about five children making claims of sexual abuse in three different cities. They had supposedly seen Aquino in the media stories about Presidio and said that he had abused them. Three were located in Ukiah, California, where Police Chief Fred Keplinger told the *Mercury News*, "the children are believable. I have no doubt in my mind that something has occurred" (McGowan 2004).

From a 1985 abuse scandal in Santa Rosa, California, Aquino was identified as being present at one of two churches: "allegations of ritual abuse erupted ... in 1985 when several children at the Jubilation Day Care Center said they were sexually abused by a number of people at the day care center and at several locations away from the center, including at least two churches" (McGowan 2004).

The Presidio story also wasn't the only child sexual abuse case to occur at a military base. The *Mercury News* stated, "by November, 1987 the Army had received allegations of child abuse at 15 of its day care centers and several elementary schools. There were also at least two cases in Air Force day care centers." Additionally, "a special team of experts was sent to Panama [in June 1988] to help determine if as many as 10 children at a Department of Defense elementary school had been molested and possibly infected with AIDS" (McGowan 2004).

Before any of this, however, was the case at West Point, which began in July 1984 after a three-year-old had a lacerated vagina, which she told a doctor was caused by a teacher at her daycare center. The *Mercury News* said about the school, "by the end of the year, 50 children had been interviewed by investigators. Children at West Point told stories that would become horrifyingly familiar. They said they had been ritually abused. They said they had had excrement smeared on their bodies and been forced to eat feces and drink urine. They said they were taken away from the day care center and photographed" (McGowan 2004).

The investigation led by former U.S. Attorney Rudy Giuliani resulted in no federal grand jury indictments. Only a year earlier, a 22-month-old child had been killed by an Army staff sergeant. After "a court martial hearing, the sergeant was given an 18 month suspended sentence and dishonorable discharge," according to the *Mercury News*.

Sexual abuse accusations occurred at over 10 percent of Army daycare centers between 1984 and 1987. These included Fort Dix, West Point, Fort Jackson, and Fort Leavenworth. There had even been a case at a site run by the U.S. in West Germany (McGowan 2004).

TED GUNDERSON & THE SATANIST

Exploring the world of SRA, there was a name that came up even more frequently than Aquino. His background provided his work with an air of authority, but his character suggested otherwise. Prior to his 1979 retirement from the force, Ted Gunderson had acted as FBI Special Agent in Charge for bureau offices in Memphis, Dallas, and Los Angeles. As he climbed the ranks of the FBI, he earned accolades in particular for his part in Hoover's COINTELPRO program, a sort of domestic Gladio dismantling dissident groups and the American left (Best 2016). In 1965, while acting as Assistant Special Agent in Charge (ASAC) in New Haven, Connecticut, Gunderson was involved in cultivating informants and infiltrators in the city's Black Panther Party (BPP), about which the FBI wrote:

> Source, a Negro, male was not a member of the BPP at the time, however through direction and guidance he was successfully admitted in membership and since then has been considered a trusted and active Panther. In addition to providing information on local BPP activity, including details of the meetings, identity of members and information concerning funds, finances, travel, etc., informant has also furnished extensive information on a national and international level. In a number of instances, he was the first informant in the country to provide such information…
>
> This informant is now in a trusted position to furnish extremely valuable information concerning BPP activities. Our most valuable weapon against Soviet intelligence and domestic extremist organizations such as the BPP is the development of quality informants such as these two informants. ASAC Gunderson's efforts in these cases is exemplary.

Gunderson was praised for his work against the BPP by Hoover himself and even given $150 as a bonus. His biggest contribution to the efforts of the FBI to destroy the party, however, came in 1969, when the group killed a member thought to be an informant. This in turn led to the arrest of several members and generally aided in tarnishing the movement in the eyes of the general public. Gunderson was specifically commended in a report on the subject:

> Following the murder of a Black Panther member on 5-21-69, New Haven instituted a vigorous, incisive investigation under the direction of Gunderson to ascertain facts concerning the murder, persons responsible, and to locate and bring to trial these individuals. As a result of these efforts, three Black Panther leaders were arrested and a number of items of evidence seized, including a taped recording of a kangaroo court held by the Black Panther Party prior to the murder of its member.
>
> …
>
> In view of the above, I strongly recommend that Gunderson be considered for reassignment to the Inspection Division preparatory to his designation as an SAC [Special Agent in Charge].

What appeared like a steady upward trajectory for the FBI agent took a drastic turn in 1979, the year in which Gunderson claimed he was passed up for a promotion to become director of the bureau. The man chosen over him was William Webster. To his new superior, Gunderson argued that Attorney General Guidelines were threatening national security by hindering bureau investigations. Rather than take his suggestion to heart, Webster reprimanded him. In response, Gunderson wrote a letter that said:

> Individual rights are of the utmost importance, but some of our citizens are going to have their individual rights blasted off the face of the earth if our intelligence community does not gird its loins "with the laudable purpose of prevention" rather than collecting evidence afterwards. I urgently request that you lend an unbiased ear to a field commander who daily witnesses Agent frustration and overcautiousness. These men and women fear they might overstep the guidelines or find themselves powerless to protect their sources from disclosure. Hesitancy is not a historic earmark of a Special Agent of the FBI.

Webster was unmoved and maintained, "I believe at this time we are able to work within [the Attorney General guidelines] and, therefore, no modifications are necessary." Soon after, Gunderson decided to leave the bureau and start a private investigation business. It was at that point that Gunderson entered the sinister world of satanism.

It began with the case of Jeffrey MacDonald, an army doctor stationed at Fort Bragg military base accused of murdering his entire family in 1970. 10 years later, Gunderson entered the scene on the side of the defense, which argued that a Manson Family-like cult of drugged out hippies had committed the crime. Gunderson muddied already dirty waters when he focused his efforts on Helena Stoeckley, the daughter of a lieutenant colonel at Fort Bragg and once considered a suspect. Stoeckley was put aside as a suspect, however, due to what the army's Criminal Investigation Division considered to be her poor testimony. When Gunderson got a hold of her, a former FBI agent involved in the case said that there was an "element of duress" with Gunderson using "unethical means and tactics in a very important case." Gunderson even "Assured [Stoeckley] that she'd be resettled in California with a new house, job, and identity – even a part in the forthcoming movie – Stoeckley signed a statement not only implicating herself in the murders but naming five other killers (later referred to as 'Black Cult' members) as well."

The details of Stoeckley's story didn't square with reality in a number of ways, but did have the effect of adding extraneous details to the case that would make it more confusing overall for the public at large.

The former FBI agent's worldview became more convoluted when, after giving a lecture about the MacDonald case, he was provided a copy of *Pawns In The Game* by William Guy Carr. The book illuminated him to the role of the Illuminati and satanism in everyday affairs. The anti-Semitic treatise claimed that the House of Rothschild had set about controlling the world in 1776 through the establishment of a group of secret elites that would secretly govern global affairs (Best 2016).

Throughout his post-bureau career, Gunderson would insert himself into a wide variety of high-profile cases. At McMartin, Gunderson led parents' private efforts to unearth the tunnels beneath McMartin preschool. He played a role investigating the Franklin scandal. He aided in Maury Terry's search for the cult behind the Son of Sam murders. He also insinuated himself in the Oklahoma City Bombing, where he worked directly with John DeCamp (DeCamp 2005). He managed his way into the PROMIS software scandal, as well (Seymour 2010).

Particularly later in life, he was known to espouse satanic conspiracy theories at far-right conventions alongside white nationalists. He made extraordinary allegations, such as "There are approximately 4,000,000 satanic cult members in the United States" and that 50,000 children were kidnapped annually and ritually sacrificed (DeCamp 2005).

One of the most intriguing details about Gunderson's story related to his involvement with an avowed satanist. Radio broadcaster and private detective Ed Opperman claimed that he had spoken to Jackie McGauley, one of the mothers from the McMartin saga. Apparently, Gunderson had established a relationship with McGauley and, in addition to selling the McMartin tunnel dig report without her permission, wound up sleeping on her couch for an extended period of time while low on funds. During that period, McGauley claimed that he spoke on the phone daily with Michael Aquino, accused pedophile from the Presidio Daycare scandal. Opperman also said that he had spoken to an unnamed client who told him that she had run into Gunderson at the Los Angeles FBI field office. She said he was working there, despite the fact that he had supposedly been retired for more than 30 years (Opperman 2020).

It was difficult to determine if Gunderson could have been working for the feds to muddy the waters of actual intelligence operations or was merely a, possibly deranged, grifter charging something like $100 an hour for investigative services.

In addition to exploiting already dramatic cases around the country, he seemed to be involved in other questionable practices and methods for making money. For instance, in 1982, Gunderson was thought to have paid a woman to plant drugs on a crucial witness in order to discredit them in an important methamphetamine investigation by the DEA, resulting in an obstruction of justice case against the former FBI agent. After Gunderson's involvement, the case began to fall apart (Best 2016).

A 1984 investigation into Gunderson suggested that he was involved in wire fraud for his role in a company called Dekla International. A memo about Gunderson once said that he was participating in "numerous suspect activities involving persons allegedly dealing in narcotics and advance fee swindles." And a later memo described him as "armed and dangerous." Nevertheless, Gunderson was never prosecuted.

He turned up in Washington state in 1989 fraternizing with known drug dealers, throwing around his status as a retired FBI official. Mason County Sheriff Holter told the FBI that he looked "somewhat disheveled in expensive clothing and alleges to be involved in some kind of clandestine project" (Best 2016).

50 SHADES OF RED

If there were truth to the idea that the powerful were engaged in satanic child abuse, it seemed as though someone like Michael Aquino was key. I tried to put the pieces together as best I could.

I determined that the elite had a long history of association with the occult and what could have been perceived as satanism, particularly through intelligence services. In the case of the grandfather of modern occultism, Aleister Crowley was an asset for British intelligence. However, the Process didn't necessarily seem involved. That didn't rule out Son of Sam or the Manson Family, the latter of which definitely appeared to be linked to the deep state. It also seemed to be the case that Hollywood stars flirted with the occult at the very least, possibly even engaging in mutual sadomasochism or, worse, torture and abuse.

Tentatively, I imagined that Aquino could have been involved in all of these child abuse cases of which he was accused. I had no evidence of it, but if he had, it could have indicated some Army-wide child abuse program. Why the Army would allow a satanist to assault children across the country took the form of a vague blur, edges difficult to decipher. As I got closer to the shedding chrysalis at the center of this hellscape, I could make out two, symmetrical wings.

PART 4

MIND CONTROL

Sidney Gottlieb, Sept. 21, 1977
Rzfrie, Creative Commons

CHAPTER NINETEEN

A BRIEF OVERVIEW OF MKULTRA

In the basement of some New York City hospital was something that was obviously only a gangway to other, more dangerous laboratories. Some of the experiments were performed in the expected dungeons where they kept the undesireables, but others were conducted in penthouse apartments in Manhattan or large homes outside of D.C. Anywhere and everywhere. I toured them like a ghost from the present.

To be honest, when a couple of Gundam said they were looking into it, I was scared to research Monarch. On the one hand, I fretted that it was fake and I would get suckered into believing in it. On the other, I worried that it was real and our world was filled with horrors beyond anything the Nazis could have dreamed of. I opened the book @KetracelBlack was reading, *The Illuminati Formula to Create an Undetectable Total Mind Control Slave*, by Fritz Springmeier and Cisco Wheeler, and was confronted with this:

> WARNING, READ THIS FIRST BEFORE READING THE BOOK: IF THERE IS ANY CHANCE you the reader have had mind-control done to you, you must consider the following book to be DANGEROUS (Springmeier & Wheeler 1996).

It was a silly warning, but how was I supposed to know if I had ever been brainwashed? There were the countless advertisements, video games, tv shows and movies I'd been exposed to my whole life. Not to mention the U.S. public education system, college and grad school. Paulo Freire taught that education was used as a means of indoctrination, with each economic class receiving the type of learning that would best prepare them for their stations in life; in my case, that would seem to be sort of a middle management type. Plus, there was the pornography I'd watched as an adolescent and young adult and god knows what that did to my subconscious. Anyway, I wasn't taking any chances. I closed the book and decided I'd better start with the basics. What was MKULTRA?

When MKULTRA was made public in the early 1970s through a combination of investigations on the part of journalist Seymour Hersh and the U.S. congress, this program showcased just a fraction of the depravity that the CIA and other intelligence organizations would indulge in to achieve their objectives of power (Hersh 1974). Only 20,000 pages of documentation survived the more than 20-year program. The rest were destroyed at the orders of CIA Director Richard Helms in 1973 (Church Committee 1976). As a result, there was a mixture of actual documented evidence, other public disclosures on behalf of victims and executors of the program, and wild speculation. Sometimes, there was a mixture of all three.

The program began in 1950 with research into "truth drugs" during World War II under what was then called Operation Bluebird (Rockefeller Commission 1975). In 1951, Bluebird became ARTICHOKE, which could have been boiled down to this question asked of the CIA's Medical Office chief: "Can we get control of an individual to the point where he will do our bidding against his will and even against such fundamental laws of nature [like] self-preservation?" (Albarelli 2011, Ch. 3).

The CIA hoped to perform such strange tasks as hiding messages within the minds of their spies, wiping memories from individuals without their knowledge, inserting false memories into people, and programming assassins.

By 1953, MKULTRA was developed alongside ARTICHOKE and would be led by Sydney Gottlieb. The goal had mind control at its center, but was so broad that it also involved the development of chemical and radiological weapons as well as seemingly general studies of sociology. It would grow to more than 150 subprojects encompassing over 80 institutions, ranging from colleges and universities to hospitals, prisons, and pharmaceutical companies (Horrock 1977). Test subjects and targets, witting and unwitting, spread across a similar gamut: from addicts, prisoners, mental patients, and sex workers – "people who could not fight back," as they were described by one CIA officer – to college students, artists, musicians, political leaders, and, even, some evidence indicates, an entire French town (Albarelli 2011, Ch. 9).

These were just some of the drugs deployed: LSD, psilocybin, mescaline, cocaine, AMT, DMT, heroin, morphine, temazepam, mescaline, scopolamine, alcohol and sodium pentothal (Marks 1979). They explored the impacts of these substances in a wide array of complex scenarios that could only be described as experimental torture. In fact, much of it would inform the CIA's torture manual, KUBARK, which served as the basis for the "enhanced interrogation" techniques still in use today (Hajjar 2012).

Though stories about the program percolated previously, the first major public revelation about the program came from a series of investigative articles published by Seymour Hersh in 1974. This was followed by the 1975 Church Committee of the United States Congress and Gerald Ford's United States President's Commission on CIA activities within the United States (better known as the Rockefeller Commission). In 1977, some 20,000 documents were uncovered from a Freedom of Information Act request, which resulted in Senate hearings that year (Joint Hearing before the Select Committee on Intelligence and the Subcommittee on Health and Scientific Research of the Committee on Human Resources 1977). Further documents were declassified over the years, including in 2001 and 2018 (Whalen 2018).

Some objectives included:

- Substances which will promote illogical thinking and impulsiveness to the point where the recipient would be discredited in public.

- Substances which increase the efficiency of mentation and perception.

- Materials which will prevent or counteract the intoxicating effect of alcohol.

- Materials which will promote the intoxicating effect of alcohol.

- Materials which will produce the signs and symptoms of recognized diseases in a reversible way so they may be used for malingering, etc.

- Materials which will render the induction of hypnosis easier or otherwise enhance its usefulness.

- Substances which will enhance the ability of individuals to withstand privation, torture, and coercion during interrogation and so-called "brain-washing."

- Materials and physical methods which will produce amnesia for events preceding and during their use.

- Physical methods of producing shock and confusion over extended periods of time and capable of surreptitious use.

- Substances which produce physical disablement such as paralysis of the legs, acute anemia, etc.

- Substances which will produce "pure" euphoria with no subsequent let-down.

- Substances which alter personality structure in such a way the tendency of the recipient to become dependent upon another person is enhanced.

- A material which will cause mental confusion of such a type the individual under its influence will find it difficult to maintain a fabrication under questioning.

- Substances which will lower the ambition and general working efficiency of men when administered in undetectable amounts.

- Substances which promote weakness or distortion of the eyesight or hearing faculties, preferably without permanent effects.

- A knockout pill which can be surreptitiously administered in drinks, food, cigarettes, as an aerosol, etc., which will be safe to use, provide a maximum of amnesia, and be suitable for use by agent types on an ad hoc basis.

- A material which can be surreptitiously administered by the above routes and which in very small amounts will make it impossible for a person to perform physical activity (Senate Select Committee on Intelligence and Committee on Human Resources 1977)."

MKULTRA burgeoned to include MKSEARCH in 1964, which spent at least $10 million ($87.5 million adjusted for inflation) on developing over 26,000 biological, chemical, and radioactive materials for controlling people's behavior (Lee & Schlain 2007).

Both MKULTRA and related projects demonstrated that the U.S. military was not adverse to testing on an ignorant public. Through an MKULTRA project called Midnight Climax, agency-hired sex workers brought johns back to a CIA apartment outfitted with recording equipment and a two-way mirror, behind which agents could observe the effects of drugs such as LSD secretly fed by the prostitutes to their unwitting clients (Albarelli 2011, Ch. 11). An Army program called Operation Seaspray saw bacteria dispensed on large groups of people, including along the coast of San Francisco and dropped from light bulbs on New York City subways (Carlton 2001). There was even evidence to suggest that the CIA was involved in dosing the small French town of Pont-Saint-Espirit with LSD, which led to mass hallucination, injuries and death (Albarelli 2011, Ch. 9).

Ewen Cameron, one time president of the Canadian and American Psychological Associations, the most prestigious psychological organizations in each country, represented just a sample of the torture conducted under the MKULTRA program. Paid $69,000 from 1957 to 1964 (modified for inflation US$579,480 in 2021) for his MKULTRA work, Cameron invented what he called "psychic driving," a process by which he exposed mental health patients at the Allan Memorial Institute of McGill University to LSD, electroshock at 30 to 40 times the normal voltage, paralytic drugs, sleep deprivation and more as a means of "erasing" their memories. They would then be held in drug-induced comas for weeks on end, up to three months in at least one instance, with tape recordings of sounds or repetitive statements played continuously as a means of constructing new identities. Instead, these test subjects, who often came to the facility for minor problems such as depression, were left shattered, with memory problems and incontinence (Marks 1977).

Meanwhile, the CIA conducted similar experiments not just on victims in North America but at secret detention centers around the world, including Japan, Germany and the Philippines (NPR 2019). This evolved into the interrogation centers the U.S. maintained today, such as Abu Ghraib and Guantanamo Bay, where prisoners had been given high doses of the antimalarial mefloquine, taking advantage of the drug's ability to induce psychosis (Kaye 2015).

Reading about this work, I wasn't only shocked that these psychedelics – which I was taught were means of opening the minds and hearts of innocent partiers – were used to torture people, to death in some cases. I also kept having the oddest thought that maybe people like Sidney Godfried, who admitted to taking acid personally some 30 times, or Allen Dulles had used them to see truths about our reality that only LSD or some top secret variant could reveal. And they were then applying those truths to enhance their torture techniques and gain more power. These could have then been combined with the massive amount of psychological and sociological data the CIA connected to understand life on earth. Because they weren't just studying drugs and torture, but Marxism and modernism and Maoism and ESP and more. As his neighbor in Switzerland, what did Dulles learn from Carl Jung? Sending his wife and mistress to one of the fathers of psychoanalysis for therapy, was Dulles gaining insights into the human psyche and collective unconscious that would aid him in his quest to control the mind on a massive and deep scale?

Worse yet, maybe they saw themselves as improving the state of things by enacting the will of negative forces in some Yin-Yang mechanics underlying the universe. That by being evil, humanity would unleash the demons of its collective unconscious, thus uniting the opposites as the Process believed or integrating the shadow as Jung theorized. Giving themselves moral permission to behave like monsters, how would Dulles and Gottfried have treated our children?

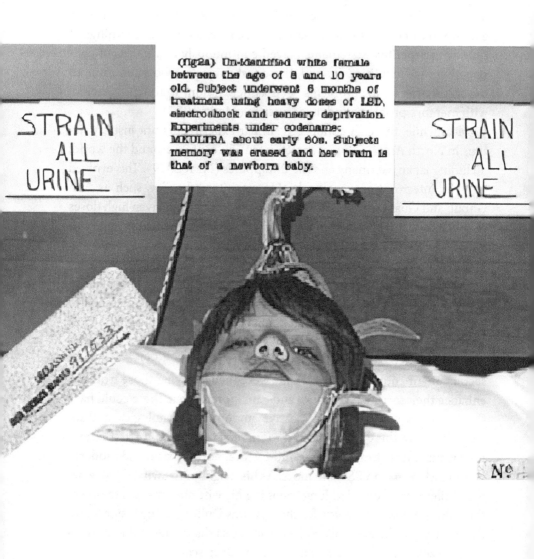

(fig2a) Un-identified white female between the age of 8 and 10 years old. Subject underwent 6 months of treatment using heavy doses of LSD, electroshock and sensory deprivation. Experiments under codename: MKULTRA about early 60s. Subjects memory was erased and her brain is that of a newborn baby.

STRAIN
ALL
URINE

STRAIN
ALL
URINE

CHAPTER TWENTY

MKULTRA's EXPERIMENTATION
ON CHILDREN

As horrific as the experiments on adults were, there was evidence that the CIA and its accomplices had a similar no-holds-barred approach to children as young as three years old. What I could find about the exact nature of this work was very limited. What became public were verified survivor stories.

One of the most notable practitioners that experimented on children for the MKULTRA program was Dr. Lauretta Bender, a neuropsychiatrist with a focus on children who worked at Bellevue Hospital in New York City. She was probably best known for the Bender-Gestalt Test for assessing the motor skills of children (*Gale Encyclopedia of Medicine*) and was likely less known for the LSD experimentation she performed on "schizophrenic" and "autistic" children with funding from the CIA (Albarelli & Kaye 2010).

Before this work began, Bender was an expert in the field of electro conductive therapy. She applied electroshock procedures to 100-500 children between three and 12 years old. This research saw her in contact with a cadre of MKULTRA scientists that included Alfred Hubbard, Joel Elkes, Paul Hoch, Harris Isbell, Max Fink, James Cattell and Harold A. Abramson.

This last was an allergy doctor who posed as a psychiatrist and may have played a role in one of the most well-known MKULTRA-related deaths, that of CIA researcher Frank Olson. Hoch and Cattell were responsible for the other most well-known MKULTRA death, injecting lethal amounts of a psychedelic amphetamine called 3,4-Methylenedioxy amphetamine into Jewish tennis star Harold Blauer at the New York State Psychiatric Institute. Elkes was an early experimenter of LSD in Europe who went on to work hand in hand with the CIA, Pentagon and MI6 on drug research in the UK and U.S. Fink, whose work Dr. Bender admired, was the godfather of electroshock treatment and a CIA consultant, applying his expertise for use in CIA interrogations. He told the agency in one document that "an individual could gradually be reduced through the use to electroshock treatment to the vegetable level."

Hubbard was not a medical doctor, though he was referred to as such. The "Johnny Appleseed of LSD," Hubbard was responsible for spreading the drug's use around the world, even jailed at one time for smuggling the substance across national borders. A paper published by New York Medical College in 1961 stated that Hubbard's work exposing "children, primarily delinquents" to LSD "to have been 85% successful." Bender cited Hubbard's early work in LSD to have been "very substantial and beneficial."

While she publicly boasted of the effectiveness of electroshock on treating children with "autistic schizophrenia," Bender privately expressed dissatisfaction with the long-term effects, with one six-year-old shifting from shyness to aggressive violence and and a seven-year-old becoming catatonic after too much electroshock. In the very long-term, one patient went to prison as a "multiple murderer," the worst of a number of Bender cases that had wound up in prison as adults.

Even by medical standards of the time, Bender's work was problematic. A study published in 1954 looked at the effects of her treatment on roughly 50 children, determining that the overwhelming majority were in even worse condition than before, including some that had grown to have suicidal tendencies. Among the subjects of the study was Guy Susann, the son of Jacqueline Susann, author of *Valley of the Dolls*. After being diagnosed with autism, Guy was placed in Bender's care at three years old. When he returned to his family, his mother said he had been "destroyed." He spent the rest of his life in institutions (Albarelli & Kaye 2010).

Bender began her experiments using LSD on children in 1960, with partial funding provided by a CIA front group called the Society for the Investigation of Human Ecology (SIHE). In a memo from the CIA's Technical Services Division (TSD) to the head of the SIHE, former U.S. Air Force psyops officer James L. Monroe raised questions about the "operational benefits of Dr. Bender's work as related to children and LSD," asking to be "closely appraised of the possible links between Dr. Bender's project and those being conducted under separate MK/ULTRA funding at designated prisons in New York and elsewhere."

The work was performed at the Children's Unit of Creedmoor State Hospital in Queens, New York, where she received LSD from Sandoz, the originator and initial supplier of the drug to the CIA. Bender began with 14 children ages six to 10 and diagnosed as schizophrenic, though the diagnostic criteria at the time made it difficult to determine what they might or might not have been diagnosed with today. After injecting them with LSD, "The two oldest boys, over ten years, near or in early puberty, reacted with disturbed anxious behavior. The oldest and most disturbed received Amytal sodium 150 mg intramuscularly and returned to his usual behavior," Bender wrote.

Those two boys were then removed from the experiment and the other 12 exposed to further doses of 25 mcg before the dose was kicked up to 100 mcg injected once a week. "Then it was increased gradually to twice and three times a week as no untoward side-effects were noticed…. Finally, it was given daily and this continued for six weeks until the time of this report," Bender wrote.

Bender believed the results were positive. She wrote:

> "In general, [the children] were happier; their mood was 'high' in the hours following the ingestion of the drug … they have become more spontaneously playful with balls and balloons … their color is rosy rather than blue or pale and they have gained weight." She went on to write. "The use of these drugs [LSD, UML-401, UML-491] … will give us more knowledge about both the basic schizophrenic process and the defensive autism in children and also about the reaction of these dilysergic acid derivatives as central and autonomic nervous system stimulants and serotonin antagonists. Hopefully these drugs will also contribute to our efforts to find better therapeutic agents for early childhood schizophrenia."

Bender went on to publish an article in 1970 about two "mildly schizophrenic" adolescent boys who were dosed with LSD and began to hallucinate that researchers were making faces at them, that their pencils were "rubbery," and one said the face of the other had become green. The boys grew concerned about being experimented on, but Bender gave them 150 mcg more for each day of the project. She determined one of the subjects "benefited very much," but grew up to become "a disturbed adult schizophrenic." They terminated the project with the other subject "because of the boy's attitude towards it" due to "his own psychopathology."

As Bender continued her research on the use of LSD on children throughout the decade, she went on to test other drugs, including a dreamier, longer lasting type of psychotropic called UNL-491, also developed by Sandoz. Other psychotropics she used included amphetamines, anticonvulsants, sub-shock insulin dosing, and Metrazol, a circulatory and respiratory stimulation drug. Bender also tested psilocybin, the key ingredient in magic mushrooms, in experiments on "six pairs of matched, pre-puberty, schizophrenic boys."

I learned that, at extreme doses, Metrazol resulted in seizures. At the public mental health site Vermont State Hospital, CIA asset Dr. Robert Hyde tested Metrazol on patients "to address overly aggressive behavior." Deaths at the clinic jumped during the same period in which the drug was prescribed. Metrazol finally had its FDA approval pulled in 1982. Under Bluebird and Artichoke, the CIA and Army Counter-Intelligence Corps (CIC), with the assistance of "former" Nazi scientists injected the drug into enemies in front of their compatriots as a means of terrorizing them during interrogations. These might have been combined with LSD, heroin, other drugs and electroshock.

In addition to the aforementioned CIA-linked researchers, Bender also consulted with Ronald A. Sandison, Thomas M. Ling and John Buckman, who worked at the Chelsea Clinic and Potwick Hospital in the U.K. Sandison was responsible for introducing LSD to Hubbard, as well as to England as a whole. Using funds from the CIA, MI6 and the Macy Foundation, he opened a department at Potwick dedicated to dosing schizophrenic patients with LSD under the guise of what he called Psycholytic Therapy. Over ten years, he and his colleagues provided 900 patients with over 15,000 doses of acid.

Buckman was one Chelsea Clinic doctor that treated children with LSD. One example was that of 13-year-old Marion McGill (a pseudonym) and her 15-year-old sister. Their parents had become "quite taken with the benefits of LSD and thought that we would also benefit from the drug (Albarelli & Kaye 2010)."

Marion said:

> As a 13-year old at the time, my decision-making capacity was very limited. I was, by nature, fairly compliant and docile, rather eager to please my parents. I understood nothing of what was being suggested for me and my 15 year-old sister – namely that we participate in some sort of "research" that both our parents had also participated in. Whether the word "experiment" was used, I don't recall. The term "LSD" was vaguely familiar, however, because my parents were "taking" this drug as a form of "quick therapy" – their term for it – that had been recommended by my uncle, a psychiatrist at a well known east coast medical school.

Marion said that, while her parents were in need of therapy, she did not:

My sister and I, however, were about as "normal" as any two teen-agers could be. We were at the top of our classes in school; both of us had lots of friends, participated in extra curricular activities. We didn't need "therapy." We were told we would get a day off from school after each overnight stay at the clinic for this LSD. It was perhaps the prospect of a day off from Catholic girls' school that persuaded us to do it. I wasn't aware of making a "decision." The purpose of this program was never explained. There were to be 10 sessions – once a week for 10 weeks. I believe they started in Jan-uary 1960.

She received her doses at the instruction of Buckman, who would "[provide] no information about what to expect from the LSD. There was no mention, for example, of hallucinations or perceptual distortions or anything frightening. I was not informed of any persistent effects, such as nightmares. Certainly the possibility of lasting damage was not men-tioned. The word 'experiment' was not used. There was, in other words, no informed consent whatsoever. I was not told that I could refuse to participate, that I could quit at any time (as provided in the Nuremberg Code). Since I was below the age of consent, my parents would have been the ones to agree to this. Indeed, they were the ones to suggest that we be used in these experiments. It would not otherwise have happened. But my parents would never discuss this in later years and never explained why they did it."

Marion said that, with each of the ten sessions in which she received injections of LSD, she and her sister were kept in two separate, darkened bedrooms, usually with some unknown person present and, sometimes, with her mother there.

"At times, I was so frightened by the hallucinations that I screamed and tried to escape from the room. I remember once actually reaching the hallway and being forcibly put back into the bedroom by my mother. I saw a wild array of images – nightmarish visions, occasionally provoking hysterical laughter, followed immediately by wracking sobs. I had no idea what was happening to me. It was terrifying," Marion said.

When the sessions were over, there was no "debriefing" nor any coun-seling.

"Why I did not refuse to participate after I first experienced it, I don't know. But as an adult and later as a professional medical ethicist, I recog-nized this lack of resistance as a function of childhood itself. Most chil-dren who are victims of parental abuse do not know how to resist. They

239

fear rejection by parents more than they fear the abuse, it seemed. The 'power differential' is huge between parents and children and the dependence on parents is virtually absolute. We were also, living in London at the time, away from our friends. My sister and I had been told not to talk about what we were doing. We were Catholics, obedient to parents, etc. Our father was a doctor, after all – it was hard to grasp that he would do harm to us or that our mother would. Children just don't think this way initially. A child's dependency usually means trusting one's parents or caregivers," she explained.

Marion said the impact of the LSD "unfolded gradually" after the sessions were over, including regular nightmares and "visions of crawling insects, horrible masks, etc. I couldn't sleep. I was afraid to shut my eyes. I became afraid of the dark. My parents were dismissive and unsympathetic. Their attitude was, in some ways, more disturbing to me than the experiments themselves because it meant that my parents had known full well that the experience would very likely be frightening – and hadn't cared."

The apathy of her parents led to a fracturing of their relationship with Marion. Two years later, her sister suffered a nervous breakdown while a freshman in college.

> I discovered that my parents were dishonest and unfeeling in ways that I could not comprehend. They told my sister and me never to talk about the LSD experiences, never to disclose what had happened in London. This further ruptured our relationship with them, a relationship that was, by then, permanently damaged. I was still dependent on them, however and so was my sister.
>
> I don't know the extent to which the LSD may have precipitated this. But my parents' response to what was probably a mild breakdown from which my sister could have recovered, was coercive and drastic. She had been asking questions about the LSD at this time. She was angry about it. We both were. We talked about it together, but I was afraid to confront our parents. My sister was not. The angrier she became, the more she was "diagnosed" as a "psychiatric" case and the more medication she was given. To this day, my sister is heavily medicated. She never fully recovered from that first episode.

Marion said that the "treatment" her sister was put through as a result "seemed to me to be a form of ongoing abuse and torture."

The status of their father and their uncle made it "impossible to expose them or go against them. Their reputations were more important to them than the health and well being of my sister." In turn, Marion simply left home as she learned more and more the ways her father had lied to her and prevented her from exposing the story. When she confronted him with the knowledge that LSD was tested as a weapon by the CIA, "he dismissed his participation by saying that it was an 'enlightening experience, like visiting an art gallery.' When I pointed out that this was not my experience as a child, he dismissed it, including the presumption that I must be a 'conspiracy theorist' to propose such a thing. At the age of 91, he finally admitted that it had perhaps not been a very good idea to subject my sister and me to LSD."

When Marion found Buckman working on the faculty of a medical school in the U.S., she said:

> I asked him what he thought about the ethics of using children in an LSD experiment. At first, he didn't seem to realize who I was. I identified myself as one of his "subjects" and gave him my business card as a Medical Ethicist and lawyer. He was clearly shocked, stood up, refused to talk to me and told me to leave his office. Shortly thereafter, I received a phone call from my father. His brother, the psychiatrist and colleague of Dr. Buckman, had been alerted to my impromptu visit. Subsequently, both my uncle and my father threatened me, saying they would make sure I lost my university faculty position if I disclosed anything publicly about the LSD experiments in London.
>
> "You will never work in bioethics again," they said. (Albarelli & Kaye 2010)

Another researcher who didn't shy away from experimenting on children was Jose Delgado, who was funded by the Office of Naval Intelligence for work on mind control. Delgado was notorious for the development of the Stimoceiver, a small electrode that could receive and transmit electrical signals within an animal's brain. The Stimoceiver was made famous when Delgado implanted the device into the cranium of a bull. Playing the matador, he stepped into a ring with the animal, which charged at him at full speed, then suddenly stopped and turned around. A quick push of a button on the researcher's remote control had stimulated a spot in the bull's brain to make him stand down (Ofgang 2017).

Delgado concluded that his projects "support the distasteful conclusion that motion, emotion and behavior can be directed by electrical forces. Humans can be controlled like robots by push buttons (U.S. Congress)."

The Yale professor applied his technique not only to animals, like monkeys and cats, but humans, as well – adults and children alike. In an 11-year-old, "[e]lectrical stimulation of the superior temporal convolution induced confusion about his sexual identity." The result was repeatable and exact. The child said, "I was thinking whether I was a boy or a girl," and "I'd like to be a girl." One stimulation caused the child to immediately talk about marrying the male interviewer (Delgado 1959).

A similar desire to marry the therapist was generated in two adult female patients as well. Another patient was made to giggle and joke with a therapist upon stimulation of their temporal lobe.

Delgado's colleagues, Vernon Mark and Frank Ervin, implanted electrodes into patients at Harvard hospitals, including an 18-year-old girl who could be made to smile or pound the wall in rage at the push of a button (Mark & Ervin 1976).

Another MKULTRA doctor involved in electrode experimentation was Dr. Robert G. Heath, Chairman of the Department of Psychiatry and Neurology at Tulane University. While his work on children was unknown, what was known was that he attempted to "cure" homosexuality through electro stimulation. He gave one gay man a box with which he could stimulate his own pleasure center via implanted electrode. The subject, dubbed B-19, stimulated himself 1,500 times in three hours (Horgan 2017).

"During these sessions, B-19 stimulated himself to a point that he was experiencing an almost overwhelming euphoria and elation, and had to be disconnected, despite his vigorous protests," Heath wrote.

Details were scarce on other programs involving children, but Alfred M. Freedman at New York Medical College experimented with LSD on "12 autistic, schizophrenic children who were attending a day school" (Albarelli 2011, Ch. 6). Allergist-turned-CIA-hypnotist Harold Abramson used LSD on six children between five and 14 years-old. It was also thought that Frank Olson "may have been connected to work connected to the testing of psychoactive drugs" by "government-sponsored physicians [in Norway], on people in Oslo mental institutions, including children who were classified as disenfranchised war babies," according to former Camp Detrick officials.

Chapter Twenty-one

Hypnosis as Mind Control

I was getting sleepy, lulled into a complacent gaze as they lowered me deeper into the collective unconscious. Back into the muck I went, watching exactly how they toyed with my mental apparatus.

From what I could tell, hypnotism was regarded with a great deal of skepticism by the general public. And I remembered in psychology class, there was about one paragraph – at most a page – devoted to the topic in my textbook. It was true that the psychological community agreed that not everyone was susceptible to the practice, but it also agreed that there were a minority of people who were particularly willing to enter trance states brought about by hypnotism.

One-time head of the Psychology Department at Colgate University, George "Esty" Estabrooks, thought of himself as a pioneer in the use of the technique for military applications. He believed that it was this minority of individuals who could be hypnotized into acting against their waking beliefs to commit crimes or reveal enemy secrets. "I can hypnotize a man, without his knowledge or consent, into committing treason against the United States," Estabrooks once said (Albarelli 2011, Ch. 4).

In 1939, Estabrooks performed an FBI experiment along with Milton Erickson, another prominent U.S. hypnotist who also did work for the CIA. The project appeared to demonstrate an uncanny ability to remember by subjects put into trance states. Erickson recounted the research this way:

> At the end of an hour they asked me to awaken Tommy, to bring him out of the trance, talk awhile, then put him back into the trance, and reorient him to that first trance. They had a program of exact movements, and they asked me … to have him visualize the entire procedure. Tommy gave a blow-by-blow account of the first hour, including the exact time in which so-and-so uncrossed his legs, when he re-crossed them, when he shifted his hat over to one side, when he lit the other fellow's cigarette, when the other fellow lit his cigarettes.

It seemed absurd at first, given the lack of credibility hypnosis was given in Psych 101, but it turned out that hypnosis was a crucial area of research under MKULTRA and, based on CIA documents, was more successful than I thought. Document 190691 stated that one subject was hypnotized to shoot another subject with an unloaded pistol:

> [Redacted] was then instructed (having previously expressed a fear of firearms in any fashion) that she would use every method at her disposal to awaken [redacted] (now in a deep hypnotic sleep) and failing in this, she would pick up a pistol nearby and fire it at [redacted]. She was instructed that her rage would be so great she would not hesitate to 'kill' [redacted] for failing to awake. [Redacted] carried out these suggestions to the letter, including firing the (unloaded pneumatic) pistol at [redacted] and then proceeding to fall into a deep sleep. After proper suggestions were made, both were awakened and expressed complete amnesia for the entire sequence. (1954)

Document 190527 stated that a subject was hypnotized into placing an incendiary device in an office desk drawer.

> [Redacted] being in a complete SI state at this time, was then told to open her eyes and was shown an electric timing device. She was informed that this timing device was an incendiary bomb and was then instructed how to attach and set the device. After [redacted] had indicated that she had learned how to set and attach the device, she was told to return to a sleep state and further instructed that upon concluding the aforementioned conversation, she would take the timing device which was in a briefcase and proceed to the ladies room.
>
> In the ladies room, she would be met by a girl whom she had never seen who would identify herself by the code word "New York." [Redacted] was then to show this individual how to attach and set the timing device and further instructions would be given the individual by [redacted] that the timing device was to be carried in the briefcase to [redacted] room, placed in the nearest empty electric-light plug and concealed in the bottom, left-hand drawer of [deleted] desk, with the device set for 82 seconds and turned on.
>
> [Redacted] was further instructed to tell this other girl that as soon as the device had been set and turned on, she was to take the briefcase, leave [redacted] room, go to the operations room and go to the sofa and enter a deep sleep state. [Redacted] was further instructed that after completion of instructing the other girl and the transferring to the other girl of the incendiary bomb, she was to return at once to the operations room, sit on the sofa, and go into a deep sleep state.

For a matter of record, immediately after the operation was begun it was noted that a member of the charforce was cleaning the floor in the ladies room and subsequently, both [redacted] and [redacted] had to be placed ... once again in a trance state and instructions changed from the ladies room to Room 3. It should be noted that even with the change of locale in the transfer point, the experiment was carried off perfectly without any difficulty or hesitation on the part of either of the girls. Each girl acted out their part perfectly, the device was planted and set as directed and both girls returned to the operations room, sat on the sofa and entered a deep sleep state. Throughout, their movements were easy and natural. (1951)

Things became even more disturbing when looking at document 140393, which cited interviews with an agency-contracted hypnotist who boasted of his ability to hypnotize women and have sex with them, a form of rape.

On July 2 1951 approximately 1:00 PM the instruction began with [redacted] relating to the student some of his sexual experiences. [Redacted] stated that he constantly used hypnotism as a means of inducing young girls to engage in sexual intercourse with him. [Redacted], a performer in [redacted] orchestra was forced to engage in sexual intercourse with [redacted] while under the influence of hypnotism. [Redacted] stated that he first put her into a hypnotic trance and then suggested to her that he was her husband and she desired sexual intercourse with him. [Redacted] further stated that many times while going home he would use hypnotic suggestion to have a girl turn around and talk to him and suggest sexual intercourse to him and that as a result of these suggestions he spent approximately five nights a week away from his home engaging in sexual intercourse. (1951)

These experiments, conducted under the guidance of the agency's Morse Allen in 1954, were designed to meet the ultimate goal of creating a programmed assassin, or Manchurian candidate, that could kill a political leader without having any memory of the event afterward and, therefore, would have been unable to divulge any connection to the CIA even under sever torture. In discussing Estabrooks idea for "the Agency utilizing] couriers that had been hypnotized," Allen told SRS Chief Paul Gaynor, "We [CIA] ourselves have carried out much more complex problems than this and in a general sense I agree that it is feasible" (Albarelli 2011, Ch. 4).

He added, "There is no proof whatsoever that the hypnosis cannot be broken by another competent hypnotist." When asked about whether or not an asset might be broken with third-degree interrogation and drugs, Allen said, "We don't know at this point in time, but we expect to have answers to this issue soon as a result of planned experiments that are soon to be carried out."

About a hypnotized individual's ability to be "made to commit murder," Allen said that the agency's experiments so far demonstrated "promising results," noting that "long ago raised problems of moral inhibitions blocking hypnosis" were not "that great a problem at all." When an "actual demonstration" was requested by Gaynor, Allen said, "there have already been a number of successful tests with [name redacted, but believed to be Milton H. Erickson] that showed religious and moral inhibitions were not problematic." Allen further added that an Agency employee had been made to "commit harm to fellow employees on a number of occasions … resulting in physical violence."

Allen said he'd meet with Estabrooks about his idea, but worried that the "things Estabrooks is proposing, he [Estabrooks] has never carried out in any fashion except in laboratory-type experiments."

Allen did not refer to having deployed these tactics in the field, though they may have been redacted, but one story regarding Jolly West suggested that it may have been a possibility.

West was one of the earliest researchers in this field, having worked with 83 prisoners of war returning from Korea. He and his team were thought to have reversed the brainwashing done to some of these men, including their claims that the U.S. had used biological weapons in the war. But it was his application of hypnosis in dealing with criminal interrogations that demonstrated the lengths West would go.

In 1954, three-year-old Chere Jo Horton went missing outside of Lackland Air Force Base sometime after midnight. A search party soon discovered a pair of her underwear hung from the door of a car. Alerted by shouting nearby, they found two construction workers who had been startled by an Air Force pilot who emerged from the darkness of the night bloody, shirtless and covered in scratches. The man was said to be "trance-like" and asked the crew, "What's going on here?" He didn't know where he was, how he had gotten there, and wasn't able to provide any explanation for the blood all over his person. The search party then found the body of the girl in an adjacent gravel pit, raped and with a broken neck (O'Neill 2020).

Authorities learned that the man was 29-year-old Jimmy Shaver, who had no history of violence or criminal record. Though he had been at the bar from which Horton was abducted, he'd left with a friend who said he wasn't drunk at the time. The friend did tell police, however, that Shaver seemed high on something. Military police ordered local authorities to hand him over, at which point he was examined by two doctors and an Air Force Marshall at the base, who determined that Shaver wasn't drunk. A doctor said during the eventual criminal case that Shaver "was not normal … he was very composed outside, which I did not expect him to be under these circumstances."

Shaver's wife saw him at the county jail, where he was sent for rape and murder, but she was completely unrecognizable to the prisoner. Additionally, in a statement to the police, Shaver said that in trying to remember the night, he could conjure up an image of a man with blond hair and tattoos that he believed was responsible for the crime. Upon a visitation from the Air Force Marshall, he contradicted his belief in the blonde-haired man by signing a statement accepting responsibility for the crime.

After two months, Shaver still didn't remember the event, at which point Jolly West, stationed at Lackland Air Force Base at the time, subjected him to two weeks of tests, including a visit to the crime scene, hypnosis, and the use of sodium pentothal. During a trance in which multiple doses of sodium pentothal was given, Shaver admitted to the murder, saying the girl had triggered repressed memories of his own sexual abuse at the hands of a cousin named "Beth Rainboat." After drinking at home on the night of the crime, Shaver "had visions of God, who whispered into his ear to seek out and kill the evil girl Beth."

Though his supposed cousin wasn't brought in for questioning, Shaver was brought to trial, with West testifying on behalf of the defense. West suggested under oath that the confession provided under the influence of the "truth serum" was the most valid, with the defense hoping to get Shaver acquitted based on a temporary insanity ruling. While West argued that the man was no longer insane, a newspaper said that, during the trial, Shaver "sat through the strenuous sessions like a man in a trance," without ever getting up to smoke, despite being a known chain-smoker.

Much like the therapists in the McMartin case, West had relied on leading questions while examining Shaver, which could only be exacerbated by the trance state. This included statements like: "Tell me about when you took your clothes off, Jimmy" and "After you took her clothes off what did you do?" to which Shaver replied, "I never did take her clothes off." West even pushed the memory repression angle, asking, "Jimmy, do you remember when something like this happened before?" According to Tom O'Neill, the middle third of the recording of this session wasn't captured, but when the recording returned, West said, "Shaver is crying. He has been confronted with all the facts repeatedly." He then questioned Shaver, saying, "Now you remember it all, don't you, Jimmy?" Shaver answers, "Yes, sir,"

According to one psychiatrist who worked with West during the sessions with Shaver, he had never been told that the airman had been hypnotized. In the end, Shaver proclaimed his innocence, but despite this, Shaver was convicted of murder and, the day he turned 33, was executed by electric chair.

O'Neill pointed out that the case of Shaver mirrored that of Jack Ruby in 1963. Upon shooting alleged JFK shooter Lee Harvey Oswald, Ruby had no memory of the event such that when he was tackled to the ground, he asked "What am I doing here? What are you guys jumping on me for?" In 1963, George Estabrooks argued that Lee Harvey Oswald and Jack Ruby "could very well have been performing through hypnosis."

Ultimately, Ruby testified that he must have committed the crime to defend the honor of Jackie Kennedy, but Ruby's lawyer, Melvin Belli, believed this was a "confabulation" to fill "a blank spot in his memory," saying that possible motivations for the crime "had been poured like water into the vacuum in his pathologically receptive memory and, once there, had solidified like cement."

Eventually, Jolly West was brought on Ruby's case as well and, after two days of time alone with the mobster-turned assassin, the doctor claimed that Ruby had had an "acute psychotic break." West wrote:

> Last night, the patient became convinced that all Jews in America were being slaughtered. This was in retaliation for him, Jack Ruby, the Jew who was responsible for "all the trouble." The delusions were so real that Ruby had crawled under the table to hide from the killers. He said he'd "seen his own brother tortured, horribly mutilated, castrated, and burned in the street outside the jail. He could still hear the screams. … The orders for this terrible "pogrom" must have come from Washington.

The judge in the case noted that the change in Ruby was extremely abrupt, particularly after numerous other psychiatrists had examined Ruby and determined that he was sane. He therefore called in an impartial doctor to make an assessment. Dr. William Beavers saw Ruby two days after West and agreed with the conclusion drawn by West, that the man had suffered a break. But Beavers also thought the mental disintegration occurred too rapidly, writing, "The possibility of a toxic psychosis could be entertained, but is considered unlikely because of the protected situation."

When asked by O'Neill if West would have been willing to brainwash Ruby, Dr. Jay Shurley, a good friend of Dr. West for 45 years and a colleague at Lackland, said, "I feel sort of disloyal to Jolly's memory, but I have to be honest with you, my gut feeling would be yes. He would be capable of that (O'Neill 2020)."

Another example of the lengths military programs had gone to – and potentially succeeded at – in creating programmed assassins was made public by U.S. Navy psychologist Lt-Commander Thomas Narut while speaking at a NATO conference in 1975. To train soldiers to cope with the stress of killing, increasingly disturbing films of violent murder and injuries were shown to the men in order to induce dissociation. The recruits for this program included not only submarine crews and paratroopers, but also convicted murderers from military prisons. When asked if he was implying that murderers were being trained as assassins, Narut said, "It's happened more than once." After a few weeks of processing at a lab in San Diego or Naples, these commandos were passed on to other departments, including to U.S. embassies around the world. Specifically, Narut mentioned the embassy in Athens during the end of the Yom Kippur War (*Sydney Morning Herald* 1975).

Even this *Clockwork Orange*-style treatment seemed mild compared to the ideas proposed by Estabrook, involving the deliberate splitting of a person's mind to compartmentalize information from the various identities formed:

> … multiple personality [can] be both caused and cured by hypnotism. Remember that war is a grim business. Suppose we deliberately set up that condition of multiple personality to further the ends of military intelligence. (McGowan 2004, Introduction)

He later put it this way:

> … everyone [can] be thrown into the deepest state of hypnotism by the use of what [I] termed the Russian method – no holds barred, deliberate disintegration of the personality by psychic torture…

> The subject might easily be left a mental wreck but war is a grim business. (McGowan 2004, Introduction)

But Estabrooks didn't just suggest that these types of procedures be carried out. He claimed to have performed them:

> We know that dual, and even multiple, personality can be both caused and cured by hypnotism.... Moreover ... the Dr. Jekyll and Mr. Hyde combination, is a very real one once it is established ... the key to creating an effective spy or assassin rests in splitting a man's personality, or creating a multiple personality, with the aid of hypnotism.... This is not science fiction.... I have done it. (McGowan 2004, Introduction)

A 1971 article by Estabrooks went into further detail:

> During World War II, I worked this technique with a vulnerable Marine lieutenant I'll call Jones. I split his personality into Jones A and Jones B. Jones A, once a "normal" working Marine, became entirely different. He talked communist doctrine and meant it. He was welcomed enthusiastically by communist cells, and was deliberately given a dishonorable discharge by the Corps and became a card-carrying party member. Jones B was the deeper personality, knew all the thoughts of Jones A, was a loyal American and was "imprinted" to say nothing during conscious phases. All I had to do was hypnotize the whole man, get in touch with Jones B, the loyal American, and I had a pipeline straight into the Communist camp. It worked beautifully. (Estabrooks 1971)

O'Neill uncovered a document in Jolly West's archive in which the good doctor said, "Certain patients requiring hypnosis in therapy, or suffering from dissociative disorders (trances, fugues, amnesias, etc.) might lend themselves to our experiments."

He also found a document from the University of Oklahoma indicating that West had been looking into "a number of dissociative phenomena" on humans "in the lab," including an exceptionally rare clinical disorder known as "latah," "a neurotic condition marked by automatic obedience (O'Neill 2020)."

Outside of West's work, I came across one MKULTRA subproject, number 136, interested in dissociative states and multiple personalities. According to document 17395 submitted for funding on July 9, 1951, the agency hoped to explore "[l]earning models will be instituted in which the subject will be rewarded or punished for his overall performance and reinforced in various ways – by being told whether he was right, by being told what the target was, with electric shock etc. … In other cases drugs and psychological tricks will be used to modify his attitudes. The experimenters will be particularly interested in disassociative states, from the abaissement de niveau mental to multiple personality in so-called mediums, and an attempt will be made to induce a number of states of this kind, using hypnosis" (1951).

Pin-up photo of Candy Jones for the Nov. 30, 1945 issue of *Yank*, the Army Weekly.
Public Domain

Candy Jon

YAN

CHAPTER TWENTY-TWO

THE MONARCH PROGRAM: THE CIA'S UNREAL PLAN TO CREATE SEX SLAVES

My story may be hard to believe for most, but here it is:

I spent the first 17 years of my life enslaved within a military-political trafficking ring located in Central Texas. There was extreme child sexual abuse, torture-based mind control, necrophilia, cannibalism and snuff. I spent the ages of 7-17 systematically fighting my way out and fighting for others who were enslaved. My parents were high-level members of the "hierarchy" who looked like everyday, upper middle class white suburban professionals to most. They were secretly sexually abusing me, selling and programming me and countless others for "hierarchy use." By day, I was trained to become an Ivy League educated debutante and astrophysicist. By night, I was trained as a "Snuff Queen" and a mind control programmer.

I have been "awake" for almost 4 years now and deeply deprogramming, am "no contact" with my family and anyone I know to be involved in organized abuse, and still working to break others free. Ask me anything (Reddit).

"What are you reading?" Cindy asked. "More CIA stuff?"

"Kinda." I wanted to tell her, but didn't want to traumatize her with the exact details. We had two young boys and, once motherhood kicked in, she became the best, most protective mother possible. Was reading about this my way of being a good dad? Probably not.

"What's it about?"

"Well, so there are some people who think that you can brainwash people with multiple personalities by programming each personality to behave differently."

"Oh. Hm. I could see that, I guess."

"Yeah, well there's this thing people think is related to MKULTRA, only with kids and it involves Satanism – "

"Honey, I've got to ask: are you becoming one of those Qanon people?"

My blood pressure began to rise as I sensed the conflict coming. I scraped at the thick, gelatinous wall of the inner chamber, hands becoming coated in the pink, translucent ooze. The stuff embedded itself beneath my fingernails as I dug away at it. Sweating, I saw a small opening in the chrysalis, I was reinvigorated with purpose and kept hacking until large chunks of the mass began to fall away.

On the other side, I immediately saw them: rows upon rows of children in cages lining a dank concrete room. It was eerily silent, except for the sound of my soft footsteps padding the hard, stone floor. As I passed by them, I realized why. They were entranced. Conditioned to no longer scream or even utter a whimper. This was hell. This was Monarch.

From what I could tell, one of the earliest mentions of the Monarch Project came from a 1992 lecture by Dr. Corey Hammond titled "Hypnosis in MPD: Ritual Abuse" at the Fourth Annual Eastern Regional Conference on Abuse and Multiple Personality, in Alexandria, Virginia (Hammond 1992). This speech would come to be known among Monarch researchers as "the Greenbaum Speech."

According to Hammond, as a part of the CIA's Operation Paperclip to recruit Nazis for the U.S. rockets and weapons program, the agency also rescued doctors conducting mind control research in the camps. Among that group was a teenage Hasidic Jew with knowledge of Cabala who'd managed to survive by collaborating with his captors.

When the Americans came to liberate the camps, this prisoner-turned-torturer was brought over to the U.S., where he Americanized his surname from Greenbaum to Green and became a doctor. He then assisted the CIA in conducting mind control experiments on children to break their psyches and create multiple identities, within which a variety of programs could be installed.

The method by which this programming would be installed involved traumatizing children as young as possible in the most frightening ways possible continuously throughout their young lives. The evolutionary need for these kids to maintain attachments to their caregivers while also suffering abuse from those protectors and nurturers would result in a fracturing of identity. The resulting multiple personality disorder, later referred to as dissociative identity disorder (DID) was leveraged for multi-level programming. It was possible, according to Hammond, to hypnotize individual alternate identities (often called "alters" in the DID community) such that each one could execute different programs when called up by the practitioner/torturer.

In his Greenbaum Speech, Hammond told the audience about a time in which he encountered another therapist dealing with a victim of Dr. Green:

> In the middle of talking about some of this all the color drained out of one social worker's face and she obviously had a reaction and I asked her about and she said, 'I'm working with a five-year-old boy,' and she said, 'Just in the last few weeks he was saying something about a Dr. Green.' I went on a little further and I mentioned some of these things and she just shook her head again. I said, 'What's going on?' She said, 'He's been spontaneously telling me about robots and about Omega.' I think you will find variations of this and that they've changed it, probably every few years and maybe somewhat regionally to throw us off in various ways but that certain basics and fundamentals will probably be there. I have seen this in people up into their forties including people whose parents were very, very high in the CIA, other sorts of things like that. I've had some that were originally part of the Monarch Project which is the name of the government Intelligence project.

Notorious Monarch "victim" Cathy O'Brien described her introduction to the program:

> Soon after we moved, my father was reportedly caught sending kiddie porn through the U.S. mail. It was a bestiality film of me with my Uncle Sam O'Brien's Boxer dog, Buster. My Uncle Bob, also implicated in manufacturing the porn, out of apparent desperation informed my father of a U.S. Government Defense Intelligence Agency TOP SECRET Project to which he was privy. This was Project Monarch. Project Monarch was a mind-control operation which was "recruiting" multigenerational incest abused children with Multiple Personality Disorder for its genetic mind-control studies. I was a prime "candidate," a "chosen one." My father seized the opportunity as it would provide him immunity from prosecution. In the midst of the pandemonium that ensued, Jerry Ford arrived at our house with the evidence in hand for a meeting with my father.
>
> "Is Earl home?" he called to my mother, who nervously stood behind the screen door, hesitating to let him in.

"Not yet," my mother replied, her voice shaking.

"He should have been home from work by now – I know he's expecting you."

"That's OK." Ford turned his attention to me. I was standing outside on the front porch, and he crouched down to my level. Patting the large, brown envelope containing the confiscated porn tucked under his arm he said, "You like doggies, huh?"

…Not long after that my father was flown to Boston for a two-week course at Harvard on how to raise me for this off-shoot of MK-Ultra Project Monarch, When he returned from Boston, my father was smiling and pleased with his new knowledge of what he termed "reverse psychology."

This equates to "satanic reversals," and involves such play-on-words as puns and phrases that stuck in my mind like, "You earn your keep, and I'll keep what you earn." He presented me with a commemorative charm bracelet of dogs, and my mother with the news that they "would be having more children" to raise in the project. (I now have two sisters and four brothers ranging from age 16 to 37 who are still under mind control.) My mother complied with my father's suggestions, mastering the art of language manipulation. For example, when I could not snap my own pajama top to the bottoms in a childish effort to keep my father out of them, I asked my mother, "please snap me." She did. she would snap her forefingers against my skin in a stinging manner. The pain I felt was psychological as this proved to me once again that she had no intention of protecting me from my father's sexual abuse.

Also in keeping with his government-provided instructions, my father began working me like the legendary Cinderella. I shoveled fireplace ashes, hauled stacked firewood, raked leaves, shoveled snow, chopped ice, and swept – "because," my father said, "your little hands fit so nicely around the rake, mop, shovel, and broom handles."

By this time, my father's sexual exploitation of me included prostitution to his friends, local mobsters and Masons, relatives, Satanists, strangers, and police officers. When I wasn't being worked to physical exhaustion, filmed pornographically, prostituted, or engaged in incest abuse, I dissociated into books. I had learned to read at the young age of four due to my photographic memory which was a natural result of MPD/DID.

Government researchers involved in MK-Ultra Project Monarch knew about the photographic memory aspect of MPD/DID, of course, as well as other resultant "super human" characteristics.

Visual acuity of an MPD/DID is 44 times greater than that of the average person. My developed unusually high pain threshold, plus compartmentalization of memory were "necessary" for military and covert operations applications. Additionally, my sexuality was primitively twisted from infancy. This programming was appealing and useful to perverse politicians who believed they could hide their actions deep within my memory compartments, which clinicians refer to as personalities.

Immediately after my father's return from Boston, I was routinely prostituted to then Michigan State Senator Guy VanderJagt. VanderJagt later became a U.S. Congressman and eventually chairman of the Republican National Congressional Committee that put George Bush in the office of President. I was prostituted to VanderJagt after numerous local parades which he always participated in, at the Mackinac Island Political Retreat, and in my home state of Michigan, among other places.

My Uncle Bob helped my father decorate my bedroom in red, white, and blue paneling and American flags. He provided assistance in scrambling my mind according to Project Monarch methodologies. Fairy tale themes were used to confuse fantasy with reality, particularly Disney stories and the Wizard of Oz, which provided the base for future programming.

I had personalities for pornography, a personality for bestiality, a personality for incest, a personality for withstanding the horrendous psychological abuse of my mother, a personality for prostitution, and the rest of "me" functioned somewhat "normaily" at school. My "normal" personality provided a cover for the abuse I was enduring, but best of all it had hope – hope that there was somewhere in the world where people did not hurt each other (O'Brien & Phillips).

While Cathy O'Brien was probably the most well-known of the sources for Monarch lore, Hammond may have been the first to lay the groundwork. The name "Dr. Green" came up in numerous Monarch stories, as did the specific programming Hammond described, suggesting that the same torturer or network of torturers were utilizing the same routine.

Alphas appear to represent general programming, the first kind of things put in. Betas appear to be sexual programs. For example, how to perform oral sex in a certain way, how to perform sex in rituals, having to do with producing child pornography, directing child pornography, prostitution. Deltas are killers trained in how to kill in ceremonies. There'll also be some self-harm stuff mixed in with that, assassination and killing. Thetas are called psychic killers. You know, I had never in my life heard those two terms paired together. I'd never heard the words "psychic killers" put together, but when you have people in different states, including therapists, ring and asking, "What is Theta," and patients say to them, "Psychic killers," it tends to make one a believer that certain things are very systematic and very widespread. This comes from their belief in psychic sorts of abilities and powers, including their ability to psychically communicate with 'mother' including their ability to psychically cause somebody to develop a brain aneurysm and die. It also is a more future-oriented kind of programming. Then there's Omega. I usually don't include that word when I say my first question about this or any part inside that knows about Alpha, Beta, Delta, Theta because Omega will shake them even more. Omega has to do with self-destruct programming. Alpha and Omega, the beginning and the end. This can include self-mutilation as well as killing themselves programming. Gamma appears to be system-protection and deception programming which will provide misinformation to you, try to misdirect you, tell you half-truths, protect different things inside (Hammond 1992)."

How would Hammond discover this programming? It was determined that, because it was installed through a combination of torture, drugs, and hypnosis, hypnosis was the best way to uncover it. He would put DID patients into a trance and ask them to tap their fingers to answer "yes" or "no" to questions. This meant that, even if the patient voiced an answer, their hands might answer differently, representing unconscious programming.

The way that I would inquire as to whether or not some of this might be there would be with ideomotor finger-signals. After you've set them up I would say, "I want the central inner core of you to take control of the finger-signals." Don't ask the unconscious mind. The case where you're inquiring about ritual abuse, that's for the central inner core. The core is a Cult-created part. "And I want that central inner core of you to take control of this hand of these finger-signals and what it has for the yes-finger to float up. I want to ask the inner core of you is there any part of you, any part of Mary," that's the host's name, "who knows anything about Alpha, Beta, Delta, or Theta." If you get a Yes, it should raise a red flag that you might have someone with formal intensive brainwashing and

programming in place. I would then ask and say, "I want a part inside who knows something about Alpha, Beta, Delta, and Theta to
come up to a level where you can speak to me and when you're here
say, 'I'm here.'"

Hammond reiterated that many patients had been programmed by
cults, the mafia, and the U.S. government. "The interesting thing is how
many people have described the same scenario and how many people that
we have worked with who have had relatives in NASA, in the CIA and in
the Military, including very high-ups in the Military," Hammond said.

Of course, Hammond's claims appeared absurd, possibly inspired by
science fiction. However, the things he discussed became widespread
enough to inform a niche group of academics and therapists within psychology. I looked through journal articles from the 1990s, when SRA was
still a hot topic, and found a number dedicated to this torture-based programming.

In the Sept./Oct. 1991 of *The California Therapist*, David W. Neswald,
M.A. M.F.C.C., along with Catherine Gould, Ph.D. and Vicki Graham-Costain, Ph.D., published an article titled, "Common Programs
Observed in Survivors of Satanic Ritualistic Abuse," in which the authors
discuss the various ways in which DID patients could be trained to enact
certain behaviors, such as self-harm, suicide, assassination, reporting to
their cults, and more.

At the The Sixth Western Clinical Conference on Multiple Personality
and Dissociation in Irvine, California in 1993, John D. Lovern, Ph.D. discussed a novel type of training people with DID he called "spin programming." Based on interviews with seven DID patients, Lovern described
how their tormentors would use a "combination of physical spinning,
cognitive and imagery training, and repetition and practice aimed at creating an internal multi-alter spinning "mechanism" that can transmit the
pain or affective components of numerous traumatic memories simultaneously to large groups of targeted alters." The goal, according to Lovern,
was to "spread effects such as pain, painful emotions, and other feelings
or urges globally throughout a patient's personality system for purposes
of either designing and building a young victim's personality system, or
harassing older victims and disrupting psychotherapy."

However, academia on this topic continued decades later. In a 2011
book titled *Ritual Abuse and Mind Control: The Manipulation of Attachment Needs*, published by Karnac Books, Ellen P. Lacter was the author

of a chapter on "Torture-based mind control: psychological mechanisms and psychotherapeutic approaches to overcoming mind control," in which she specifically called out the CIA as operating a program dedicated to mind control through the creation and manipulation of DID.

Lacter defined "torture-based mind control as the systematic application of (1) acute torture, including pain, terror, drugs, electroshock, sensory deprivation, oxygen deprivation, cold, heat, spinning, brain stimulation, and near-death, and (2), conditioning, including coercive hypnosis, directives, illusions (staged tricks, film, stories), spiritual threats, manipulation of attachment needs, and classical, operant, and fear conditioning, to coerce victims to form altered mental states, including (a) hyper-attentive blank slate (tabula rasa) mental states that arise spontaneously in response to perceived threat to physical survival, and are completely attuned to external stimuli, ready to do whatever is needed to survive; (b) self-states that spontaneously form in response to threat to psychic survival, that is, levels of mental anguish that exceed the tolerance of all previously existing ego states, and that are mentally registered apart (dissociated) from previously existing ego-states; (c) ego-states that develop more gradually through conditioning, all three of which are subjected to 'programmer' strategies to define, control, and 'install' within them perceptions, beliefs, fear, pain, directives, information, triggers, and behaviours, to force victims to do, feel, think, and perceive things for the purposes of the programmer, including execution of acts that violate the victims' volition, principles, and instinct for self-preservation, and to cause ego-states that usually have executive control of mental functions (the host, front, or apparently normal personality) to have no conscious memory for the torture, conditioning, programming, controlled ego-states, or executed programmed behaviours."

Some of the strongest corroborative evidence for torture-based mind control I found was a 2007 Internet survey in which 1471 people from at least forty countries responded as survivors to the Extreme Abuse Survey (EAS). This included a list of reported mind control phenomena:

"1. Torture to induce the formation of receptive/programmable dissociated self-states. Of 1012 EAS respondents who replied to the item: 'My perpetrator(s) deliberately created/programmed dissociative states of mind (such as alters, personalities, ego-states) in me,' 640 (63%) said "Yes."

2. Torture to influence the host with no conscious awareness. The host experiences unexplained behavioural compulsions to perform

particular behaviours, and programmed self-states take executive control to follow programmed directives, unbeknown to the host.

3. The perception of "structures," that is, mental representations of objects, usually inanimate, in the body or internal landscape in the mind. Often-reported structures include buildings, walls, containers, grids, computers, and devices of torture. Structures often serve organizational purposes for programmers, such as containing groups of self-states that serve particular functions, storing files of information, serving as barriers (walls, caps, seals) to separate groups of self-states, and hiding deeper levels of programming and structures. Dissociated selfstates perceive themselves as trapped behind, within, or attached to structures, often reliving the pain, suffocation, electroshock, etc., used to "install" the structure.

4. Perceived explosive devices, electroshock wires and devices, and vials capable of releasing toxins and drugs, in the body of specific self-states, or in the internal landscape, to control behaviour.

5. Perceived internal monitoring devices to watch or 'read' and transmit thoughts, e.g., all-seeing eyes, microphones, and microchips.

6. The perception of internal programmers, abusers, demons, and human spirits, to watch and control the victim. Of 996 EAS respondents who replied to the item: "Perpetrators have on at least one occasion made me believe that external entities/spirits/demons had taken over my body," 530 (53%) said "Yes."

1000 respondents answered the item "Secret government-sponsored mind control experiments were performed on me as a child." Of those, 257 (26%) said "Yes." 219 of those 257 claimed to have seen their abusers wearing white doctors' coats (Lacter 2011).

Outside of the descriptions by these academics, there were numerous people claiming to be survivors of this sort of abuse as programming.

THE MONARCH VICTIMS?

Before Hammond invoked the word "Monarch" in his Greenbaum speech, there was a precedent for the type of mind control he described. The earliest example may have been that of Candy Jones, a pinup model born to a wealthy family that she claimed subjected her to physical and sexual abuse. Passed from relative to relative, she was reportedly kept in dark rooms and developed an imaginary friend named "Arlene" to cope with these times (Bain 1976).

Achieving runner up status in the Miss America pageant, Jones was able to become a leading pinup model, landing on the cover of 11 different magazines in just one month in 1943. Between this time and her eventual claims of mind control, Jones married, had three sons, divorced, opened a modeling school, and joined NBC's *Monitor*, a weekend radio news show.

On New Year's Eve of 1972, she married radio host Long John Nebel after dating for just one month. She soon became the co-host of his overnight talk show dedicated to the paranormal and other strange topics. Nebel claimed that, not long into their marriage, he noticed drastic mood swings in his new wife, almost an entirely different personality.

Several weeks into their marriage, Jones had supposedly told her husband that she worked for the FBI and would sometimes have to leave the city without saying why. He wondered if this alternate personality had anything to do with the FBI trips. Upon hypnotizing his wife, he discovered that she had a separate identity called "Arlene." While in these trances, she went on to reveal that she'd been programmed by the CIA at colleges on the West Coast.

The model-turned-radio-host said that she had some recollection outside of hypnosis, claiming that a retired army general she knew from her days touring with the USO had initiated the work in 1960 by asking to use her modeling school's address to receive some mail. At one point, she was asked to carry a letter to a Dr. Jensen in Oakland, California. To her surprise, the doctor happened to be the same man who treated her for an illness while on her 1945 USO tour in the Philippines. Jensen and a colleague, Dr. "Marshall Burger," said they'd provide ample sums of money for her to work with them, which she agreed to due to her desire to keep her sons in private school.

Jensen reportedly crafted "Arlene" as a personality while Jones was under hypnosis. She would then act as a courier, traveling to locations like Taiwan to deliver messages. Jones said that she was put through extreme torture to determine how well the Arlene identity would hold. She even believed a 1970 USO trip to South Vietnam may have tried to utilize Arlene to free prisoners of war held captive in North Vietnam.

In 1976, the couple's story was published in Donald Bain's *The Control of Candy Jones*, from Playboy Press. Because Nebel had a reputation for playing practical jokes, some members of his radio audience were hesitant to believe their claims. However, Bain had some evidence beyond their tale to provide some credibility to the story. For instance, colleagues of Jones from her modeling school days noted that she did take business trips that seemed to lack any actual business performed. Bain also came across a passport for an "Arlene Grant" in which Jones was pictured "in a dark wig and dark makeup," though the former model claimed not to remember dressing for the portrait. The couple additionally had an answering message left on their home line on July 3, 1973 that played:

"This is Japan Airlines calling on oh-three July at 4.10 p.m. ... Please have Miss Grant call 759-9100 ... she is holding a reservation on Japan Airlines Flight 5 for the sixth of July, Kennedy to Tokyo, with an option on to Taipei. This is per Cynthia that we are calling."

Jones called the number and requested to speak with Cynthia, only to be told there was no Cynthia at that number. She also reportedly provided a letter to her lawyer, William Williams, in the case of her death or disappearance, but was unable to tell him what was inside. Bain said that the lawyer verified the existence of this letter.

Jones would be the first in a series of individuals claiming to have survived CIA mind control experiments with similar stories. Claudia Mullen testified at a 1995 hearing from the Advisory Committee on Human Radiation Experiments. She referenced a Dr. Greene, who was Dr. L. Wilson Greene, Technical Director of the Chemical Corps at the Chemical and Radiological Laboratories at Edgewood Arsenal, where much of the MKULTRA research was headquartered.

Mullen claimed that she was first sexually abused by her adoptive mother from age two-and-a-half to seven before she was taken by the CIA and experimented on for almost 30 years. Much of the abuse she described was along the lines of the "torture-based programming" discussed by Hammond, Lacter and others. She said that, through her programming, she developed a photographic memory and that the doctors were also careless in identifying themselves.

"Dr. L. Wilson Greene, who claimed to have received 50 million dollars to his army chemical and radiological corporation as part of TSD (Technical Science Division) of the CIA, once described to my monitor, Dr. Charles Brown, that children were used as subjects because they were more fun to work with, and cheaper too. They needed lower profile subjects than soldiers or government people, so only young, willing females will do. Besides, he said, "I like scaring them; they and the agency think I'm a God" – creating subjects and experiments for whatever deviant purposes SID (Dr. Sidney Gottlieb) and James (Dr. James Hamilton) can think up," Mullen testified.

She also referenced The Human Ecological Society, a front for the CIA established as a conduit for agency funds to psychological and socio-logical research, as well as Dr. John, Dr. Cameron, Dr. Robert G. Heath, Richard Helms, Dr. Gottlieb, George White, Morse Allen, Dr. Stephen Aldrich, and Martin Orne. Her testimony included details of physical, emotional and sexual abuse by a variety of methods. She said:

> By the next year, when I turned nine, I was sent to a place in Mary-land called Deep Creek Caverns to learn how to "sexually please men." I was taught also how to coerce them into talking about themselves, and then I had to prove my accurate recall. Richard Helms, Dr Gottlieb, George White and Morse Allen all planned on entrapping as many officials, agency targets, heads of academic institutions and foundations. Later, if the funding started to dwin-dle or the head of the agency, John McCone, decided he could no longer tolerate children being tortured, abused and shot full of bi-ologicals and radiation, then he would be forced to continue the projects at all cost. I was to become a regular little "spy" for them after that summer, entrapping many unwitting men with the use of hidden cameras. I was only nine when this began (Mullen 1996).

The next year, in 1996, was when Cathy O'Brien self-published her book *Trance Formation of America* co-written with her husband Mark Phillips. The story was very similar to that of Mullen, told in explicit and disturbing detail. She pointed to a long list of prominent people as being involved in her abuse as a trained spy, drug mule and sex worker. These included George H.W. Bush, Gerald Ford, Senator Robert Byrd, Pierre Trudeau, and Hillary Clinton, among others. Much of her later abuse oc-curred under the cover of the country music circuit while she was sup-posedly married to ventriloquist and stage hypnotist Alex Houston. One of her programmers was supposedly Michael Aquino and at times in-volved advanced technology. Other Monarch victims she encountered in her life included country singer Loretta Lynn, Dodger pitcher Fernando Valenzuala, and comedian Jack Benny.

"Bush apparently activated a hologram of the lizard-like 'alien,' which provided the illusion of Bush transforming like a chameleon before my eyes," she wrote. "In retrospect, I understand that Bush had been pains-takingly careful in positioning our seats in order that the hologram's effec-tiveness be maximized." This was different from another scene in which Bush was high on heroin "kissing the sky" and repeating to his friend, "You look just like Elmer Fudd!"

It wasn't until her future husband, Mark Phillips, rescued her and her daughter, that she was able to get freed from her life of sex slavery. Phillips was supposedly a Department of Defense subcontractor who was involved in MKULTRA and helped "deprogram" O'Brien (O'Brien & Phillips 2001).

Then there was Paul Bonacci, the Franklin scandal victim with DID. At age 22, Bonacci was imprisoned at Lincoln Correctional Center when Franklin investigator Gary Caradori found him. In November 1989, Bonacci was charged with two counts of sexual assault on a thirteen and nine year old boy. He said that, just before he was imprisoned, someone told him not to talk to anyone and stay away from the Franklin investigation.

Bonacci's court-appointed psychiatrist Dr. Beverley Mead was asked to examine him to see if he was a "mentally disordered sex offender." After six interviews that ended in April 1990, she determined that that wasn't the case. Instead she diagnosed him with Multiple Personality Disorder, saying that he had "20 or more alternates, several of them well-formed, as much or more so, than Paul himself…." Each alter had an "individual identity, a different name, and certain individual characteristics." Some alters were homosexual, others heterosexual. She even learned that there were those that were colorblind.

She concluded that the "principal personality Paul has no wish to molest children, is quite religious, and is not inclined to have homosexual interests." Bonacci, according to the doctor, was previously unaware of having more than one identity. Mead wrote, "[H]e is still mystified by the situation and finds it difficult to accept."

Mead determined that Bonacci's childhood was in line with the theories that MPD was caused by a "very disorganized childhood," featuring "severe and often repeated abuse." As the second youngest of six children, Bonacci saw his parents separate when he was young and, as a result, did not see his biological father during this time. His stepfather would beat him and his siblings and, according to Mead, even chop the children's toys with an axe. His mother and stepfather got a divorce after she experienced physical abuse and she remarried to someone who ignored Bonacci altogether, but did not beat him.

In the meantime, Bonacci was continuously abused sexually by a neighbor at the age of six. His complaints to his mother and stepfather were dismissed. By the third grade, Bonacci started blanking out on things that he had done, which Mead described as "the first experiences of having an alternate personality takeover."

Around nine- or ten-years old, Bonacci's peers introduced him to a playground where he could make money from pedophiles in exchange for sexual acts. Mead determined that his main personality did not experience pleasure from this. It was at this point that he entered a life of drugs and prostitution, and around age 12, satanism entered the picture as well. Mead wrote that he went to "a lot of parties where he served as a young male prostitute."

The psychiatrist concluded her report by saying, "Without treatment, it is conceivable (and this is probably what happened in the contact with the little boy) that if placed in an unusual circumstance, an alternate personality might temporarily take over and commit such an act of fondling, although it is also true that such behavior will be stopped, or at least quickly checked, by another alternate personality which would disapprove of such behavior. It all gets quite complicated" (DeCamp 2005).

Numerous others had also come forward with stories like Bonacci, O'Brien, and Mullen's ranging from similarly self-published authors like Carol Rutz to random YouTube users with less than one hundred views. In addition to abuse by the CIA, the mob, satanic cults, or groups like the KKK from a very young age, some stories discussed so-called bloodlines or family histories of DID, child abuse, and sex slavery. For instance, O'Brien claimed that, due to a family history of child sexual abuse dating back multiple generations, she was genetically predisposed for Monarch programming. Others modified the Greenbaum story, explaining that Dr. Green was actually a code name for the Nazi Angel of Death, Dr. Josef Mengele.

Wandering through the noosphere and considering the horrors of human imagination, I wondered if what I had encountered could have been authentic. After all, MKULTRA was certainly real and it did involve experimenting on children. Child trafficking had been a blackmail tool of intelligence agencies for decades. The elite even seemed to have dabbled in the occult on occasion, though the extent to which satanic ritual abuse was involved was difficult to determine. There was plenty of background to suggest that, if it were possible to create mind-controlled sex slaves from children at a very young age for intelligence purposes, the CIA likely wouldn't have been averse to it.

CHAPTER TWENTY-THREE

THE REALITY OF DISSOCIATIVE
IDENTITY DISORDER

At the core, was this concept of multiple personalities. The possibility of splitting children's personalities, hypnotizing them and brainwashing individual alters rested on the question of whether or not DID was real in the first place.

Included in the Diagnostic and Statistical Manual of Mental Disorders (DSM-5), DID was a disturbance of identity in which at least two enduring identities controlled a person's behavior at different times. Most often, the dominant identity (or "host") would not remember some events that took place while an alter was in control. Individuals with DID could have as few as two identities or over 100 (the average is about 10), with different mannerisms, genders, and preferred styles of dress. Some could even be different species – even elves or aliens. In some cases, alters could have physical differences, including which hand was dominant, eyeglass prescriptions and even allergies. Those with DID may not have been aware that they had alternate identities, but suffered lapses in memory, interacting with strangers that recognized them, ending up in locations with no memory of getting there, and buying things they had no memory of buying. Based on that criteria, DID was said to occur in about 1% of the population (Bhandari 2020).

Surprisingly, there wasn't exactly a scientific consensus on whether or not DID was an authentic disorder or a miscategroization of something more common, such as borderline personality disorder. In part, the reason for the controversy related to the concept of "repressed memories," specifically, memories that had been unconsciously blocked from conscious perception due to the trauma associated with those experiences.

In turn, there were two broad schools of thought on DID: 1.) the "iatrogenic theory" that DID was a miscategorization related to faulty therapeutic techniques that led patients to disclose false memories that they believed to be real, formerly repressed memories, combined with pop culture phenomena (media about people with DID, etc.) that drove the ways that a patient expressed their mental illness (Brown et al 1999), and, 2.), the "trauma theory" that DID was an authentic disorder in which traumatic experiences, usually repeated abuse at a very young age, caused one's identity to fragment, resulting in the inability of all aspects of one's identity to access memories from other aspects (Apter 2019). As a method of dealing with the extreme trauma, these individuals were thought to dissociate before a connected sense of identity could be formed and, instead, develop alternate identities. It was thought that there was a genetic predisposition to dissociating, combined with disorganized or disrupted attachment caused by one's environment. The trauma theory for the existence of DID was the same dynamic that "Monarch survivors" claimed they were subjected to.

According to skeptics, the diagnosis of multiple personality disorder (MPD), as it was first called, gained serious attention with the publication of the 1973 bestselling book *Sybil,* in which psychiatrist Cornelia Wilbur discussed her treatment of a "multiple," a patient named Shirley Mason. Pop culture around the topic then boomed.

However, as much attention as the case brought to MPD as a disorder, *Sybil* was thought not to be based on a genuine diagnosis. Psychiatrist and hypnotherapist Herbert Spiegel said he saw Mason when Wilbur was out of town and the patient asked him if he wanted her to switch personalities. She was relieved when he said no, telling Spiegel that Wilbur asked her to express alternate personalities in sessions for therapeutic purposes (Paris 2012).

The concept of MPD had a life of its own, however, and the incidence rate of the disorder appeared to grow at a surprising rate. A pioneer in the field was Dr. Bennett Braun, who claimed to have encountered his first case of MPD in 1974 (Hanson 1998). By 1980, he claimed to have treated 70 cases, before he'd even completed his residency or become board certified. In 1984, Braun co-founded the International Society for the Study of Dissociation (ISSD), a professional group dedicated to the study of MPD. By 1986, his book *The Treatment of Multiple Personality Disorder* became a textbook for the specialty. That same year, with his colleague Roberta Sachs, Braun launched the first psychiatric unit dedicated to treating patients with MPD, located at Rush-Presbyterian-St. Luke's Medical Center in Chicago, Illinois.

There they would take in such patients as Patricia Burgus, who entered the unit as a 29-year-old mother with 20 different personalities, which included the low self-esteem "Garbage" and the determined and courageous "Super Kathy." With a daily combination of hypnosis and sedatives, the number of personalities burgeoned to 300 as she recalled her life being raised in a satanic cult. The memories that came back to her were so horrific that she eventually recalled her Roman Catholic father, manager of a Coca-Cola plant, grinding human remains into hamburger meat and serving them at a family picnic.

Over the course of six years in treatment, more than two of which were spent as an in-patient in Braun's ward, Burgus broke off ties with her family, tried to kill herself, and lost custody of her children, who spent three years in the hospital for MPD themselves. It wasn't until she was an outpatient in 1992, on lower doses of medication and free from hypnosis, that she believed these memories to be false. A year later, she sued Braun for malpractice and ultimately accepted a settlement of $10.6 million.

The story began when, after suffering postpartum depression, Burgus saw psychiatric social worker Ann-Marie Baughman. When she had a false pregnancy in 1984 and started to refer to herself and the baby as "we," Baughman diagnosed Burgus as having MPD and began labeling her various moods, such as "Super Slow" for when she couldn't make a decision and "Religious One" for when she felt hopeful. The therapist began to put her through role-playing that exacerbated the diagnosis, telling Burgus to imagine how she would behave as a child if she were upset, including how she would sound. This led Burgus to use a child's voice, which Baughman responded with, "That's how Little Patty always wanted to talk."

Soon, the patient began to use different voices and mannerisms for each personality. As these identities began to show up outside of therapy, Burgus's husband, Mike, believed they were individual personalities, too. Apparently, Baughman had rejected the opinions of six different psychiatrists who disagreed with her diagnosis. Nevertheless, the Burgus family accepted it as an explanation for her issues.

After seeking an in-patient solution to her illness, she found herself at Rush hospital. Key to Braun's treatment was a technique that bore a striking similarity to that of Hammond of Greenbaum Speech fame. While under hypnotic trance, the patient would use different fingers to mean "yes," "no," and "stop" so that, as a patient was asked certain questions under hypnosis, the fingers would give one answer even while the patient provided a different answer vocally. This signified an alter personality disagreeing, so that Braun could probe further.

After two years in the program, Burgus was allowed to leave the facility for half the day, and was also on medications prescribed to her by Braun:

a hypertension medicine he thought would help her anxiety called Inder-al, and an addictive sleeping medicine called Halcion. While suffering from nightmares, sluggishness and on a dose of Inderal ten times that used to treat hypertension, she began to speak about her involvement in a satanic cult.

Things spun out from there, as she recalled acts of cannibalism, her family's history of satanism dating back to the 1600s, and her rape, mur-der, torture and eating of 2,000 children per year. She believed herself to be the "high priestess" for a nine-state network of satanists. In addition to tales of being raped by tigers and gorillas at the zoo, as well as stories about sleeping with JFK, she said she'd taught her young sons how to commit ritual human sacrifice.

When out of Braun's treatment, she believed all of this to have been implanted by the therapist through a combination of hypnosis, meds, and leading questions. In some cases, when Braun thought sessions would trigger a violent reaction, such as when recovering memories of ritual abuse, he would have her locked in restraints, sometimes for 24 hours. Some of the details for her memories, according to post-recovery Burgus, came from absorbing the stories recalled by other MPD patients in the ward. They would recall to one another their histories of violent satanic rituals, thus contributing to even more graphic details to their peers' con-fabulations.

Burgus believed her recollections with such fervor that she cut off ties with her parents, claimed that she'd abused her own children, and drew up lists of cult murderers she knew from her home state of Iowa. Her hus-band couldn't fathom how she'd managed to participate in all of this cult activity from a purely logical standpoint, saying, "I couldn't figure out how, time-wise, she could do it, and I didn't think she was capable of do-ing it. But [Braun] told me a personality did it, and if she didn't cooperate, then our children would have been murdered. [Braun] had explanations for everything."

Braun also seemed to believe it, as he'd even taken a barbecued burg-er Mike brought in from a Burgus family picnic and had a lab test it for the presence of human meat. The results, according to Braun, were in-conclusive, despite a lack of human proteins discovered in the burger. In turn, Braun requested raw meat used by Pat's mother to make the burgers, which she conceded to, though she didn't believe that her daughter had MPD. The sample, according to Braun, was lost in the lab, however.

At another point, Braun asked Burgus to strip naked and requested that one of her child alters draw the satanic symbols they'd encountered on her body. When Pat came to, she was covered in sharpie triangles and squiggles. He then presented pictures of her nude, inked body at an ISSD conference as evidence of satanic behavior.

Things became even more frightening when Braun grew afraid that Pat's four-year-old son Mikey would be sacrificed by the cult one Halloween evening, which led to Mikey's hospitalization at Pat's request. Soon both of her sons were in the children's ward at the hospital and, a year on, Burgus, overwhelmed at what had become of the children's lives, attempted to hang herself. Braun prescribed her sodium amytal as a tranquilizer – without the consent of the patient or her husband – writing in her chart, "I feel the need to shut her down outweighs the risk of death. In his testimony during the lawsuit, he said, "At a time like this, with this degree of agitation, you don't bother to seek a court order. You do what it takes to take care of the patient."

A turning point came when Burgus acted out during a session with Braun. She had conjured one of her child personas and refused to comply when Braun asked her to stop. He decided to kick her out of the program and moved her to outpatient therapy.

Her children, however, remained at Rush. While Braun gave the okay for the kids to exit in-patient care, the child psychiatrist who oversaw them, Elva Poznanski, believed Burgus might abuse them. The doctor called the Department of Children and Family Services and gained emergency custody over them. Later on, even after she was sued by the Burgus family, Poznanski maintained that the children required her care, saying they were highly sexualized and testifying. "They were the most disturbed kids we had on our unit," Poznanski said

When the children first came in, Poznanski claimed the older son, five year old John, was robotic and nonsensical. Consulting on the case, Braun helped her diagnose him with MPD. The younger son, four-year-old Mikey, didn't have MPD, according to Braun, but suffered from amnesia and went into trances. Both were thought to have been abused by the cult of which their mother was a leader. They were given Inderal and Lopressor, medications normally reserved for adults. This was followed by Halcion and Xanax, all of which led to a range of side effects.

According to Poznanski, John tried to peek up her dress, spread her legs, and once asked her to masturbate him. Mikey would try to grab nurses' breasts. They both played with anatomical dolls in a sexual way, with Mikey trying to perform oral sex on one. The child psychiatrist took these all as signs of sexual abuse, though the Burguses denied any abuse ever

271

occurred. Given the cross-contamination that occurred in the adult ward with MPD patients, it would not have been altogether surprising if living in the children's ward exposed John and Mikey to the specialized or troublesome behavior of other young patients.

At one point, Braun brought several firearms to a group meeting with the kids, reasoning that, if their stories of a satanic cult were true, they wouldn't be afraid of the guns as they were likely already accustomed to them. Without alerting the hospital to his plan, Braun showed the boys the weapons and allowed them to handle them, including a .9mm handgun. The psychiatrist later testified about the experiment, "John handled the gun like someone who knew what he was doing. [He] wasn't afraid of it."

The children spent 20 more months at the hospital after the gun incident until a custody battle ensued between the Burgus parents and Poznanski, with Braun testifying against his colleague and on behalf of the boys' mother and father. When the judge finally granted custody to Pat and Mike Burgus, the children had already spent 1,200 days in the hospital. Ultimately, the boys fell behind academically and had to attend a private school for children with learning disabilities, due to their three years at Rush.

From 1993 to 1998, over 100 patients in the U.S. sued therapists for their MPD treatment. Braun was sued by seven patients before he had his license to practice in Illinois revoked. He next headed to Montana, where he practiced well into the 2000s until having his license in that state removed, as well, upon several more lawsuits. The first in-patient unit dedicated to dissociative disorders was shut down in 1998, as his cofounder, Roberta Sachs, was sued by patients for similar treatment. In one case, she was sued alongside Braun and Cory Hammond, of the Greenbaum Speech.

According to Herbert Spiegel, the psychiatrist who discovered the misdiagnosed MPD of Shirley Mason, aka Sybil, Braun's ISSD group contributed to the overproliferation of MPD diagnoses. At a conference held by the group, Spiegel noted social workers claiming to treat tens of MPD patients at the same time, somehow discovering people with an otherwise rare disorder. "A large number of Braun's followers were low-level therapists with an agenda," Spiegel said. "They're almost like a cult, because they tend to see what they want to see (Hanson 1998)."

This network of mental health workers appeared to be spread out around the country. Judith Peterson, in Texas, sent patients of hers who'd gotten MPD from abuse at the hands of a satanic cult to Braun and Sachs in Chicago for treatment. Peterson was sued numerous times and became the first psychologist charged criminally in a recovered memory case.

George Greaves was another member of the ISSD who had his license revoked in 1994 when he "hypnotized [a] patient on numerous occasions during therapy sessions and while the patient was under hypnosis, would masturbate himself or engage in acts of sexual intercourse and fellatio with her (Grey Faction 2021)."

Diane Humenansky had her license revoked for implanting false memories of ritual abuse. Richard Kluft was another therapist sued for his implantation of memories of ritual abuse. These were just a handful of a list of professionals, including therapists and lawyers, who promoted the concept of DID, repressed memories, and satanic abuse, according to a website called the Grey Faction. A spin-out project of the Satanic Temple, the Grey Zone sought to educate visitors to the site about the satanic panic of the 1980s and its effects into the present, such as the fact that many of the professionals on that list were still practicing.

From an outside perspective, the acts of Braun, Sachs, and the others seemed questionable and abusive, but I thought the Grey Faction may have gone too far in tying DID and repressed memories to satanic ritual abuse too closely. Even if many of the professionals on its list did practice extremely unethical and abusive methods on patients driven by a seemingly irrational belief in a network of satanic cults, did that mean I should write off DID and repressed memories as a whole?

THE MEMORY WARS AND THE GASLIGHTING OF CHILD ABUSE VICTIMS

Closely related to the debate about the validity of DID as a diagnosis were the so-called "memory wars" of the 1990s. As illustrated with the story of Bennett Braun and his colleagues, the idea of "repressed memory" was a potentially problematic one. After all, an irresponsible or even pernicious therapist could potentially convince a vulnerable, mentally unwell person into believing a variety of untrue things about their past, using hypnosis, drugs and their own authority to create false memories. In fact, these were the very things people like Jolly West were attempting to perform under the MKULTRA program.

Developing alongside Braun and the ISSD was another organization with its own collection of professionals that combated what it called "false memory syndrome," something that, unlike DID, was not recognized by the DSM. Dubbed the False Memory Syndrome Foundation (FMSF), the group's fight against this "syndrome" was particularly fierce when it came to accusations of sexual abuse against children (Heaney 2021). The FMSF was established by Pamela Freyd, a high school teacher, and Peter Freyd, a mathematician, when their daughter Jennifer, a psychology professor, privately accused her father of childhood sexual abuse. Jennifer's memory of the abuse came not from coercive therapeutic techniques, but when her sister asked her if she knew that their grandfather had sexually abused their own father, Peter. Suddenly, Jennifer recalled with shock as a wave of memories of her own childhood abuse came flooding back.

Though her daughter made the allegations privately, Pamela decided to take action by writing an article describing what she considered false accusations. The characters in the story were meant to be anonymous, but the author included enough details that those in the psychology community could determine who was referenced. Pamela then sent the story on FMSF letterhead to Jennifer's colleagues. As Jennifer Freyd was up for a promotion at the time, the story caused enough of a stir as to potentially disrupt her career. Instead of siding with her, some of Jennifer's colleagues actually joined the FSMF board.

The professions of the Freyds was worth noting because Jennifer was a psychologist, but her parents had no training in mental health, which meant that, for FMSF to pull any weight, it needed some psychologists involved. The first was Ralph Underwager, a psychologist and Lutheran minister, who, along with his wife Hollida Wakefield, joined with accused parents and recruited a diverse group of academics to lend some authority to the organization (McMaugh 2020).

Enhancing its credibility was its "Scientific and Professional Advisory Board," which included the father of cognitive therapy, Aaron T. Beck, as well as Elizabeth Loftus, a pioneer in false memory research. These experts were contrasted with the addition of celebrity skeptic and magician James Randi (Van der Reijden, n.d.).

Though a psychologist with name recognition, Underwager himself was a controversial figure. Known for acting as an expert witness in such high profile child sexual abuse cases as McMartin, Underager claimed both in interviews and in court that 60% of women sexually assaulted as children had reported that the abuse was "good for them." When psychologist Anna Salter dissected his published work misrepresenting child sexual abuse, Underwager unsuccessfully attempted to sue her. Worse still, Underwager and his wife gave an interview with Dutch pedophile magazine *Paidika*, in which he said:

Paedophiles can boldly and courageously affirm what they choose. They can say that what they want is to find the best way to love. I am also a theologian and as a theologian, I believe it is God's will that there be closeness and intimacy, unity of the flesh, between people. A paedophile can say: "This closeness is possible for me within the choices that I've made."

Underwager resigned from the FMSF board after the stir caused by the interview, while his wife stayed on.

Perhaps more interesting than them, however, were the number of FMSF science advisors and board members that had ties to the CIA (Van der Reijden n.d.). Martin Orne, for instance, was a key MKULTRA scientist that joined the Scientific Advisory Board. He worked for the Office of Naval Intelligence, Air Force Intelligence, and the CIA's Human Ecology Foundation. According to a 2000 obituary in *the New York Times*, "Dr. Orne, who was also a psychologist, was considered an expert in a variety of fields, including multiple personality disorder and what is popularly known as brainwashing. Yet what most interested him was how people behaved when, in the hands of an accomplished practitioner, they were lulled into trance-like states (Nagourney 2000)."

One-time director of the FMSF board was professional skeptic Ray Hyman, who provided his services to the Department of Defense to investigate the claims of psychics, as well as to the CIA for its "remote viewing" psychic visualization program (McMaugh 2020).

Another board member was Dr. Jolly West, who served as an MKULTRA scientist for the CIA, as well. Dr. Margaret Singer was also on the board and, like West, studied prisoners-of-war returning from the Korean War, in her case at the Walter Reed Army Institute of Research in Maryland.

Despite the lack of an official recognition of a false memory syndrome, the foundation was able to proliferate, with affiliated groups forming globally, including the Australian False Memory Association, the British False Memory Society, as well as groups in Germany, France, Israel, New Zealand, Belgium, Canada, The Netherlands and Sweden.

ELIZABETH LOFTUS, MEMORY WARRIOR

Distinguished Professor of Psychological Science; Criminology, Law and Society; Cognitive Science; and Law at the University of California at Irvine, Elizabeth Loftus was considered a leading expert in memory research. She was also a vocal opponent of the concept of repressed memories.

Loftus broke much ground while researching how memory worked and the impact of leading questions on eyewitness recall. Her misinformation effect paradigm demonstrated how exposure to incorrect data about an event via leading questions could cause a witness to misremember what they saw, such as in recreating an automobile accident. This was followed by the now famous "lost in the mall study," used as an example in countless Psychology 101 textbooks to demonstrate how easy it can be to implant false memories in an individual. Inspired by an undergraduate student's class project, Loftus created an experiment in which caregivers would tell their adult children a false story about a time they got lost in a mall when they were young. Approximately one quarter of the participants went on to believe that the event had taken place when it had not (Heaney 20201).

The research of Loftus established her as a leader in the field, resulting in her becoming a very prominent expert witness for high profile legal cases. She provided the first professional testimony on eyewitness memory in Washington State in 1975, which would ultimately build her career as an expert in over 250 cases, including some of the most famous in modern U.S. history (Wilson 2002). For instance, Loftus provided her expertise in the McMartin preschool trial, as well as cases related to O.J. Simpson, Ted Bundy, Oliver North, the Los Angeles police officers accused of beating Rodney King, the Bosnian War trials in the Hague, the Oklahoma City bombing, Michael Jackson, Lewis "Scooter" Libby, the Duke University Lacrosse team, Harvey Weinstein, Bill Cosby, and Jerry Sandusky (Neimark 1996, York 2020, Aviv 2021)).

In 1997, Loftus went so far to demonstrate her attitude toward memory repression that she investigated a "Jane Doe" delayed memory case published by psychiatrist David Corwin. She first uncovered the identity of the victim to be Nicole Taus and dug through public records and interviewed people linked to Taus to learn information that wasn't included in the original article. The information, according to Loftus, suggested that her recovered memories were false (Constantine 1996)

When Taus alerted Loftus's employee, the University of Washington, to the psychologist's breach of her privacy, the school took Loftus's files and spent 21 months investigating her. The University of Washington finally allowed Loftus to publish her findings. This resulted in a lawsuit by Taus against the school, Loftus and several others, making claims of defamation, fraud, emotional distress and invasion of privacy. In the end, the Supreme Court of California dismissed 20 out of 21 counts. The last fraud count was related to the fact that Loftus had misrepresented herself as David Corwin's supervisor to convince Taus's foster mother to be interviewed. Loftus's insurance company ultimately agreed to a nuisance settlement of $7,500 on this count.

Outside of the Taus case, two women, Jennifer Hoult and Lynn Crook, filed ethics complaints with the American Psychological Association (APA) against Loftus in regarded to her published statements about their legal cases related to delayed memories of childhood sexual abuse. Both women had won lawsuits against their childhood abusers, introducing corroborative evidence sufficient for judicial proof of their allegations.

In a 1995 article for *Skeptical Inquirer*, published by the Committee for the Investigation of Claims of the Paranormal (CSICOP), Loftus explored a handful of cases about delayed memory and child sexual abuse, comparing them to the Salem witch trials. At first providing anonymity to Hoult by calling it "the case of Jennifer H," Loftus went on to cite Hoult v. Hoult, thus leaking the victim's last name.

Among her complaints against Loftus, Hoult believed that the psychologist misrepresented herself as an expert on the subject of child sexual abuse given that she never worked as a clinician, meaning that she didn't have experience with child psychology, child sexual abuse, trauma, or the analysis of alleged sex offenders. For this reason, Hoult suggested that Loftus had violated APA guidelines relating to honesty and claiming authority outside of her training.

Other complaints included blatant inaccuracies in Loftus's article. For instance, Loftus wrote, "Jennifer was a 23-year-old musician who recovered memories in therapy of her father raping her from the time she was 4," when, in fact, the woman was an artificial intelligence programmer at the time, the majority of her memories were recalled outside of therapy, and Hoult never claimed that she was four when the abuse began.

The psychologist also said that the victim "remembered one time when she was raped in the bathroom and went to her mother wrapped in a towel with blood dripping," when Hoult never claimed to remember a "rape" and never said that the towel was soaked in blood, but only mentioned a small amount of blood between her legs.

Lynn Crook won a suit against her parents after recalling her childhood sexual abuse, with the judge awarding her $149,580 in damages. Loftus was an expert witness on the side of the Crook parents. In a later interview, Loftus appeared to suggest that Crook's accusations grew progressively more absurd in the courtroom, a claim made by another FMSF board member, Richard Ofshe, acting as an expert during the trial itself. These allegations were rejected by the judge, a fact that Loftus did not mention in her interview. Loftus also failed to point out that Crook won and had corroborating testimony from two of her sisters who recalled abuse by their father.

At the time that Crook and Hoult made their complaints to the APA, Jeffrey N. Younggren was the chair of the APA Ethics Committee and played a similar role to Loftus as an expert witness. He would testify on behalf of the accused in cases involving claims of sexual abuse or on the side against therapists charged with implanting "false memories." In fact, when the complaints were filed against Loftus; Younggren and Loftus were performing this very role on the same side of the same case (Constantine 1996).

Loftus's reputation had been increasingly called into question, as had some of her experiments and the FMSF as a whole. The latter finally shuttered its doors at the end of 2019. As for Loftus's "Lost in a Mall" study, a powerful rebuttal experiment essentially copied the original experiment point for point, only instead of trying to convince participants they had been lost in a mall as children, researchers attempted to convince them that they had received rectal enemas when they were young. The result was that not a single participant believed this story. The big difference between the two scenarios was that being lost in a mall seemed feasible to participants and was very easy to imagine. In contrast, a rectal enema was more extreme and more unlikely (Belli 2012).

While both studies were interesting indicators of how human memory may have worked, they represented only small pieces of a larger puzzle of memory. The truth was that, on the one hand, it was possible to forget and later remember very traumatic events and, on the other, it was possible to implant false memories of traumatic events.

THE RECONCILIATION OF THE MEMORY WARS

The memory wars were raging in the 1990s and early 2000s, but seemed to have concluded in large part by the succeeding decades. That wasn't to say that there weren't still holdovers from the wars who continued to play out either side of the argument, but that some degree of reconciliation had transpired and a scientific consensus had been established.

The conclusions were that it was possible to recover memories that either weren't encoded in a traditional manner when the events took place or that were subsequently forgotten in the same way non-traumatic memories were. There was extensive scientific evidence to explain and describe how memory recovery could occur. Part of the issue with misunderstandings about this concept was that some underlying and incorrect assumptions were made about the nature of memory and trauma. This included the idea that traumatic events were necessarily encoded wholly and completely in memory and that, afterward, they didn't fade as non-traumatic memories did (DePrince et al 2011).

Jennifer Freyd, daughter of the founders of FMSF, went on to establish a well-founded concept for how trauma could be ignored or forgotten in part due to the survival instinct of a victim and their relationship with a caregiver:

> Betrayal trauma theory (BTT) proposes that the way in which events are processed and remembered will be related to the degree to which a negative event represents a betrayal by a trusted, needed other. Full awareness of such abuse may only increase the victim's risk by motivating withdrawal or confrontation with the perpetrator, thus risking a relationship vital to the victim's survival. In such situations, minimizing awareness of the betrayal trauma may be adaptive.

BTT suggested that, in order for children to maintain a relationship with their caregivers, evolutionarily necessary to survive even in the face of abuse, it may have been required that they forget, dissociate or overlook the trauma inflicted by their caregivers. The ability to ignore or forget this abuse in childhood was a skill that became more powerful with exercise so that, by adulthood, the repression of memories became a conditioned response to attempts to recall those memories. In turn, the recollection of these victims was overall impaired. The ability to inhibit retrieval of negative memories appeared to be a powerful coping mechanism in the short term but detrimental to memory in the long term.

Because identity formation occured at a very young age and was based in large part on autobiographical memories, intense and repeated trauma at the hands of a caregiver could disrupt the formation of a cohesive sense of self, leading in extreme cases to the development of distinct identities, i.e, DID.

There was also evidence that memory was imperfect and that, even in some extreme scenarios, false memories could be implanted through highly suggestive therapeutic techniques. This was particularly true with highly suggestive individuals that were exposed to extreme manipulation, hypnosis, and drugs.

"[W]hen Pezdek, Finger, and Hodge tried to implant a false memory in adults of receiving a childhood enema, the error rate was zero. Although some adults, including with trauma histories, agree with schema-consistent false suggestions about childhood events, when it comes to taboo acts of a sexual nature, Goldfarb, Goodman, Larson, Eisen, and Qin again found zero false memories. Many suggestibility/false memory studies use creative coding, such as when 'partial false memories' ('That never happened to me, but if my mother said it did, it could have been at the mall') are nearly buried in statistics reported," Freyd and her co-authors wrote. "That said, we acknowledge the reality of false abuse memories in some individuals as possibly induced or encouraged by therapists, particularly those who use hypnosis or psychotropic drugs (e.g., in combination with religious or other doctrines; Bottoms, Shaver, & Goodman, 1996). Still, it is unclear that clinicians should refrain from discussion with clients about lost memory (a term we prefer because it does not invoke 'repression' mechanistically), given that therapy can help memory: Child victims who sought therapy during/soon after legal involvement (vs. did not) had more accurate long-term memory for abuse a decade later" (Goodman, Goldfarb, Quas, & Lyon, 2017) [Goodman et al 2018].

Some findings that added nuance to the debate included evidence that it was easier to alter a detail in a memory for a real event than to implant an entirely new memory for an event that didn't occur at all. Relateldy, learning about sexual abuse could color the recollections of those who were already aware of their own otherwise dysfunctional relationships. Also, learning about abuse caused people *without* dysfunctional relationships to become *less likely* to have their memories influenced (DePrince 2011).

Additionally, it was possible to discriminate a false memory from a real one due to the fact that "memories for experienced events are stored and embedded in memory within an elaborate informational network that typically includes a significant quantity of perceptual details (e.g., color, sound, and smell) and contextual information (e.g., time and place). On the other hand, memories for imagined or otherwise non-experienced events typically include less perceptual and contextual information and rather have more information about the cognitive processes that produced them (DePrince et al 2011)."

However, in a small group of people where false memories were particularly compelling, even trained judges were unable to distinguish between the reporting of a memory of a true event compared to a false one.

Victim advocates provided overwhelming data that the implanting of false memories occured far less than the delayed memory of childhood sexual abuse. The best evidence was the fact that there were cases, often in legal settings, in which corroborating evidence, such as police reports, could be found.

Authors of a paper that included Jennifer Freyd pointed out that those on the side of denying delayed memories of abuse were, in part, working on behalf of a system that privileged the voices of authority, such as psychological researchers, over those of victims. Trauma, particularly sexual assault and abuse, was underreported not just to police, but to scientists, as well. Freyd wrote:

> While a higher proportion of people may disclose their experiences to researchers when they are asked about victimization than they spontaneously disclose to law enforcement, certainly not all do.

They went on to say:

> Particularly in the face of social pressures to discount abuse survivors and to privilege researcher voices (which may or may not be survivor voices) over lay survivor voices, which lack the tonalities or the authority of the academy or the laboratory (DePrince et al 2011).

DISSOCIATIVE IDENTITY DISORDER IS A REALITY

A meta examination of almost 1500 studies suggested that there was very little evidence for the iatrogenic model – that poor therapy techniques, leading questions, hypnosis, and the influence of media did not explain the overwhelming majority of DID cases. The researchers determined that effect sizes from a relationship between trauma and dissociation were so strong as to conclude that the trauma theory was valid, whether third-party verified abuse (police reports, court documents, etc.) or self-reported abuse was used. The report also found that suggestibility wasn't a factor, meaning that DID individuals weren't more likely to be led by their therapists to believe they'd been abused (Brand 2016).

Some research suggested that, even where DID was not a widely known phenomenon, the diagnosis could be made. For instance in China, where DID was not in the psychiatric diagnostic manual, researchers found DID in patients based on structured interviews. A study in Turkey found four cases of DID, all reporting childhood abuse or neglect, in a study of over

900 women. Additionally, upon reviewing the childhood records of adult patients only being treated for DID as adults, researchers found dissociative symptoms in childhood and adolescence. Adult patients with DID had also been highly correlated with severe childhood abuse.

Other findings included the fact that DID simulators and those diagnosed with DID could be differentiated in a variety of ways, including via neurological differences exposed with brain imaging techniques:

> Several recent controlled studies have found that DID simulators can be reliably distinguished from DID patients on a variety of well-validated and frequently used psychological personality tests (e.g., Minnesota Multiphasic Personality Inventory–2), forensic measures (e.g., Structured Interview of Reported Symptoms),and neurophysiological measures, including brain imaging, blood pressure, and heart rate. (Brand et al 2016)

In fact, the neurological evidence of the existence of DID may have been the most convincing. A 2018 study published in the *British Journal of Psychiatry* determined that machine learning could be used to distinguish between the brain scans of individuals with DID and those without from a sample of 75 participants with 73% accuracy. DID patients are said to have

> …smaller cortical and subcortical volumes in the hippocampus, amygdala, parietal structures involved in perception and personal awareness, and frontal structures involved in movement execution and fear learning. DID patients also show larger white matter tracts that are responsible for information communication between somatosensory association areas, basal ganglia, and the precuneus. These neuroanatomical changes appear to be associated with common DID symptoms such as host dissociation, neurotic defense mechanisms, and overall brain activation/circuitry recruitment… The neuroanatomical evidence for the existence of DID as a genuine disorder is growing and the structural differences seen in DID patients' brains, as reviewed in this report, contribute to that growth (Bilhar et al 2020)."

In some cases, researchers recorded differences in EEG readings between alter states. One study found that beta activity in the frontal and temporal lobes of a DID subject were of greater difference between two alters than EEG records of a single control subject, though not as distinct from two separate controls. Comparing functional MRIs (fMRIs), another study found "increased perfusion in the dorsomedial prefrontal cortex, primary somatosensory cortex, and motor-related areas" for alters compared to the host personality and compared to actors role-playing different identity states (Schlumpf et al 2014). One study compared the fMRIs of a woman who could voluntarily switch between her host personality – a middle-aged, high-functioning woman – and an alter described as between four and six years old. Conducted months apart, the fMRIs showed the same areas activated during a switch:

> ...the primary sensory and motor cortex, likely associated with characteristic facial movements made during switching; the nucleus accumbens bilaterally, possibly associated with aspects of reward connected with switching; and prefrontal sites, presumably associated with the executive control involved in the switching of personalities (Savoy 2012)."

In one remarkable case, a woman who "after 15 years of diagnosed cortical blindness gradually regained sight during psychotherapeutic treatment. At first only a few personality states regained vision, whereas others remained blind. This was confirmed by electrophysiological measurement, in which visual evoked potentials (VEP) were absent in the blind personality states but normal and stable in the seeing states (Waldvogel et al 2007)."

Mark Phillips and Cathy O'Brien
https://trance-formation.com/

CHAPTER TWENTY-FOUR

QUESTIONABLE CHARACTERS

It was difficult to find any biographical information about Cathy O'Brien and her husband/deprogrammer Mark Phillips outside of the couple's own writings and interviews, but even then there were internal inconsistencies that demonstrated the problematic nature of their almost absurd and graphic narrative.

While most "serious" scholars and laypeople alike write off the story without second thought, Ufologist Martin Cannon attempted to examine it with a somewhat sympathetic eye, only to come up empty handed and frustrated (Cannon 1996).

"Little about the basic Monarch theory struck me as technically implausible – indeed, this putative project seems, in many ways, the logical extension of MKULTRA. I therefore initially found the O'Brien/Phillips story quite intriguing. But I also found Mark and Cathy exceptionally frustrating to deal with."

Cannon went on to describe a number of discrepancies in their narrative. He wrote, "Mark Phillips has offered varying descriptions of how he first learned about Monarch programming. At one point, he said he had worked for an unnamed 'DIA contractor,' in which position he came across various materials detailing the government's mind control projects. But in a letter to me (June 1, 1991), he claimed to have discovered the operation during his 'tenure in the '60s and '70s at NASA (Huntsville, Alabama) and Woodland Hills R&D; (Woodland Hills, California).'"

Other issues included the fact that, though Phillips claimed to have had classified documents related to Monarch programming, he never released any. He also never proved his prior employment with a government contractor. "Independent background checks have revealed only that he has held far less impressive jobs, such as selling recreational vehicles," Cannon said.

A researcher named Mike Knight reportedly confirmed that O'Brien had been married to Alex Houston, a country entertainer she claimed to be her handler for the CIA. Houston denied any involvement in any CIA operation. Cannon wrote, "Houston reports that he and Phillips once traveled to China to sell capacitors, and were briefly detained on suspicion of espionage by the Chinese government. After returning to the United States, Houston found that Cathy had gone off with Mark."

Knight also reportedly called Arkansas entertainment director H.B. Gibson, who O'Brien claimed was involved in Bill Clinton-related drug trafficking. According to Knight, Gibson had no idea who O'Brien or once-husband Alex Houston were. Cannon also pointed out that, though the pair had been spinning yarn throughout 1991, it wasn't until Bill Clinton won the 1992 Democratic primaries that he and his wife began to show up in their stories.

When Phillips was called in front of a Grand Jury in Tennessee, he reportedly told Cannon "that the Grand Jury had falsely accused him of threatening President George Bush. This assertion made no sense: Anyone accused (even falsely) of posing a presidential threat would first confront the Secret Service, not a Grand Jury. Later still, I discovered that the Grand Jury had merely called in Mark Phillips as a potential witness in a matter unrelated to either Bush or Monarch."

Cannon concluded his article on the subject by saying:

> At this point, an honest investigator can only feel aggravated and dispirited – which may be the entire point of this charade. In fact, ritual abuse claimants throughout the country had spoken darkly of a "Project Monarch" well before Mark and Cathy came on the scene. Now, skeptics can posit that Mark Phillips contaminated the testimony of others, even though the chronology argues against this scenario...
>
> How, then, do we assess their allegations? Some believe that Cathy's testimony is essentially true, while others damn it as a pack of lies. Still others suspect that Mark and Cathy have played out a clever disinformation gambit, mixing fact and fiction in order to discredit any genuine victims who "break program" (Cannon 1996).

Then there was Paul Bonnaci. Bonacci's own role in the lore related to Monarch and satanic ritual abuse was somewhat suspicious. Out of all of the victims, he provided the most extreme examples of abuse, going far beyond the satanic ritual described by Shawneta Moore and including the graphic scene of a pregnant woman having sex with her two-year-old son and then being given a c-section before having that same son climb inside her woman as she died. It was Bonacci who discussed being forced to participate in the making of a snuff film at Bohemian Grove. He also corroborated Eulice Washington's seeing George H.W. Bush at a sex party in Chicago. He was one of the call boys who was personally given a midnight tour of the White House.

By including everything and the kitchen sink in his story, he managed to both corroborate details provided by other victims and exaggerate them, muddying the waters so that what was real and what was false were near impossible to distinguish. His stories could very well have been true or they could have been exaggerations of what actually happened to him. Or none of it could have been true.

Some of his story seemed validated by psychologist testimony and the opinion of psychiatrist Beverly Mead, described previously. However, some of it appeared invalidated by other details. One important bit of information was provided by a man named John Gosch Sr., whose son Johnny, a newspaper boy, disappeared in 1982 in West Des Moines, Iowa. The story was both well-known, as it popularized the idea of putting photos of missing children on milk cartons, and quite involved, with many theories attempting to determine what happened to 12-year-old Johnny Gosch. These ideas ranged from a kidnapping that led to murder to the trafficking of Johnny in an international pedophile ring. (DiMeo 2018).

One character that added confusion to the mix was Paul Bonacci, who claimed that he was involved in the kidnapping of Johnny Gosch. Being held captive with another boy named Mike by a man named Emilio, Bonacci was forced at gunpoint to cooperate as Johnny was pulled into Emilio's car. Bonacci's role was to put the chloroform over Johnny's mouth as the vehicle sped off to its next destination, a remote home in Colorado. There, Johnny was sold to "the Colonel," who turned out to be Lt. Col Michael Aquino.

Bonacci's lawyer, John DeCamp, first made the Gosch family aware of Bonacci in 1991. DeCamp wrote:

> I had noted that one of the events Paul described reminded me of the case of Johnny Gosch, which I had read about years earlier. I went to the library, and confirmed the similarity of the details of the case, with what Paul said. I then contacted the Gosch family. They advised me that they had had their fill of false leads from people who claimed to know something about their missing boy, and people who claimed to have information for sale but did not seem genuinely interested. But a couple of weeks later, Mr. Gosch did come to Omaha (DeCamp 2005)."

In a *Des Moines Register* article, DeCamp was quoted as saying, "I am convinced this kid is telling absolutely the truth.... He never varied on the time. He gave a description of Johnny's pants, names on his shirt, scars on the body (DeCamp 2005)."

The reason it took so long for DeCamp to make the Gosch connection was that Bonacci had never given a last name to the Johnny he'd kidnapped, just referencing an "incident" with a newspaper carrier. The article quotes DeCamp as saying, "I went to the library and checked on Johnny Gosch. I wrote to the Gosches and told them I don't know if there is any validity, but the dates coincide and he talks about someone from Iowa (*Des Moines Register* 1991)."

Johnny's mother, Noreen Gosch, said that Bonacci knew "some incredible things" about her son's case. She told the *World-Herald*, "There were photographs taken of Johnny prior to the kidnaping. We know this because a woman reported it to police. We're convinced Bonacci saw those pictures. He accurately described the location [from where he was kidnapped], which is not far from our home. He described many things about the pictures which we have never publicly talked about" (*World-Herald* 1991).

He was also apparently able to describe a mark on her son's body that was not made public. In turn, Noreen Gosch seemed to be convinced of Bonacci's story, which became more complicated when he added that he actually saw Johnny again, several years after the kidnapping, at a farm in Colorado where he was being kept by a gay man and gay woman in their thirties. He'd been branded by the couple when he tried to run away and Bonacci was able to sketch the marking.

What added notes of legitimacy to the tale was that, on an episode of *America's Most Wanted*, Bonacci was able to take the production team to the ranch in Colorado. He became visibly upset as they pulled up to the site, with Bonacci recalling details of his trauma. After the episode aired, the producers reportedly received letters from viewers claiming to confirm the existence of the ranch and even saying they had the same symbol branded on them that Johnny Gosch had (Belinson et al 2016).

Noreen Gosch appeared to believe Bonacci, but John Sr. was less impressed. He said that the first thing he asked Bonacci was how tall Johnny was. When the inmate gave a grossly inaccurate estimate to the boy's height, very tall for a 12-year-old, John Sr. claimed he immediately doubted Bonacci's tale. He said he then asked a guard about the inmate, who said Bonacci had newspaper clippings about the Gosch story all over his prison cell, suggesting the whole thing could have been a con (DiMeo 2018).

DeCamp told the *Des Moines Register* a completely different story:

"DeCamp said John Gosch, the boy's father, met with Bonacci, 'and started getting chills. I believe he believed him,' DeCamp said (1991)."

The West Des Moines police "have not interviewed Bonacci and have no plans to do so," reported a 1991 article in the *Des Moines Sunday Register*. "We are aware of what's going on," said Lt. Gerry Scott, responsible for the Gosch investigation. "We're not going to reinvent the wheel. This has been investigated in Nebraska. When things need investigating, here, they will be investigated."

The Gosch family suggested that the police never did an adequate job in investigating their son's disappearance. The decision not to interview Bonacci could have been a continuation of that pattern or it could simply have been related to a lack of veracity to Bonacci's claims. One would think that there would be no harm in interviewing Bonacci, regardless of whether or not he was telling the truth.

Bonacci's abuse by Larry King was at least partially validated. In a lawsuit against the prominent Republican, in which King did not show up for court, the judge awarded Bonacci a $1 million judgement. In his decision, Judge Urbom wrote:

> Between December 1980 and 1988, the complaint alleges, the defendant King continually subjected the plaintiff to repeated sexual assaults, false imprisonments, infliction of extreme emotional distress, organized and directed satanic rituals, forced the plaintiff to "scavenge" for children to be a part of the defendant King's sexual abuse and pornography ring, forced the plaintiff to engage in numerous sexual contacts with the defendant King and others and participate in deviate sexual games and masochistic orgies with other minor children. The defendant King's default has made those allegations true as to him. The issue now is the relief to be granted monetarily. The now uncontradicted evidence is that the plaintiff has suffered much. He has suffered burns, broken fingers, beatings of the head and face and other indignities by the wrongful actions of the defendant King. In addition to the misery of going through the experiences just related over a period of eight years, the plaintiff has suffered the lingering results to the present time. He is a victim of multiple personality disorder, involving as many as fourteen distinct personalities aside from his primary personality. He has given up a desired military career and received threats on his life. He

suffers from sleeplessness, has bad dreams, has difficulty in holding a job, is fearful that others are following him, fears getting killed, has depressing flashbacks, and is verbally violent on occasion, all in connection with the multiple personality disorder and caused by the wrongful activities of the defendant King (DeCamp 2005).

In response, DeCamp said, "I don't think the judge would have given Paul a million dollar award if he didn't think he was telling the truth."

King appealed the judgement, before retracting that appeal. The $1 million in damages awarded to Bonacci was never collected.

In addition to the potential for interfering directly in the case, De-Camp helped drive along the satanic aspect of the narrative. He quoted Gunderson at length in his self-published book, *The Franklin Coverup*, and also contributed to the idea of the Monarch Project. He described Franklin victim Paul Bonacci as a subject of Monarch:

> The story told by Monarch victims – one of whom is Paul Bonacci – is that they were tortured for the purpose of creating "multiple personalities" within them. These multiple personalities could then be programmed as desired – as spies, "drug mules," prostitutes, or assassins.
>
> *Because of legal cases still pending, I am severely limited in what I can say about the Monarch Project. Suffice it to say at this point:*
>
> *Major intelligence programs in this country did and do exist for the purpose of protection of this country and to learn what other countries, particularly our Cold War enemies, were doing in this area of mind control"* (2005).

DeCamp used then-deceased former CIA director William Colby to validate the existence of the program, quoting Colby as telling him:

"There was no particular program called 'Monarch,' contrary to what you want to think. 'Monarch' was merely a name that some participants in the program – who knew very little about it, other than from their own limited participation – were given to identify themselves. But, as far as the CIA was concerned, there was no such program named 'Monarch.'"

Due to the aforementioned "legal cases still pending," DeCamp said that he had "deposited extensive documentation on the Monarch Project with people who have the means, the motivation, and, most importantly, the guts, to print the entire story, should I suffer an 'accident' before I get around to it." However, he never did publish anything on Monarch or release any documentation.

He then went on to quote an "investigative reporter" named Anton Chaitkin, History Editor of Lyndon LaRouche's publication, *Executive Intelligence Review* (EIR). LaRouche, of course, was a well-known disinformation agent and EIR was one of his most well-known outlets. Chaitkin was involved in causing fissures on the left in the 60s and 70s as a part of the LaRouche movement and continued his disinformation activities up through the Barack Obama presidency, in which he claimed:

> President Obama has put in place a reform apparatus reviving the euthanasia of Hitler Germany in 1939, that began the genocide there.... Dr. Ezekiel Emanuel and other avowed cost-cutters on this panel also lead a propaganda movement for euthanasia.... They shape public opinion and the medical profession to accept a death culture ... to let physicians help kill patients whose medical care is now rapidly being withdrawn in the universal health-care disaster. (Blumenthal 2009)

DeCamp said, "Chaitkin showed up one day in my Lincoln law office. I told him, 'Look, I know you have been in some tough spots before, but are you really sure you want to poke around in this? This question of 'mind control' – the Monarch Project – is the most scary and dangerous thing I have ever encountered.'"

After the meeting, Chaitkin published a story linking the Franklin scandal to the Monarch program for another LaRouche publication called *The New Federalist*. The story included the following:

> Offutt is the headquarters for the Strategic Air Command, and has had a cadre of thousands of intelligence personnel. At Offutt, and later at other military installations, Paul [Bonacci] says this ring "trained" him by tortures, heavy drugging, and sexual degradation, while instructing him in military arts including assassination. In fact, his personal knowledge in these realms can scarcely be accounted for other than by crediting the indictments he has made...
>
> Larry King, FBI agent Gerry Wahl, Alan Baer, Harold Andersen, and former Omaha Police Chief Robert Wadman have all been reported as collaborators with this Satanic military-based ring...
>
> Professionals probing the child victims of "Monarch" say there are clearly two responsible elements at work: the government/military, and cooperating Satanic (or more exactly pagan) cults. These are multi-generation groups, where parents donate their own children – who are proudly called "bloodline" or simply "blood" cultists – to be smashed with drugs and electric "shock, and shaped.

Other children are kidnapped and sold into this hell, or are brought in gradually through day-care situations."

Paul Bonacci and other child victims have given evidence in great depth on the central role of Lt. Col. Michael Aquino in this depravity. Aquino, alleged to have recently retired from an active military role, was long the leader of an Army psychological warfare section which drew on his "expertise" and personal practices in brainwashing, Satanism, Nazism, homosexual pedophilia and murder (DeCamp 2005).

Chaitkin then described the same origin story for Monarch as Cory Hammond, involving a Jewish turncoat who helped the Nazis conduct brainwashing experiments before becoming the infamous Dr. Green for the CIA.

The only Gundam more deeply immersed in Franklin than I thought I had been was @ShaggyTooTrope, who was based in Nebraska. Neither of us could determine the truth behind Bonacci's story. We both believed he was abused, but couldn't figure out if he truly had DID or was some sort of intelligence asset planted in the story to add confusion and blow up the proportion of the scandal with seemingly absurd details.

Chapter Twenty-Five

Is Monarch Real?

My cheeks became flush with warm, pink blood. "Huh? What? No, no, no. I'm not a Qanon person."

"You promise? You've been reading a lot of weird stuff lately. I'm just worried – you know, there's stories of these people getting divorced because the husband becomes obsessed with Internet conspiracies…"

"No, I swear. I'm trying to be as reasonable as possible."

"I just want to make sure you don't start caring about this stuff more than us. Maybe you should try reading something less intense."

"Listen, I'm going to want to read what I want, okay? But that doesn't mean I'm going to go crazy and leave you guys."

Somehow, the conversation became heated and Cindy took off with Prez into our room, while I drove around trying to get Misha to sleep. I was still hot with blood. Was I wrong? Maybe I was. There was one thing she was definitely right about. I was obsessed.

But it was hard not to be. I felt like I had begun to understand the contours of the thing – this system in which we operated. And I was at the center of it, the mental site where they kept the children. I just couldn't tell if there the kids were being held under lock and key by satanists programming them to kill or if it was the more quotidian type of prison. The type Louis Althusser described as the "Ideological State Apparatus" that chained us psychologically. Or both.

Trying to determine if the Monarch Program was real was a difficult thing to do.

The thing was: if the CIA could create child sex slaves, it would. There was evidence that it had aided in the trafficking of children, sought to and likely succeeded to an extent at controlling people's minds, and had been involved in the occult.

The CIA also did protect Nazis, scientists and otherwise, from justice after the war. As a part of Operation Sunrise, Higher SS Police Chief for Italy Karl Wolff, responsible for the deaths of 300,000 Jews, was shielded from the Nuremberg trials (Talbot 2016). Operation Gladio and associated programs rescued Reinhard Gehlen, chief of Nazi intelligence for the Eastern front, as well as countless other fascists for its "anti-Soviet" stay-behind armies (Francovich 1992). Operation Paperclip saw over 1,600 Nazi scientists, from rocket engineers and biological and chemical warfare experts to death camp torturers, taken to the United States (Jacobsen 2014). This included doctors at Dachau, who experimented on prisoners using mescaline as a possible interrogation tool.

There were allegations that the U.S. rescued the Angel of Death himself, Josef Mengele. While there was no smoking gun, there was some evidence to suggest the possibility. In addition to the general collusion of U.S. forces with the Nazis at the war's close, including aiding their escape to South America, the U.S. did have Mengele in its captivity at one point only to lose him (Drozdiak 1985). But was he Dr. Green, as some so-called "Monarch survivors" claimed?

As mentioned before, in his book on the Franklin scandal, John De-Camp said that he asked William Colby, his former superior and once director of the CIA, about Monarch. Colby was reported as saying, "There was no particular program called 'Monarch,' contrary to what you want to think. 'Monarch' was merely a name that some participants in the program – who knew very little about it, other than from their own limited participation – were given to identify themselves. But, as far as the CIA was concerned, there was no such program named 'Monarch.'"

Desperate to know if "Monarch programming," as some people referred to it, was possible, I reached out to DID expert, Michael Salter, Scientia Associate Professor of Criminology at the School of Social Sciences at Western Sydney University. When I asked him if it was possible to intentionally cause the development of DID and then train individual alters for specific tasks, he replied:

> I think the question is too specific. Let's put it another way: Can an adult torture and terrify a child into doing what the adult wants? Once the child has been terrified and tortured, is that child likely to be compliant and obedient to the wishes of the adult? The answer is: yes, of course.

Dr. Salter continued,

> The child will dissociate to cope with severe abuse, whether the abuser knows it or not. Some abusers are aware of this to some extent. They may not know the specifics of dissociation or DID, but they will naturally observe changes in the child's mental state, and

find ways to manipulate that. A dedicated abuser will try to interfere with the child's mental state through various practices, including drugging, hypnosis and the misuse of religious ritual and belief.

Salter also pointed out the significance of the cultural context of abuse, saying that it might not be considered DID by the perpetrator of abuse.

> Some people with DID describe being raised in subcultures of sexual trafficking, where the child is a commodity and they are subject to practices designed to ensure their compliance and pain tolerance. This can include electroshock, near drowning and so on. The child dissociates in order to cope, and this process appears to be actively encouraged and manipulated by the traffickers. Again, the abusers may not know about DID; they may instead believe that the child is possessed, for instance.

Salter said.

> Notions of "brainwashing" and "mind control" emerged during the Cold War and have similarities to the processes I've described above. I'm an Australian and the speculation around covert organisations in the States are not relevant to me or my country. We don't need conspiracy theories to explain why paedophiles want to brainwash and control children. It's a distraction when we need to focus on addressing the contemporary realities of child sexual exploitation.

He was also able to reframe my understanding of DID with less bizarre language that wasn't anchored in the Cold War tropes I was accustomed to.

> It just depends on the theory of mind that you adopt. A multi-model theory of the self suggests that we all develop function-specific states (i.e. at work I act/feel/present in one way, at home I act/feel present in another way) but we experience continuity between them.

Salter said.

> Children with DID also develop function-specific states but they do not experience continuity between them (each state has amnesia for the other state). Those states include the roles they are forced to play in sexual exploitation, which are very different from the roles they adopt when they go to school, etc.

"An abuser forces a child into those roles. Does this mean that they 'hypnotise' them or 'create new identities' etc? This kind of language makes the dynamics of abuse and exploitation sound like science fiction (Personal correspondence 2021)," he concluded.

In other words, Salter suggested that children under extreme abuse would do whatever necessary to survive and please their abusers. In some cases, the perpetrators would be able to exploit their victims as they dissociated. And while bizarre methods of torture might be deployed, including electroshock or religious rituals, these might simply be used to further obtain obedience and desired behaviors.

So, DID, was real and was largely caused by repeated childhood abuse. What more traumatic way to cause DID in a child than something like satanic ritual and sexual abuse? An additional benefit for the abuser would be the fact that satanic ritual abuse was not particularly believable. The stories were so far-fetched that they stretched the imagination beyond the boundaries of what most ordinary people were willing to believe.

This made me wonder, if SRA did occur even infrequently, perhaps it provided the added incredulity to already incredulous stories of experimentation and child trafficking that really did take place. In turn, it polluted those genuine stories, rendering them completely unbelievable. For instance, if the Epstein tale had included details about satanic orgies, in addition to talk of presidents and celebrities, it might have been written off to begin with.

PART 5

DUTROUX AS A SYNECDOCHE OF EVERYTHING

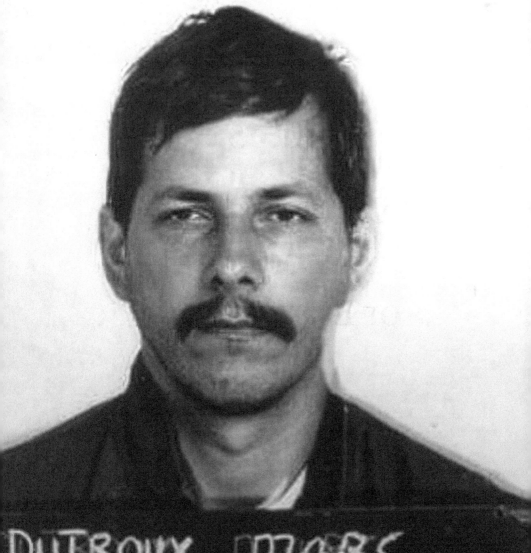

DUTROUX MARC
ixeLLes   006-777-556
1m 817   ⊙ bruns chatair

CHAPTER TWENTY-SIX

THE BEAST OF BELGIUM

A pparently, it wasn't over yet. Somehow I had managed to wander into a side room off the center of the complex. Slowly the screams faded as I plodded into a corridor of absolute darkness. Suddenly, a strange brightness illuminated the space. In bioluminescent lights read the name "Dutroux," blinking before an amphitheater or, more accurately, a surgical theater. A performance was about to play out in grim and gory detail.

In June 1995, two eight-year-old girls went missing. This would be followed two months later by the disappearances of 17-year-old An and 19-year-old Eefje went missing (Trouw1996). The last thing the teens had done was attend a performance by a notable magician, where they had been hypnotized. Though authorities quickly determined he was not a suspect, his career was ruined (van der Reijden 2007).

The Bewakings-en opsporingsbrigade (BOB), part of the former Belgian gendarmerie and more or less equivalent to the FBI of the United States, essentially ended its search for the girls later that year, but a foundation established a few years prior, kept the cases alive. Nevertheless, the girls weren't found by the time even more children disappeared. This included 12-year-old Sabine in May and 14-year-old Laetitia in August of 1996. As an atmosphere of fear arose around parents' concern for their children, faith in the authorities began to drop (Dernière Heure 2018).

The investigation was headed by magistrate Jean-Marc Connerotte under the leadership of prosecutor Michel Bourlet, a pair who had already earned reputations for the public's belief that the duo had been prevented from solving the 1994 murder of socialist politician Andre Cools (van der Reijden 2007). During Connerotte's first day on the case, there was a major breakthrough, with two witnesses reporting a white van cruising the streets of the town of Beatrix, where Laetitia went missing. This led to the arrest of a man who would become known as the Beast of Belgium, Marc Dutroux, along with his wife Michele Martin and his accomplice Michel Lelievre. With the kidnappers in custody, the whereabouts of Sabine and Laetitia were uncovered and the girls were retrieved from Dutroux's basements (van der Reijden 2007).

But the story wasn't over. Soon, it would become evident that not only had the authorities refused to arrest Dutroux in previous years, but that he was likely only a brutal henchman for a network that spread to the very top of Belgian society, which included a pair of powerful banking brothers, a far-right political leader, and a former prime minister. More surprising still, this network was linked to the "strategy of tension" executed by NATO and the CIA throughout Europe.

Prior to Dutroux's capture and the rescue of Sabine and Laetitia, the Beast of Belgium was actually under the close watch of the BOB. The authorities had significant reason to suspect his involvement in the kidnappings, as he had initially been convicted in November 1988 for the kidnap, torture, and rape of five girls aged 11 to 19. He was additionally convicted of torturing an older woman, inserting a razor blade into her vagina and attempting to rob her. He was released just four years later through the approval of a Minister of Justice, though others in the justice system did not share the opinion he should go free. One of those that advised against his release was his own mother (van der Reijden 2007). Upon leaving prison early, Dutroux's doctor provided him with ample sleeping pills and other sedatives with which he would ultimately feed his victims (Waterfield 2009).

For a petty criminal, Dutroux owned a surprising surplus of 10 homes. It was at his house in the town of Charleroi, however, that he spent most of his time and where he constructed a dungeon in which the girls would be found. Dutroux's mother reported anonymously to authorities the suspicions she had about her son's activities there. He had blacked out his windows, filled his yard with used tires, and two girls around "16 or 18 years old" were seen on the property at night (van der Reijden 2007).

Another home he rented to a minor crook, who would tell the authorities prior to Dutroux's arrest that the Beast of Belgium made an unusual and incriminating statement to him. When two girls walked by,

Dutroux was triggered to say, "If you want to kidnap them, you'll make 150,000 francs [roughly 4000 euros] … Grab them from behind, put a sedative drug under their nose, pull them into the car, and lock the doors."

Dutroux then elaborated his plan to kidnap girls, imprison them in his dungeon before trafficking them out of the country. As a police informant, the petty criminal reported what he'd heard to the cops, who searched Dutroux's homes months later. Though they found a renovated basement, they could not find any missing children. When searched again the following summer, Dutroux's basement had completed its remodel. A year later, Dutroux was sued for illegally stretching a hole to his basement to install a venting tube. When Julie and Melissa went missing, the petty crook went to police once more to repeat his story, but they simply asked for more evidence (van der Reijden 2007).

Under the command of officer Rene Michaux, BOB finally launched Operation Othello in 1995. Between August 10, 1995 and January 1996, the authorities were meant to surveil Dutroux for any signs that he may have been involved in any of the kidnappings. Despite this fact, and numerous bits of evidence, the BOB and Michaux failed to catch their suspect(s) and allowed numerous victims to be murdered under their watch (van der Reijden 2007).

For instance, the team only applied the use of video recording for two percent of the complete surveillance period, with observation ceasing at 10 PM every night. In turn, the BOB was unable to catch the monster as he kidnapped An and Eefje and imprisoned them in his basement. Three days later, they somehow missed it when Eefje was able to gather her clothes, push through a bathroom window, and scream for help before Dutroux grabbed her and yanked her back into the house just moments later. Finally, the police never got a glimpse of Dutroux taking the girls out of the home several weeks later to kill them (van der Reijden 2007).

During the timespan of Othello, Dutroux was also arrested for stealing a truck and then kidnapping and torturing three teenagers he believed to have stolen that same vehicle from him. One of the teens was able to escape and inform the police. A week later, December 13, 1995, Rene Michaux conducted a search of Dutroux's homes. At that time, the officer and the locksmith he used to open the doors heard what sounded like the cries of children. They went to the basement in search of the sound's source, only to discover a recently renovated room (Frenkiel 2002). Not finding anyone, Michaux determined the cries to have come from outside of the home, though the parents of one girl would later claim that it was possible to communicate through the modified walls of the basement dungeon. While there, Michaux also discovered a speculum for spreading and examining human orifices, vaginal cream, chains, chloroform, and videos that would later be revealed to have shown the criminal building the basement and raping girls. One cassette was labeled "Perdu de Vue, Marc" ('Lost From Sight'), a program about missing kids, including Julie and Melissa (van der Reijden 2007). Without watching the videos, Michaux had them returned to Dutroux's wife (Bates 1999). Worse still, several months after his arrest for picking up and torturing the teenagers who he thought stole his stolen truck, Dutroux was released for "humanitarian reasons" because his wife was going to give birth (van der Reijden 2007).

After the failed search of Dutroux's home, Michaux met with a police officer to discuss a mysterious white Mercedes that had been trailing and taking pictures of school girls. The officer relayed that an informant had told him that the vehicle was a part of a pedophile ring tied to a business based in a suburb of Brussels. The informant said the photos being taken were for catalogs from which customers could purchase a child to be abducted and imprisoned in Belgium until the kid was shipped to Thailand or Eastern Europe for a price of roughly 7500 euros. Nevertheless, Michaux did nothing with the information.

The police officer later said, "I remember that Michaux told me that Dutroux went to countries in eastern Europe ... The sums he mentioned for the kidnappings were similar to those given to me by my informant ... Even today this still keeps me awake at night. I feel responsible. Afterwards, in 1996, I looked into Dutroux ... You just felt it. This was the man we were looking for!"

The business would turn out to have been incorporated by a frequent partner of Michel Nihoul, a businessman and radio host. Among the firm's known frequenters was Nihoul, as well as Dutroux's friend and later murder victim, and Dutroux's wife, Michele Martin. When the company went bankrupt in 1994, the building was found to have five mattresses and baby milk inside. At the same location Nihoul's associate registered another firm with five white Mercedes with French plates.

The fact that Dutroux was carrying out catalog-style order requests was corroborated by his accomplice Lelievre, who said, "Marc always told me that he kidnapped girls for people who had placed an order with him. When he came out of prison in March 1996, I asked him who did the orders when he was in jail. He answered that somebody else did that and that he certainly wasn't the only one. When we went to pick up a girl, Marc wanted that she corresponded with the order, small hips. He gave me a description of the girl that we were looking for. [One day] I asked him why they [An and Eefje] were still with him even though he claimed he had an order. He told me that the people who had placed the order had come, but that they weren't interested in them.... Dutroux explained to me that he conditioned the girls to be obedient and submissive when they arrived at customers..."

Upon Dutroux's arrest, authorities confiscated an unknown number of videos, with realistic estimates circling around 100. In addition to showing Dutroux's brutal crimes, reports circulated that they featured high-profile

members of Belgian society. The criminal's entry point into this high society seemed to have been Michel Nihoul, according to Dutroux's wife.

> By the way, Marc told me that he went more and more to Brussels
> and met an increasing number of people in light of his activities
> with Michel Nihoul," she said. "Nihoul always gave me the impres-
> sion that he had many connections that he could count on. Marc
> Dutroux told me that Nihoul had taken care of many of Lelievre's
> problems: he had prevented that he was arrested, he had worked
> out his fines and solved his money problems. Marc had accurate-
> ly sensed that he would benefit from continuing to see Nihoul,
> because of his connections and those of his wife, the lawyer. The
> more they saw each other, the more they opened up of course. I
> think that at a certain moment a mutual trust was built. I see ev-
> idence of that in a conversation between Lelievre and Marc that
> I coincidentally heard and in which Dutroux said that they had to
> bring back a girl for Nihoul. I think that Jean-Michel had influence
> on Marc Dutroux. Marc often told me that he was impressed by the
> connections Nihoul had.
>
> Nihoul was arrested when it was learned that he freely provid-
> ed 1,000 pills of ecstasy to Dutroux's accomplice, Lelievre, the day
> after Laetitia was abducted, which police thought was payment for
> the deed. Nihoul had no alibi for his whereabouts the day before
> the kidnapping. On the contrary, witnesses saw him near the spot
> where Laetitia was taken and near Dutroux or his van. Dutroux's
> wife claimed that one of Dutroux's clients was Nihoul, saying, "I
> have heard Marc personally telling Lelievre that he should bring
> a girl for Michel Nihoul. If I haven't mentioned that before, that
> is because I'm afraid of that gang, I mean Nihoul, Marc Dutroux
> and others in Brussels. I mean well-placed individuals who Nihoul
> knew. The connections of Nihoul made me fear for my children
> and myself.... I was afraid, because Jean-Michel Nihoul, Marc
> Dutroux and Michel Lelievre were part of a gang that was involved
> in all kinds of business, like drugs, pills, girls and forged papers. I
> have to say that at the time of the kidnapping of Sabine and Laeti-
> tia, Michel Nihoul, as I already stated, often called to, to my home.
> He was looking for Marc Dutroux. He didn't call for me. When
> Nihoul tried to reach Marc he always remained vague. I never knew
> why he called so often to Marc Dutroux. Over time I became more
> and more convinced that Marc Dutroux and Jean-Michel Nihoul
> did things that couldn't stand the light of day and which I was not
> supposed to know about.

Lelievre seemed to implicate Nihoul, as well, but refused to provide details out of fear. "I would like to reveal other things about Jean-Michel Nihoul, but I don't want that these testimonies are taken up in the dossier. As I said, I fear for my life and those around me. I remind you that Nihoul told me the following: 'if you cross me, I will destroy you'. With those words he made it known to me that he would kill me or have me killed," Lelievre said (van der Reijden 2007).

It was reported that a nightclub frequented by Nihoul, the Dolo, was a location often attended by individuals in the child abuse network. The Dolo was also visited regularly by high ranking members of the police, as well as lawyers, heads of business, and politicians who were thought to interact with members of the underworld. The former valet of the club testified in 1997 that Nihoul participated in a child kidnapping and abuse ring. One police report noted: "[A witness] heard Nihoul and Doudou speak about cages for children, to make them suffer. Videos from the USA would show black children in cages in which they were tortured and burned (van der Reijden 2007)." Nihoul was ultimately convicted for human trafficking, as well as drug trafficking and financial fraud, but not for any crimes related to Dutroux's kidnapping and murder of girls (La Libre 2010).

In many cases, the testimonies of the surviving victims of the network were difficult to fathom. However, there was enough corroborating evidence to consider them significantly credible. To protect their identities, each victim was named with an X and a number for the order in which they came forward. Among these, the figure that became the most well-known was X1, whose real name was eventually revealed to be Regina Louf.

Later diagnosed with DID, X1 lived with her grandmother, the owner of a brothel catering to pedophiles and torturers that filmed child pornography and where Louf was abused from a very young age. At four, she was pimped out by a man named Tony, who shopped her around for further abuse (France 3 2017). It wasn't until she was able to meet a boy with whom she married that she would escape the fate of starring in a snuff film, the future that awaited most of the children in the network who aged past 16 or 17. However, even then, the abuse continued. When her husband was on the road as a truck driver, Tony would return to abuse her or force her to abuse others (van der Reijden 2007).

Another possible sufferer of DID, Nathalie C., or X7, was tracked down based on information from Louf and confirmed that she was once

X1's best friend and knew of her sexual relationship with Tony. Sexually abused by her father at a young age, she would go to the home of Louf's grandmother, where she was not allowed to enter the first floor. Another victim, X4, picked out X7 as having been in child pornography, providing corroboration (van der Reijden 2007).

Chantal S. was also found by the BOB based on X1's information. Her grandmother was a practicing satanist and she was sexually abused by her parents, who brought her to the brothel of Louf's grandmother, where she was also abused and forbidden from entering the first floor. She corroborated X1's testimony that one of the abusers had the nickname "Monsieur" and also saw Louf threatened by her grandmother with a revolver. When Chantal's testimony triggered a fight between her husband and her parents, her father conceded that he brought Chantal to the brothel. She was also identified by X4 as being forced into child pornography.

Victim-witness X2 was actually a police officer working on the Dutroux case. It was when X1's story was brought up in a meeting at the station that she became visibly upset and told her superiors about her own history of child abuse. As she grew up, X2 ultimately became the mistress of a magistrate before later acting as a mistress with a high level Justice Department member. She noted that these two figures were part of a sexual abuse ring she was subjected to in the mid-to-late 1980s. While she wasn't tortured to the same extent as some victims, the future police officer learned from others about child murders and claimed to have been at a party where children were hunted. She named some of the same perpetrators and locales as X1 and other victims who provided testimony. X2 became a witness at first, but pulled out when she believed that the investigation was being thwarted.

X3's testimony was starkly different from the rest in that the abuse she testified to occurred between 1950 and 1962, as opposed to the 1980s and 90s. She was abused in her own home between three and 12, at which point she was introduced to her father's larger network of powerful people, which ultimately included the Belgian royal family.

X4's mother allowed a pimp to film her in sadomasochistic child pornography. She was able to recognize two of X1's childhood friends and identified some of the same abusers. It was learned that X4's parents were neighbors of Regina Louf's grandmother.

In February 1996, six months prior to Dutroux's arrest, Nathalie W. spoke to the police but they would not write down her testimony. Several months later, in July, more cooperative police recorded her story, which included her father raping her from the age of six on. He then brought her to various homes in Waterloo before, at 10-years-old, she was given to a prince and his assistant. She corroborated participation in the pedophile ring by Nihoul and X1's pimp, Tony.

A gang member given the label "VM1" came forward to speak of his abuse, which included being picked up by a local juvenile court judge who took him to parties in Brussels. He then became a child prostitute at a high-end club called Le Mirano, attended by Nihoul and other men named by witnesses. He claimed to be threatened by someone on the street two days after coming forward to the police (van der Reijden 2007).

The Ghent Law Court at least held up the fact that X1 had been in a sexual relationship with her pimp, Tony, as a minor, with her parents' consent. However, the court suggested that it was Louf, a child at the time, who pushed the relationship and manipulated her parents into allowing it and giving Tony a key to their home. Judge Soenen noted in 1998:

> It has been established that Regina [X1], between her twelfth and sixteenth year, had a sexual relationship with a much older and grown man, named Antoine V.... Her mother knew about this, allowed the relationship and even encouraged it. Her mother at least felt a platonic love for this same V.... Regina had this relationship WITH her consent and not AGAINST her will.

Tony seemingly had sexual relationships with X1's mother and housekeeper. Regina Louf's classmate, Marlene, had apparently witnessed abuse and said, "there were sexual contacts between X1, that Tony, the mother of X1 and the housekeeper." The housekeeper not only confirmed this with investigators, but told them she believed Louf's accounts. She also said she left that house when her 18-month-old had been abused.

Tony's girlfriend from the 1980s, "Odette," said about him,

> He liked to give people the feeling that he could blackmail them ... I don't know what to think about the whole X1-affair and I find it hard to believe that Tony had something to do with those child murders. But still. When I read the book of X1, I cannot deny that everything she wrote about Tony is accurate, down to the smallest details. That was a shock to me.

Other corroborating details included the fact that X2 pointed to two locations of abuse that were also indicated by Louf, as well as a street that faced the brothel of X1's grandmother. Some perpetrators named by X2 were named by X1, as well. This included Vanden Boeynants, Baron de Bonvoisin and the Lippens brothers, all of whom I would come to learn much more about. Vanden Boeynants was also named by X3.

X4 said her parents lived adjacent to a site where X1 claimed to have been abused with Carine Dallaert. X4 was able to pick out friends of X1, Chantal S. and Nathalie C., as other abuse victims. Witness Nathalie W. knew the names of X4's sister and mother, while X4 identified Nathalie in turn.

X1's best friend from age 10 to 14, Nathalie C., was aware of the sexual relationships between Tony and Louf and mother. She had been to her grandmother's home and was not allowed to visit the first floor.

Louf also named Nathalie W. as a victim of abuse, recognized her father, while Nathalie W. picked out "Anthony" as X1's pimp and a friend Nihouls. Both X1 and Nathalie W. referred to Nihoul as "Mich."

Chantal S. said abuse happened at X1's grandmother's home and that she was not allowed on the first floor. X4 identified Chantal S. as having been abused by the same group as herself. Witness Kristelle M. was a schoolmate of Regina Louf and said that she was sexually abused and impregnated by Tony. Anja D. corroborated that Tony abused X1 and took her places. The parents of a classmate of Regina Louf said that their child had been told by Louf about the abuse at X1's grandmother's home. They then had Louf tell them herself and believed that she could not know those stories without them being true. They then told the school principal, to whom X1 repeated the details and revealed bruises on her neck. This led the principal to call Louf a "fantasizer" and send her to parents. They were never asked to testify (van der Reijden 2007).

House, owned by Marc Dutroux in Marchienne-au-Pont, Belgiumw.
IIVQ / Tijmen Stam, Creative Commons

CHAPTER TWENTY-SEVEN

CHILD TRAFFICKING AND MURDER

The torture these victims underwent was unimaginable. It included being subjected to freezing showers, physical and sexual abuse with sharp objects, and being raped with or by animals, such as dogs and snakes. X1 claimed that, before, during, and after giving birth to a child, she was raped in various ways by extremely powerful people, including a pair of brothers involved in banking, a former prime minister, and the assistant commissioner of police. Six weeks later, the baby was taken from her, only to be seen by her again later at a factory where Louf was abused and snuff films were made.

When victims reached the "end circuit" around the age of 16 or couldn't satisfy a customer, X1 claimed they could be murdered. Other witnesses, including X2, X3, X4, Nathalie W., VM1, and individuals named Jacques Thoma and Pascal Willems, mentioned the killing of children, some of which was said to be captured in snuff films and sometimes shown at parties (van der Reijden 2007).

X1 reported seeing some 60 children murdered, providing the first names of roughly 35 of them (van der Reijden 2007). To determine her credibility, the police reopened the cases of four dead girls. It turned out that some of her descriptions were astoundingly accurate.

She was able to select an image of one Veronique Dubrulle from a collection, correctly noting her year of death as 1983. She claimed that the girl had been sadistically abused with a knife until she died at a party attended by Nihoul, Tony, and others. Though the death certificate said that she passed from cancer, it was signed by a neuropathologist and neurosurgeon that X1 claimed to see at abuse parties held by a family that owned a textile business, and that one of the doctors had raped her.

However, Louf never had a chance to pick the perpetrators out from photographs. Veronique's case was closed shortly after, around the time that the X investigations were beginning to be publicized. Police learned that Louf's pimp, Tony, had called Veronique's father, the manager of a cinema business owned by a wealthy Belgian family corporation, three times after these initial stories were published. It was later reported by the authors of a book on the Dutroux affair, *The X-Dossiers*, that the two were friends.

Another victim Louf claimed to have seen murdered was a girl three years older than her that she referred to as "Clo." X1 said that during the second half of 1983, Tony picked her up from school and took her to a home in Gent, where Clo was delivering a baby on a bed. During the process, Clo was sexually assaulted and abused, finally dying from blood loss, with the baby taken away. Louf was able to provide police with the name of the school that Clo attended, giving them the necessary information to find class photos and show them to her.

Louf picked out the deceased Carine Dellaert as Clo. While looking at the class photos, X1 reportedly indicated another girl, "V.," and said, "they killed her too." Dellaert had gone missing in August 1982 and her body was found in a state of extreme decomposition in a cesspool in 1985. It was confirmed that Carine was three years older than X1. The autopsy report on the girl also corroborated Louf's statement that Clo wore "an ankle bracelet ... a chainlet." Moreover it included the presence of a laminaria tent in the girl's pelvis, for opening her cervix for childbirth. The victim's mother also learned that her daughter had maternity clothing with her after she went missing.

The home where Louf said that Clo had died was formerly a brothel called the International Club that catered to upper class clientele. X4's parents happened to live next door. Starting in 1991, the home was rented from the same owners who had the property in the 1980s to the owner of the Co-Cli-Co nightclub, where X1 said she'd been abused with Clo by Tony's customers. The Co-Cli-Co, found listed in Tony's diary, went bankrupt in 1984, largely indebted to a video shop owned by Tony as well as a firm owned by an infamous pornography producer named Gerard Cok. Cok was in league with an even larger pornographer named "Fat" Charles Geerts, previously accused of producing child pornography. In addition to these details, several sources confirmed the accuracy of X1's description of the home where she claimed Clo died, including the researchers who wrote *The X-Dossiers*, a police investigator, and a judge.

An additional witness, Fanny V., was a friend of Carine's that said the victim told her about sexual abuse by her father and his friends. Another witness, Louf's classmate Kristelle M., corroborated that Tony was Louf's pimp and that X1 told her she'd been impregnated by him. Kristelle told police that Louf would frequently go out with someone named "Christine, Carine, Caroline or Claudine," with other classmates of X1 saying that Carine went by "Clo."

In fact, Carine's father was originally a suspect in the girl's disappearance due to the fact that he had already been accused of incest by his wife in 1977, had been suspected of sleeping with a minor in 1965, and had waited a week before telling the police that Carine was missing. Moreover, he'd taken erotic pictures of her. Carine's Girl Scout group also said that the father and daughter acted more like a romantic couple than father and daughter. They also said Carine became terrified of the forest and heard her shrieking leading up to her kidnapping (van der Reijden 2007).

A third girl X1 described as a murder victim was named Christine. Based on Louf's details, the police were reminded of Christine Van Hees, a 16-year-old who had been discovered in February 1984, abused to death. X1 claimed that the victim had become involved with Nihoul in October 1983 before Christine learned how dangerous he was and feared for the safety of her family. Her friends reported that around that time, she had in fact begun to act strange (Frenkiel 2002).

Christine was forced into orgies and sex with X1, according to Louf. She claimed to have told Christine to try to speak to her parents about the sex trafficking, but, in the meantime, another girl told Nihoul and Tony about X1's advice to talk to her family. In turn, Christine and Louf were taken to an abandoned mushroom farming facility where the former was killed.

According to X1, Dutroux was present, though she perceived him as being on the outskirts of the abuse group's social circle. Researchers learned that Dutroux and an accomplice visited a skating rink that Christine attended. His wife, Michele Martin, said he often went there alone because it was easier to "seduce girls." Christine also went on a date with a "Marc" before her disappearance. Her friend who lived on the same street, Nathalie Geirnaert, was able to pick Dutroux out in two photos as someone Christine was seen with (van der Reijden 2007).

Nathalie also said that her friend had become terrified of something in the time leading up to her disappearance and that Christine asked Nathalie to accompany her on walks back home. She additionally testified that, on the night the girl was taken, there was an odd black car with a man behind the wheel sitting in front of Christine's home. A week later, a black car with four people who worked at Nihoul's radio station were seen observing the mushroom facility where the girl was murdered.

Other details included the fact that the victim regularly swam at a pool located in the same building where Nihoul hosted his radio show. This occurred in a town called Etterbeek, where Nihoul regularly attended the

Dolo club. Apparently, there was an anonymous tip to the police that suggested this club was essential to understanding the death of Christine.

At the time of the girl's death, her friend told investigators that Christine was involved in orgies and sadism with a dangerous collection of individuals. She reported to the police in February, 1984:

> We got to know each other in October 1983. Over time our discussions became more and more intimate. Christine told such unbelievable stories that I slowly became convinced that she made things up. She told me that she had gotten to know a group of people. She regularly saw them at an abandoned house close to her house. She regularly saw these people in the months October and November 1983. These people were older than Christine. She explained to me that meetings were held in that house, to which a road led about nobody knew. Other girls were in the group.
>
> Sometimes, she said, she went alone to the house to write her diary. Christine never spoke about this with girls from her school class. I was bewildered when she told me what happened there. She told me that if she ever spoke about this with her parents or brothers, her so-called friends would kill her and burn down the house. She told that in the group free love is practiced.... She told me that this group attracted and frightened her at the same time.
>
> In early 1984, I noticed that Christine had changed a lot. She had lost weight, was paler and in any case took less care of herself. She said she wanted to blow up all bridges because very bad things had happened. I noticed that she had bruises, and a cigarette burn on her arm. She then explained that it had started as a game, that those games had started slowly, but then became violent. Christine had come into conflict with one of the other girls in the other group. She felt very much attracted to a member of the gang. She told me that it was possible to feel sexually attracted to a man, without really loving him. She truanted from school. About her friends she said: "They are pigs, but I feel good with them." She said me that, once you ended up in that milieu, you never got out. It was of little use, she said, to talk about it with someone, because no one would believe her (van der Reijden 2007).

X1's description of the murder matched details from the actual case files and more. Louf said she was blindfolded and shoeless as she was forced out of a car, where she felt gravel beneath her feet before entering what smelled like a moldy location. The mushroom farming facility where Christine's corpse was found was indeed on a gravel lot and, due to the fact that it hadn't been in operation since 1972, a dank smell was reasonable.

In a 2003 Dutch documentary called 'De X-dossiers," the former owners of the site went through X1's descriptions and were blown away with her detail because the facility was very unique in architecture:

> The doors. We had very special, hand-made doors. Old doors with ornaments, which she described perfectly. She knew all that. She drew the chimney and the living room. It matched quite well. The chimney looked like it. She drew the rose window. A rose window is a rose window. It could well be our rose window. What she told about the champignonniere was accurate. I showed the description [of X1] to one of my brothers. That girl had to have been there. There's no other way. (Zembla 2003, translation van der Reijden 2007)

In the book *The X-Dossiers*, the authors described how the son of the facility owner was shown descriptions of the site from Regina Louf and a police officer that found Christine's body. He responded:

> That police officer has not been inside there, your witness X1 was. The police officer in question, Jacques Dekock, is summoned that evening and immediately confronted with the son. The confrontation doesn't last long. It's true, he admits. He was so dismayed by the body that evening that he hardly looked at the rest of the building. The complex was demolished in 1989. Nowhere information is available about how the building looked in 1984. It was such a complex clew of houses, hangers, driveways, halls and basements that all who would try to do a little guessing on describing the place would be seen through immediately. And that is what is so bizarre. The inspectors just couldn't figure it out how X1 told them that she got there by car, stepped out, stumbled.… The son of the owner had no problems with this. Almost immediately he could tell exactly through where X1 entered the building and how she reached the basement. That she stumbled in the hall is logical, he says. More people used to do that. By rebuilding two houses into one, a connection had been created with two stairs: the first one going down, then up again. 'In reality she was in the kitchen', the son deducts from the description of the wallpaper and the tiles which also is perfectly accurate. He went through it with his family. 'There are things we read in her testimony that reminded us of details that

we ourselves had long forgotten, like the motif on the tiles', he later says. Indeed, from the kitchen there was a separate doorway to the basement. And those flesh hooks? Yet another detail that only now recalls memories. "Of course, then she was in the scullery," the son says. His uncle made meat pies and had created a sort of industrial kitchen in the adjacent building. With a pen in his hand the son draws the route that X1 must have travelled that night. The rugged wooden table, the rain barrel. … Yes, yes, his father had left that when he moved out. It is extraordinarily, no question about it (Bulté 1999, translation van der Reijden 2007)."

X1 also noted that a tampon had been used to absorb Christine's blood. The police in 1984 had in fact found a blood-soaked tampon in the building with Christine's blood type. Louf remembered seeing a rope and a gas can and said the only light came from a candle, all of which police had also found at the scene. X1's recollections about the girl's body matched the descriptions of police: that she had been tied to a metal bar, that she had been severely burned, and that she had a hollow metal bar 30-cm long hammered through her wrist (van der Reijden 2007).

A final victim that Louf described and investigators matched with a missing girl was 15-year-old Katrien. She went missing in December 1991 and was found murdered in June 1992. X1 picked her picture out from a series and said that she believed Katrien was picked up by Tony and seemed to lack the same experience that other girls had. The victim was then abused at a party at a castle before being murdered. Among the perpetrators were Tony and Nihoul. X1 was able to give an accurate description of Katrien's hair color and length. However, police did not believe that she had identified the girl. Part of the reason may have been that one of the officers responsible for dismissing her testimony about Katriens seemed to have been close to Louf's pimp, Tony. This same officer was instructed to investigate Tony, as well, despite protests from other police who knew of their friendship.

Based on X1's description, the police were able to track down the site of the abuse as Castle Kattenhof of the de Caters family. In fact, the de Caters had buildings on some of the streets Louf identified. The adjacent castle belonged to famous art collector Axel Vervoordt, who had not only been accused of pedophilia, but was a good friend of Marina Abramović and possibly the Podestas.

CHAPTER TWENTY-EIGHT

A FLAWED INVESTIGATION

At the start, the case against Dutroux and Nihoul was being led by two figures already liked by the Belgian public for their role in investigating the death of socialist leader Andre Cools. Before prosecutor Michel Bourlet and examining magistrate Jean-Marc Connerotte could close in on the politician's killer, they were removed from the case. When they rescued Sabine and Laetitia upon the arrest of Dutroux, they were seen as heroes.

In September 1996, Connerotte selected BOB officer Patriek De Baets to head the investigation, operating directly under him and with little interference from the BOB at large. However, in October 1996, Connerotte was taken off of the case, ostensibly for attending a fundraiser for parents of missing children for just an hour and, thus, demonstrating a lack of objectivity in the case. This was despite the fact that he was on leave that day, insisted on paying for his meal, declined to meet the family of the girls and rejected their gift of flowers (Reuters 1996). Bourlet, who also attended, could not be removed due to his specific government position, but it would have been Connerotte who managed the investigation on the whole. When Connerotte was taken off the case, he was replaced by an inexperienced prosecutor named Jacques Langlois.

As the public had already believed the story would be covered up, the removal of Connerotte led to a massive outcry with some 275,000 people taking to the streets of Brussels in what was called the White March (Reuters 1996). Nevertheless, Langlois dismissed any suggestions of pedophile rings, neglecting evidence and directing his team down dead end leads (Bates 1999).

Then, in December 1996, the disparate investigation teams that had worked independently under Connerotte were brought into a single unit under the leadership of a single Gendarmerie Commandant Jean-Luc Duterm, ensuring that he managed the investigators under him. While Duterm went back and reinterpreted the existing testimony from the various witnesses and victims, Langlois pursued leads that his predecessor believed to be misdirection, such as the highly publicized investigation into a Satanic cult called Abrasax. Additionally, investigators previously trusted by the victims were replaced by aggressive, combative officers. This resulted in such disastrous effects as driving Nathalie W. to leave the case and attempting to discredit X1 (van der Reijden 2007).

Louf said of the new team:

> The two BOB officers with whom I have to work from now on come to pick me up for an "informal" talk…. The three of us go and sit at a table in a village cafeteria…. Eddy voices my suspicions in the following words: "We don't care if it is true or not. The only thing that matters to me is my paycheck at the end of the month.." I smile worryingly. Am I psychic after all? The discussion proceeds in the expected direction. The security – and investigative brigade of the gendarmerie thinks that the ball is in my court. I am the one who has to come up with evidence, they won't do any field – or investigative work anymore. In these words they ask for my cooperation. When I state that I do not have the authority to conduct searches, nor that I can come up with evidence if they are not willing to investigate, they just laugh at me…. Eddy begins to insinuate that it all couldn't have been so bad. Because, look, I have a husband and four kids, I have everything that I wish and also, I can laugh…. "Come on," Eddy says rather loud, "you also enjoyed it, didn't you? You can't say that everything was bad? You were in love with Tony, weren't you?" After exactly one year of hearings, in which I was treated with respect, I politely try to explain my feelings. I wasn't "in love" with him, I loved him; like a daughter loves her father [at least, that's what she tried to convince herself of as a young girl] …

She also said:

> I am only really disheartened when Eddy and his colleague interrogate my friend Tania. This happens in such a dehumanizing manner that I begin to feel sick. Her hearing is not recorded on video, and they know it. The two BOB officers eagerly use their power position to destabilize and intimidate Tania by bringing up her personal life. They question her in an office where every BOB officer walks in and out of, and where my supposedly well-protected dossiers are up for grabs. Tania asks what her personal life has to do with the case. After all, she did nothing more than encourage me to testify, and made the first telephone contact with Connerotte…. Are you also a victim? Were you also in the network? You're not going to tell me that you didn't have anything to do with the network of Ginie? Have you known De Baets a long time? Was this really

the first time you spoke to him, the 4th of September 1996? Are you sure you never were in the prostitution? Are you really sure? The discussion continues along these lines the whole afternoon. Tania is intimidated. Tania even became so scared that she comes to me in the late afternoon, looks silently at me for a while and then advises me to stop testifying. For the first time my friend understands my words just before she phoned up Connerotte in '96: "This is too big, Tania, I can't do anything against my perpetrators." (van der Reijden 2007)

Duterme also didn't seem to have a firm grasp of Louf's native language of Dutch. Independent Dutch researcher Joël van der Reijden wrote:

Duterme would continually ask questions about passages which would be completely clear to anyone speaking perfect Dutch [like van der Reijden, the author writing the passage]. Duterme probably made one of his biggest mistakes when he concluded from one of X1's statements that her grandmother had also been present at the murder of Christine Van Hees. The only thing that X1 had said here was: 'My grandmother also had those in her scullery' [referring to meat hooks she had seen in the champignon factory]. In another case, Duterme did not understand that the word "bus" has more than one meaning in Dutch. He apparently knew that it could refer to a vehicle that drives on the road, but forgot that it can also refer to a small container in which things can be put (a "can" or "small box," usually metal). Describing the location where Christine Van Hees had been murdered, X1 at some point spoke about a "bus" containing a liquid. In another place she called this object a "jerrycan." Duterme wrote next to the sentence containing "jerrycan" that this is a different object than the "bus containing liquid" described earlier, which is complete madness. Baudouin Dernicourt, who had come up with the false statement that De Baets and Hupez had not filed an official report of X1 misidentifying Christine Van Hees, made even worse "mistakes." Pertaining to Carine "Clo" Dellaert which X1 was to identify from a set of pictures, X1 at one point stated: "Not that I saw, but…" and "… she wasn't in there also." In Dernicourt's translations this became: "I know that I saw her…" and "Wasn't she in there also?" Just incredible. There are numerous other incorrect statements from the rereaders that were echoed all over the media. (2007)

To discredit X1, some of her statements were neglected, misinterpreted, or taken out of context while false ones were completely invented.

This negative portrayal of the victim was then fed to the press. Louf's friend, Tanja V., had her home searched for incriminating evidence and the BOB used helicopters to capture footage of a home the new investigators claimed were a part of a conspiracy between X1 and the old BOB officer, Da Baets, to invent the entire pedophile ring story. Da Baets was ultimately acquitted of this so-called conspiracy.

Demonstrating the extent to which he could influence public perception of the X dossiers, Langlois met with the producers of an important French language TV show called *Au Nom de la Loi* which went on to make four shows that aired between 1997 and 2000 in which Nihoul was portrayed as innocent in the crimes of Dutroux.

CHAPTER TWENTY-.NINE

PERPETRATORS IN HIGH PLACES

The victims not only accused the police of involvement in the abuse network. In fact, supposed perpetrators reached to the highest echelons of Belgian society, accusations that were corroborated by overlapping accounts in some cases. X1, X2, X4 and two anonymous letter writers identified the Lippens brothers, two powerful businessmen in Belgium, as abusers.

Count Maurice Lippens managed the large Belgian bank Société Générale de Banque and the Belgian branch of the Fortis Bank, as well as established SN Brussels Airlines, all of which he did alongside Viscount Etienne Davignon. Davignon was a powerful player on the international stage, acting as a director of the large Belgian chemical company Solvay, the first president of the International Energy Agency, Vice President of the European Commission, a member of the Council on Foreign Relations, the Trilateral Commission, and an honorary chairman of Bilderberg. He was also a good friend of Henry Kissinger, a director of Kissinger Associates, and worked in partnership with the Rockefellers. Maurice Lippens too attended Bilderberg and the Trilateral Commission.

Maurice Lippens and his brother Leopold, a long-standing mayor of the city of Knokke, were accused of some of the most vicious crimes, including child abuse and the making of snuff films. Their relative Count Francois Lippens, honorary consul general of Belgium, was also mentioned in one message. It read: "Transmitted to examining magistrate Mr. LANGLOIS in Neufchâteau, his dossier 86/0/96 [April 22, 1998] ... Annex 161. A note on the existence of a SNUFF network of which Mr. GLATZ of the CIDE would have had knowledge and in which one would find a certain François LIPPENS, who is close to the mayor of Knokke, whose name is often mentioned in very horrible activities. I conducted no verification or crosscheck."

According to X2, Davignon and the Lippens brothers were present at a party that was attended by minors: "Parties with underage girls in the Cromwel hotel in Knokke. Present: Delvoie – Karel – X2 – Lippens – Van Gheluwe – Etienne Davignon. The girls knew where to go and with whom. Lippens hits the little girls. Several meetings between Karel and Davignon in the Memling hotel with the two Lippens."

X2 also mentioned two different Karels, a government official at a court in Brussels to whom she served as a mistress and Dr. Karel van Miert, a Socialist politician and one time director of Solvay, involved in child abuse. Van Miert was a member of European Parliament, an advisor to one of the largest Dutch banks, Rabobank; German utility company, RWE; manufacturing giant Philips; Goldman Sachs and Eli Lilly.

Other elite figures mentioned were members of the House of Merode, the most prominent family of Belgian nobility. X4 and Nathalie W. mentioned Prince Alexandre de Merode as being involved in satanic child abuse and killings, while X2 listed the "Merode brothers," including Prince Baudouin de Merode and his brother Lionel, as participating in sadistic child abuse (van der Reijden 2007).

Dutch writer Joël van der Reijden pointed out that Solvay had numerous connections to child abuse and trafficking. For instance, a lawyer in Brussels named Charles De Selliers De Moranville was accused of child abuse, with suspicions of building a tunnel for transporting children. His family had some Solvay connections, according to van der Reijden. More explicitly, two major Solvay shareholders, the Boël and Janssen families, were accused of trafficking drugs and children. X2 named another abuser who happened to be a quality and innovation manager at Solvay. A groundskeeper at the Solvay family castle was also accused of child abuse and the Solvay's Chateau des Amerois was said to be a location where abuse occurred.

Members of the Belgian royal family that cropped up in the Dutroux affair included Princess Liliane de Rety, whose property was said to have children buried on it. This site was purchased by shareholders of Solvay, the Delaware family, in 2004. X2 said she'd seen Prince Laurent, the brother of the country's crown prince, masturbating at child sexual abuse parties. X3 named the son of King Albert I, Prince Charles, as well as the son of King Leopoldo III, King Baudouin and either King Albert I or II as being involved in child abuse. However, her testimony covered a much earlier timeline, from the 1950s to the 1960s, and thus could not be matched with the stories provided by other witnesses and victims (van der Reijden 2007).

THE INTELLIGENCE CONNECTIONS

Michel Nihoul indicated just how much sway he had in Belgium after he was released on parole in 1999. In a 2001 interview with *Der Spiegel*, he said,

> I control the government. … Everyone has compromising dossiers on one another, to be used as leverage in the right situation.… This is the Belgian disease.… Give me another 20.000 Marks, and I give you a serving minister who is embroiled in a murder.… I know the killer and will have him contact the minister by telephone. You can listen along, okay?

After he believed the reporter's voice recorder to be turned off, he added that, for a six-digit price,

> I will give you a picture in which Prince Albert jumps a 16 year old girl. Naked. Shot at the second floor of the Mirano Club 20 years ago [where a pedophile blackmail ring allegedly was situated, according to other witnesses].… Then I do have to leave Belgium" (van der Reijden 2007).

Nihoul's connections were indeed deep. In addition to the aforementioned links to Belgian high society, the pedosadism ring described by the victims were part of a broader intelligence operation. This could be seen from the BOB on up. Here's just a brief description of the corruption within the legal system:

It was learned that one of the BOB officers that took over the investigation from less corrupt officials was a drug runner for Nihoul, while another was involved with the CIA's Gladio operations. Jean-Luc Duterme, who oversaw the Dutroux unit, was accused by police officer and victim X2 of being involved in the abuse network. Duterme's superior, Commandant for the Brussels BOB, lied to Connorette in saying that the BOB did not have files on Michel Nihoul. His other superior, head of the Neufchateau gendarmerie, was instructed in 1986 by Nihoul not to investigate a business partner of his linked to Italian mob and fascist groups. Additionally, this superior's good friend, the police commissioner of Brussels, was accused of participation in the abuse ring by X2 and Nathalie W. The commissioner's ally, too, was accused of torturing children and once directed a Gladio-affiliated fascist think tank called CEPIC that was within the country's Social-Christian Party (PSC).

CEPIC was a crucial part of the Belgian Gladio network. Investigator Connerotte's successor, Jacques Langlois, was a strong backer of the PSC, as was his family. The party's one-time minister Joseph Michel appointed him as magistrate in 1993. Michel, a founding member of CEPIC, also helped secure Nihoul an early release from jail after he was contacted by him in 1978.

More importantly, the think tank was managed by Paul Vanden Boey-nants, former prime minister of Belgium and Minister of Defense, along-side Benoît, Baron de Bonvoisin, a far right activist involved in illegal campaign financing for Vanden Boeynants. The politicians were highly involved in right-wing terrorist operations in Belgium under the CIA's Gladio program. They were both also pedophiles and sadists.

X1, X3 and X4 all accused Vanden Boeynants of extreme abuse of chil-dren or of participating in the hunting of children. He was seen at Ni-houl's preferred club, the Dolo, with X2 noting the presence of Vanden Boeynants's personal chauffeur there as well. The driver was apparently chatting with an infamous mobster, both of whom were accused of child abuse by Regina Louf.

De Bonvoisin, nicknamed the Black Baron, was seen as one of the big-gest monsters in the ring by X1 and X2. His sister married a Count Herve d'Ursel, who Louf said was also involved in the pedophile ring. The Black Baron's other sister married Bernard de Merode, who was said to have been involved in satanic ritual abuse according to X4 and Nathalie W. X2 claimed that her pimp set up a meeting attended by the Prince and Princess of Chi-may, as well as the de Merode, d'Ursel and de Bonvoisin families. She also said that children were hunted in the woods at the Chimay estate.

First chairman of the PSC in 1961, Vanden Boeynants then became the country's prime minister from 1966 to 1968 and again in 1979. In between these two stints he was defense minister from 1972 to 1978. A long time fascist sympathizer, Vanden Boeynants helped revive the PSC while attempting to run an anti-communist campaign and fight the labor wing of the party. Together with Baron de Bonvoisin, Vanden Boeynants helped drive the Belgian wing of the fascist Gladio program, which would cultivate a strategy of tension in the country in order to increase the pow-er of the national security apparatus and stifle the left-wing.

This began in part when Vanden Boeynants established the Cercle des Nations in 1969 with Baron de Bonvoisin and Paul Vankerkhoven. The Cercle des Nations was a monarchist, fascist organization made up of just 80 or so members. The group held an event to honor the fascist military that ruled Greece, another to celebrate Papa Doc's 10th year of autocratic rule in Haiti, and promoted dictatorships in Spain, Argenti-na, and Portugal along with African apartheid in its publication, *Nouvel Europe Magazine* (NEM). Vankerkhoven had his own additional right-wing credentials as the founder of the Belgian branch of the World An-ti-Communist League and secretary-general of CEDI, an anti-communist, Catholic hub founded by the last crown prince of Austria-Hungary, Otto von Habsburg.

The Cercle des Nations was followed by the creation of CEPIC, which had similar goals of squashing a left-wing within the PSC. Meanwhile, fascist organizations developed around the NEM publication, ultimately resulting in the formation of a militant group called Front de la Jeunesse (FJ), which operated fascist training camps and had Baron de Bonvoison's advisor Francis Dossogne as its leader. Then, in 1974, the private military intelligence organization, Public Information Office (PIO), was created with the fascist Major Jean-Marie Bougerol selected by Vanden Boeynants and de Bonvoisin as the head. Bougerol in turn acted as an advisor to Francis Dossogne of the FJ.

The fascist tendencies of these groups could be evidenced in part by the fact that Bougerol and CEPIC director Bernard Mercier attended Franco's funeral in Spain. A Nazi-turned U.S. Defense Intelligence Agency and NATO operative named Paul Latinus also joined PIO and FJ in the late 1979s, where he was the leader of the military police-only squadron Group G. Group G, along with other units across the Belgian state apparatus, such as the Royal Military School, the Special Intervention Squadron (Diana Group), and the BOB's narcotics division attempted to infiltrate and subvert the government (van der Reijden 2007).

When a confidential State Security memo was published by *De Morgen* in 1981, it was revealed that Baron de Bonvoisin, Jean Bougerol and CEPIC were building up a fascist network. Interestingly, the memo neglected to mention the most powerful member of this group, Prime Minister Paul Vanden Boeynants. The excerpt read:

> It was determined that certain members of the board of the C.E.P.I.C. (x) in the past have lent their cooperated to the publication and the editorial office of NEM, were part of the NEM-clubs of the F.J. and maintained contact with board members or supporters of the two latter mentioned groups. Amongst others, it concerns: Jean Breydel, secretary-general of the C.E.P.I.C., Benoit de Bonvoisin, treasurer of the C.E.P.I.C., Joseph (Jo) Gerard, Paul Van Kerkhoven, Joseph Franz and Bernard Mercier. The board, the administration and the editorial office of the NEM, which has been published under this name since 1971 by the "Compagnie Internationale des Editions Populaires" (C.I.D.E.P.), is located at no. 5 of the Dekenstraat in Brussels. ... Furthermore, at this address was located the secretariat of the 1972 founded NEM-clubs, as well,

until 1978, the seat of F.J. … . The seat of C.E.P.I.C. is located at no. 39 of the Belliardstraat in Brussels. This building also contains the Belliard auditorium, the seat of "Mouvement d'Action pour l'Unite Europeenne" (xx), just as the offices of the "Societe de Promotion et de la Distribution Generale" (P.D.G.), supervised, through a go-between, by Benoit de Bonvoisin. … The NEM is supported by Benoit de Bonvoisin, who pays the rent of the in the Dekensstraat located offices and hires the editor in chief as an advisor … Francis Dossogne, head of the F.J., was paid in the same way, until he left the NEM. The partnership P.D.G., and consequently de Bonvoisin, through a gobetween finances the magazine "INFOREP" which claims to be a "daily paper for party leaders," but in reality is a bi-language magazine with strong anti-communist leanings. From 1976 to 1978 its editor in chief was Major Jean Bougerol, a higher career officer working for the headquarters of the domestic armed forces. Jean Bougerol has spoken at lectures organized by the NEM-clubs. … This officer, who keeps in close contact with Bernard Mercier, board member of the C.E.P.I.C., was mentioned as one of the organizers of the transport from Antwerp to the seat of the C.E.P.I.C. in Brussels of a wanted neo-nazi terrorist. This person had to be taken by Bernard Mercier to a domain in the Ardennes belonging to de Bonvoisin and subsequently to France. The German was intercepted by State Security during the trip from Antwerp to Brussels. … According to unverifiable sources the F.J. would have approached several foreign governments and opposition-movements for financial support. (van der Reijden 2007)

It was in the aftermath of the memo that CEPIC was ended, as was de Bonvoisin's life in government. When the FJ was shut down in response to the memo, it was reborn as Westland New Post (WNP), led by the former head of the FJ, Paul Latinus. A DEA agent was also said to be in the WNP, as were military police and BOB officers. The head of security for WNP was not only a murderer but an employee of the U.S.-intelligence-linked Wackenhut Corporation. Other members of the WNP included the secretary of the International Drug Enforcement Association and the founder of Belgium's National Bureau for Drugs. In addition to providing intelligence to the CIA about the country's leftists and dissidents, he was accused of participating in pedophilic orgies. Another WNP member was acting as director of Wackenhut Belgium, whose past included being involved with terrorists that attempted to assassinate de Gaulle in France.

In turn, the individuals involved in this group continued in their covert, fascist activities and played roles in the Gang of Nijvel robberies between 1982 and 1985. The Gang of Nijvel, also known as the Brabant killers, were a group of criminals thought to have committed a series of violent robberies in the Belgian province of Brabant. This included such crimes as robbing grocery stores and restaurants, stealing weapons and cars, and committing murder. The spree saw some 28 people killed and 22 injured (BBC 2017).

Joël van der Reijden pointed out that some victims were former members of the CEPIC, knew of secret plans of subversion, or had been involved in sex parties, suggesting that assassinations were buried within what was made to look like a spree of random crimes. The group may have also played a role in the Cellules Communistes Combattantes bombings that took place around the same time in 1984 and 1985. This group was said to have targeted property representing capitalism, rather than individuals, such as American companies Litton Industries and Honeywell, a NATO support group, police stations and banks. This would essentially fit the pattern of false flag attacks carried under Gladio in other countries.

It was learned that some of those within this network were actually a part of the CIA's Gladio operations in Belgium, suggesting that these attacks were a part of a strategy of tension, as occurred in Italy and elsewhere. In response to the robberies and bombings, the Belgian government deployed about 1,000 soldiers from the Belgian army onto the streets.

Van der Reijden cited an October 14, 1997 regular session of the Belgian Chamber of Representatives as follows:

"Around 1981, Paul Latinus testified more than once that he worked for the American intelligence services. Also his assistant, Marcel Barbier, claimed to work for an international organization of which he never wanted to give the name.... On top of that, Paul Latinus testified in 1983 that his organization, the WNP, to which Libert, Barbier and others belonged, worked for an unnamed allied power and countered the Soviet infiltration in Belgium."

One WNP member said: "One received orders. We can go back to, say, 1982. From 1982 to 1985. There were projects.'[I was told:] You, Mr. Libert, know nothing about why we're doing this. Nothing at all. All we ask is that your group, with cover from the gendarmerie, with cover from Security, carry out a job. Target: The supermarkets. Where are they? What kind of locks are there? What sort of protection do they have that could interfere with our operations? Does the store manager lock up? Or do they use an outside security company?'" Seemingly referencing the Gang of Nivel robberies, the member said, "We carried out the orders and sent in our reports: Hours of opening and closing. Everything you want to know about a supermarket. What was this for? This was one amongst hundreds of missions."

An early member of Group G and acquaintance of Paul Latinus, said, "When I joined the Gendarmerie, I became a devout fascist. At the Diana Group I got to know people who had the same convictions as me. We greeted each other like the Nazis.... " He elaborated on the fascist plans for the network, "During the gatherings of the Front a plan was developed to destabilize Belgium and to prepare it for a non-democratic regime. This plan consisted of two parts: a political terrorism cell and a gangsterism cell. I worked in the gangsterism cell. I was one of the specialists who had to train young guys with rightist leanings, to knead them into a well trained gang prepared to do anything. After that I had to break all contact with them, so they could exist as an independent group and do robberies without them realizing they were part of a well-planned plot.... " He continued, "They'd have two plans. The first one was to organise gangs to hold up hostages, you know, killing; the second one was to organise the so called 'Left movement' who will do a terrorist attempt just to make believe, make the population believe that these terrorist attempts were done by the Left."

In addition to these admissions, there was strong evidence that other associates of the CEPIC and related fascist groups were involved. Jean Bultot, assistant director of a prison in Brussels, helped link Nazis within the prison to the fascist network outside its walls. He was an associate of the head of FJ, Francis Dossogne, and the owner of a fascist club. Within the burnt wreck of a car stolen by the Gang of Nijvel was a scrap of paper from a speech Bultot had given at a shooting competition he had arranged. The words were in the handwriting of Butot's girlfriend who worked for the ministry of a former member of the CEPIC. Her boss, along with the secretary of state who was also a former CEPIC member, had attended Bultot's event. In the same month and at the same venue, Bultot had shown off the bullet proof material known as Kevlar, a new product at the time that happened to be found in the doors of the same burned out vehicle (van der Reijden 2007).

In addition to being closely tied to the aforementioned fascist networks, CEPIC was allied with foreign intelligence agencies. Its director was not only involved in resurrecting the PSC but also in drawing up a plan to assassinate Patrice Lumumba when Belgium lost control of the Congo. Another CEPIC director allowed the WNP to board militants and store documents. He additionally convened often with members of foreign intelligence agencies. Like Director Vankerkhoven, he liaised with Aginter Press, a CIA-controlled fascist group in Portugal. This group was linked to key members of the Gladio network, former SS-Obersturmbannführer in the Waffen-SS Otto Skorzeny and Italian neo-Fascist terrorist Stefano Delle Chiaie. Aginter Press was founded by Yves Guérin-Sérac, whose OAS attempted to kill De Gaulle. Documents retrieved from Aginter Press in 1974 echoed the strategy of tension pursued by CEDIC:

> In the first phase of our political activity we must create chaos in all structures of the regime. Two forms of terrorism can provoke such a situation: blind terrorism (committing massacres indiscriminately which cause a large number of victims), and selective terrorism (eliminate chosen persons). This destruction of the state must be carried out as much as possible under the cover of "communist activities." After that, we must intervene at the heart of the military, the juridical power and the church, in order to influence popular opinion, suggest a solution, and clearly demonstrate the weakness of the present legal apparatus.... Popular opinion must be polarized in such a way, that we are being presented as the only instrument capable of saving the nation. It is obvious that we will need considerable financial resources to carry out such operations" (van der Reijden 2007).

Baron de Bonvoisin, co-founder and treasurer of CEPIC, claimed that he had an important ally in U.S. intelligence. He worked on their behalf and, in return, they forced his antagonist, Belgium's head of State Security, out of office.

> Besides his political role within the CEPIC, Benoît de Bonvoisin exerted an influence in Zaïre [Congo; Belgian colony until 1960], firstly in the struggle against communism and secondly attempting to curb corruption, with friends from the American administration. Van den Boeynants assigned General Roman and Benoît on a number of missions in order to counteract the Soviet influence in Belgium.... Through a number of people with whom he was in touch in the United States and France, B. de B felt it necessary to try and get the Belgian intelligence services under democratic control. He considered it urgent, since this was the only secret service to es-

cape control … [bashes Albert Raes, head of Belgian intelligence] Largely because of B. de B, Raes was forced to resign in 1990 … B. de Bonvoisin was highly regarded by the head of the French secret services, Alexandre de Marenches, but the latter had no esteem for Albert Raes … [bashes Albert Raes a bit more] … he [Raes] tried to associate B. de B with the extreme right, a trick often used by the Soviet secret services…. Professor Lode Van Outrive concluded that: "Several times the Americans tried to convince Raes to concentrate first and foremost on the Eastern block countries whereas he seemed more interested in targeting extreme right wing movements. This clearly bothered the Americans who got him to resign" (van der Reijden 2007).

As demonstrated, Benoît de Bonvoisin and Paul Vanden Boeynants were part of a right-wing, often Catholic network that stretched across Europe. These individuals shared overlapping memberships in a variety of groups that included the Opus Dei, Knights of Malta, Mouvement d'Action pour l'Union de l'Europe, l'Institut Europeen de Developpement, Académie Europeene des Sciences Politiques, Ordre du Rouvre, the Ligue Internationale de la Liberte (WACL), Cercle des Nations, and the Pinay Circle (Le Cercle).

Established by French prime minister Antoine Pinay and his fascist intelligence agent Jean Violet, Le Cercle had convened with powerful, right-wing players, including CIA directors William Casey and William Colby, to concoct a unified strategy around the world. With funding from Otto von Habsburg, Violet was really the brains behind Le Cercle and, through Belgium's Cercle des Nations, worked with Baron de Bonvoisin, Paul Vanden Boeynants, and Paul Vankerkhoven to help enact the Belgian aspect of the strategy of tension. Like Colby, Casey and von Hapsburg, Violet was also a member of Opus Dei and the Knights of Malta and performed intelligence on behalf of the Vatican.

Two BOB officers were provided information by two aristocrats in Opus Dei that some nine members of the Catholic group were strategizing to undermine the Belgian government. Among these nine were Paul Vanden Boeynants and the general of the military police, who was suspected of pedophilia and incest himself. They were thought to have hatched this plan at the Opus Dei meeting at Castle Dongelberg, a location that both X2 and Nathalie W. cited as locations of child abuse. X4 also claimed that individuals from Opus Dei were the most violent of those who abused her.

In a trove of notes X1 had written over the course of six years before coming forward, she described one perpetrator who consistently donned brown sunglasses, a military police officer who she had also seen in *Humo* magazine. BOB officers suspected this was Madani Bouhouche, due to beliefs he may have been involved in the Gang of Nijvel. Being shown 40 pictures of various gendarme officers, including some thought to have been linked to the crime spree and others not involved, Louf picked eight, four of which were either from the far right or tied to the Brabant killings. One was Madani Bouhouche, who was selected alongside former gendarme officer Christian Amory, gendarme colonel Gerard Lhost, and gendarme colonel Rene Mayerus. Bouhouche was advised by the WNP and FJ, who were in turn a part of the network run by Baron de Bonvoisin and Paul Vanden Boeynants, who worked closely with the CIA, DIA, DEA and Wackenhut.

Bouhouche, according to X1, had taken her to "the factory" where abuse occurred and snuff films were recorded. Amory carted her and other victims to locations where children were hunted, such as parks and recording studios. Louf placed Vanden Boeynants' private driver, as well as Baron de Bonvoisin, Michel Nihoul, Tony the pimp, former prime minister Wilfried Martens and others at the factory where sadistic abuse occurred. During the investigation, she took BOB officers to the location, where they learned it was a factory owned by the Boas family, good friends of Paul Vanden Boeynants. X1 saw a man named Roger at the factory, who turned out to be CEDIC and Cercle des Nations member Roger Boas. This firm turned out to be a defense firm owned by Roger Boas and tied to the Israeli military.

Bouhouche was known to attend the fascist Jonathan Club, frequented by Nihoul. The venue's owner was also an associate of Nihoul. Bouhouche was arrested in 1986, at which point he chose a CEPIC council member to be his lawyer. This attorney was also an associate of Nihoul, worked as a lawyer for fascists Francis Dossogne and Paul Latinus, and was accused of being in the abuse network.

Amory was a gendarme officer within Bouhouche's Nazi clique and responsible for investigating the Barbant spree. In 2003, he, Baron Benoit de Bonvoisin, and Pierre de Bonvoisin were prosecuted for creating false KGB documents in an attempt to demonstrate the existence of a "vast left-wing conspiracy" on behalf of State Security against de Bonvoisin (van der Reijden 2007).

Despite the suspicious nature of these figures, Joël van der Reijden noted:

> Even though there are plenty of reasons to be suspicious of these men, it should be remembered that the accusations against Mayerus, Lhost, Amory and Bouhouche are less powerful than many other aspects of X1's testimony. Bouhouche was already Belgium's most famous gangster and his face had appeared in the media here and there. And unfortunately, neither the authors of the book *The X-Dossiers*, nor the Dutroux dossier summary, reported how many of the 40 pictures portrayed real suspects. X1 misidentified three, and possibly four pictures, which at best gives us a 60% accuracy rate" (2007).

The intelligence network then tied all the way back to the pedophile ring itself. Not only did it serve the monstrous needs of the Belgian far right in a sadistic manner, but also for gaining leverage in political society. X1 described the roles of children in sexual blackmail operations:

> Since I was 8 or 9 years old, Mitch [Nihoul] would often enough take me with him and give me the assignment to hang around a certain customer. I liked doing that. I enjoyed seeing them shamble around, their efforts to stay out of my way unnoticed. I smiled when Mich asked me to stand next to a customer to make a picture, and how the customer reluctantly smiled and put a weak arm around my shoulder.... The glances which were then exchanged between the one taking the picture and the customer were priceless. The customer knew he was trapped.... In the night they had been the boss, now they were prey.... Too bad that most of them, once they knew they had been trapped, went to experiment even more during the night...
>
> In Brussels there was a villa in which a room was set up with built-in cameras. Even in the 1970s these cameras were so discrete that only the people who maintained them and the child- prostitutes knew where they were located.... Why did I had to get those guys clearly in the picture, why was I supposed to get them to hit me and brutally rape me? Why was "regular" sex often not enough? ... Blackmail, the word that was never mentioned, I only started to really understand when I was thirteen, fourteen years old...
>
> Contracts between the business milieu and the political world, contracts between businessmen amongst each other, fraud with subsidies or licenses, setting up fake firms, criminal contracts like arms trade ... everything was possible. And it always ended with

sex and children. ... Pictures were taken, in jest, to keep both parties to their contracts. ... The men were brought to ideas by child pornography movies that were played at parties. ... The pimps also had another tactic. They invited a person who could be useful to them. They went to dine with him, and took him – after he had been liquored up – to a "party." Men from the top layer of society are used to visiting or getting offered prostitutes. They usually knew that something like this would follow, and the prostitutes they would see upon entering would be slightly older girls, between 16 [sexually mature in Belgium] and 18 years old. More booze and cocaine would be supplied, for ambience. And only then the "prey" would be taken to a room where a younger girl was waiting, like me, then.

Most men probably realized only afterwards in what kind of hornet's nest they now found themselves, but by then it was far too late. ... Men were introduced to the network by colleagues, friends or family members. Carefully or slowly, or briskly after a party. Step by step customers, who first went to bed with me cautiously, were stimulated to rougher sex. I was forced to help them with that ... They became complicit and at the same time their mutual connections became tighter. Not one of these people was still inclined to sign contracts with individuals outside the network. If that happened one could make them pay dearly for that ... (van der Reijden 2007).

About Louf's description, van der Reijden said, "To summarize, extreme sadomasochist (SM) obsessions combined with blackmail appear to be the most obvious reasons for the existence of the abuse networks. Judging by some of the names, the extreme abuse almost seems like the ultimate admission test for some aspect of what [senior officials of the CIA-affiliated BCCI bank] once termed 'the black network'" (2007).

Location of former house of Marc Dutroux in the Rue Daubresse 63, Jumet, Belgium. The house has been demolished and replaced with a small monument.
IIVQ / Tijmen Stam, Creative Commons

CHAPTER THIRTY

DID AND SATANISM

A s noted, several of the victims that came forward may have suffered from DID, most notably X1. She reported that a number of her alters had the same age as when they were formed. Louf described her experience in this way:

> More than ever I discovered that I was missing time. I turned out to have gone to school, get good grades, I even turned out to know several classmates who spoke to me, but somehow this all had gone past me. It seemed as if someone else took over from me as soon as the door of my house closed behind me. It seemed as if the abused Ginie was put away until Tony again stood at my bed or at the school gate. The abused Ginie hardly was aware of school and family life, the other Ginie seemed not present during the abuse, and so lived "normal."
>
> … It had always been this way. In Knokke, at grandmother's, the adults had noticed that I talked to the voices in my head, that I often rapidly changed moods, or even began to speak with another voice or accent. Even though I was only 5 or 6, I understood that something like this was weird and that it was not allowed. I learned to hide my voices, my other "selves." After what had happened to Clo, the voices, and the bizarre feeling that I at times was led by the inner voices got stronger. After the initiation I no longer resisted against the voices. It was blissful to disappear into nothingness, and only to become conscious again if Tony was there. The pain seemed more bearable.

As X1's pimp, Tony was described as nurturing the girl's alters. There was Kenny, who endured some of the more sadistic abuse. Stone responded only to Tony and was used to manage Louf's fear. Moon was formed as a means of handling the most freezing of cold temperatures.

> Tony was the only adult who understood that something was "wrong" in my head. He didn't get mad about it, but cultivated it. He gave me different names: Pietemuis, Meisje, Hoer, Bo. The names slowly started to become part of me. The strange thing was

that if he mentioned a name, the mood that fit that name was immediately called up. Pietemuis [Small Mouse] became the name of the little girl that he brought home after the abuse – a scared and nervous girl that he could comfort by talking to her in a caring and fatherly kind of way. Meisje [Girl] was the name of that part of me that only belonged to him. If he abused me in my bed in the early morning, for example, or if there was no one around us. Hoer [Whore], the name of that part of me that worked for him. Bo, the young woman who cared for him if he was drunk and needed to be looked after, X1 explained. "Now you just leave that to me," he said when I asked him curiously why he gave me so many names, "daddy Tony knows you better than you know yourself." That was also true (van der Reijden 2007).

In the Dutroux affair, there seemed to be credible claims of occult abuse, as well as obviously bizarre forms of torture that would have easily fit into the category of "satanic panic" used by promoters of the witch hunt narrative in the U.S. in the 1980s. According to Joël van der Reijden, these details were interspersed with a larger, more absurd story involving a Luciferian religious order, called Abrasax. He used an article from a December 29, 1996 issue of the the *Sunday Times* as "one of the best examples in which some of the most accurate (albeit hard to believe) information appears to have been strategically mixed in with a central piece of disinformation" (2007). The article read:

> SATANIC sects involved in bizarre rites including human sacrifice are being linked by Belgian police with this summer>s string of grisly paedophile murders in which at least four children died. Five witnesses came forward last week and described how black masses were held, at which children were killed in front of audiences said to have included prominent members of Belgian Picture of Abrasax headquarters in the small, stuffy home of Francis «AnubisMoloch» Desmedt and Dominique «Nahema Nephthys» Kindermans where maybe 20 persons could be involved in a ritual at the same time. The profoundly negative Abrasax cult consisted of four institutes: The Belgian Church of Satan, the Wicca center, the Order for Luciferian Initiation and the Gnostic church. society. One investigator said it was «like going back to the Middle Ages».
>
> The tentacles of the sects appear to have stretched beyond the borders of Belgium to Holland, Germany and even America.
>
> The witnesses – several of whom claim to have received death threats – say that young babies were handed over by their parents

willingly in return for money. In other cases the victims were abducted. [PEHI note: The incest aspect should definitely have been described here. The "abductions" should also have been explained in more detail] The witnesses, who are believed to have identified the sites where the masses took place to the police, said organisers had also photographed participants and threatened to hand over their pictures if they went to the police.

The investigation centres on Abrasax, a self-styled institute of black magic, whose headquarters in the village of Forchies-la-Marche in southern Belgium was raided by police last week. Human skulls were among the objects removed from the run-down building.

...Police have long suspected that Dutroux, a convicted paedophile, was part of an international network which abducted children, sexually abused them and then killed them. Their activities appear to have been financed by the sale of pornographic videos filmed by members of the ring. Psychotherapy was also practiced here. Keep the following in mind: like Jumet didn't disprove the existence of a network surrounding Nihoul and the Trusgnach case didn't disprove high level involvement in abuse networks, so the Abrasax disinformation doesn't prove (high level) Satanism doesn't exist. It's important to note that there are innumerable and very similar reports of cultist or Satanic practices in combination with child abuse. Going through U.S. and UK newspaper archives since the late 1970s will turn up thousands of (mainly superficial) reports on ritual abuse and Satanism. In the XDossiers there also appears a fair dose.

...Investigators are still trying to determine the precise nature of the links between the Satanists and the paedophile groups.

In a separate twist, a Belgian newspaper claimed yesterday that a former European commissioner was among a group of judges, senior politicians, lawyers and policemen who attended orgies held in a Belgian chateau and organised by Michel Nihoul, one of Dutroux>s alleged accomplices. La Derniere Heure, which claimed to have a guest list, did not name the commissioner but said he «came with a girl, Josette, nicknamed Jojo, the Bomb (van der Reijden 2007)».

Van der Reijden went on to comment on how highlighting the Abrasax cult served to muddy the picture of the actual investigation:

Everything mentioned in this article is accurate, meaning that this is what a number of anonymous (to the public) witnesses were testifying about in Neufchateau at that. Although not all spoke about Satanism, at least half of them did. But besides the exaggerated focus on Satanism, the disinformation here is that this whole Satanic or sectarian aspect of the investigation centered around the Abrasax cult. The X-Dossiers had absolutely nothing to do with Abrasax and even though there might have been some circumstantial Dutroux/Weinstein-related evidence against the cult to justify a house search some day (144), there's no good reason why, with all those other promising leads, this questionable and highly delicate one had to be picked out for a premature house search. Unless, of course, the aim was to discredit the whole investigation, which is what Connerotte and his chief investigator De Baets have publicly stated (145). The basic idea was to discredit any future claims of Satanism and extreme abuse by bringing up the (soon to be discredited) Abrasax affair. This motive also becomes obvious when one learns that Duterme, with the consent of Langlois, scrapped all of the 43 house searches recommended by De Baets and Bourlet. Their list was based on the most promising information supplied by the X-witnesses, which indeed included "a former European commissioner … judges, senior politicians, lawyers and policemen" (2007).

One victim who claimed to have been abused in an occult ritual was Jacques Thoma, former treasurer of the youth wing of the PSC and employee of CEPIC member Jean-Paul Dumont, accused of child sexual abuse. He said that between 1985 and 1986, he was sexually abused in satanic rituals under the guise of initiation into the Catholic society, Opus Dei. At one ritual, he said he saw 13-14 year old "girls from a country in the East" before

> … [h]e was drugged [and] taken into a room with masked people who had dressed in black robes. The participants drank blood. He was placed in the presence of a naked little girl laying down on an altar – she had died.
>
> He encountered the grand master, Francois-Joseph, who told him that he was a police informant and that he had to be careful … Francois-Joseph is a notary implicated in the trafficking of girls for prostitution from the East.
>
> He wanted to leave but was drugged again. He woke up the following day in his car.

Thoma then quit the PSC party and filed a report with the Special Investigations Unit of the military police.

X4 was another victim who said she'd been made to participate in Satanic black masses. Psychotherapist Pascal Willems claimed that PSC member, Melchior Wathelet, a protege of Paul Vanden Boeynants said by X1 to be involved in child abuse, may have been involved in black masses.

> Since 1992, Brassine was in contact with Pascal Willems, a fellow psychotherapist. Willems looked after two children (8-10 years) who were victims of child molesters and Satanists.... The children would have participated in a combined feast and orgy organized by Melchior Wathelet in a castle located in the region of Verviers. The castle belongs to a private association. Willems would be in the possession of an invitation.... This [abuse] went on until the children were put to death. The children came from a children's home with a complicit director.
>
> At the time, Willems spoke about the affair to the adviser of the SAJ [Les Services de l' Aide à la Jeunesse, or youth support] of Verviers, who told him to keep quiet. He has been intimidated or has been threatened by telephone by the boss of the judicial police in Verviers and by the advisor of the SAJ, and by an anonymous person. Contact between Brassine and Willems in October-November 1995 and at the end of 1996. Brassine speaks of it to Denayer (judicial police in Namur). Following that, Willems was threatened with 'suicide' [by a superior of Mr. Denayer].... The 2 files of the SAJ would have disappeared ... Willems hid the relevant documents in a safe place at this office ...

PSC member Jean-Pierre Grafe, a former board member of CEPIC, was also accused of child abuse, possibly in an occult setting or manner:

> Sectarian or satanic activities at the Valmont castle in Merbes-LeChateau [Chateau de la Roquette]. Owner of the chateau = Pierre Ferbus (07/01/42). Homosexual-banker BBL [Banque Bruxelles Lambert]. Di Rupo and Graffe would have been seen at these parties.... A report of the Police of Lobbes [nearby town, to the north] received the same information concerning Jean-Pierre Graffe.... A rapport of the BSR [Special Investigations Unit of the Gendarmerie] in Thuin [another nearby town] contains approaching information (van der Reijden 2007).

Reading about the Dutroux Affair, a name that seemed designed to distract from the other players involved and instead focus on a single Beast of Belgium, I had found a sort of synecdoche for everything that I'd tried to research until that point. The story was one in which a society's elite had participated in extremely sadistic child abuse. The accounts appeared highly credible, as were the claims of a coverup. There were even credible accounts of occult rituals under the guise of a Catholic secret society. If I were to believe all or most of it, and I was inclined to, I had to acknowledge that the powerful not only didn't have the best interests at heart but would go to extreme lengths to protect their own. Worse still, they participated in some of the most grotesque forms of torture one could fathom.

Van der Reijden's assertion that the use of a satanic cult to distract from stories of occult abuse also resonated. Perhaps ritual abuse occurred in some elite circles, but was not as widespread or cartoonish as suggested by the likes of Ted Gunderson or Cathy O'Brien. In fact, given Gunderson's role in the FBI, he, and others like him, could have deliberately exaggerated occult aspects of ritual abuse so as to obscure more believable accounts of elite abuse of children, sometimes in ritualistic settings.

Had they really hidden hell within more hell? Through the fake screams, I could hear the authentic cries of agony. Behind the actors feigning sacrifices to Satan, there were the actual children being sacrificed to Satan. Beyond the mind controlled robot assassins were the real manipulated victims and murderers.

The sounds grew increasingly louder, the images more violent, the pace faster as we raced toward a flaming planet. Unable to bear it any longer, I twisted away and staggered into some unknown direction. I was getting weaker. My life force was escaping my body as I fled the facility. The shrieks followed while I slammed into the walls of a dank hallway until I landed my fingers on a cold and wet metal knob and turned. I hurled my body through the door. Ahead of me was a chute, from which emanated the worst stink I'd ever known. I lunged forward into the thing.

PART 6

HANGOUTS &
STRATEGIES OF TENSION

Cover of The Satanic Bible: custom,
hardcover leather bound.

CHAPTER THIRTY-ONE

SATANISM AS DISTRACTION

Spit out into some sort of sewer system, I was covered in shit, blood and other bodily fluids. The feces was all around and had reached near knee level as I sloshed through the muck and darkness. The tide of sewage continued to rise, however, and I could no longer walk nor breathe. I swam, gasping for air above the waves of waste, taking in the last molecules of oxygen I could before it all went black.

I tried to keep my research to myself in the waking world as best I could, but it just wasn't in my personality. Whether it was about politics, a TV show, or conspiracy theories regarding global satanic pedophile networks and mind control, there was always a crack in the dam. And when there was, a flood would soon break through. So, Thanksgiving proved particularly difficult for me.

It was our first holiday without my mom and we spent it at an Airbnb in Florida, a sort of beachside getaway to distract us from her absence, since it had always been her favorite holiday. As I tended to do, I drank a few beers and, as tended to happen at family gatherings when it was assumed everyone maintained the same politics, someone brought up Trump.

"Did you hear what he said about the fires in California?" my dad asked.

"Yeah," my sister laughed. "He said you could rake the forest floor to stop them."

The family erupted in hysterics. I chimed in, "Actually, a friend of mine in the forest service just told me that you do have to clean up the debris on the forest floor so there's less dry brush to fuel fires. So, I think he was probably just misinterpreting something some scientific advisor said or something."

There was some more critiquing of Trump that mostly ignored my comment, but the next thing I knew, I had somehow managed to talk my dad and 10-year-old niece into a corner.

"So, the whole Qanon thing isn't actually as ridiculous as it seems. I mean, I don't know about the whole Satanism angle. Have you heard about Project Monarch?"

From the corner of my eye, I caught Cindy on the other side of the room moving her hand across her neck, universal sign language for both "cut it out" and "you're dead meat." I realized I had done it again. I was alienating people with esoterica. Not only that, but I was coming off as a Republican. Just then, I noticed that our baby, Misha, now about six months old, was crying and I realized I had been bouncing him around in my arms for who-knows-how-long as he was bawling his eyes out.

It was around then that I decided to log off the Internet. Not entirely, but to at least ditch social media, which meant I would more or less be ditching the Gundam, too. Instead, I would try to focus on consensus reality. That didn't mean giving up my research altogether. But I did want to focus on the things that really mattered to me, which was my wife and kids and our beautiful life, isolated from the pedophilic satanists of the world.

However, there was something I would need to do before I could really focus. I had to wrap up all that I had been researching for the past couple of years. I needed to get it out of my head. So, I decided to write it all down. The only thing was, I wasn't sure what conclusions I had drawn. I had no firm ideas about the most important and/or absurd aspects of the investigation, like Satanism and Monarch.

And that is exactly how *They* wanted things to be. They wanted it so muddy that you couldn't tell what was what. It was actually some of the Gundam that introduced me to a key weapon of psychological warfare used to obfuscate the truth: the "limited hangout."

A former special assistant to the Deputy Director of the CIA, Victor Marchetti, described a limited hangout as "spy jargon for a favorite and frequently used gimmick of the clandestine professionals. When their veil of secrecy is shredded and they can no longer rely on a phony cover story to misinform the public, they resort to admitting – sometimes even volunteering – some of the truth while still managing to withhold the key and damaging facts in the case. The public, however, is usually so intrigued by the new information that it never thinks to pursue the matter further" (Marchetti 1978).

Some had argued, for instance, that the Pentagon Papers, leaked by RAND Corporation contractor Daniel Ellsberg, were a limited hangout that directed public attention toward the military atrocities committed in Vietnam as a means of deflecting attention away from CIA atrocities committed in Vietnam (Valentine 2017).

The concept could also be taken a step further with a "modified limited hangout," in which misinformation was combined with facts in order to muddy the waters and prevent further investigation (Dean et al 1973). One very clear example of a modified limited hangout might have been a broadcast by conspiracy entertainer Alex Jones when saying that the chemical atrazine was "turning the friggin' frogs gay" (Sommerland 2018). Through the use of colorful language, Jones had exaggerated the very real effects of the chemical inducing hermaphroditism in amphibians (Hayes et al 2002).

The Gundam had many times brought up the possibility that the satanic panic and #pizzagate were modified limited hangouts of actual operations by intelligence services. Barring documentary evidence, this would have been a difficult theory to prove. In fact, it was a rare event when limited hangouts were ever explicitly exposed as such, but there had been at least one documented example in the field of ufology.

UFOs, A TEMPLATE FOR CONTROLLED OPPOSITION

To understand how how #pizzagate and the Satanic Panic may have become modified limited hangouts, I wanted to understand how a limited hangout was created. Information about this technique was not widely available for many forms of disinformation, including the Satanic Panic, but one writer, Mark Pilkington, had done a great deal of excellent research on how it was applied to the ufology movement in his book *Mirage Men*. There may have been a possibility that visitations of spacecraft from other planets were real, but there was strong evidence that, in most cases, spotted UFOs were actually experiments in military technology. To throw people off the trail, pieces of disinformation were deliberately sewn into the larger public UFO narrative.

In a 1952 report from the CIA's assistant director for Scientific Intelligence, H. Marshall Chadwell, to Director Walter B. Smith, Chadwell noted that the phenomenon of UFO sightings could be exploited for "national security" reasons:

> [T]he flying saucer situation contains two elements of danger which, in a situation of tension, have national security implications. These are: a) Psychological – with worldwide sightings reported, it was found that, up to the time of the investigation, there had been in the Soviet press no report or comment, even satirical, on flying saucers. ... With a State-controlled press, this could result only from an official policy decision. The question, therefore, arises as to whether or not these sightings: 1) Could be controlled 2) Could be predicted 3) Could be used from a psychological warfare point

of view, either offensively or defensively. The public concern with the phenomena, which is reflected both in the United States press and in the pressure of inquiry upon the Air Force, indicates that a fair proportion of our population is mentally conditioned to the acceptance of the incredible. In this fact lies the potential for the touching off of mass hysteria and panic. b) Air Vulnerability – the United States Air Warning System will undoubtedly always depend upon a combination of radar screening and visual observation. The USSR is credited with the present capability of delivering an air attack against the United States.

... At any moment of attack, we are now in a position where we cannot, on an instant basis, distinguish hardware from phantom, and as tension mounts we will run the increasing risk of false alerts and the even greater danger of falsely identifying the real as phantom.

Chadwell then went on to say that a "study should be instituted to determine what, if any, utilization could be made of these phenomena by United States psychological warfare planners and what, if any, defenses should be planned in anticipation of Soviet attempts to utilize them." He believed that public perception of flying saucers should have been controlled in order to "minimize the risk of panic" (Pilkington 2010).

While the language was couched in concern for national security, intelligence operations such as MKULTRA or Gladio exhibited just how an ostensibly "defensive" program could go off the rails to become totally offensive. More likely, even the framing that a study of the implications of UFOs for psyops purposes were defensive to begin with was just a pretense to protect their asses if and when these programs were uncovered. Therefore, it was crucial to wonder how intelligence agencies may have exploited UFO phenomena against civilians. In the case of William Moore, Richard Dowty, and Paul Bennewitz, the primary goal of manipulating public belief in UFOs seemed to be to provide cover for military operations.

In the 1980s, the interest of the U.S. military in the culture surrounding UFO sightings shifted into disinformation overdrive when a prominent voice in the community was recruited by the Air Force Office of Special Investigations (AFOSI). William Moore wrote the bestselling book *The Roswell Incident*, which reintroduced the story of the 1947 Roswell "spacecraft" crash to the public imagination and aided in making the UFO community more presentable. But it was a speech he gave at the 1989 Mutual UFO Network (MUFON) Conference that would shed new light on UFO research altogether.

There, Moore told his compatriots that he had been working with the AFOSI to not only spy on the UFO community, but had also been feeding them disinformation on behalf of Air Force intelligence. In exchange, Moore was told he would be provided with genuine documentation of human contact with alien life and the U.S. government's strategy to cover it up.

One of the ways that Moore injected false information into ufology was through a military contractor named Paul Bennewitz who took notice of strange activity around Kirtland Air Force Base near his home in New Mexico. In 1979, Bennewitz started filming strange lights flying over the Manzano mountains. He also became convinced that he was intercepting electronic signals from alien spacecraft on his homemade receivers.

As a patriotic American, he presented the information to Kirtland's head of security, Major Ernest Edwards, in October 1980. Edwards then tapped AFOSI Special Agent Richard Doty to handle Bennewitz. To describe what followed, Mark Pilkington cited internal documents from Kirtland Air Force Base, released via the U.S. Freedom of Information Act:

> On 26 Oct 1980, [Special Agent] Doty, with the assistance of Jerry Miller [a] Scientific Advisor for Air Force Test and Evaluation Center ... interviewed Dr. Bennewitz at his home in the Four Hills section of Albuquerque, which is adjacent to the northern boundary of Manzano Base. Dr. Bennewitz ... produced several electronic recording tapes, allegedly showing high periods of electrical magnetism being emitted from Manzano/Coyote Canyon area. Dr. Bennewitz also produced several photographs of flying objects taken over the general Albuquerque area. He has several pieces of electronic surveillance equipment pointed at Manzano and is attempting to record high frequency electrical beam pulses. Dr. Bennewitz claims these Aerial Objects produce these pulses. ... After analysing the data collected by Dr. Bennewitz, Mr. Miller related the evidence clearly shows that some type of unidentified aerial objects were caught on film; however, no conclusions could be made whether these objects pose a threat to Manzano/Coyote Canyon areas. Mr. Miller felt the electronical [sic] recording tapes were inconclusive and could have been gathered from several conventional sources. No sightings, other than these, have been reported in the area (Pilkington 2010).

Next, Bennewitz was asked to present his research to higher-ups at the base, including officials from the NSA and AFOSI who learned from his talk that he'd been receiving transmissions from their own experiments. To understand how he was pulling it off, the physicist was allowed to keep up his investigation. However, to ensure that his work wouldn't lead anywhere near the truth, they decided to interfere with his interference.

William Moore was first brought to the offices of AFOSI in November 1980 to brief them on the ufology community's understanding of the technology. Moore was also provided by Doty a document labeled "SE-CRET" that contained the photographs taken by Bennewitz. The paper read:

> (S/WINTEL) USAF no longer publicly active in UFO research, however USAF still has interest in all UFO sightings over USAF installation/test ranges. Several other government agencies, led by NASA, actively investigates [sic] legitimate sightings through covert cover. (S/WINTEL/FSA) One such cover is UFO Reporting Center, U.S. Coast and Geodetic Survey, Rockville, MD 20852. NASA filters results of sightings to appropriate military departments with interest in that particular sighting. The official U.S. Government Policy and results of Project Aquarius is still classified top secret with no dissemination outside official intelligence channels and with restricted access to "MJ Twelve." Case on Bennewitz is being monitored by NASA, INS, who request all future evidence be forwarded to them thru AFOSI, IVOE (Pilkington 2010).

The problem with this document was that there was no Project Aquarius. Nevertheless, Doty instructed William Moore to pass it along to Bennewitz. Moore did so and Bennewitz accepted the report as validation of his research, that the Air Force and NASA believed the physicist may have caught evidence of actual extraterrestrial activity. Bennewitz went on to warn the world, communicating with the ufology community and writing letters to local politicians and even President Reagan.

He also developed a method for decoding the electrical signals he was picking up, with repeated patterns converted into such vocabulary as "spaceship," "abduction," and "UFO." He then turned the broadcasts he translated over to the Air Force. This project was exacerbated when he was visited by notable astronomer and ufologist Allen Hynek, who gifted Bennewitz not only with further validation about his UFO research but a new computer from the Air Force. The device was loaded with special software capable of "improving" the physicist's translations. Bennewitz's decoded transmissions included such missives as 'VICTORY OUR BAS-ES OBTAIN SUPPLIES FROM THE STARSHIP METAL TIME IS YANKED TIME IS YANKED MESSAGE HIT STAR USING REJUVI-NATION [sic] METHODS GOT US IN TROUBLE SIX SKYWE RE-ALIZE TELLING YOU ALL MIGHT HELP YOU.'

It appeared likely that Hynek, who was widely respected in the UFO community, was aiding the Air Force in leading Bennewitz further astray. And Bennewitz, in turn, led the UFO community astray, all guided by the AFOSI. Bill Moore would then provide Air Force intelligence with regu-lar updates on its PSYOP campaign.

Meanwhile, they were influencing the subculture through William Moore directly as well. Pilkington described one incident in 1983 in which Moore was "told that he would soon receive some important infor-mation. A bizarre wild goose chase followed, in which he was instructed to fly to airports all around the country until finally reaching a hotel in New York State. A courier came to his room with the inevitable manila en-velope and gave him nineteen minutes to study its contents, during which time he was able to photograph the documents inside and read them into a tape recorder. The papers purported to be a UFO briefing for President Jimmy Carter, who had once promised to reveal to the public everything the U.S. government knew about the subject. Further references were made to Project Aquarius and the Majestic 12 (MJ-12) group mentioned in the fake AFOSI document from 1981. The message presented by these new documents was that a clandestine government agency, MJ-12, had been set up to engage with UFOs and their occupants, and to keep the reality of the ET presence a secret, since at least the early 1950s."

At his 1989 speech, in addition to coming clean about his work for the feds, Moore revealed what he thought to be the truth about the UFO situation:

- A highly advanced ET civilization is visiting planet Earth and is actively manipulating our awareness of its presence here.

- Elements of at least two government agencies are aware of this and are conducting highly classified research projects. One of these projects has the data to prove that some UFOs represent some-body else's highly advanced technology.

- USG counter-intel people have been conducting disinformation about the UFO phenomenon for at least forty years. High-level op-eratives in at least two agencies are behind it and are co-operating to some extent. They are creating false documents and gathering information on researchers and experiencers within the UFO community using informants. Why are they doing this? The disinformation provides security cover for a real UFO project that exists at a very high level and is known only to an elite few.

- *It is useful for diverting attention away from USG R&D projects.*

- *It aids those groups, such as the Trilateral Commission, who are using the UFO phenomenon to try to bring about world unity in the face of an unknown threat from space.*

- *It provides a convenient way to train counter-intelligence agents in deception and disinformation.*

- *It is a manipulation by the aliens themselves to gradually make human society aware of their presence* (Pilkington 2010).'

Either Moore was intentionally participating in the disinformation campaign created by his handlers in Air Force intelligence, or as Pilkington put it, "Moore still demonstrated an unshakeable faith in the reality of the ET presence on Earth."

Meanwhile, as Bennewitz began to suspect an oncoming alien invasion at a secret alien facility he called Dulce Base, he reported his findings to the ufology community. By 1988, the researcher had drawn up a plan dubbed Project Beta on how to attack the site. Pilkington described the state of Bennewirz's mind at this point:

> He was intensely paranoid, installing extra locks on doors and windows and hiding guns and knives around the house. He told Moore and Doty that the aliens were climbing into his bedroom at night and injecting him with drugs that made him do strange things. Bennewitz would sometimes wake up behind the wheel of his car, having driven out into the middle of the desert. According to Greg, both Doty and Moore independently told him that they had noticed what looked like needle marks dotting his right arm; he wondered whether one or other government agency was injecting Bennewitz with drugs, then driving him out into the desert to pump him full of more alien horrors and absurdities. Doty thought Bennewitz was either harming or injecting himself, though he also claims to have seen ladder marks outside a first-floor window of the Bennewitz home, right where Paul claimed the aliens were entering the house.
>
> Things finally came to a head in August 1988. Bennewitz, aged sixty-one, was barely functioning. His business, Thunder Scientific, was being run by his two adult sons. Back at home, he was accusing

his wife Cindy of being in the control of the extraterrestrials. The final straw came when he barricaded himself in their home with sandbags.

It couldn't go on. Paul's family had him sequestered at the mental health facility of the Presbyterian Anna Kaseman hospital in Albuquerque, where he was held under observation for a month. When Doty went to visit his old friend, Bennewitz didn't even recognize him.

Doty's role in driving an American citizen to insanity was only one piece of understanding what the intelligence community was capable of achieving through sophisticated psyops campaigns on U.S. soil. The disinformation operation most relevant to my research had to do with a story passed around ufology circles about a planet called Serpo.

Substitute teacher Victor Martínez managed an email group that would predate Qanon by over a decade. It was made up of about 200 members including individuals with backgrounds in military, intelligence, and science, all with intense interest in UFOs. The email list would be taken by storm when Martínez was sent a message on November 1, 2005 that read:

> First let me introduce myself. My name is Request Anonymous. I am a retired employee of the U.S. Government. I won't go into any great details about my past, but I was involved in a special program…

The user had, according to Martínez, been lurking on the email list for six months before making this introduction. Then, he began pouring out increasingly long messages over the course of three years. In 31 "releases," Request Anonymous wrote tens of thousands of words, including excerpts from a supposedly top secret 3,000-page document made by the Defense Intelligence Agency in the 1970s, about close government encounters with extraterrestrial species from a planet called Serpo.

According to the enigmatic user, the report detailed how, in 1947, two alien spacecraft crash-landed in New Mexico, killing six and sparing one otherworldly passenger. This creature, EBE 1, was taken to Los Alamos National Laboratory, where he attempted to communicate with his home world of Serpo until he died in 1952. Only after he passed did Serpo and its race of Ebens answer his call. This was the start of a decades-long relationship with the Ebens, who sent another emissary, EB 2, to live on Earth, while 12 humans were taken on an Eben craft to Serpo, located thirty-eight light years away in the Zeta Reticuli star system.

The brave Earthling explorers on Serpo found a planet smaller than their own, but with two suns. They learned that the Ebens had won an intergalactic battle with another civilization, which saw their own world made uninhabitable and drove them to seek out a new home. While EB 1 had wound up as a scout on Earth, some 650,000 Ebens ended up migrating to Serpo. There, they lived a semi-communist existence, with about 100 autonomous communities connected by a central hub that served as the industrial center for the society. The humans finally returned to Earth in 1978, though two had died and two more had decided to live on Serpo, providing contact with Earth over the years until 1988. The remaining eight suffered from the extreme radiation of Serpo's two suns and succumbed to death, the final intergalactic traveler dying in 2002.

The messages from Request Anonymous never described how the Ebens actually looked, though they were replete with details about the Eben planet and their society. The user also promised photos of the creatures, including one of them playing a soccer-like game, but those never materialized. Request Anonymous finally provided a photo of Serpo, featuring two suns, but some people on Martínez's chain believed them to be poorly photoshopped concoctions.

Martínez said he would not reveal the identity of Request Anonymous, for fear of losing the intel the user provided. Meanwhile, two individuals on the Martínez list were able to verify the anonymous user's claims. Paul McGovern was said to be a former DIA security chief at Area 51, while Gene Lakes was another member of the DIA. Unfortunately, the identities of neither man could be corroborated outside of the mailing list. There was a third individual who supported the claims of Request Anonymous: Richard Doty.

As the Serpo story expanded beyond the confines of the Martínez email list, Doty published a story in the February 2006 issue of *UFO Magazine*, the only publication in the English-speaking world dedicated to UFOs that was sold on newsstands. In it, Doty wrote:

> My name is Richard Doty retired special agent, Air Force Office of Special Investigations (AFOSI), and now a private citizen living in New Mexico. I've been an avid reader of UFO Magazine for the past several years.... In early 1979, after arriving at Kirtland Air Force Base as a young special agent with AFOSI, I was assigned to the counter-intelligence division of AFOSI District 17. I was briefed into a special compartmented program. This program dealt with United States government involvement with extraterrestrial biological entities. During my initial briefing I was given the complete background of our government's involvement with EBEs.

> This background included information on the Roswell incident ... basically, this was exactly the same information that Mr Anonymous released."

According to Mark Pilkington, Doty would chime in on the Martínez email list with his own details to support the Serpo tale. Given the level of information, misinformation, and disinformation in the mix, the exact source of the Request Anonymous messages was difficult for Pilkington to determine, but there was substantial reason to believe that Doty himself was the man behind the email account – or, if not *the* man, then at least one of them.

A British computer network expert named Steven Broadbent had become wrapped up in the Serpo saga and began investigating its roots, only to find that the original emails from Request Anonymous, as well as those from Doty, Paul McGovern and two others claiming to be members of the DIA and backing up the Serpo story had all come from the same IP address in Albuquerque, New Mexico. This address made it possible to assume that all of these figures were on the same computer network. Given Doty's residence in New Mexico and past work in UFO disinfo, he seemed like a likely suspect.

Pilkington wrote:

> Broadbent's findings appeared to show that Rick Doty had sent Victor Martínez the original "Anonymous" postings that had set the Serpo machine in motion; Rick had then followed them up with corroborative emails from himself and the other fake Pentagon UFO insiders. Alternatively, somebody had actively manipulated these emails to make it look as if Rick had sent them – something well within the bounds of possibility, especially if there was an intelligence component to the Serpo saga. It was difficult for us to believe that Rick could have generated the voluminous Serpo material alone, though he may have had a hand in it."

In trying to determine the reason behind the Serpo op, Pilkington wondered:

> Disinformation. Noise. Was this what Serpo was about? An attempt to use the Internet to seed information within the UFO community, much as AFOSI had done, using faked documents in the Bennewitz affair? Were we seeing an obscure new salvo in the information war? Were Serpo and the Martínez list a vivarium for information? Was Serpo a sociological or psychological research project being carried

out by one or other intelligence agency, or a university – perhaps by a member of Martínez's list? We might think of it as memetic tracking: following the paths that information follows over the web would be a useful exercise in our data-saturated age. Like attaching a transmitter to a whale, or tracking a barium meal through a hospital patient's digestive system, it can teach us a lot about both what is being followed and the territory it's travelling through – in intelligence lingo, this is called a "marked card." If Serpo did have its origins in the intelligence world, and it looked to many observers as if it might, it may have had nothing to do with UFOs. Perhaps sensitive information was encoded within the releases, or perhaps it was what the intelligence world calls a "false flag" operation, made to look as if it was the work of UFO insiders and intended to lure foreign or industrial spies into its web. Was it just a coincidence that there were so many intelligence and military personnel on Martínez's UFO list? Was Serpo an attempt to flush somebody out of hiding? One interesting idea raised online, then swiftly shot down, was that Anonymous had actually stumbled on to genuine government documents, but ones that had originally been created in order to fool somebody else – the Russians, for example.

The Serpo narrative bore remarkable similarities with Qanon: a government insider leaking top secret information using the web tools of the day available. The result was a stoking of bizarre theories related to government encounters with alien life within a group already prone to fantasy. I would soon learn that there was another strange tale that contained elements resembling the Qanon storyline. And, like theories of government participation in satanic ritual abuse, this conspiracy theory sang a siren song to draw plenty of deep politics researchers toward a yawning Charybdis of obsession – an endless rabbithole that distracted, confused and sometimes enlightened. By some, it was called the Octopus. To others, it was known as the PROMIS scandal.

PROMIS AND THE 5TH COLUMN

PROMIS branched off into a variety of dark spaces, from Iran-Contra to 9/11, even to Michael Aquino. This piece of software was developed in the 1980s as a data management tool for the U.S. Department of Justice by Bill Hamilton's Inslaw Corporation. However, when it was modified by the CIA and/or Israel's Mossad at a Wackenhut facility on a Native American reservation, it became a powerful spy tool. Once installed into a computer system, PROMIS acted as a backdoor, allowing anyone with access to spy on that system. Over time, it would evolve to become the PRISM tool used by the NSA to surveil computer users worldwide.

An abbreviation of "Prosecutors' Management Information System," the software was meant to trace financial transactions related to illegal activity as funds passed through laundering and wire transfers. With some tweaks, it was able to extend this tracing through to the banks and shell companies leveraged by drug dealers and terrorists, an obviously useful skill for those who wished to level justice at international criminals. It was also useful for achieving total information awareness and dominance for the powers that operated it.

To enable this, a young and brilliant computer scientist named Michael Riconosciuto claimed he was hired to transform the program into a spying tool that, when installed on a computer, could monitor the user's activities. In turn, the CIA relied on a number of front organizations to have it installed on the networks of some 88 world governments. In the USSR, this meant employing Robert Maxwell to get it across the so-called Iron Curtain. Ultimately, the Department of Justice decided not to pay Inslaw Corporation and its founder, former NSA agent Bill Hamilton, the $6 million it owed for the powerful software platform. In turn, Hamilton went on to fight the DOJ in courts of law and ultimately became a leaker of information about the software.

Some Gundam, @ElResisto in particular, ventured onto strange detours on the PROMIS pathway. For instance, by researching PROMIS, he learned how MCA Records may have been involved in smuggling drugs into Yosemite National Park (Seymour 2010). At one point, I came across some article relaying the possibility that wunderkind computer programmer Michael Riconosciuto was actually recruited as a child by pedophiles in a honeypot scheme only to later develop cyberweapons for the CIA. The most well-known victim of the PROMIS conspiracy was Danny Casolaro, a journalist who got so wrapped up in his investigation of what he called "the Octopus" that he wound up dead with wrists slashed in a West Virginia hotel room from what was deemed a suicide, despite the journalist's fear of blood and generally positive outlook on life.

But what drew me in in particular was an element that one of the Lone Gundam, @Gumby4Christ, introduced to our club. It was something called the Fifth Column, a group of five retired intelligence officers set up to take out corrupt members of the deep state. At least that's what former CIA agent Charles Hayes claimed when he was arrested by an FBI SWAT team for hiring an undercover agent to kill his own son.

Circa 1998, before Hayes's attempted murder trial kicked off, the story had been circulating around early Internet sites and message boards, as well as a right-wing publication called *Media Bypass*. The tale went like this: the Fifth Column had used a supercomputer to hack into some 3,000 secret foreign bank accounts used by U.S. politicians to store illegal funds they'd received from drug and arms dealers and the like. More than that, they had supposedly wire-transferred $4 billion worth of this money to "escrow holding funds" at Federal Reserve banks. They then quietly told members of Congress and foreign governments what they'd discovered, which supposedly led to the retirement of roughly 60 U.S. senators and representatives ahead of the 1996 elections (Russell 1997).

Though the CIA denied that Hayes worked for them in any capacity, he presented his ID number and cover name at trial. His shadowy background suggested he had some deep-state ties, as well. The 1991 telephone records of Danny Casolaro included many calls to Hayes the month leading up to his grisly death. A year later, Hayes testified before a grand jury about the Inslaw affair, which was followed by an extensive 1996 deposition about Inslaw. During Hayes's 1998 trial, FBI Special Agent David Keller provided testimony saying that he was acquainted with Hayes from the bureau's investigation of Inslaw.

A 1992 report from the House Judiciary Committee described Hayes this way: "Mr. Hayes is a surplus computer dealer with alleged ties to both United States and foreign intelligence communities. Mr. Hayes first came to the attention of the Committee during August 1990, following assertions that excess Haris-Lanier word-processing equipment he had purchased from the U.S. Attorney's office for the Eastern District of Kentucky, located in Lexington, contained the PROMIS software."

The Justice Department then took the machines from Hayes. In turn, it couldn't be used as evidence in Inslaw's lawsuit against the Justice Department.

In a 1995 letter to the director of the NSA, the chairman of the House Banking Committee, Rep. Jim Leach, specifically mentioned PROMIS and Hayes while asking for the "agency's help in verifying or laying to rest various allegations of money- laundering in Arkansas in the late 1980s."

According to a *High Times* article from the time, "Several of Hayes' associates back up his contention that he's being framed, in an attempt to put the Fifth Column out of business. One well-placed source, who requested anonymity, affirms that Hayes was a CIA asset, adding, 'I think Hayes has been set up to the nth degree to discredit him.'"

Hayes told *High Times* that he'd started the crusade wanting to track the laundering of funds from drug dealing operations due to the way his son had "cooked his mind on drugs." There was also an Arkansas Committee that focused on Contra-related drug smuggling at Mena Airport in the state, which saw the Committee's Mark Swaney speak frequently with Hayes. Swaney told *High Times*, "A lot of what [Hayes] told me about Mena turned out to be true."

According to 1992 notes from Swaney, Hayes claimed that the federal government and state police participated in drug running from Mena. Hayes said that Clinton did not seem to be directly involved, but that his associates were. How did Hayes know so much about drug running from the tiny Arkansas airport? He was supposedly one of the Air Force pilots that shipped packages of what he thought were weapons from Mena for the CIA. Upon learning that he was actually trafficking drugs and not arms to Aruba, he said he threw the cocaine on the runway. This resulted in a shoot-out that ended the lives of several individuals.

Hayes reportedly told Bill Hamilton, founder of Inslaw, that PROMIS was "in the CIA, DEA, FBI, everywhere." He then told Hamilton that he and a partner, both of whom had the code name "Running Fox," were a part of an intelligence unit called Squad D trained "to be able to take apart and put back together, without any diagrams, the Cray supercomputer." The elite unit was described by intelligence asset Bob Woodward in his book *Veil: The Secret Wars of the CIA, 1981-1987*, as being created under the guidance of Reagan CIA Director William Casey for the purposes of cyber warfare: "There was penetration of the international banking system allowing a steady flow of data from the real, secret sets of books kept by many foreign banks that showed some hidden investing by the Soviet Union," Woodward wrote.

Back in Kentucky, Hayes established a company dedicated to salvaging computer parts. Working with him was Michael Riconosciuto. Together, they built the Cray Model 3B supercomputer using components bought from Department of Defense auctions, with Hayes claiming that he was doing so under the auspices of the government. Supposedly, the Fifth Column was able to grab data from more than 50 intelligence organizations globally. When Riconosciuto was arrested for a meth manufacturing operation in 1992, Hayes learned that the computer whiz had installed a second set of back doors into PROMIS, possibly for his own chance at robbing the money laundering accounts. After closing Riconosciuto's port, Hayes's team established its own entryway. It used the supercomputer to comb through the information it downloaded as quickly as possible.

When the CIA "didn't hold up their end" of an undisclosed deal, the Fifth Column went out on its own with no one else able to access their own version of the software. Hayes claimed that the team found a bribe to Panamanian dictator Manuel Noriega from the Cali drug cartel and, when the Column found cover accounts used by the Salinas family in Europe, they supposedly sent the information to the DEA. In this way, it was suggested that the Fifth Column had supplied what they found to the proper authorities.

The story became even more involved when I considered the reporting of former *Forbes* senior editor James Norman on the saga. According to Norman's sources, White House deputy counsel Vince Foster and Hillary Clinton's Rose Law Firm may have had ties to PROMIS. Norman suggested that bank data company Systematics, managed by Arkansas billionaire Jackson Stephens, helped funnel money for covert activities by the CIA and NSA. Norman's sources purportedly told him that Vince Foster oversaw Systematics operations for the NSA while working at Rose Law Firm.

Norman said that Hayes claimed to have uncovered Foster's Swiss bank account while scrounging through Mossad files. Foster was reportedly selling information related to encryption and data security to Israel. Norman wrote for *Media Bypass:* "Foster's first indication of trouble came when he inquired about his coded bank account at Banca Della Svizzera Italiana in Chiasso, Switzerland, and found the account empty. Foster was shocked to learn from the bank that someone using his secret authorization code had withdrawn all $2.75 million he had stashed there, and had moved it to, of all places, the U.S. Treasury." The responsible for taking Foster's funds was the Fifth Column.

In a 1995 letter to the White House press secretary, Norman warned of the details of his upcoming article, then scheduled for publication in *Forbes.* These included allegations that Foster learned from Hillary Clinton that he was under CIA scrutiny, that Clinton was receiving money from Foster's overseas account, and that Systematics was party to money laundering related to Mena drug running.

When *Forbes* publisher Caspar Weinberger, former Secretary of Defense under Reagan, dropped the story, Norman was forced to bring it over to the right-wing outlet, *Media Bypass.* In the meantime, Norman learned that Barry Seal, who smuggled cocaine for the CIA, died with a string of numbers in his suitcase that a friend of the *Forbes* writer believed was linked to a Swiss bank account. When Norman shared the number with Hayes, Hayes claimed to trace it to a Union Bank of Switzerland account linked to Caspar Weinberger himself. Supposedly, he next sent a message to the publisher by removing $2.3 million from the account and dropping a note into Wein-berger's PO Box in Maine that read, "You have been had."

Norman provided evidence of trips by Vincent Foster to Switzerland to the editor of *Forbes*. He also provided copies of the documents found in Barry Seal's trunk along with a message:

> If you have any doubts about the ability of the CIA's Fifth Column to raid foreign bank accounts and withdraw funds, just ask Caspar Weinberger. The clear implication is that Caspar Weinberger, while Secretary of Defense, was taking kickbacks on drug and arms sales. A cosignatory on this account appears to be connected with [a rel-ative of] Howard Metzenbaum, the retired senator from Ohio. We are talking about bipartisan payola. Which helps explain why Con-gress is so squeamish about investigating this stuff.

Norman was then more or less let go from *Forbes*, at which point he met up with Hayes, who told him that there would be some shake ups in Congress. He explained that the Fifth Column was dropping off discrete letters to politicians with documentation of their secret bank accounts. Soon enough, members of Congress began to retire from office in large numbers, including Maine senator William Cohen and Colorado senator Pat Schroeder, according to Hayes's courtroom testimony.

Norman said, "He would make allusions to some geographical area or other way of describing people other than by name, who invariably would announce they weren't going to run again. It became almost like pin-the-tail-on-the-donkey."

As the Fifth Column continued its shenanigans, handing numerous doc-uments over to Ken Starr's Whitewater investigation or transferring money from the accounts of Oliver North, Nancy Reagan and Henry Kissinger to the U.S. Treasury, the FBI began to close in on Hayes. In October 1997, the feds set up a sting in which FBI agent Don Yarborough played the part of an assas-sin and reached out to Hayes to set up a hit on an ordinary phone line. Record-ings of the call captured Hayes saying he was willing to pay $5,000 for his son's murder. In court, Hayes testified that he "figured the government was getting ready to set up something, so I thought it would be a good time to reverse it on 'em.... I figured I would be able to get them caught in a trap." However, there was a court battle between Hayes and his son over $800,000 in property from the will of Hayes's mother that suggested the hit was more than a ploy.

The jury ultimately found Hayes guilty and he was sentenced to 120 months in prison. Hayes was quoted as saying, "Hey, I love my government. They trained me well. And the Fifth Column ain't out of business yet (Russel 1997).

Again, there were overlaps with the Qanon story. A secret group of intelligence officials had taken it upon themselves to undo the corruption embedded in the deep state, with a focus on the Clintons, among others. Though Norman and Hayes had claimed a large number of political officials had been taken down through the compromise material collected by the Fifth Column, those individuals were hard to verify. Once Hayes went to prison, there didn't seem to be any more activity from the covert group.

Additionally, this plotline was actually just one in a larger narrative about PROMIS, a complex web of information and disinformation. At its heart, there was the fact that it was used to spy on global governments and computer users, which seemed to be verified by the existence of PRISM decades later. There were also stories of gun and drug-running related to Iran-Contra mixed in, with Wackenhut using the Cabazon reservation to develop and test new weapons, which also seemed to be verified with the Iran-Contra scandal made public later on.

But there were additional claims that Osama bin Laden got ahold of PROMIS to track the movement of money through the dark financial network made visible by the software. In some versions of the story, bin Laden shaved his beard, went under the alias Tim Osman and performed secret work on U.S. soil.

Michael Riconosciuto was a suspicious character, as well. Outside of his claims of being recruited to the CIA as a child for use in pedophike operation (De Brosse 2007), he said he had inside information about a satanic cult and pushed his own UFO stories, including that he'd witnessed an alien autopsy. As for Michael Aquino, his main connection seemed to be that, among Riconosciuto's things was a large box labeled "Ted Gunderson" that was filled with writings by the Satanic PSYOPS officer.

So, as with Paul Bennewitz and the Satanic Panic, the PROMIS affair possibly had true elements combined with sensational ones to create a modified limited hangout. The idea that the U.S. government could be involved in drug and arms trafficking, as well as spying on everyone in the world, would seem ridiculous alongside tails of UFOs and satanic cults.

And, if you took a bit from Request Anonymous, a bit from the Fifth Column, and a bit from the Satanic Panic, you'd get everything you needed for Qanon. The only thing missing was a personality around which to build the narrative.

CHAPTER THIRTY-TWO

QANON AS LIMITED HANGOUT

I awoke in a fog, literally and figuratively. My thinking was a bit hazy from being unconscious, but I also couldn't see much of anything through the particulate matter. It was visual noise. Tiny dots of filthy atmosphere designed to occlude the senses. I waved my hands through the clouds in an attempt to feel something familiar. It wasn't until I planted my face into his damp, fleshy chest that I could locate myself in the physical universe. I tilted my head up only to see:

Donald Trump's relationship with conspiracy theories seemingly began during Barack Obama's 2008 presidential campaign, when he pushed the rumor that Obama was not a U.S. citizen, making him ineligible for the presidency. He wasn't the only one driving this conspiracy theory. Members of Hillary Clinton's campaign staff (Emery 2016), the right-wing *National Review Online* (Tumulty 2008), former member of the Democratic State Committee of Pennsylvania Philip J. Berg (Hinkelman 2008), and NPR (Quist-Arctom 2008), among others also played a role in sowing this disinformation.

When Trump began flirting with the idea of running for President in 2011, he went on a number of television programs, such as *The View* (*WSJ Staff 2011*), *Good Morning America* (Marr 2011), and *NBC News* (AP 2011), and repeated the idea that he was skeptical of Obama's citizenship or that he thought there was information on his birth certificate that Obama didn't want released.

However, one of Trump's allies, Steve Bannon, was more versed in the world of conspiracy, via his media site, *Breitbart,* which would come to aid in the propagation of a number of right-wing conspiracy theories. In fact, its namesake and founder, Andrew Breitbart, had planted the seeds for pizzagate much farther back than most people had taken note of. On February 4, 2010, Breitbart turned to Twitter to ask why John Podesta hadn't yet been labeled an "underage sex slave op[eration] cover-upper-er." He had been referring to the 2009 ACORN "prostitution" scandal he had fabricated with the help of his operatives James O'Keefe and Hannah Giles, daughter of far right media personality Doug Giles.

Breitbart had paid the duo to visit a variety of offices of the Association of Community Organizations for Reform Now (ACORN), a nearly 40-year-old non-profit involved in voter registration and community organizing with low-income people. Posing as a pimp and a sex worker, respectively, O'Keefe and Giles asked staff how they might smuggle underage girls from El Salvador to the U.S. for prostitution. Two employees at the non-profit's Baltimore office, Shira and Tanja, provided their advice.

O'Keefe asked, "Is [prostitution] against the law in Maryland?" to which Shira replied, "Anything that the government isn't getting money from is always against the law." The video was then cut and jumped to a new question, in which O'Keefe asked about how to deal with taxes when handling "lots of cash."

Next, Shira brought in Tanja to help them set up their enterprise, saying, "She's going to make a legal business." Tanja began looking for the proper business code for their endeavor, with O'Keefe asking, "A code for prostitution?" To get around the illicit nature of their work, Tanja offered alternative business types, like "independent artist" and "dancing." Shira elaborated, "She's gonna make a legal business."

The quick cuts of the video made it clear that the exact order and full context of the questions were impossible to know, with Shira appearing and disappearing from the scene after some jump cuts, for instance. Tanja seemed to not want to discuss prostitution specifically, avoiding questions about whether or not condoms could be deducted for tax purposes. She also didn't seem to be an expert at how to turn prostitution into a legal business.

After another editing cut, O'Keefe asked Tanja about "girls from El Salvador," stating that they "don't want to put them on the books." Confused, Tanja replied, "Why are y'all even gonna do taxes?" When they said they wanted to buy a house with their funds, Tanja looked upset, leaning into her hand and making a frustrated face. O'Keefe then followed, "Everyone else has been discriminatory." To which, Tanja replied, "If they don't have social security numbers, then you don't have to worry because they can't file taxes anyway."

Shira was later edited in, providing advice on how to keep the Salvadoran girls off the government radar, by saying, "Do not discuss [sex trafficking] ... you've still got a lot to learn. You never, never talk ... about business in front of people." Another jump cut and Shira was saying, "It's not gonna damage us because we're not gonna know."

"Train them to be careful," Shira said, and to "keep their mouths shut, always have eyes in the back of your head – always be squeaky clean" (ACORN Baltimore Transcript 2009).

Based on this heavily edited video, it seemed clear that the behavior of these employees was not the norm and that O'Keefe and Giles weren't received the same way at every ACORN office. Tanja and Shira were fired as soon as the video was made public (Fenton 2009). However, the damage was already done. As right-wing outlets like Fox News covered the story, donors withdrew from ACORN and the organization had to close its doors (Neumeister 2010).

Breitbart's operation was successful and he leveraged the fabricated prostitution scandal to direct it at Podesta. As Trump added Steve Bannon as chief executive officer of his presidential campaign in 2016, he had fully embraced right-wing theories, with Bannon's *Breitbart* website acting as a leading voice in racist ideologies. Meanwhile, Roger Stone, Trump's long-time friend, lobbyist, and an advisor for his campaign in 2015, also began to promote conspiracy theories on behalf of Trump. On *InfoWars*, Stone told Alex Jones that, if elected, Trump would investigate 9/11 and the possible involvement of the Bush White House in the collapse of the World Trade Center, which, regardless of any validity to the claims, was a form of signaling to Jones's increasingly right-wing audience.

This momentum continued so that, as the 2016 election approached, the promotion of conspiracy theories and parapolitics alike had become co-opted by a right-wing audience. This was demonstrated in part by the alliance of WikiLeaks with the Trump campaign. A publisher of classified media, the site previously had an anti-establishment or activist appearance due to the fact that it shared such media as the "collateral damage" video leaked by Chelsea Manning, which showed U.S. soldiers gunning down civilians from a helicopter as if joyfully playing a video game.

WikiLeaks seemed to throw its weight behind Trump by tweeting about #pizzagate on November 4, 2016, just days before the election:

> The Podestas "Spirit Cooking" dinner? It's not what you think.
> It's blood, sperm and breastmilk.
> But mostly blood. wearechange.org/spirit-cooking...

The article linked to by the WikiLeaks tweet was authored by right-wing writer Cassandra Fairbanks. As I learned, the deep state activities that the #pizzagate theory was based upon weren't inherently conservative. However, in retrospect, it seemed that WikiLeaks was potentially

QANON AND THE PIZZAGATES OF HELL

supporting Trump, if only to spite Clinton. Assange ultimately threw a conspiracy theory about Seth Rich into the mix, implying that the dead Clinton staffer could have provided WikiLeaks with the Podesta emails (Nieuwsuur 2016).

Heather Marsh, the former editor of *Wikileaks Media*, the news publication begun by the Wikileaks team, suggested that WikiLeaks had used #pizzagate to distract from her authentic work in documenting child trafficking. In an interview, Marsh said that she had always had a "shaky" relationship with Wikileaks founder Julian Assange and that she had limited control over her work or that of her writers. After she left, she said Wikileaks "acted in direct opposition to what I and my writers worked towards on the site." One example she gave was #pizzagate:

> "They helped Trump and others deflect from my crowd sourced OpDeatheaters investigation into human trafficking and paedosadism with the decoy 'pizzagate' noise, very specifically targeting and attempting to counter and discredit my work," Marsh said. "As soon as I left, they threw out all my years of meticulous work establishing the credibility of everything I published by backing obviously false and biased reporting (pizzagate as just one example)" (Marsh 2019).

Similarly, Twitter user @Soychicka claimed #pizzagate was meant to distract from existing child trafficking, specifically the child rape case involving Trump and Epstein and a girl identified as "Maria." When @Soychicka called the police department in Waterbury, Connecticut, to learn about missing 12-year-old Maria, #Pizzagate shortly followed:

> The first mentions of Pizzagate started 11/4, within 8 hours of my first call to report I had identified an open missing person's case matching the abduction of Trump's 12-year-old victim known as 'Maria'
>
> *It exploded after I contacted [law enforcement].*
>
> *Check the numbers. Check the timing,*" @soychika tweeted, including a photograph of their phone records that would seem to show a call to the Waterbury police.

The spread of the #pizzagate theory seemed to occur throughout an increasingly powerful conservative alt media apparatus that toyed with or outright disseminated extreme right-wing conspiracy theories, drowning out any legitimate information that existed and weaponizing it for

Trump and beyond. This was signaled in part by the fact that, on February 1, 2017, Alex Jones gave his first appearance on the *Joe Rogan Experience* podcast, gaining nearly 4 million views in two months. Jones passed along the idea that the emails contained coded messages in which items of food referred to sexual products. Rogan seemed to strongly consider the possibility, saying:

> Maybe it is ["hot dogs" as code for "male prostitutes"], but what I'm saying is, anybody who is skeptical, anybody who is looking at this and is saying, "You guys are so fucking crazy. You're making such gigantic leaps of faith." No leaps, just look at all the weird code in those emails. There's definitely some code in those emails.

Assisting alt-media personalities like Jones in spreading the theory were people like Jerome Corsi, who had previously aided in the dissemination of the idea that Obama wasn't a U.S. citizen. According to Corsi, "a group of generals" approached him about launching a coup against Obama. They then "reconsidered" after recruiting Trump to run for president and execute his own coup against the deep state.

As Corsi explained to Alex Jones on April 11, 2018:

> Trump had agreed he would run, and they agreed that if he would run, they would conduct their coup d'etat as a legitimate process, rooting out the traitors within the government. And that pact between the military and Donald Trump has held, as we have been interpreting and watching, and Alex has been following QAnon (InfoWars 2018).

Of course, there's no evidence this is true. But Q followers seized on the fact that on April 10, the day before Corsi's "revelation," Trump tweeted a picture of himself surrounded by military officers, including Secretary of Defense James Mattis:

> 204) #Qanon asked who was standing next to Trump and Pence at the special dinner for the military leaders the previous night.
>
> Admiral Rogers is to their left, General Mattis is to the right. pic. twitter.com/9z1rcfQjnm
>
> – Praying Medic (@prayingmedic) April 10, 2018

Other Trump affiliates that seemed to be involved in the #pizzagate operation included Erik Prince, whose sister Betsy DeVos went on to be Trump's Secretary of Education. Prince himself worked closely with military intelligence via collaborations between his mercenary firm, Blackwater, and Joint Special Operations Command. Worth considering was the fact that Prince himself had been involved in child trafficking operations via Blackwater (Schwellenbach & Leonnig).

Others close to Trump who had seemingly endorsed Qanon included Trump's deputy chief of staff and social media director Dan Scavino (Rosenberg & Haberman 2020), who tweeted ticking clock memes three times, a reference to a countdown to the "Storm" the Qanon community believed Trump would be executing. Rudy Giuliani, Trump's lawyer, tweeted posts using the hashtag #QAnon several times and followed at least 224 Qanon accounts at one point on Twitter (Sommer 2019). Trump's son Eric tweeted a promotion for a rally of his father's that included a large "Q" along with the Qanon motto "where we go one, we go all" in the summer of 2020. He then deleted it (Stanley-Becker 2020).

According to David Brock's *Media Matters*, Trump retweeted or mentioned at least 152 QAnon-affiliated Twitter accounts at least 265 times (Kaplan 2019). This was before Trump was asked specifically about Qanon on August 19, 2020, to which he replied, "I don't know much about the movement, other than I understand they like me very much, which I appreciate. But I don't know much about the movement (Miller et al 2020).

Later, he was asked by a reporter if he could support the idea that he "is secretly saving the world from this satanic cult of pedophiles and cannibals." Trump responded, "Well, I haven't heard that, but is that supposed to be a bad thing or a good thing? (Itkowitz 2020)." Then, during a town hall event on October 15, 2020, he was urged to denounce the movement. Instead, he noted that QAnon opposed pedophilia and that no one can could know whether the premise of QAnon's conspiracy theory was true. "They believe it is a satanic cult run by the deep state," the reporter replied. She then asserted that this wasn't true. Trump responded, "No, I don't know that. And neither do you know that" (Bump 2020).

CHAPTER THIRTY-THREE

QANON AS A STRATEGY OF TENSION

More interesting than these individuals, however, was a man who would become a regular InfoWars guest named Steve Pieczenick. Journalist and documentary filmmaker Robbie Martin noted that Pieczenick really set up the Qanon/Fifth Column element that Trump and his coterie were fighting the deep state within the #pizzagate narrative (Martin 2020). On November 1, 2016, ahead of the election, Pieczenick published a video to his YouTube channel, which did not yet have many subscribers. The video was titled "The Hillary Clinton Takeover of the United States," and established a story that there was a secret element in the deep state that wanted to overthrow the existing corrupt order:

> November 1, 2016, Hillary and Bill Clinton and an entourage of assistants affected a civilian coup – in contrast to the usual concept of a coup, where the military is involved and takes over the White House and communication centers. Very much like the scenarios you see in a movie, this coup was done silently and very effectively through two methods, corruption and co-optation. The Clintons have been involved in co-opting our White House, our judiciary, our CIA, our Federal Bureau of investigation, our Attorney General Loretta Lynch, and our Director of the FBI James Comey for some time. Now, what they've done is to make sure that they were part and parcel of a group of people who were interrelated through political cronyism. However, in order to stop this coup we in the intelligence community and others involved have informally gotten together. And with their permission, I am beginning to announce that we've initiated a counter-coup through Julian Assange and WikiLeaks.
>
> What has happened in effect when Comey had to open up the case of Hillary Clinton and discuss the emails that were involved with the Anthony Weiner case. It was not the case itself that was as important as the fact that this was the entree for many of us in the counter-coup to say to the administration, 'We have your number. Not only do we have your number, we're going to stop you from making Hillary the president of the United States. And at the same

time, we will convict and indict the President of the United States, Loretta Lynch, and many others who were involved in the coverup of the massive corruption that occurred under the Clinton Foundation.

Now, in both cases, their coup was silent and our counter-coup was silent. It was all transgressed – or occurred – on the Internet. And this is probably the first time in the history of any country where a coup was initiated on the Internet and a counter-coup was initiated through the Internet.

I am just a small part of something far bigger than myself. It was the brave men and women who were in the FBI, the CIA, the director of intelligence, the military intelligence and men and women in 15 other intelligence organizations who were sick and tired of seeing this corruption in the White House and the Justice Department and an intelligence system. And we decided that there was something we had to do in order to save the Republic. So, we initiated a counter-coup through Julian Assange, who has been very brave and, and really quite formidable in this and his ability to come forth and provide all the necessary emails that we gave to him in order to undermine Hillary and Bill Clinton.

Again, America, we're doing through a major, major transition, and quite frankly, a second American revolution. We do not have guns. We do not have weapons. We do not intend to kill anybody. We do not intend to harm anybody, but we, the American public and those of us who serve as veterans and in the intelligence service, like myself, will stop the Clintons from assuming power that they don't deserve. At the same time, we will make certain that Obama leaves without any trail of a pardon or any other act of treason in effect.

We want a peaceful transition in this great American Republic. I bring you this news, and I want you to understand what has happened. A moment of history is occurring right now in front of us, and I'm proud to explain it."

The video was published on the front page of the popular right-wing blog, the Drudge Report, earning it 3 million less than 24 hours later. This was followed by another video by Pieczenick titled "the Clinton pedophilia connection":

"I've just talked to you about the ongoing coup and counter-coup that is being initiated by the Clintons on the one hand and the counter-coup by the FBI, the New York Police Department, and other branches of our intelligence community. The important part to remember is that not all the information has come out with regards to Weiner and his sexting to a 15-year-old North Carolina teenager. The real issue underlying a lot of Bill Clinton's nefarious activities, as well as Hillary Clinton's sexual activities, is the fact that we know that both of them have been a major part and participant of what's called the Lolita Express, which is a plane owned by Mr. Jeff Epstein, a wealthy multimillionaire who flies down to The Bahamas and allows Bill Clinton and Hillary to engage in sex with minors. That is called pedophilia. And as a result of the excellent work that the New York Police Department does in tracking a pedophilia. They also have a record of both Hillary, Bill and other people associated with the Clintons with regard to pedophilia.

"So, not only will she be charged with obstruction of justice, with lying to a prosecutor and the FBI, she will also be charged with pedophilia sex with minors and other perjury issues. Bill might be brought up again on certain charges because those charges still relate to American crime and prosecutorial issues. But I do want to inform you that we are well aware in the intelligence community that they're activities haven't stopped. And we're not talking about one trip to The Bahamas. We're talking about a multiple of 20 or 30 trips that Bill and Hillary did take separately and together on the Lolita express to engage in sexual activities with minors (Pieczenik 2016)."

As Martin explained in his program, *Media Roots Radio*, this was essentially the Qanon narrative and it was published before Erik Prince went on Breitbart or Cassandra Fairbanks mentioned spirit cooking. Pieczenik's first video, as well as the Cassandra Fairbanks story and Erik Prince's interview with Breitbart Radio, were all hosted on the front page of *Drudge*.

Pieczenik actually had the deep state credentials to inform his theories. He served as Deputy Assistant Secretary of State under Henry Kissinger, Cyrus Vance and James Baker (Kaye 1995), in the administrations of Gerald Ford, Jimmy Carter, Ronald Reagan, and George H. W. Bush (Romano 1992).

While with the State Department, Pieczenik played the role of a "specialist on hostage taking" (Geyer 1980), which included working on such high profile situations as the hijacking of TWA Flight 355 in 1976 and the kidnapping of the son of the president of Cyprus in 1977 (Toth 1978). He claimed that, in 1978, he was involved in secret negotiations that led to the Camp David accords (Kaye 1995) and, in 1979, he resigned after the failed negotiations related to the Iran hostage crisis (Taubman 1981).

Before he did, however, he was involved in a task related to the Gladio operations in Italy in 1978. Pieczenik worked on the "crisis committee" as a negotiator to handle the kidnapping of Italian Prime Minister Aldo Moro by the ostensibly communist Red Brigade. It was this negotiation process that lessened Moro's chances of safe release, in that Henry Kissinger warned Moro's wife not to compromise with his abductors, saying, "You will pay dearly for it." The crisis committee then released a false statement from the Red Brigades saying that Moro was already dead.

The Daily Telegraph reported on this false statement in 2008: "Mr Pieczenick said that this had a dual purpose; to prepare the Italian public for the worst, and to let the Red Brigades know that the state would not negotiate for Moro, and considered him already dead." The article relayed that "Pieczenik said that Moro had been 'sacrificed' for Italy's 'stability."" As with the violence that occurred with Gladio operations across Europe, there was evidence that the kidnapping was a false flag pinned on the left (Moore 2008).

Pieczenik's other notable positions included working as a psychiatrist treating CIA employees (Taubman 1982), a psychiatrist with the National Institute of Mental Health (The Annual Report of the Superintendent 1976), and a consultant for the United States Institute of Peace and the RAND Corporation (United States Institute of Peace 2012). Pieczenik was also a member of the Council on Foreign Relations (CFR) until his name was removed from the online members list in late fall of 2012. Interestingly, he had also worked with author Tom Clancy to write some of his novel series.

Along the line, Alex Jones began to add the Pieczenik storyline to the Q plot. In an interview, Jones was asked how he was able to get Donald Trump on InfoWars. Jones replied with the following:

> [There are people] I know that are part of Delta Force and I know people that are part of covert action in the Defense Department and the CIA. And, quite frankly, they've given me authorization to talk about this. I have never been in the CIA. I've never been part of covert operations, but I was basically contacted by groups inside Special Forces operations in Florida, inside breakaway groups, inside the Central Intelligence Agency and groups basically behind American industry that wanted to defeat the globalists and their plan to bankrupt America. And so they told me that they were advising Trump on the globalist takeover and that they understood from their demographics and their studies that we actually had conservatively 15 million people a week visiting infowars.com and tens of millions watching our videos and that that they had briefed the president, then candidate Trump. And that they wanted to attempt a counter-coup against the globalists.

But this is what got Donald Trump to say, I gotta be on this guy show.

Donald Trump was advised by the special forces command out of Florida.... They said, they said, "Sir, you need to go with Alex Jones. And you need to rally the troops." And they briefed him. They showed him the documents and they said, "We need you to run."

Pieczenick wasn't the only part of the Qanon apparatus that was associated with Gladio. The other Gladio connection came through the mentor of Q-linked Ezra Cohen-Watnick, Michael Ledeen.

Cohen-Watnick was a member of the Defense Intelligence Agency (DIA) with General Michael Flynn and then joined Flynn in Trump's National Security Council (Gray 2017). There, he was accused of leaking information to Representative Devin Nunes suggesting that the Obama administration had spied on the Trump campaign ahead of the 2016 election (Miller & DeYoung 2017). By summer 2017, Cohen-Watnick was taken out of the National Security Council and working at tech giant Oracle. Then, in 2018, he returned to government as an advisor on counterterrorism and counterintelligence for the Department of Justice (Goldman 2018).

A single Q drop brought Cohen-Watnick into the conspiracy. Posted on September 2, 2018, it read simply, "Ezra Cohen-Watnik." This event was followed by the emergence of a number of Twitter accounts that claimed to be him sending mysterious messages out to the Qanon community. "It is only at the precipice that true and lasting change will occur," said one tweet. "In order to fully expose the 'Invisible Enemy,' we had to bait them into a very contentious, bright light."

These users were shut down, purportedly on behalf of Cohen-Watnick himself, arguing that he was being impersonated online. However, new accounts would pop up only hinting at being him, such as a user named "@YourFriendlyE." They were, therefore, able to get around Twitter's anti-impersonation policies. Q followers would then claim that these new accounts were Cohen-Watnick.

The government official later told *Politico* that he was not behind these accounts and was not at all related to Qanon. He even claimed that someone had hacked into an old, disused Hotmail account of his and set up a meeting with Bill Binney, a former National Security Agency employee.

"The funny thing is, at the time, I wasn't even living in D.C. And I got a call from somebody saying, 'Hey, you stood up Bill Binney.' And I said, 'What are you talking about?'" Cohen told *Politico*. "You can imagine getting your email hacked into and having somebody lure people into coming to meet with you is very alarming" (Gerstein 2021).

I would later learn of the importance of his possible networking with Binney, but it was his connection to Michael Ledeen that first made me question his innocence in the affair. Cohen-Watnick was a protege of Ledeen, a neoconservative historian, who had once operated as a propagandist for the Gladio network.

The career of Michael Ledeen began when he was a historian of Italian fascism and, while living in Italy, he worked on a variety of intelligence projects. For instance, in 1976, he co-authored an article with Claire Sterling alleging that the Italian Communist Party, the primary target of Operation Gladio's anti-left campaign in the country, was secretly funded by the Soviet Union (Landis 1979). The article was published in Robert J. Myers' *New Republic*. Myers was closely associated with former chief CIA analyst Ray Cline, who was at the time the executive director of the right-wing Center for Strategic and International Studies (CSIS) think tank. In a 1978 congressional hearing about CIA activities, Myers said, "The reciprocal relationship between the CIA and the American press has been of value to both parties and often to the individuals themselves whose careers may have mutually benefited by such connections."

Just ahead of the Italian elections, the article was published once more in the CIA-funded *Rome Daily American*. Its authors went on television from 4 PM to 2 AM that night to act as commentators to reiterate the points of their article on Channel 1. The station was managed by the Christian Democrat Party, who received the majority of the CIA's funds in Italy (Landis 1979).

In 1980, he continued to work with *The New Republic*, while also reportedly executing black propaganda operations with right-wing Italian intelligence agents. According to a 1985 *Wall Street Journal* article, the Italian military secret service, SISMI, paid Ledeen $120,000 (Unger 2006). SISMI was heavily involved with Gladio terrorist activities, including the 1980 bombing of the Bologna train station that saw 85 people killed and 200 injured, which were then pinned on the Italian communist party (Monzat 1992).

Michael Ledeen was known to be a friend of Lucio Gelli, head of the Propaganda Due (P2) lodge used to plan and fund Italy's Gladio operations. In 1981, Ledeen made an attempt to purchase a list of P2's members when it was taken from Gelli's villa during a police raid. Barbara Honegger noted in *October Surprise*:

When the Italian police raided (P2 Lodge founder) Gelli's home in March 1981, it was Michael Ledeen who, at the instigation of Alexander Haig and Henry Kissinger, offered to buy the list of 953 P2 members in an apparent attempt to keep it from becoming public. Henry Kissinger had also reportedly sent Ledeen to Italy to try to squash an investigation into his and Haig's involvement in the founding of P2 (1989).

Ledeen became a close friend of General Michael Flynn, who shared a hatred for Iran, and his daughter, Simone Ledeen, worked for Flynn in Afghanistan at the office for the director of national intelligence. She was also employed in the DIA, conducting research on threat assessment.

Michael Ledeen went on to co-author a book with Flynn called *The Field of Fight: How We Can Win the Global War Against Radical Islam and Its Allies*, which urged action against Iran. He then consulted Flynn when the general joined the Trump administration, looking at the executive orders of former President Obama and suggesting "which ones should be cancelled, which ones should be expanded, and so on." In particular, Ledeen was focused on Iran, saying, "I've been agitating for thirty years to go after Iran. Now all of a sudden we've got a national-security adviser, a Secretary of Defense, and the head of the C.I.A. who all agree" (Schmidle 2017).

In 2016, Cohen-Watnick was introduced to Flynn by Michael Ledeen's wife, Barbara, who he knew from his younger years growing up in the Washington area. After connecting with Flynn, the young intelligence agent rose to prominence under the general's leadership (Gray 2017).

While I initially thought that #pizzagate was some sort of limited hangout to cover up and distract away from Trump's involvement in the Epstein affair, the presence of figures such as Pieczenik and Ledeen in the Qanon circle made me wonder if there was something else at work.

Noting another interesting figure that entered the scene to promote Qanon, I wondered if something even more insidious was at work. He was U.S. Army Maj. Gen. Paul E. Vallely, who went on the talk show "AmeriCanuck Internet Radio of Canada" to claim:

> QAnon is tied to information that comes out of a group called "The Army of Northern Virginia." This is a group of military intelligence specialists, of over 800 people that advise the president. The president does not have a lot of confidence in the CIA or even the [Defense Intelligence Agency] much anymore. So he relies on real

operators, who are mostly special-operations type of people. This is where "Q" picks up some of his information.

Vallely was a 1961 graduate of West Point who rose to the ranks of Deputy Commanding General for the U.S. Army Pacific in 1991. He was deployed in Vietnam twice and went on to command the 351st Civil Affairs Command from 1982-1986, which included the Special Forces, Psychological Warfare, and Civil Military units in the Western U.S.. After retiring in 1991, he worked as a military analyst for FOX News (Guffey 2020).

Also relevant to the fact that he had essentially endorsed a theory about the President taking down a cabal of deep state satanic pedophiles was that Vallely himself had been close to his very own deep state satanic pedophile, Lt. Col. Michael Aquino. He had commissioned the alleged child abuser and Temple of Set founder on a paper titled "From PSYOP to MindWar."

Aquino described the circumstances in a 2003 introduction added the document:

> In the later 1970s, Psychological Operations (PSYOP) doctrine in the U.S. Army had yet to emerge from the disappointment and frustration of the Vietnam War. Thus it was that in 1980 Colonel Vallely, Commander of the 7th PSYOP Group, asked me, as his Headquarters PSYOP Research & Analysis (FA) Team Leader, to draft a paper that would encourage some future thought within the PSYOP community. He did not want a Vietnam postmortem, but rather some fresh and innovative ideas concerning PSYOP's evolution and application.
>
> I prepared an initial draft, which Colonel Vallely reviewed and annotated, which resulted in revised drafts and critiques until he was satisfied, and the result of that was this paper: From PSYOP to MindWar: The Psychology of Victory.
>
> Colonel Vallely sent copies of it to various government offices, agencies, commands, and publications involved or interested in PSYOP. He intended it not as an article for publication, but simply as a "talking paper" to stimulate dialogue. In this it was quite successful, judging by the extensive and lively letters he received concerning it over the next several months.
>
> That should have been the end of MindWar: a minor "staff study" which had done its modest job.
>
> With the arising of the Internet in the 1980s, however, Mind-War received an entirely unexpected – and somewhat comic – resurrection. Allusions to it gradually proliferated, with its "sinister"

title quickly winning it the most lurid, conspiracy-theory reputation. The rumor mill soon had it transformed into an Orwellian blueprint for Manchurian Candidate mind control and world domination. My own image as an occult personality added fuel to the wildfire: MindWar was now touted by the lunatic fringe as conclusive proof that the Pentagon was awash in Black Magic and Devil-worship.

Now that this absurdly comic opera has at least somewhat subsided, I thought that it might be interesting to make a complete and accurate copy of the paper available, together with an Introduction and some historical-hindsight annotations to place it in reasonable context. After all it did – and perhaps still does – have something worthwhile to say (Guffey 2020)."

Vallely's willingness to link Q to an enigmatic collection of military intelligence officials in Northern Virginia took on a new meaning in the context of his affiliation with Aquino and "MindWar." Some of the possibilities included that he was telling the truth and 800 military intelligence specialists had aligned with Trump to fight the deep state, or he was lying to bolster the believability of the Qanon narrative, or the Army of Northern Virginia did exist but that they were involved in Qanon in another capacity. Given Vallely's interest in Aquino's psyops philosophies, one could wonder if the Army of Northern Virginia or simply Vallely and anyone he was working with was conducting some sort of MindWar on the American people and beyond.

Poster of Jesus wearing Maga Hat paraded at January 6, 2021 during the storming of the United States Capitol, with QAnon "WWG1WGA" slogan.
Creative Commons.

Chapter Thirty-four

Qanon as Right-Wing MKULTRA Cult

U nlike the Satanic Panic, Request Anonymous, or the Fifth Column, Qanon featured an addictive quality only possible with the advent of the Internet and gaming. The community of anons that began to worship the enigmatic Q were hooked by the puzzle-like nature of solving Q's riddles, such as a drop made on November 2, 2017:

> Senator McCain and others roundly criticized Rep. Michele Bachmann in 2012 when she and four members of the House Permanent Select Committee Intelligence and the House Judiciary Committee cited Ms. Abedin in letters sent to the Inspectors General of the Department of Defense, Department of State, Department of Justice, Department of Homeland Security, and the Office of the Director of National Intelligence, warning about Muslim Brotherhood infiltration of the United States government.
> Why is this relevant?
> Who took an undisclosed trip to SA?
> What was the purpose of a f2f v phone call?
> Alice & Wonderland."

These questions would allow players to rack their brains to answer them and fit them into a larger context while trying to decipher such enigmatic phrases as "Alice & Wonderland." And when hints were provided to aid in the investigation, the player was dragged further along. The question "Who took an undisclosed trip to SA?" was answered with such a hint in a November 3, 2017 drop that read:

> "Where is John Podesta?
> Where is Tony Podesta?
> Did one or both escape the country and was let out?
> WHERE IS BO?
> WHERE WAS BO YESTERDAY?
> What is the difference between commercial and private re: security clearance for departure?
> Who is the TSA head?

Which party did he contribute to?

What is of particular interest when researching?

How does HS interact w/ TSA?

What updated post 9-11 protocols were put in place to prevent/ stop inbound/outbound C-level targets?

What local airports are in close proximity to DC?

What happened shortly after 9-11 (specifically with all aircraft)?

Who was authorized to depart? ONLY 1 PLANE was authorized during this 'mandatory forced grounding'.

Who SPECIFICALLY authorized this?

What airport did the departure take place at?

Why is this relevant?

How does it tie together?

Podesta's plane has military escort (i.e. tag) and is being diverted (forced down).

Short delay.

This will be leaked.

Watch the news.

Have faith.

What fake news anchor will not be on air tonight?

Why is this relevant?

What was stated in the past?

Where did the $18b from Soros go?

Why?

Can it be used by bad actors (escape, bribes, rogue contractors, etc.)? Slush fund?

Did the U.S. gov't seize/stop/track other slush funds that prevent or create risk to operate?

Why did JK travel to SA recently?

What is SA known for?

Where do the biggest donations originate from?

Why is this relevant?

What else is relevant w/ SA?

Safe harbor?

Port of transfer?

Why was there a recent smear campaign against JK and POTUS?

Why is the timing important?

Who released the article?

The council of Wizards & Warlocks cannot be defeated.

Nice view up here.

Q"

There were obvious guesses as to who and what the "JK" and "SA" in "Why did JK travel to SA recently?" could have been. The riddle was seemingly answered, like a trivia card flipped over, in October 2017 when news stories came out that President Trump's son-in-law, Jared Kushner, had taken an unannounced trip to Saudi Arabia.

Not only did learning the answer produce some sense of satisfaction, but this seemed to be proof that Q really did have access to insider knowledge. This was what came to be known as a "Q proof," evidence that Q was indeed close to the President of the United States (mi5terp n.d.).

The proofs ranged from somewhat plausible to broader stretches of the imagination. For instance, a user asked Q on January 29, 2018 if Trump could work the phrase "tip top" into the State of the Union. Though it wasn't the State of the Union, Trump did mention in an April speech that the White House was kept in "tip top" shape. Q followed up by posting on 8chan, "It was requested. Did you listen? Q (Moore 2018)."

In another Q proof, the eponymous user posted what some considered to be evidence that someone behind Q was aboard Air Force One with the President. On November 9, 2017, Q published a photo looking out of the window of an airplane. The same day, the President tweeted that he was traveling from China to Vietnam and tweeted once again when he landed. The timing of the Q proof just so happened to occur during this timeframe. The file name of the image was "AF1_5A_2," implying that it was named for its location aboard the president's aircraft. And, because no one could seem to find the same photo with an image-based search engine online, they believed the photo to be wholly new and authentic (mi5terp n.d.).

In the video program of a prominent Qtuber, Tracy Beanz, Jerome Corsi claimed that another Q post, featuring a photo of a Montblanc pen on a desk, proved the figure's proximity to Trump.

"That's the Laurel desk," Corsi told Beanz. "It's the one that Obama used and apparently Trump is also using at Camp David. That's the desktop at Camp David. The pen is a Montblanc ink pen that Trump has used for a long time. That's Camp David over the weekend and that picture had to have been taken by somebody who was there with President Trump. His pen on the desk; that pretty much authenticates that QAnon is very close to Donald Trump and present in some of these really important inner circle White House meetings" (Mantyla 2018).

The result of these riddles was a consistent flow of dopamine that kept Qanon players going, continuous shots of the habit-forming neurotransmitter as their meaning-making brains worked on Q's codes. This was followed by larger doses when they were validated by these so-called Q proofs.

There was some precedence for such an online game in the recent past. It was an alternate reality game (ARG) called Cicada 3301 and it began with an image file consisting of a brief note, written with white text on a black background, and published to 4chan on January 4, 2012:

> Hello. We are looking for highly intelligent individuals. To find them, we have devised a test.
> There is a message hidden in the image.
> Find it, and it will lead you on the road to finding us. We look forward to meeting the few who will make it all the way through.
> Good luck.
> 3301"

To solve it, a user first had to use steganography software to extract a message embedded in the graphic. Next they would need to rely on a shift cipher to find that each letter in the message corresponded with a different letter. Once this was decoded, a URL could be found that led to a picture of a duck that could be further deciphered with steganography tools. This led to another URL with another puzzle and so on.

In the end, those actually capable of solving the riddles would end up applying a combination of cryptography, knowledge of Mayan numerology, and some familiarity with cyberpunk fiction to ultimately break out of the computer and into the physical world. This included hints recorded on the answering machine of a Texas phone number as well as flyers attached to telephone poles across 14 cities around the globe. Finally, the player would wind up on the dark web at a Tor site where they supplied their email address to supposedly receive contact from the 3301 team.

The first puzzle lasted for a month before the hidden site displayed the message, "We have now found the individuals we sought." Subsequent puzzles were hosted on January 4 of 2013 and 2014, the last of which was never solved (Hartigan 2015). The mystery of who was behind Cicada 3301 also continued, however one person stepped out of the shadows to claim ownership.

In an October 2020 video, *Financial Times* spoke with an early developer of ARGs (also referred to as "LARPs), Jim Stewartson, who said that, after its first year, Cicada was "gamejacked." Someone had launched a new puzzle under the same banner as the original Cicada 3301. This person was Thomas Schoenberger, a self-described musical composer and polymath. When

Schoenberger took the reins of the popular LARP, the symbols of Cicada morphed from the mildly esoteric to the weirdly occult. It incorporated references to Aleister Crowley, William Blake and runic figures.

As bizarre as this was, it became more surreal when, according to Stewartson, the composer employed someone named Lisa Clapier to draw Cicada players to Qanon in 2017 (Kaminska 2020). They weren't the only ones involved, however. Former Technical Director of intelligence for the NSA William Binney and ex-CIA agent Robert David Steele, along with other members of the Veteran Intelligence Professionals for Sanity (VIPS) activist group, supposedly joined Schoenberger to create Qanon. This was the same Bill Binney would may or may not have met with Ezra Cohen-Watnik during a time when many suspected Cohen-Watnik of being Q (Bicks 2021).

Behind the Scenes?

Trusting the specifics of the Q operation was extremely difficult for many reasons. The most obvious was the fact that the Internet was filled with misinformation, ranging from mainstream media pushing corporate and state agendas to the fact that anyone with a website could publish whatever they wanted without any verification. Then, there was the fact that Qanon itself seemed to be a psyop intentionally filled with dubious data. And, finally, the suspects involved were, by their own reputations, untrustworthy.

When I looked up Thomas Schoenberger, much of what I found were stilted employees and friends, claiming to have been manipulated by him in one way or another. Some claimed that he used "sock puppet" accounts online – that is, alternate personas – to reinforce his own agenda. Working with others virtually and remotely, he may have had multiple identities representing other project team members so that he could spy on those around him over email, online chats, and on social media.

One of Schoenberger's close associates, Manuel "Defango" Chavez III, was also considered a notorious troll, making some of his accounts untrustworthy, as well. However, even Defango claimed that Schoenberger had manipulated him.

Moreover, Defango was one of several people who claimed that they had been involved in the launch of Q. He wrote in a 2018 blog post:

> I knew he was setting me up from the start to take the fall for this QAnon thing. I believe he thought I was going to stay quite [sp]

and let the thing happen. I decided to leave Texas out of fear for my life when I discovered this deal with sony [sp] was going threw [sp] and he was making the cut happen. I tried to call him and get business going but he completely blocked my calls and just keep [sp] telling folks the plan to take me down. It was sad to see it happen but at least I understand how to fix this (Bicks 2021)."

Another person suggesting Schoenberger's involvement was Richard Miller, a coder who had been involved in creating puzzles for Cicada after Schoenberger gamejacked it. In a blog post, Miller said that he was working with Heavy.com on an article about Q and could be presumed to be the publication's source who designed Defango as "a notorious Internet troll who worked for political campaigns and Schoenberger, who was closely associated with the 2016 [Qanon precursor] FBIAnon (Miller 2020)."

Miller wrote, "Heavy.com created a piece with researchers I am working with highlighting Schoenberger's connections to QAnon, and either gamejacking the movement, or LARPing (pretending to be) the person from the movement. Thomas Schoenberger, however, solemnly swears he was not involved as heavy.com has reported, and that he will sue them. In contrast, in personal e-mails to me, he has shown to be involved with and colluding with people who may have gamejacked the QAnon movement."

He further wrote, "I received a confession from Lisa Clapier (PistisSophia/SnowWhite7IAM on Twitter) that she is 'behind Q.'"

Moreover, he claimed that Schoenberger implicated the participation of Ezra Cohen-Watnik in Qanon and Schoenberger's various lawsuits:

> Schoenberger confesses that "Eyethespy" aka "EtheFriend," a notorious account on Twitter spreading Q conspiracy is Ezra Cohen-Watnick. This is either Thomas in collusion with [Cohen-Watnick], or in collusion with an individual impersonating a government official. Thomas Schoenberger also reveals a confession of intentionality of disrupting civil suits (Manuel Chavez III, Gabe Hoffman, et al.) by "asking a favor" with positional interference from Ezra Cohen-Watnick. He claims this will net him $7,000,000 dollars. Thomas also says he wants to "destroy" these people and "spend money foolishly."

In his blog post, Miller described how Schoenberger and Lisa Clapier seemed to have manipulated at least one minor, encouraging them to obtain money from their parents.

I regret to say, early 2019 (1/31) I was randomly introduced to a child who I really had no clue what he was talking about and just kind of "went with it." He was 11 which I was not fully aware of. TS was sending him very adult-oriented and scare manipulation images. As well as feeding him promises of trust in himself, as well as putting him up to and guilt-tripping him for not being able to donate to me raising money for a concert in 2019. The child also said "he does not want to be hurt again, he's sorry and Thomas put him up to apologizing for being unable to donate to me." I have ignored this child's e-mails after I became more aware of who he was.

The child also frequently says "Long live PistisSophia" in e-mails to me. PistisSophia is Lisa Clapier. … There is also evidence that they lied to him about Lisa dying, and that other children are involved. He still e-mails me to this day and it is heartbreaking. A 60-year-old man [Thomas Schoenberger] has no place doing such things to a child.

Additionally, Schoenberger used Pistis Sophia as a proxy to other minors, which he fed lies to and pretended to be his own secretary "Jane." He then claims "Jane" was real, though I have e-mails confirming she is not."

As evidence, Miller included an email between the child and Schoenberger. Miller said that some sort of cult-like status had emerged between Schoenberger and Clapier and their followers, including the minor:

Back to 2015, I was introduced to a woman, Iona Miller who showed me her blogs and ramblings essentially worshipping Thomas Schoenberger as the living incarnation of St. Germain, which he claims as well. These blogs had several testaments to this cult-like influence Schoenberger had over a large number of Authors. Friend/Girlfriend Lisa Clapier "PistisSophia" was also involved with this cult-like worship as well.

Miller – along with a film producer named Gabe Hoffman, who produced a documentary exposing authentic accounts of pedophilia in Hollywood called *An Open Secret* – claimed that Schoenberger had a relationship with Isaac Kappy. This was the same Isaac Kappy I had begun my journey into hell reading about. The one who had accused Seth Green of child sexual abuse before committing suicide.

Hoffman made a series of tweets referring to Schoenberger as Kappy's media handler and saying that the key to understanding Kappy's death was examining Schoenberger. According to Heavy.com's source, likely Richard Miller, "Hoffman was then attacked online by a massive gang of trolls for months." Schoenberger claimed that Hoffman had murdered Kappy himself to cover the tracks of a pedophile ring. In turn, Hoffman sued Shoenberger for defamation (Becks 2021).

In June 2018, about a year before his death, Kappy was on a podcast called *Lift the Veil*, in which he claimed that "there's a lot of other people involved in [Q]," adding that he participated on an 8chan board with the people behind Q. He then said that Thomas Schoenberger, from Cicada, connected him with people.

The show's host, Nathan Stolpman, replied that he knew Schoenberger, as well, and that the composer tried to recruit him. He added, "I'll just tell you to be very very cautious about who you trust. Even Thomas" (Becks 2021).

These seemed to be the people involved in Qanon at first, but it was difficult to trust their accounting. Then, there were other individuals that either participated with Schoenberger or took the operation over from him, such as Ron Watkins. Once Q was chased off of 4chan, the team behind Q was reliant on Jim Watkins, the owner of a different message board site called 8chan, and its administrator, Jim's son, Ron.

In an HBO documentary series, *Q: Into the Storm*, filmmaker Cullen Hoback made a convincing case that, at some point after this transition from 4chan to 8chan, Q's posts were being performed by Ron. The admin nearly admitted as much in the final episode of the series, when discussing his personal transition from using 8chan to Twitter.

Ron told Hoback, "I've spent the last, what, almost 10 years doing this kind of research anonymously. Now I'm doing it publicly, that's the only difference … don't think for a second that half the threads on /pol/ [the political page of 8Chan] weren't like, me digging. So thinking back on it, like it was basically three years of intelligence training teaching normies how to do intelligence work. It's basically what I was doing anonymously before… but never as Q" (Hoback 2021, Ep 6).

The exchange came after Ron had spent the entire documentary flipping between playing dumb about the Qanon phenomenon and presenting in-depth knowledge. Hoback made a convincing case that Ron Watkins, and likely his father, Jim, were involved in Q, at least when it started on 8chan. He also seemed to be able to link other 8chan users, such as Paul Ferber and possibly Tracy Diaz, as participating in the Qanon project.

This seemed to be validated by someone calling themselves "QBRD_ BAKER," whose email about Qanon was published online and dated Sunday, May 6, 2018 12:11 AM (UNIRockTV 2018).

According to this user, there was a group of users who published as Q that "started this to rally up patriots for a common cause. Yes, we had good intentions – in the beginning. We wanted to create something positive even it was a bit deceptive (it was for a good cause we thought).

"And I say this with so much guilt, No, there is no real Q member or members within the government or in the military giving us intel. It's the truth!"

QBRD_BAKER said that a number of 4chan and 8chan users actually posted as Q and worked with Jerome Corsi to spread Q's message:

"Pamphlet Anon [Coleman Rogers], Pam's wife [Caroline Urso], Baruch the Scribe [Paul Ferber], Farmer Funk, Code Monkey [Ron Watkins], Obobo, Rain, Tracybeanz [Tracy Diaz], and to a big extent Dr Corsi (unknowingly at first, but I'm sure Corsi was let on to the truth later on, IDK for sure because I had left the group but I'm pretty sure he knows the truth) are the major players that you know of…" they wrote.

The user claimed that the Q operation was born out of frustration, saying:

> Prior to the elections some members had started sending letters to the president complaining about the problems in our government. It was time we got measurable change – is what they wrote. We also called it Quality and Quantitative change! This is where Q came from. We called ourselves Q patriots in every letter and made it clear that we were wanting change and that we were rooting for him and promised to help him gain votes to make this possible. We sent lots and lots of letters hoping he'd acknowledge us.
>
> Regarding the famefagging – look back to see who reached out first to inforwars, tracy and many other truthers for interviews. The truth is out there. They've even been caught saying that Q told them directly to do this (BULLSHIT AGAIN). This is when Tracy came on board too and Corsi."

When members of this clique became too problematic for whatever reason, they were cut off from the ability to run Q or participate in the program. QBRD_BAKER went on to explain how they were able to provide drops that closely coincided with reality. They said that the group of Q users relied on a specific website dedicated to showing all of Trump's tweets, called Trump Twitter Archive. Apparently, at one point, the site loaded the President's tweets about five to 15 minutes more quickly than they would appear to the public on Twitter. The group was, therefore, able to post Q drops that included words from his tweets on the chans before they went live for the Twitter public.

"But really it was all because there was a code that twitter provided to capture the tweet off the server (it's how media websites would capture and embed them too). Twitter eventually fixed this and it's why you no longer see the POTUS tweets prior to him posting them on twitter. This coding was all code monkey [Ron Watkins] with the help of a few others," the user claimed.

A lot of the direction for Q drops was provided by a user called Pamphlet Anon, whose real name was Coleman Rogers. He and his wife, Christina Urso, ran a YouTube channel called Patriot's Soapbox dedicated to Qanon. It live-streamed a Discord chat room and featured a variety of moderators and commentators. According to QBRD_BAKER, Rogers would research Jerome Corsi's books to come up with fodder for the Socratic method-style questions that Q posted. For pictures such as the Mont Blanc pen at Camp David, QBRD_BAKER said that they found images online and modified them so that they would not appear in a reverse image search.

QBRD_BAKER even said that the group hacked a server that journalists sent their breaking news to in order to distribute stories across the media. "It was and has been a gold mine of info. It's also how we found out about some of the real on-goings with POTUS. We just added more BS to it all. It made what we were dropping on the chans really look like intel. It wasn't. We were either diligent at what we planned, very lucky or both every time," they claimed.

Before signing off the email, QBRD_BAKER apologized for leading people on and pointed out the absurdity of the Q project, noting Hillary Clinton still hadn't been arrested.

DIGITAL SOLDIERS

Perhaps more interesting were Thomas Schoenberger's ties to the Qanon community's second biggest hero after Trump, General Michael T. Flynn. Flynn was the former head of the Defense Intelligence Agency (DIA) and Trump's first National Security Advisor. He had already become loved among right-wing voters when he led chants of "Lock her up!," referring to imprisoning candidate Clinton, at Trump's rallies. Flynn was made to resign less than a month after becoming National Security Adviser when it was exposed that he had lobbied on behalf of Turkey without formally registering as a lobbyist, a not uncommon practice for influence peddlers in D.C.

Schoenberger was linked to Flynn indirectly through his marriage to Iranian American musician Faranak "Fara" Shahroozi. Shahroozi's cousin was Nasser Kazeminy, founder and chairman of NJK Holding Corporation. Together, Schoenberger and Kazeminy established Amadeus Investors LLC in 2005, from which Schoenberger was paid over $100,000, according to *Heavy* (Becks 2021). The *Washington Post* reported in 2017 that Flynn received "$140,000 for [his] work as an adviser and consultant to Minneapolis-based NJK Holding Corp. That firm is led by Nasser Kazeminy, an Iranian-born businessman now living in the United States (Hamburger & Gold 2017)."

That wasn't Schoenberger's only connection to Flynn and Schoenberger may not have only been a composer. In a 2015 deposition, Schoenberger said that, in 2011, he was involved in a covert operation for use in Afghanistan with Bijan Kian, a partner at Flynn Intel Group (Becks 2021).

If Flynn was involved in Qanon, the military use of ARGs wasn't completely new. A 2013 *Wired* article described how the Department of Defense's Intelligence Advanced Research Projects Activity (IARPA) was exploring how ARGs could enable the DoD to enhance their understanding of human psychology and social behavior (Beckhusen 2013). Before that, Joseph Matheny, a developer of the early ARG Ong's Hat, said that the U.S. Navy had asked him if they could study his game and the synchronicity experienced by its players. Ong's Hat players had reportedly felt that the game was alive, with events in their lives somehow coinciding with events in the ARG in such a way that was either extremely disturbing or revelatory for the players. Matheny reportedly rejected the offer, but something he noted in an interview foreshadowed things to come with Qanon: "Unfortunately, what we've discovered is that there are certain personality types [for whom the game] can trigger a flight into destructive fantasy" (Michael 2019).

Another possible component of Qanon could have been related to Psy-Group, an Israeli firm founded by Joel Zamel. The online perception management company provided Trump campaign official Rick Gates with a quote for $3,125,000 for its services, such as manipulating social media and conducting opposition research, honey traps and clandestine on-the-ground activities (Mazzetti et al 2018).

This included the use of the "dark web" for such purposes. The dark web usually referred to the use of encrypted overlay networks in which Internet use was typically anonymous and, therefore, a prime method for conducting illicit business such as buying and selling drugs, weapons, assassination services, and child pornography. However, there was a possibility that Psy-Group was referring to the chans, given their relative obscurity on the traditional Internet.

In a Trump Tower meeting three months later, Erik Prince, Donald Trump Jr., and George Nader met with Joel Zamel. The meeting followed with Nader paying Zamel $2 million soon after (Klippenstein 2018). (Interesting side note: Nader was convicted of child trafficking, providing another link between Trump and the pedophile networks he was meant to stop.)

Joel Zamel was introduced to Flynn by Bijan Kian, the aforementioned partner at Flynn Intel Group (Klipperstein 2018). Zamel's Psy-Group went on to partner with a now-infamous firm called Cambridge Analytica, invested in by Trump supporter Robert Mercer and owned by private intelligence company and self-described "global election management agency" SCL Group (Tau & Ballhaus 2018). The goal of the partnership was to deradicalize people sympathetic to ISIS on behalf of the State Department's Global Engagement Center.

SCL Group had an extensive history with the military industrial complex, specifically the U.K.'s conservative Tory establishment. One former board member was Geoffrey Pattie, former parliamentary under-secretary of state for defence procurement and director of Marconi Defence Systems. A shareholder in the firm was Lord Marland, pro-Brexit trade envoy under Prime Minister David Cameron (Cadwalladr 2017).

The publication Fast Company noted that SCL had "developed a set of techniques to battle extremism and disinformation for a range of defense agencies, including the British Foreign Office, the Norwegian Government Defense Research Agency, the Kingdom of Saudi Arabia, the British Army's 15 Psychological Operations Group, and multiple U.S. agencies." In one instance, this included collaborating with the top secret Sandia National Laboratory on "an in-depth behavior change study in relation to violent extremism in South and Southeast Asia (Pasternack 2019).

One of its most valued tools was something called Target Audience Analysis (TAA), developed by the company's research lab, Behavioral Dynamics Institute (BDI), which had "invested over £19m in developing scientific approaches for 'influencing a target audience.'" The research group claimed on its since-deleted website, "Using advanced research techniques, the BDi can accurately diagnose an audience from within (in theatre) or remotely," using the language of the military.

It also stated, "The Behavioural Dynamics Institute can tell you how 'difficult' an audience is likely to be, how best to influence the audience and then can actually produce the communications or triggers that will change the audience."

Steve Tatham, once head of psychological operations for the U.K. in Afghanistan, worked with SCL and wrote a paper for the U.S. Army explaining that TAA was meant for targeting "key groups – who may not yet have emerged – through accurate behavioral profiling of groups," giving them rankings based on their influence ability and ability to be influenced. In a NATO strategic communications journal, he also noted that "TAA can be undertaken covertly. Audience groups are not necessarily aware that they are the research subjects and government's role and/or third parties can be invisible."

SCL even taught a two-month course on TAA at the NATO StratCom Center of Excellence dedicated to "scientific application, [that] involves a comprehensive study of audience groups and forms the basis for interventions aimed at reinforcing or changing attitudes and behavior."

The work SLC's subsidiaries performed involved applying its expertise in audience manipulation to aiding right-wing efforts globally. In Saudi Arabia, a "psychological road map" of the population was created to determine the impact of possible reforms to be enacted by Crown Prince Mohammed bin Salman, such as allowing women to drive. Another project was a re-election campaign for the president of Kenya. Yet another was focused on diplomats in the United Nations General Assembly in New York, targeting them with posts containing the hashtag #BoycottQatar on social media. Countries where SCL conducted surveys and political campaigns included India, Pakistan, Iran, Yemen, Indonesia, South Africa, and Nigeria, the last of which featured a "voter suppression" operation, according to the company's website.

As for right-wing affairs in the U.S., the company already had some familiarity with General Flynn, as SCL analyzed the population of Afghanistan under Flynn in 2010. Just before joining Trump as his first national security advisor, Flynn was a consultant for SCL's defense unit in 2016. At that same time, SCL Group obtained a $500,000 deal with the U.S. State Department to work on counter-terrorism.

It was after a fortuitous 2013 meeting that future Trump backer and hedge fund manager Robert Mercer invested $15 million into launching Cambridge Analytica, with future Trump campaign manager Steve Bannon made a Vice President and board member. The subsidiary's first operations in 2014 were dedicated to providing assistance to the election campaigns of numerous right-wing candidates backed by the super PAC of ultra-conservative, anti-Iran Bush veteran John Bolton, who would go on to be one of Trump's national security advisors.

A 2014 post-election report by Cambridge Analytica, made public by the Center for Public Integrity noted, "Primarily concerned with promoting [Bolton's] agenda with regards to national defence and foreign policy, the PAC made use of significant input from SCL on messaging and target audiences, with positive results. Respondents [who] had been targeted with Bolton Super PAC messaging on foreign policy and national security showed a significant increase in their awareness of these subjects."

Specifically, Cambridge Analytica had generated voter profiles by combining material from Facebook data, focus groups, psychographic models, phone surveys and its AggregateIQ software. With this, they were able to craft ads tailored to the anti-immigration, pro-war policies of such Bolton-backed candidates as Tom Cotton, Cory Gardner, and Thom Tillis.

In 2016, Cambridge Analytica added presidential candidates Ben Carson, Ted Cruz and Donald Trump to their portfolio. In 2018, the world learned that Cambridge Analytica had bought the data of 87 million Facebook profiles to assist the Trump campaign.

Then, of course, there was the Brexit campaign for the U.K. to leave the European Union. When SCL got into military work after 9/11, the company aimed to demonstrate to governmental customers the ways in which media might be implemented "to help orchestrate a sophisticated campaign of mass deception" on a large population, such as that of London. It was no coincidence then that Target Audience Analysis (TAA) was used for the Brexit campaign. SCL executive Julian Wheatland wrote in a December 2015 email to the CEO of Leave.EU:

> As we discussed, we will make sure that the Target Audience Analysis (TAA) suits the purposes of Leave as well as [UKIP, the UK Independence Party] and we will try to seed some questions into the survey that will help inform future study of insurance risk profiling. Once we have completed the TAA and matched it to the Experian data we will be in a position to start microtargeting and, at that time, we would propose that we start digital outreach and a program of voter engagement and fundraising.

Bannon was not only able to assist in the U.S., but in the U.K., as well, when he was included in a number of emails during Leave.EU's campaign. According to an interview with *the New York Times*, Bannon's goal with Brexit was to radically alter the country's culture. "He believes that to change politics, you have to first change the culture. And Britain was key to that. He thought that where Britain led, America would follow. The idea of Brexit was hugely symbolically important to him," *the Times* wrote (Cadwalladr 2017).

Knowing what SCL and Cambridge Analytica were capable of doing, it would be possible to imagine the companies gathering data on a sub-segment of impressionable people who didn't hold much allegiance to the Republicans or Democrats and target them with specific messages, perhaps bordering on the conspiratorial.

It could even be possible to funnel them into Qanon-style content. The game-like nature of solving Q's riddles could have further addicted them to the cause. If SCL, Cambridge Analytica, and Psy-Group were willing to go far enough, they could even jump onto obscure websites ideal for introverted homebodies, like 4chan and 8chan and build a movement that might trickle outward to mainstream sites like Facebook.

THE FBI ON 8CHAN

If U.S. intelligence agencies were operating on the chans, it may not have been the only time. Outside of co-opting members of Anonymous, an activist group that began on 4chan, the FBI had used the chans to sow disinformation related to the Russian government. According to an independent researcher going by the moniker HenryKrinkle, a federal agent used 8chan to "redirect the users' conspiracy theories against the Russian government instead of the CIA or Mossad."

The researcher found this in exploring the contents of an application by FBI Special Agent Michael Rod for a search warrant on 8chan's servers. The warrant request came after an April 27th, 2019 shooting at a California synagogue by white supremacist and 8chan user John Earnest, who posted his manifesto to the site. In the warrant application, HenryKrinkle found screen grabs of an 8chan thread leading up to the shooting. The screenshots were from the perspective of an 8chan user with the phrase "(You)" appearing after the 8chan user's anonymous ID to let them know that they were looking at their own posts.

By submitting these screenshots as evidence for obtaining the warrant, Special Agent Rod seemed to have outted himself as 8chan user ID "8f4812." By looking at an archived version of the thread, HenryKrinkle found all of the other posts made by the FBI agent. This included a post suggesting that the Russians had promoted the synagogue shooter's manifesto:

> "Guys. Read my posts. I believe that the shooter did post on here
> but there is also more. Ive been here all day. There are at least two

others that are posting in a bot, shilllike fashion to promote this. This theead never would have made the first page, where I found it this morning.

Think there is outside involvement. Likely Russian.

In the posts not attributed the man himself, these two not only hyped this thread in an awkward way, they continued an odd pattern of posts to keep this thread alive. Look at the parallel language and style. pol does not talk like that.

Look at the memes chosen in these posts. Not even a fucking clown.

While I believe John may have been motivated by hia own beliefs and reasons, I believe that there are other forces at work here that may have provoked him.

The original link leads to a Tarrants Lads group In russian.

He may have been rightfully upset with the way the world is, but he may have been manipulated into this by something that is not.

I'd blame Mossad, the CIA and FBI too, but this time I am not so sure. We know all three of them can meme because we are shilled all day long by them.

He chose a crappy pistol. Anyone would have planned a litte more thoroughly. If BT is a hero to him as he describes, he would have learned from this mistakes, or at a minimun made an effort to emulate him and do the same. To walk in there completey unprepared with a single pistol sends off even more red flags,

This is very unusual. This is not the typical $((($conspiracy$)))$ and I am worried. I dont believe this is the end of this.

I hope some one else takes it upon themselves to investigate what I posted above as well."

HenryKrinkle explained that the FBI poster made a similar attempt to attribute the shooting to the Russians:

"This was posted by one of the shills that
knew of the shooting prior. Notice screen shot is at 20:00. That correlates with ukraine and western russia if you do the math

Seriosuly, one of you has to dig on this. Please review this thread. There is some russian/ukranian involvement."

The user was later accused of being a Mossad agent, to which the agent replied, "No. Not mossad. Stop attacking the board and sliding this thread. Sloppy job putin. Dick (HenryKrinkle 2019)"

HenryKrinkle then went on to elaborate on the many times that the FBI had collaborated with extremists, from mentally unstable individuals to right-wing groups. This included a 2015 incident in which an FBI agent texted an ISIS sympathizer named Elton Simpson to "tear up Texas" just days before Simpson tried to execute a mass shooting at a "Draw Muhammed" event in Garland, Texas. According to one study, 55 percent of all terrorist prosecutions by the government were manufactured by entrapment. The more dangerous, the more manufactured they seemed to be and only nine percent of total cases were deemed genuine threats (Norris 2015).

While the FBI's entrapment of the mentally unstable may have just been part of a self-filling cycle that justified the bureau's existence, the impact of arresting "would-be terrorists" constituted a form of domestic Gladio, false flags initiated by U.S. intelligence to generate tension and, therefore, cause Americans to demand greater security. If the chans were similarly leveraged to create right-wing extremists, this could have been part of the motivation behind Qanon. That would potentially explain any participation by Steve Pczieneck or Michael Ledeen. After all, the operation continued long after Trump won the 2016 election. In fact, it gained much more steam and built up to outbursts of violence in the physical world.

Z Speaks

It was particularly difficult to understand Schoenberger's role in all of this. Had he concocted Q before it was taken over by Ron Watkins and his crew? Or was Schoenberger never involved and he tried to gamejack it? The waters were very muddy.

I reached out to Richard Miller, who went by the pseudonym Z, to see if I could gain a better understanding. Finding his email on Twitter, I wrote, "I was hoping to get the timeline of events and the players down correctly. Do I have this right? First, some coders – that didn't include you, Thomas Schoenberger, Defango, or any of the others that would become wrapped up in Q – developed the original Cicada puzzle in 2012. At some point after that, around 2014, Thomas gamejacked it with Defango, then brought you and others on board. At some point after that, these people (which included Paul Ferber, Pamphlet Anon and his wife, Farmer Funk, Ron Watkins, Obobo, Rain, and Tracybeanz) came up with the idea for Qanon in a Discord chat and launched it on 4chan. Then, for greater control over the project, they shifted it over to 8chan. Is any of that right or is it all off lol?"

Z replied, "Your timeline is spot-on!" In a subsequent email, he clarified, "Thomas was not involved with Cicada prior to gamejacking in 2015 with the BBC cicada fake puzzles, then 2016 with pi.mobi, and 2017 with myself which I had already known about him at that time. He says in official court docs his 'partner' of Cicada and himself began working together in 2014, two years after Cicada's original puzzles."

Z was also able to provide emails that Lisa Clapier claimed to be involved in Q. Miller emailed Clapier to say that he did not want Cicada 3301 to be associated with Q, writing:

> "I'm not sure why 3301 imagery is being tied to Q. It shouldn't be. From what I understand you reached out to Beth about tying the puzzles with Q. Also CC'd was Mindy, TS, Lestat, Genki, Hamilton, and Tanya. I was not, Nov. 8th, 2018.
> Why is that? What does it accomplish?
> Beth does not create the puzzles. Michael held half the copyright. Why was he not CC'd?
> Your SnowWhite persona is inherently counter-productive to my own wishes. I teach and inspire. I do not deal with conspiracy or LARPs.
> I do not believe you are connected to EtheFriend, as has been brought up, nor the StreamRift account. You are all pushing different ideologies.
>
> But, the point still stands. I was not informed of this decision, nobody came directly to me despite the fact that I am personally a stakeholder and was the most active member of 3301 when Q came around.
> I was the member personally contacted by Q as well.
> I denied Q, the trademark, and the press for this reason – I do not want propaganda based ideologies to permeate the puzzles. They are exclusive.
> If you truly want a revolution as you claim, understand that these types of campaigns have come and tried and failed numerous times. What sparks revolution is not information nor misinformation, it is action.
> Go and protest, just please don't mingle renaissance inspired art projects with conspirators."

Clapier responding by saying:

> There are reasons for anonymity which none of the stalkers comprehend benefits them too. I protect the lives of witnesses who end the cabal. Not ideally, literally. It is not a theory there is a conspir-

acy against humanity. The criminal elite are the game. The people have the power & the Truth stands as their solid foundation.

Not a single stalker trying to convince you in those threads, have any factual proof of anything. So let that sink in ... how is guessing then doxing, invading other people's privacy, trashing, defaming, bullying, stalking, photoshopping fake evidence ... a good thing? For anyone. They tag the puzzle. I do not.

I recognize you were not aware I am behind Q. People's lives are on the line, rely on me, it isn't something I share lightly, with anyone.

Anonymity has ended now because strangers played a game, took "their" lies to major media.

Miller challenged her on being Q by writing: "You are not Q. You're involved in the pushing of Q. There is a difference. As I said, I was contacted months prior to the first Q posting, in March and then again in May."

When I asked about any involvement by government officials that Z might have been aware of, he told me, "The only government official i know of being connected is Robert David Steele, if you count him." There were emails published online that showed Schoenberger interacting with Steele, confirming ax's claims.

Because Schoenberger was a clear link between Qanon and Michael Flynn, I had to make sure I knew what the self-described composer's role was in the operation. Z reiterated that Schoenberger had gamejacked Q. He told me, "[T]here's something important to note here – Thomas inserts himself (and usually his friends as well) into things to attempt to gain notoriety. This was the case with Cicada, Seth Rich, Kappy, and then Q. Thomas has been attempting to half-assed backpedal his way out of the Q nonsense, but essentially, it is all gamejacking to attempt to, in my opinion, spread an anti-zionist and anti-semitic narrative."

From whom he gamejacked Q I struggled to understand. However, one thing that Miller said completely changed how I looked at the parties involved. I asked, "So, it sounds like, as far as you know, Clapier just helped spread Q propaganda online and Thomas attempted to gamejack Q, but neither may or may not have actually ended up actually participating in the back room operations of how Q worked, right? This is important because of Thomas's possible links to Bijan Kian and, therefore, Flynn."

Z replied, "Yes, it's more likely that Thomas gamejacked Q and lied under oath about Kian." In other words, Schoenberger didn't work for Kian in Afghanistan, in Miller's estimation. Of course, this was just the opinion of one person who knew Schoenberger well, but it suggested the possibility that Flynn nor Cambridge Analytica and SCL were involved in creating Q with the help of Thomas Schoenberger.

So, then, maybe Q really started as a LARP by some random Internet users and not a deep state government conspiracy. However, even if that was the case, that didn't mean government-affiliated individuals didn't take advantage of the movement that followed. In addition to people like Pczieneck and Trump, Flynn really did build on the momentum of the Qanon community.

There was the general support of the community for the military figure, sometimes shown by Twitter users adding three stars to their bios to reflect Flynn's three-star status. But there was also the general's reciprocation, which included posting to his Twitter account a video of himself leading a small group of people in a "digital soldier" oath that concluded with the QAnon motto, "Where we go one, we go all" (Connolly 2020)." This resulted in Qanon followers copying Flynn with the hashtag #TakeTheOath, though Flynn's attorney Sidney Powell denied the oath was related to QAnon. Instead, she argued that "where we go one we go all" was just a statement engraved on a bell on John F. Kennedy's sailboat (Jarvis 2020).

Additionally, in September 2019, Flynn hosted a "Digital Soldiers Conference" about "patriotic social media warriors" for a coming "digital civil war." The announcement for the event featured the letter Q made up of stars against the backdrop of a U.S. flag. Speaking at the event were Flynn himself, along with George Papadopoulos, Trump campaign media advisor Gina Loudon, singer Joy Villa, and radio host Bill Mitchell (Friedman & Breland 2019).

HBO's *Q: Into the Storm* caught several members of the Q community mentioning that they had spoken with members of Trump's circle and other politicians. Qtber Tracy Diaz ("Tracy beanz") claimed to have spoken with Michael Flynn, who encouraged her to continue in her work (Hoback 2021, Ep. 6). Omar Navarro, a congressional candidate and Qanon believer, said that he was close with Flynn and Roger Stone and had pictures taken with them (Hoback 2021, Ep 2). Through retired Air Force vet Nick Noe, who claimed that he killed a bin Laden body double during the Seal Team Six raid in Pakistan and that Bin Laden was still alive, reportedly served as a communication bridge between Qtber Craig James and Major General Paul Vallely (Hoback 2021, Ep 5).

This suggested that, even if there wasn't a military intelligence conspiracy behind the Qanon phenomenon, they did try to benefit from that phenomenon. There was even a possibility that they could have gamejacked the LARP once its potential became clear.

CONCLUSION

MANUFACTURING CONSENT, RESTRAINING DISSENT

I found it difficult to determine the mechanics of elections and, so, didn't feel as though I could say what drove the outcome in the U.S. in 2016, but I could reason that this hysteria on the right aided in Trump's election to the presidency. Regardless, once he won, the extreme elements of his constituency wanted to see him carry through with some of the myths that had been generated during the campaign, such as "locking up" Hillary Clinton. This phrase would mean different things to different people, with progressives seeing it as reasonable to arrest Clinton for war crimes in Libya and Honduras while she was Secretary of State, liberals and conservatives not in the know believing it meant for her private email server or Benghazi-related conspiracy theories, and #pizzagate enthusiasts believing it was for child trafficking.

This last element would want to see justice served. After all, Trump was president. If #pizzagate were true, true then the candidate who somehow dodged being ensnared in it should have done something about it. Robbie Martin suggested that it was at this point that #pizzagate morphed into Qanon:

> People had nowhere to go with this energy of wanting to expose this deep state pedophile network that they thought existed, right? There was really nowhere they could take it. You know, these 4chan Reddit researchers, 8chan people were still researching things and still, you know, believing in this idea that the deep state was going to go down. And that Trump was behind the scenes sort of secretly doing things to address it and that he was going to arrest Hillary Clinton still. There was this strong belief that that still was going to happen, but people were losing hope. There wasn't much evidence out there that it was actually going to happen. Now, how long could people believe in that without much proof without any movement in that area? Well, I'll tell you how: QAnon is how" (Martin 2021).

Almost a year after Trump's win, a user on 4chan described as infodump anon used intelligence-style language to regurgitate the theories that were being espoused by Pieczenick. "Q Clearance Patriot" responded to this poster by saying:

> Hillary Clinton extradition already in motion effective yesterday with several countries in case of cross border run. Passport approved to be flagged effective 10/30 at 12:01 AM. Expect massive riots organized in defiance and others fleeing the U S to occur. USMS will conduct the operation while NG activated proof check, locate a national guard member and ask if activated for duty 10 30 across most major cities."

Obviously, none of the above happened. The Clintons were never arrested. There were no mass arrests. So, a user referred to as "Q" kept pushing the goal posts, changing the narrative. Q would leave "breadcrumbs," coded messages to string people along and essentially gamify the narrative. Along the way, it seemed as though some believers became fed up and began to take matters into their own hands.

There were a lot of instances in which Qanon believers took extreme actions, including a few that were particularly bizarre. In 2018, Matthew Wright used an armored vehicle to barricade a bridge over the Hoover Dam on the Nevada-Arizona border. Blocking traffic for an hour-and-a-half with a vehicle containing a handgun and an AR-15 rifle, Wright demanded that the U.S. Justice Department "release the OIG report" detailing the FBI's investigation into Clinton's private email server. According to one Q drop, a report released by the Office of the Inspector General (OIG) the day prior had been extensively changed and a more damning copy had been maintained by Trump (Mormon 2018).

"We the people demand full disclosure," Wright said, addressing Trump. "We elected you to do a duty. You said you were going to lock certain people up if you were elected. You have yet to do that. Uphold your oath" (Sommer 2018). He was subsequently sentenced to seven years in prison (Ruelas 2021).

In 2019, Anthony Comello believed he "was enjoying the protection of President Trump himself" when he confronted Gambino crime family underboss Frank Cali with the purported goal of performing a citizen's arrest. Thinking that Cali was part of the deep state, Comello shot Cali ten times, killing him. His lawyer said that Comello had become obsessed with Qanon, evidenced by the Qanon symbols and "MAGA forever" drawn on his hands in pen during his first court appearance (Reinstein 2019). Interestingly, the MAGA fan may have been right, in that the Gambino mob family did have extensive ties to U.S. power brokers and intelligence. This included ties to Trump and his mentor, Roy Cohn. However, Comello's conception of the deep state may have been isolated to Democrat-run pedophile rings and not the broader definition imported from Turkey by Peter Dale Scott.

Also in 2019, Cynthia Abcug attempted to kidnap one of her children that was no longer in her custody, believing they'd been taken from her by "evil Satan worshippers" and "pedophiles." Her other daughter told authorities that her mother had partnered with a weapon-carrying man who was "definitely part of this group QAnon (Slevin 2020)."

In April 2020, train engineer Eduardo Moreno drove a freight train at high speed toward a hospital ship called the USNS *Mercy* stationed in the Port of Los Angeles to handle hospital overflow from the COVID-19 pandemic. The train smashed into barriers, barreled beneath a highway overpass and screeched slowly to a halt some 250 yards from the ship. No one was injured.

The U.S. Attorney's Office said Moreno believed "the ship is [not] what they say it's for" and that "he did it out of the desire to 'wake people up.'"

"You only get this chance once. The whole world is watching. I had to. People don't know what's going on here. Now they will," Moreno told the California Highway Patrol officer who arrested him (Chappell 2020).

As voting drew near, Trump then began to suggest that the election would be fraudulent. Democratic officials also seemed to prepare for the possibility that the president would not give up his post if he lost. After he did lose, legitimately or not, Trump swapped out his Secretary of Defense with Christopher C. Miller, one of the few men with a military background, along with Generals George Marshall and James "Mad Dog" Mattis, to serve in that position. After 31 years in the military, Miller retired from the Army as a colonel. Unlike Mattis and Marshall, who were involved in conventional warfare, Miller spent his career with the Green Berets in Afghanistan – in other words, unconventional warfare, counterterrorism, and counterinsurgency. He then retired in 2014, before joining Trump's National Security Council in 2018 and later becoming director of the National Counterterrorism Center in 2020 (Lamothe et al 2020).

Within a week of becoming Secretary of Defense, Miller announced that the Assistant Secretary of Defense for Special Operations and Low-Intensity Conflict (SO/LIC), the most senior civilian post for special operations in the U.S., would report directly to the Secretary of Defense. This was unique in that only the civilian heads of the various military branches would report to the Defense Secretary. However, with Miller's move the United States Special Operations Command (USSOCOM) essentially became a new branch of the armed forces alongside the Army, Navy, Air Force, and Marines. To pull this off, Miller relied on his authority under the National Defense Authorization Act of 2017, signed into law under President Obama (Browne 2020).

Additionally, Ezra Cohen-Watnick, who was made SO/LIC in September 2020. After Miller's move, that meant a close ally of Flynn had become the civilian head of special operations forces, reporting to the Secretary of Defense (Watson 2020). Cohen-Watnick was also chosen as the Undersecretary of Defense for Intelligence (USDI), a position rivaling only the director of the CIA in terms of power within U.S. national security due to the fact that directors of the NSA, the DIA, the National Reconnaissance Office (NRO), and all military intelligence reported to the USDI (Department of Defense 2020). This put Flynn's ally in charge of all U.S. special operations forces and military intelligence, reporting only to the Secretary of Defense, who only reported to the President.

With such powerful friends as these, as well as his mentor General Stanley McChrystal, Flynn and his clique had managed to build a powerful military intelligence apparatus and may have been using such manipulative tactics as ARGs to control masses of people.

By January 6 2021, Qanon had reached what was its peak. As a part of a "Save America" rally in Washington, D.C., thousands of Trump supporters gathered to protest what they believed to be an illegitimate presidential election, demanding that Vice President Mike Pence and Congress reject the electoral victory of Joe Biden. They marched to the Capitol building, where Congress was in session to count votes from the Electoral College. With some collusion by Capitol police, a group of protestors breached a perimeter set up around the area and began to wreak havoc on the building for several hours. During that time, they looted and destroyed property, stole a laptop belonging to a member of Congress, and assaulted reporters and police. In the end, five people died and over 140 were injured (Evelyn 2021).

When the event was over, it would become apparent how important were the links between Flynn and Fort Bragg, where the Joint Special

Operations Command (JSOC) he once led were based. It was also there that Secretary of Defense Christopher Miller's Green Berets were located. So was PSYOPs officer Captain Emily Rainey, who led a brigade of protestors. In the wake of the event, it was suspected that Secretary of Defense Miller held off on deploying the National Guard to stop the riot, leading Vice President Mike Pence to call them in. He also banned the DC National Guard from taking weapons, helmets, and armor on the day of the protest and instructed them not to touch, arrest or search rioters (Summer 2021).

Also playing a role in the theatrics was General Charles Flynn, Michael Flynn's younger brother. He happened to be present when Capitol Police and D.C. officials were on the phone with the Pentagon during the protests as they requested help from the National Guard (Leonnig et al 2021). At the time, Charlie Flynn was the Army's Deputy Chief of Staff for Operations, Training, and Planning, just beneath the Army's Chief of staff, making him the senior most military figure in the Army. Toward the end of 2020, Charlie Flynn was receiving another star while his older sibling, Michael Flynn, was challenging the results of the election (U.S. Congress 2020). In fact, the day Charlie's star was confirmed by the Senate was the day after Michael was calling for martial law during a meeting at the White House (Lamothe et al 2021).

Beyond government officials, there were other suspicious elements of the protests. A senior member of the right wing group the Proud Boys, for instance, happened to be an FBI informant (Bender et al 2021). A member of the right wing militia movement the Oath Keepers had been in contact with the Secret Service just before the riot began, ostensibly to provide "security" (So 2021).

Though the mainstream media described the protests as "an insurrection," it didn't seem like one capable of making significant progress, let alone succeeding in overthrowing the government. Many Trump allies then turned their backs on him in response to the pseudo-coup. In addition to Mike Pence, this included the historically right-wing National Association of Manufacturers (NAM), which requested that Pence use the 25th Amendment to usurp Trump (Novet 2021). Secretary of Education Betsy DeVos, sister of Trump associate Erik Prince, resigned days later when Pence didn't invoke the 25th Amendment (Gaudiano & Stratford 2021). Finally, the Joint Chiefs of Staff (JCS) released a memo supporting the win of Joe Biden and instructing the armed forces to uphold the Constitution (Harkins 2021).

QANON AND THE PIZZAGATES OF HELL

WHAT DID IT MEAN?

If one connected the dots, you had a number of military intelligence officials, propagandists, and psyops agents exploiting an addictive gaming platform with known brain-warping capabilities to allow or perhaps even drive a group of susceptible people to act out in increasingly violent ways. This, in turn, led to what seemed like a reasonable reaction from the corporate-state: a crackdown on conspiracy theories and their believers, whether they posed a threat or not.

It was a strategy of tension that pinned violence on the right, rather than the left, but managed to do so in a way that created a technologically driven mind control cult. At the same time, anyone who questioned the official narrative – whether it related to 9/11, the COVID-19 pandemic, 5G technology, or the JFK assassination – was not just a delusional lunatic, but a dangerous one. This included people on the left and the right. In turn, the government and its corporate allies could spread disinformation and quiet dissent.

This actually began immediately after the 2016 election, when the idea that the Russian government had somehow managed to interfere in U.S. elections to get Trump elected permeated the media and consciousness of American liberals. To prevent future interference, various initiatives were set up to prevent "disinformation." One of the most notable was a partnership between the social media site Facebook and the Atlantic Council, an organization heavily staffed with U.S. government and NATO officials (MacLeod 2018). The Atlantic Council would aid Facebook in essentially censoring posts thought to be from troublesome foreign agents, including activist groups challenging the Israeli decimation of Palestinians. Had the U.S. government itself said it would be performing this task, the Orwellian nature of the project could have resulted in a public outcry, but because this was conducted under the guise of a third party, there was hardly any pushback. Plus, the fear of the Russians had liberals clamoring for security.

As the Trump presidency progressed, the Russia story appeared to result in nothing of note, but Qanon presented a new target for censorship. In August 2019, a document from the FBI was made public that categorized fringe conspiracy theories as a domestic terrorist problem. This group of "conspiracy theory-driven domestic extremists," according to an FBI intelligence bulletin from the bureau's Phoenix field office, was described as a growing threat. It singled out Qanon and Pizzagate and mentioned Trump by name in explaining Q as an alleged government official who "posts classified information online to reveal a covert effort, led by President Trump, to dismantle a conspiracy involving 'deep state' actors and global elites allegedly engaged in an international child sex trafficking ring" (Winter 2019).

"The FBI assesses these conspiracy theories very likely will emerge, spread, and evolve in the modern information marketplace, occasionally driving both groups and individual extremists to carry out criminal or violent acts," the report read, saying that these extremists could become increasingly active as the 2020 election approached. It also noted that "the uncovering of real conspiracies or cover-ups involving illegal, harmful, or unconstitutional activities by government officials or leading political figures" added fuel to the fire of these "extremist" groups.

Notably, the document stated, "This is the first FBI product examining the threat from conspiracy theory-driven domestic extremists and provides a baseline for future intelligence products." It categorized this "extremist" group of fringe conspiracy theorists as having beliefs that "attempt to explain events or circumstances as the result of a group of actors working in secret to benefit themselves at the expense of others" and are "usually at odds with official or prevailing explanations of events."

Nate Snyder, a former Department of Homeland Security counterterrorism official under Barack Obama, told *Yahoo News*, upon reviewing the FBI document, "The domestic violent extremists cited in the bulletin are using the same playbook that groups like ISIS and al-Qaida have used to inspire, recruit and carry out attacks. You put out a bulletin and say this is the content they're looking at – and it's some guy saying he's a religious cleric or philosopher – and then you look at the content, videos on YouTube, etc., that they are pushing and show how people in the U.S. might be radicalized by that content."

Michael German, a former FBI agent and a fellow with the Brennan Center for Justice's Liberty & National Security program, told *Yahoo News* that, with the document, the FBI was simply following a faulty theory that so-called extremist ideology could radicalize people to violence.

"It's part of the radicalization theory the FBI has promoted despite empirical studies that show it's bogus," he said. "They like the radicalization theory because it justifies mass surveillance. If we know everyone who will do harm is coming from this particular community, mass surveillance is important. We keep broadening the number of communities we include in extremist categories."

Since the report, Qanon had become a boogeyman that could represent all "conspiracy theories," regardless of their validity. As of January 26, 2021, Wikipedia linked the CIA's Operation Mockingbird with the far-right Qanon movement. The site listed under the modern usage of the phrase, "Qanon supporters, who believe a CIA program to manipulate the media still exists and that the mainstream media are responsible for spreading fake news, claim press reports they dislike are part of Operation Mockingbird." The reference supporting this entry was from an August 4, 2018 *Washington Post* article that wrote, "QAnon posters dismiss press reports they do not like by claiming they are part of 'Operation Mockingbird,'" supposedly a continuation of a 1950s CIA program to distribute propaganda through the media (Trickey 2018)."

The effect of linking what was made to look like an extremist group, Qanon, with a legitimate historical fact, Operation Mockingbird, was an instant diminishing of the importance of something like Mockingbird. The exposure of that CIA program revealed that the agency was not only operating domestically, but that it had collaborated with the heads of most, if not all, major media outlets. Given the track record of the agency, there was no reason to believe that it stopped these practices. However, if one were to attempt to use Mockingbird as a precedent for covert manipulation of the general media by a government espionage agency, one could easily be written off as a Qanon whacko.

This further extended to raising questions about any historical event, such as the JFK assassination. In February 2021, *The Independent* published an article conflating alternative theories about the death of President John F. Kennedy with Qanon, COVID-19 denial, and the anti-vaccine movement.

"The Kennedy conspiracy theory has become a respectable conspiracy theory. Almost. And the film [*JFK* directed by Oliver Stone] reinforced that. But it isn't and today's virulent conspiracies make clear that the thinking it encourages is problematic," wrote James Moore. "There might not, on the face of it, appear to be much of a link between the Kennedy conspiracy and QAnon… Yet the type of thinking that fuels the Kennedy theory even now… isn't all that different" (Moore 2021).

Joe Uscinski, an associate professor of political science at the University of Miami, had written work about conspiracy theories cited by the aforementioned FBI bulletin. According to Uscinski, "For most of the last 50 years, 60 to 80 percent of the country believe in some form of JFK conspiracy theory. They're obviously not all extremist." In fact, the House of Representatives Select Committee on Assassinations, held in 1976, determined "on the basis of the evidence available to it, that Kennedy was probably assassinated as a result of a conspiracy" (Winter 2019).

In January 2021, members of the conservative Democratic Blue Dog Coalition in U.S. Congress introduced a bil, Security Clearance Improvement Act, l meant to address the Capitol Building protest. Rep. Stephanie Murphy's (D-Fla.) Security Clearance Improvement Act would prevent Qanon supporters from getting or keeping federal security clearance. Murphy said about the Bill, "As a former national security specialist at the Pentagon, I know how dangerous it is for individuals who participated in a violent attempt to overthrow our government to receive a security clearance and access classified information. QAnon has spread far beyond the fringes, and we must now take steps to ensure these dangerous conspiracy theories don't infiltrate our government. Holding a security clearance is a privilege, not a right" (Moyer 2018). Hypothetically, such a measure could also prevent a government official with the proper security clearances from investigating possible relationships between federal agencies and Jeffrey Epstein or the Franklin Scandal.

Other fallout from the Capitol Hill protest included what seemed to be unprecedented bans from the Internet of users who participated in the demonstration. The *Los Angeles Times* reported that at least five defendants in the court cases that resulted from the protests were barred from using social media or the Internet based on federal criminal complaints, claiming the desire to prevent the spread of misinformation. While Beverly Hills esthetician Gina Bisignano was banned from the web altogether for urging followers on social media to take up arms and attack the Capitol, John Sullivan, from Utah, was only allowed to use social media while under supervision. In the past, the Ohio Supreme Court protected a defendant from being barred from social media. The federal Supreme Court struck down a law in North Carolina that would have prevented sex offenders from using social media, as well. So, there was the possibility that the Capitol Building protestors could have been protected upon appeal (Halper 2021).

Despite this strong reaction toward the group, the Qanon movement seemed to lose momentum after Biden took office. Or perhaps it was only changing shape. One bizarre feature in the wake of Qanon was the emergence of Shawunawaz and Sabmyk. The former was a mythical sword of Atlantis that was carried by heroes across the generations, from Gilgamesh and Alexander the Great to Napoleon. It was finally returned to its rightful place in 1992, when it was given by George Soros to the Persian Princess Ameli Achaemenes. Though she was said to have destroyed it to prevent its power from being abused, an entity called Sabmyk was created on December 21, 2020, the Great Conjunction of the planets, who could abolish evil from the world if it could obtain the sword. Or so the story went, as told on a number of Q-related social media and video accounts. The Sabmyk project tried to align with Trump by cutting him into its strange videos, photoshopping a Sabmyk pamphlet in his pocket and splicing footage of him saying the word "17" (Anglesey March 2021).

It turned out that Sabmyk, the "preordained ruler of the world," was actually the result of a Berlin-based artist named Sebastian Bieniek, who actually worked with Marina Abramović and was influenced by her art. Interestingly, Bieniek published a book in 2011, *RealFake*, about his use of fake social media accounts as a form of art, blurring the lines between reality and fiction (Anglesey April 2021).

The strange mythos that Bieniek introduced was a bizarre twist in the Qanon story made only stranger when the Conservative Political Action Conference (CPAC) hosted its annual event from February 25 to 28th in 2021. The event that year just so happened to be presented atop a stage in the shape of an odal rune. The rune had been adopted as an icon by the SS and, later, by the White Liberation Movement in South Africa and the National Vanguard in Italy (Snider 2021).

Perhaps the esoteric symbols of these two developments was meaningless. Or maybe it meant some rebirth of Nazi occultism as society at large teetered on the brink of collapse. Maybe the stage was being set for a form of ecofascism to take over as climate catastrophe overwhelmed existing bureaucracies. Or maybe it was just another piece of absurdity in an increasingly absurd reality. Only time would tell.

By June 2021, the FBI was continuing to describe the Qanon community as a dangerous one. On June 4, the bureau sent out a bulletin to Congress suggesting that, because Q's predictions never realized, QAnon followers "no longer 'trust the plan'" that Trump and deep state rebels would upend the system. As a result, the FBI warned that some of them "likely will begin to believe" they have an "obligation" to "serv[e] as 'digital soldiers' towards engaging in real world violence" toward Democrats and "other political opposition" (Hosenball 2021).

Soon, right-wing media pundit Tucker Carlson aired a segment claiming that the FBI had actually planned the January 6th protests. Though there was evidence that federal authorities may have actually been involved, the *Washington Post* immediately countered his segment. This provided liberal readers with a canned opinion in direct opposition to the conservative conspiracy theory (Blake 2021). Of course, Carlson's dad had been director of Voice of America, the anti-Soviet propaganda broadcaster backed by the CIA (Lenz 208). Not only that, but Carlson himself had applied to work at the CIA himself (Ankel 2020). Could he have found a new way to work for the deep state apparatus, regardless of being rejected by the Agency? Regardless, it seemed that, once again, Qanon was proving effective as a tool of dividing those ruled by the power elite.

Conclusion

When I sat down to write this book, I decided to look up Tracy Twyman once more to see if her obituary turned up online. Sadly, it did. As strange as it might have sounded, I had previously thought that she could have faked her death (WeRemember.com). As a writer who studied cryptids and the occult, it didn't seem like it would be out of the ordinary for someone like her to play such a trick. However, given the difficulty it took to pull off such a stunt and get an obituary written up, I reasoned that she was now deceased.

So, was the pedo cabal (real) sacrificing children to Moloch (dubious possibility)? It was hard to tell. What did seem to be the case was that the deep state was at least using #pizzagate and Qanon as a justification for censorship. Even more, it may have deliberately been cultivating two extreme conspiracy ideologies on either side of the political spectrum, with Russiagaters on the liberal end and Q people on the conservative. And it could then stoke these people into playing out whatever theatrics were necessary to execute their agenda.

There were numerous threads left untied, paths unexplored. Was there a relationship between Epstein and Dyncorp, the military contractor that was involved in child trafficking in the Balkans? Epstein's aircraft shared a call sign with a Dyncorp helicopter, after all (Hopsicker 2019). What was that strange social media app in Korea that was linked to child pornography and the elites (Hsu 2019)? Was there truth to the idea that Jeffrey Dahmer was affiliated with the same circles as the Son of Sam (Opperman 2015)?

What did it mean that David Ferrie, a pedophile and hypnotist thought to have been involved in the JFK assassination, was in a leadership position for Lee Harvey Oswald's Civil Air Patrol (CAP) unit when the future patsy joined at age fifteen (House Select Committee on Assassinations 1979)? This was the same CAP group that kick-started Barry Seal's career as a drug smuggler for the CIA during Iran-Contra. Was there any connection to Ferrie's pedophile ring in Louisiana and the supposedly occult rituals he performed as a priest in the American Eastern Catholic Ortho-dox Church (Snider 2016)?

As I tried to log off, I maintained contact with some of the Gundam and learned that, in my absence, they'd recruited new agents like @Geck-osDaily1, @carzonfyre, @beefytopdog, @OurHiddenHistry, @MemeV-Vitch, @mardirooster and @pisspope. I also stayed in touch with some unofficial Gundams, like @musicforcougars, who occasionally helped me find obscure documents With all of their own interests and talents, I fig-ured they'd begin investigating some of these topics and spreading what they learned online.

I would have, of course, loved some definitive proof of the reality of a satanic pedo cabal. In lieu of that, I could be unsatisfied with the less controversial answer: we were ruled by a power elite that sacrificed chil-dren in the form of the countless civilians killed by global capitalism. And, while I couldn't escape hell, I had at least carved myself out a little bit of heaven with my quaint family at the heart of the imperial core, thriving at the expense of the global south and the collapsing ecosystem.

If nothing else, I had at least exposed myself to the horrors of the col-lective unconscious, seen things I had been too afraid to look at in the past. According to Carl Jung, that was a crucial step toward integration, facing the shadow and making some form of peace. I couldn't do much to resolve any of it, but I reasoned that exposing others to the collective shadow could push us to address the hell that we had created for our-selves, do away with the institutions of torture and abuse, and begin to reintegrate the fractured portions of our collective self.

In that way, maybe we, as a teeming horde of bubbling semi-conscious, semi-unconscious entities, could manifest something resembling heaven on earth. What that would look like would be difficult to say, as it would require input from the total mass. It would also likely be driven by those who had been most oppressed by this society. What it wouldn't include, however, would be the cruel, senseless abuse of the powerless by the pow-erful. Sure, we'd still suffer and experience loss, as all creatures did, but the kind of sick predation of the Epsteins, Gottliebs, and Jolly Wests on behalf of the Rockefellers of the world would be a thing of the past.

And, though it would be hard to describe how that would look, I imag-ined that it would be something like the way I felt when a quiet breeze encircled me and my family on a warm summer night, wrapping us in a single shared airstream. It would be like that but expanded to the vast ma-jority of the world's population as much of the time as possible.

CITATIONS

PART 1

ABC 7 News. 2021. "Jeffrey Epstein's ex-girlfriend Ghislaine Maxwell pleads not guilty to new charges." ABC 7 News. https://abc7news.com/ghislaine-maxwell-update-news-jeffrey-epsteins-ex-girlfriend-jeff-epstein/10541138/.

Abramson, Alana. 2017. "President Trump's Allies Keep Talking About the 'Deep State'. What's That?" TIME.com. https://time.com/4692178/donald-trump-deep-state-breitbart-barack-obama/.

Adams, J. April 7, 2020. "The truth about adrenochrome." The Spinoff.

AlertSense. 2016. "AlertSense executive team." AlertSense. https://web.archive.org/web/20161110063635/https://www.alertsense.com/company/executive-team/.

Apuzzo, Matt, Michael S. Schmidt, and Adam Goldman. 2016. "F.B.I. Says Review Clears Clinton In Email Inquiry – Director Tells Congress Many Messages in New Trove Were Duplicates." *New York Times*, November 7, 2016.

Archiga, B. 2019. "Mythic pizza: Semiotic and ARCHETYPAL significance in the CONSPIRACY narrative known as 'Pizzagate.'" (July). https://escholarship.org/uc/item/17k1c130.

Barry, J., Eden, M., & Johnson, M. (1991, November 3). One man, many tales. https://www.newsweek.com/one-man-many-tales-201744

Beck, R. (2015). *We believe the children: A moral panic in the 1980s*. New York, NY: PublicAffairs.

Belfast Telegraph. (2016, June 02). Top secret kincora boys' home documents handed over to abuse inquiry. https://m.belfasttelegraph.co.uk/news/northern-ireland/top-secret-kincora-boys-home-documents-handed-over-to-abuse-inquiry-34760139.html

Bello, G. (n.d.). Mockingbird paper. https://www.mockingbirdpaper.com/content/columbus-where-torture-taxi-and-lolita-express-meet

Ben-Menashe, Ari (2015-10-01). *Profits of War: Inside the Secret U.S.-Israeli Arms Network*. Trine Day. p. 312. ISBN 9781634240505.

Berg, A. J. (Director). (2015, June 5). An Open Secret [Video file]. https://vimeo.com/142444429

Bernard, S., & Schoeneman, D. (2003, April 25). Dinner hosts tell their secrets – *nymag*. https://nymag.com/nymetro/news/features/n_8672/

Beth Reinhard, R. (2019, August 10). Trump and EPSTEIN Partied together. then a Palm BEACH mansion came between them. https://www.sun-sentinel.com/news/politics/fl-ne-wp-epstein-trump-palm-beach-buddies-20190731-z4aj6xux2zb6jott4deqonla4m-story.html

Bicks, Emily (September 20, 2019). "Virginia Roberts Giuffre: 5 Fast Facts You Need to Know." Heavy.com.

Bilefsky, D. (2017, September 18). Iceland's Government Falls After Letter Asking to Pardon Pedophile

Block, R. (2011, October 23). Airline swaps gun-running for Good WORKS: Southern air transport was. https://www.independent.co.uk/news/world/airline-swaps-gunrunning-for-good-works-southern-air-transport-was-run-by-the-cia-and-started-the-irancontra-scandal-but-now-its-staff-assure-robert-block-its-main-job-is-saving-somalis-1565324.html

Boadle, A. (2019, January 09). Brazil celebrity healer to face rape trial after dozens of women come forward. https://www.reuters.com/article/brazil-healer-abuse-idINL1N1YI01R

Bohrer, J. (2019, July 18). Tape shows Donald Trump and Jeffrey Epstein discussing women AT 1992 party. https://www.nbcnews.com/news/us-news/tape-shows-donald-trump-jeffrey-epstein-discussing-women-1992-party-n1030686

Briquelet, Kate. 2019. "REVEALED: We Found Billionaire Pedophile Jeffrey Epstein's Secret Charity." *The Daily Beast*. https://www.thedailybeast.com/jeffrey-epstein-has-a-secret-charity-heres-who-it-gave-money-to.

Briquelet, K. (2019, July 12). Epstein had his Own lodge AT Interlochen's Prestigious arts camp for kids. https://www.thedailybeast.com/jeffrey-epstein-had-his-own-lodge-at-interlochens-prestigious-arts-camp-for-kids-in-michigan

Brown, J. K. (2018, November 28). How a future Trump Cabinet member gave a serial sex abuser the deal of a lifetime. https://www.miamiherald.com/news/local/article220097825.html#storylink=cpy

Brown, Julie K. (November 28, 2018). "Even from jail, sex abuser manipulated the system. His victims were kept in the dark." *Miami Herald*.

Bryant, N. A. (2012). *Franklin scandal: A story of powerbrokers, child abuse and betrayal*. Waterville, ORP: Trine Day.

Burners.Me. 2019. "Another #PedoGate Researcher Suddenly Dies: RIP Tracy Twyman." Burners.Me: Me, Burners and The Man. https://burners.me/2019/07/10/another-pedogate-researcher-suddenly-dies-rip-tracy-twyman/.

Cain, Á. (2019, August 22). Jeffrey Epstein was accused of sex Trafficking young girls on his mysterious private Island. over 40 years ago, a Different millionaire escaped justice in a stunningly similar case. https://www.businessinsider.com/jeffrey-epstein-north-fox-island-francis-shelden-2019-8

Cameron Scott (1 May 2007). "Mexico's Most Wanted Journalist." *Mother Jones*.

Chaitin, Daniel (July 7, 2019). "Jeffrey Epstein arrested for sex trafficking of minors in Florida and New York." *Washington Examiner*.

Cheit, R. E. (2016). *The witch-hunt narrative: politics, psychology, and the sexual abuse of children*. Oxford University Press.

Chothia, F. (2018, August 15). South Africa's 'PAEDOPHILE' minister and a mysterious death. https://www.bbc.com/news/world-africa-45195756

Churm, S. R. (1990, June 05). Parents dig persistently for evidence : Mcmartin school: Despite skeptics, they insist they have found underground network. with the site razed for an office building, the questions may never be answered. https://www.latimes.com/archives/la-xpm-1990-06-05-me-508-story.html

Clark, A. (2007, May 08). Happy birthday Barbara. https://www.theguardian.com/media/2007/may/09/citynews.thedailytelegraph

Cobbe, Elaine (October 18, 2019). "Ex-model accuses Jeffrey Epstein's friend of rape." CBS News.

Coen, J. 2016. "Judge calls Hastert 'serial child molester,' gives him 15 months in prison." *Chicago Tribune*, April 28, 2016. https://www.chicagotribune.com/news/breaking/ct-dennis-hastert-sentencing-20160427-story.html.

Colhoun, J. (2013). *Gangsterismo: The United States, Cuba, and the Mafia: 1933 to 1966*. New York, New York: OR Books.

Colyar, Brock, Kelsey Hurwitz, Charlotte Klein, Ezekiel Kweku, Amy Larocca, Yinka Martins, Adam K. Raymond, Matthew Schneier, Matt Stieb, and James D. Walsh. 2019. "Who Was Jeffrey Epstein Calling?" *New York Magazine*. https://nymag.com/intelligencer/2019/07/jeffrey-epstein-high-society-contacts.html.

Connolly, J. (1992, September). By 1966, Wackenhut could confidently state that it had secret files on 4 million Americans. *Spy Magazine*, 6.

Crawley, Peter. "Virginia Giuffre's heartbreaking, vivid account of being told to have sex with Prince Andrew." *The Irish Times*.

Crespo, P. 2015. "The incredible story of Edmond Mulet and the children he "exported."" Plaza Publica. https://www.plazapublica.com.gt/content/incredible-story-edmond-mulet-and-children-he-exported.

Cronin, M., & Robertson, J. (2020). *Epstein: Dead men tell no tales*. New York, New York: Skyhorse Publishing.

Crowley, Aleister. *The Old and New Commentaries to Liber AL*, III, 24. (1904)

Crowley, Aleister. *Book of the Law*. 1903.

Cuhulain, Kerr (July 8, 2002). "Michelle Remembers." Pagan Protection Center. Archived from the original on May 25, 2006.

Cush, A. (2016, November 04). Trump supporters Think Hillary's campaign manager is a Satanic Occultist because of a wikileaks email about Marina Abramović. https://www.spin.com/2016/11/trump-supporters-think-hillarys-campaign-manager-is-a-satanic-occultist-because-of-a-wikileaks-email-about-marina-abramovic/

Fahrenthold, David A. (October 7, 2016). "Trump recorded having extremely lewd conversation about women in 2005." *Washington Post*

Dawson, J. 2004. "Married, with art." *Washington Post*, September 23, 2004. https://www.washingtonpost.com/archive/lifestyle/2004/09/23/married-with-art/dee9a0d0-0f0d-4505-b0ef-2f0e1b-d1e0e0/.

DeCamp, J. W. (2005). *The Franklin cover-up: Child abuse, Satanism, and murder in Nebraska*. Lincoln, Nebraska: AWT.

DeGregory, P., & Feis, A. (2019, July 10). Trump barred Jeffrey Epstein FROM Mar-a-Lago over sex assault: Court docs. https://nypost.com/2019/07/09/trump-barred-jeffrey-epstein-from-mar-a-lago-over-sex-assault-court-docs/

Delva, J. 2010. "Bill Clinton Urges solution to HAITI 'kidnap' case." Reuters.com. https://www.reuters.com/article/us-quake-haiti-missionaries-idUSTRE61503J20100206.

de Young, Mary (2004). *The day care ritual abuse moral panic*. Jefferson, N.C: McFarland. ISBN 0-7864-1830-3.

Dias, I. (n.d.). Brazilian activist's alleged suicide sparks Coverage controversy. https://www.cjr.org/analysis/brazilian-activists-alleged-suicide-sparks-coverage-controversy.php

District Court, Southern District of New York. Jane Doe v Donald J. Trump and Jeffrey Epstein (DISTRICT COURT SOUTHERN DISTRICT OF NEW YORK September 30, 2016).

Ditlea, Steve. , In New French Best-Seller, Software Meets Espionage, *New York Times*. June 20, 1997

Dorril, S. (2002). *MI6: Inside the covert world of Her Majesty's secret intelligence service*. New York: Simon & Schuster.

Drachen, Anders. 2006. "Live Action Role-Playing GamesControl, Communication, Storytelling, and MMORPG Similarities." Games and Culture 1, no. 3 (July): 252-275. 10.1177/1555412006290445.

Eberle, Shirley (1993). *The Abuse of Innocence: The McMartin Preschool Trial*. Prometheus Books. ISBN 978-0-87975-809-7

@ElResisto (2019, September 10). The robert maxell origin story. https://elresisto.wixsite.com/website/post/the-robert-maxell-origin-story

Emery, David (April 16, 2018). "Is a Hillary Clinton 'Snuff Film' Circulating on the Dark Web?." Snopes.

Erowid.org. Ask Erowid : Id 3190 : Myth Debunking: Is Adrenochrome harvested from children? (n.d.). https://www.erowid.org/ask/ask.php?ID=3190

Evans, Tim; Alesia, Mark; and Marisa Kwiatkowski (2016). "A 20-year toll: 368 gymnasts allege sexual exploitation." The Indianapolis Star.

Feinberg, Ashley. 2019. "A Running List of Jeffrey Epstein's Rich, Powerful, and Presidential Friends." Slate. https://slate.com/news-and-politics/2019/07/jeffrey-epstein-bill-clinton-donald-trump-al-an-dershowitz.html.

Friedberg, Brian. "The Dark Virality of a Hollywood Blood-Harvesting Conspiracy." Wired.

Entrepreneur.com. Samuel Bronfman. (2008, October 10). https://www.entrepreneur.com/article/197618

Faith, N. (2008). The Bronfmans: The rise and fall of the House of Seagram. New York, New York: St. Martin's.

Fairbanks, C. (2016, November 04). Spirit cooking: The most disturbing podesta email yet? (warning: Graphic content). https://wearechange.org/spirit-cooking-disturbing-podesta-email-yet-warning-graphic-content/

Feller, M. (2021, April 20). How exactly is alleged Sex Trafficker Jeffrey Epstein connected to President Trump? https://www.elle.com/culture/career-politics/a28320376/jeffrey-epstein-president-trump-connection/

Ferkenhoff, E. (2019, December 10). Fake news: CIA agent does not Blow whistle, does not say 'We Supply Elite pedophiles WITH CHILDREN'. https://leadstories.com/hoax-alert/2019/12/fake-news-114.html

Finkelhor, David; Williams, Linda Meyer; Burns, Nanci; Kalinowski, Michael (1988). "Sexual Abuse in Day Care: A National Study; Executive Summary." Durham, North Carolina: University of New Hampshire.

Fricker, R. (1993, January 1). "The inslaw octopus." https://www.wired.com/1993/01/inslaw/

Fricker, R. (2013, July 11). PRISM's Controversial Forerunner. https://consortiumnews.com/2013/07/11/prisms-controversial-forerunner/

Gage, N. (1971, February 19). Ex-Head of Schenley industries is linked to CRIME 'Consortium'. https://www.nytimes.com/1971/02/19/archives/exhead-of-schenley-industries-is-linked-to-crime-con-sortium.html

Gailey, Phil. "HAVE NAMES, WILL OPEN RIGHT DOORS." New York Times, January 18, 1982. https://www.nytimes.com/1982/01/18/us/have-names-will-open-right-doors.html.

Gass, N., S. Goldmacher, and N. Debenedetti. 2016. "Trump sharpens Benghazi attacks on Clinton." Politico. https://www.politico.com/story/2016/06/donald-trump-benghazi-clinton-224911.

genaro. "Killing the Myth: An Experience with Adrenochrome (exp51847)." Erowid.org. Mar 28, 2006. erowid.org/exp/51847

Gillu, Jack; Bridis, Ted (March 4, 2015). "Clinton ran homebrew computer system for official emails." Yahoo!. Associated Press.

Gilmer, M. (2018, August 02). How Donald Trump's own words have helped fuel the QAnon fire. https://mashable.com/article/qanon-trump-conspiracy-explainer/

Goldman, Adam (December 7, 2016). "The Comet Ping Pong Gunman Answers Our Reporter's Questions." New York Times. Archived from the original on December 13, 2016.

Golden, D. (2017, October 13). How Spy Agencies Use American Universities to Secretly Recruit Students. https://www.townandcountrymag.com/society/tradition/a12814064/spy-school-daniel-golden-fbi-cia-recruit-at-american-colleges/

Goldsmith, Samuel (June 30, 2008). "Jeffrey Epstein Pleads Guilty to Prostitution Charges." New York Post.

Goleman, Daniel (1994). "Proof Lacking for Ritual Abuse by Satanists." New York Times.

Goodman, A. 2016. "Anthony Weiner carried on a MONTHS-LONG online sexual relationship with a 15-year-old girl." The Daily Mail, September 21, 2016. https://www.dailymail.co.uk/news/article-3790824/Anthony-Weiner-carried-months-long-online-sexual-relationship-troubled-15-year-old-girl-telling-hard-asking-dress-school-girl-outfits-pressing-engage-rape-fantasies.html.

Götze, H. (2008, December 10). Springer-Verlag: History of a scientific publishing House: Part 2: 1945 – 1992. REBUILDING – Opening Frontiers – securing the future. https://books.google.com/books/about/Springer_Verlag_History_of_a_Scientific.html?id=3f1DAAAAQBAJ

Graham, Ben (December 3, 2019). "Story behind iconic Prince Andrew photo with Virginia Giuffre." NZ Herald. ISSN 1170-0777.

Grahamlester (Community forum user). "Epstein Rape Victim Was Passed on to Donald Trump by Ghislaine Maxwell." Daily Kos, June 9, 2021. https://www.dailykos.com/stories/2021/6/9/2034367/-Epstein-Rape-Victim-Was-Passed-on-to-Donald-Trump-by-Ghislaine-Maxwell.

Griffith, Janelle. 2019. "Actor Isaac Kappy dies by suicide at age 42." NBC News.

Gross, M. (2016, October 25). Inside Donald TRUMP'S One-Stop PARTIES: ATTENDEES RECALL cocaine and very young models. https://www.thedailybeast.com/inside-donald-trumps-one-stop-parties-attendees-recall-cocaine-and-very-young-models

Haberman, M. (2018, January 08). A Trump friend, unsolicited, weighs in on his mental health: Pic. twitter.com/vmr2giilsl. https://mobile.twitter.com/maggieNYT/status/950466895769210880

Haney, Stephanie. 2019. "Thor actor Isaac Kappy, 42, who made headlines for 'choking' Paris Jackson commits suicide by throwing himself off an Arizona bridge after leaving two-page note saying he 'had been a bad guy.'" DailyMail.com. https://www.dailymail.co.uk/tvshowbiz/article-7029679/Isaac-Kappy-dies-42-Thor-actor-assaulted-Paris-Jackson-commits-suicide.html.

Hartmann, M. (2019, August 09). What the Unsealed Jeffrey Epstein documents reveal About Donald Trump. https://nymag.com/intelligencer/2019/08/what-the-unsealed-epstein-documents-reveal-about-trump.html

Hastert, Dennis. 2004. Speaker: Lessons from forty years in coaching and politics. N.p.: Regnery Publishing.

Hayward, J. 2016. "Erik Prince: NYPD ready to make arrests in Anthony Weiner case." Breitbart. www.breitbart.com/radio/2016/11/04/erik-prince-nypd-ready-make-arrests-weiner-case/.

Hersh, B. (2008). Bobby and J. Edgar: The historic face-off between the Kennedys and J. Edgar Hoover that transformed America. New York, New York: BasicBooks.

Hersh, S. M. (1991). The Samson option Israel's nuclear arsenal and American foreign policy. New York, New York: Random House.

Hersh, Seymour M. (2013-10-30). The Samson Option: Israel's Nuclear Arsenal and American Foreign Policy. Random House Publishing Group. p. 260. ISBN 9780804151061.

Hoffer A, Osmond H, Smithies J (January 1954). "Schizophrenia; a new approach. II. Result of a year's research." The Journal of Mental Science. 100 (418): 29–45. doi:10.1192/bjp.100.418.29.

Hoffmann, Abbie and Jonathan Silvers, Playboy, "An Election Held Hostage," October 1988

Hooper, J. 2004. "When art and politics meet." The Age. https://www.theage.com.au/entertainment/art-and-design/when-art-and-politics-meet-20040506-gdxsnd.html.

Conspiracy: The Secret History: In Search of the American Drug Lords – Barry and the Boys, From Dallas To Mena. Ufo video, 2004. https://www.amazon.com/Conspiracy-Secret-History-Search-American/dp/B0001I555Q.

Hougan, J. (1984). Secret agenda: Watergate, Deep throat, and the CIA. New York, New York: Random House.

Howard, Dylan; Cronin, Melissa; Robertson, James (2019). "Chapter 7." Epstein: Dead Men Tell No Tales. Simon & Schuster. ISBN 9781510758230.

Hsu, Spencer (March 24, 2017). "Comet Pizza gunman pleads guilty to federal and local charges." Washington Post. Washington. Archived from the original on March 24, 2017.

Hughes & Parker in Bibby, 1996, pp. 215–30.

Hutchinson, Brian. National Post, 18 November 2011, The unbelievable life of Ari Ben-Menashe

ICMEC. n.d. "The Koons Family Institute on International Law & Policy." ICMEC. https://web.archive.

org/web/20150214011934/http://icmec.org/missingkids/servlet/PageServlet?LanguageCountry=en_X1&PageId=4345.

Jarrett, L. 2016. "Warrant: Clinton, ABEDIN emails led feds to SEIZE Weiner laptop." CNN POLITICS. https://www.cnn.com/2016/12/20/politics/hillary-clinton-anthony-weiner-fbi-search-warrant-unsealed/index.html.

Jeffrey Epstein VI Foundation. 2013. "Jeffrey Epstein Philanthropy: About." Jeffrey Epstein Philanthropy. https://web.archive.org/web/20140113083429/http://www.jeffreyepstein.org/About.html.

Jerusalem Post. "Planes for Hostages' Man Said to be an Impostor." Jerusalem Post. March 27, 1990.

Karni, A., & Haberman, M. (2019, July 10). Jeffrey Epstein was a 'Terrific Guy,' Donald Trump once Said. now He's 'not a Fan.' https://www.nytimes.com/2019/07/09/us/politics/trump-epstein.html

Katz, J. 2010. "Laura Silsby convicted in Haiti, but free to go." Idaho Press. https://www.idahopress.com/news/laura-silsby-convicted-in-haiti-but-free-to-go/article_9449e0a4-61eb-11df-97ac-001cc4c002e0.html.

Khalaj, Gabriella. 2019. "'Thor' actor Isaac Kappy dies in Arizona at age 42." USA Today.

Koernke, Mark. 1995. "America in Peril (About The New World Order)."

King, Wayne. "Fiscal Riddle Confronts Casino Panel." New York Times. April 18, 1991.

Krebs, A. (1986, August 3). Roy Cohn, Aide to McCarthy and Fiery Lawyer, Dies at 59. https://archive.nytimes.com/www.nytimes.com/library/national/science/aids/080386sci-aids.html

Kreig, A., & Madsen, W. (n.d.). New information emerges IN "maria" Trump story. https://www.justice-integrity.org/1456-new-information-emerges-in-maria-story

Lacis, Indra K. (May 2014). "Fame, Celebrity and Performance: Marina Abramović – Contemporary Art Star." Case Western Reserve University. pp. 117–118.

LaFontaine, J S. (1994). The extent and nature of organised and ritual abuse: research findings. London: HMSO. ISBN 978-0-11-321797-7.

LaFrance, Adrienne (June 2020). "The Prophecies of Q." The Atlantic. ISSN 1072-7825. Archived from the original on August 29, 2020.

Lee, Jean H. 2009. "NKorea: U.S. journalists plotted 'smear campaign.'" ABC News. https://web.archive.org/web/20090619052045/https://abcnews.go.com/International/wireStory?id=7849419.

Levenson, Eric. 2019. "https://www.cnn.com/2019/08/12/us/jeffrey-epstein-associates-possible-accomplices/index.html." CNN.com. https://www.cnn.com/2019/08/12/us/jeffrey-epstein-associates-possible-accomplices/index.html.

Lewis, S. (2019, July 12). Financier Epstein, charged with sex TRAFFICKING, has ties TO INTERLOCHEN. https://www.detroitnews.com/story/news/local/michigan/2019/07/12/financier-jeffrey-epstein-has-ties-interlochen-center-arts/1712587001/

Line, W. (2020, July 05). John Podesta torturing a Child. this video makes me Sick. #pizzagate #pizzagatelsreal #pizzagateisreal #JohnPodesta pic.twitter.com/jOFHBNeGb5. https://twitter.com/teabag_r/status/1279816639966478338?s=21

The Local SE (2008, February 26). Sweden rejects child prostitution damages claim. https://www.thelocal.se/20080226/10108/

Los Angeles Times. "McMartin Boy Says He Was Pinched With Pliers." Los Angeles Times, May 3, 1985. https://www.latimes.com/archives/la-xpm-1985-05-03-me-11887-story.html.

MacLean, Malcolm (26 September 2017). "Amels motor yacht Lady Mona K sold." Boat International.

Maeroff, Gene I. (February 20, 1974). "Barr Quits Dalton School Post, Charging Trustees' Interference." New York Times. ISSN 0362-4331.

Mangan, D. (2020, August 04). Trump banned Jeffrey Epstein FROM Mar-a-Lago after sex Criminal hit on member's daughter, book claims. https://www.cnbc.com/2020/08/04/trump-banned-jeffrey-epstein-from-mar-a-lago-for-hitting-on-girl.html

Mahle, Melissa Boyle (20 December 2005). *Denial and Deception: An Insider's View of the CIA*. Perseus Books Group. p. 29. ISBN 978-0-7867-3759-8.

Mansoor, Sanya. "'Only One of Us Is Telling the Truth.' The Biggest Moments From Prince Andrew Accuser Virginia Giuffre's BBC Interview." Time.

Mark, M. (2019, August 10). Unsealed flight logs show that Trump was on epstein's private jet in 1997. https://www.insider.com/donald-trump-jeffrey-epstein-flight-logs-unsealed-2019-8

Martineau, Paris (December 19, 2017). "The Storm Is the New Pizzagate – Only Worse." New York. ISSN 0028-7369.

McNally, RJ (2003). *Remembering Trauma*. Cambridge, Mass: Belknap Press. ISBN 978-0-674-01802-0.

Meldrum, Andrew; MacAskill, Ewan; McGreal, Chris; and Barkham, Patrick. "Tsvangirai accused of treason," The Guardian, February 28, 2002

The MIT Press (June 28, 2017). "Marina Abramović's Spirit Cooking." The MIT Press.

Mitenbuler, R. (2015, May 12). How did bourbon become "america's native spirit"? Cutthroat capitalism. https://slate.com/human-interest/2015/05/bourbon-empire-lewis-rosenstiel-and-how-bourbon-became-americas-native-spirit.html

MoMA. "Marina Abramović. Spirit Cooking. 1996." The Museum of Modern Art.

Nathan, D; Snedeker, M. (1995). *Satan's Silence: Ritual Abuse and the Making of a Modern American Witch Hunt*. Basic Books. ISBN 0-87975-809-0.

NBC News. Notorious child rapist-murderer convicted. (2004, June 17). https://www.nbcnews.com/id/wbna5233011

Newark, T. (2007). *Mafia allies: The true story of America's secret alliance with the Mob in World War II*. St. Paul, MN: Zenith Press.

Newton, Michael. *The Mafia at Apalachin, 1957*. (2012). Jefferson, North Carolina: McFarland.

Nieberg, P. (2019, July 22). More 'moral' Than NETANYAHU: Ex-israeli spook Defends lobbying for Sudanese junta. https://www.haaretz.com/israel-news/.premium-israeli-ex-intel-officer-defends-lobbying-for-sudanese-junta-1.7563126

Nogueira, Felipe (2019). "The Not So Divine Acts of Medium 'John of God.'" *Skeptical Inquirer*. 43 (4): 11–13.

NY Daily News. The Donald sans shoes. (1989, May 5). *New York Daily News*.

Office of Juvenile Justice and Delinquency Prevention. 2020. "The National Center for Missing and Exploited Children." Office of Juvenile Justice and Delinquency Prevention. https://ojjdp.ojp.gov/funding/awards/2020-mc-fx-k004.

Ohlheiser, Abby. (November 4, 2016). "No, John Podesta didn't drink bodily fluids at a secret Satanist dinner." *Washington Post*.

OnSamander. 2017. "Cheesy pizza." Urban Dictionary. https://www.urbandictionary.com/define.php?term=cheesy+pizza.

Oprah.com. 2010. "Leap of Faith: Meet John of God." Oprah.com. https://web.archive.org/web/20101120020933/http://www.oprah.com/spirit/Spiritual-Healer-John-of-God-Susan-Casey.

Parry, Robert. (2012). *America's stolen narrative : from Washington and Madison to Nixon, Reagan and the Bushes to Obama*. Arlington, VA: The Media Consortium. ISBN 9781893517059.

Parry, Robert (2012, December 12). Who Bombed Ben-Menashe's House? https://consortiumnews.com/2012/12/08/who-bombed-ben-menashes-house/

PBS (n.d.). Daughter from DANANG.https://www.pbs.org/wgbh/americanexperience/films/daughter/

Pincus, W. (1989, February 23). A chance to fill in iran-contra blanks. https://www.washingtonpost.com/archive/politics/1989/02/23/a-chance-to-fill-in-iran-contra-blanks/d21769ac-485a-470b-8990-437ed2ce0746/

Q. (n.d.). https://www.24hourcampfire.com/ubbthreads/ubbthreads.php/topics/15277434/re-q

Randi, James. 2005. "A Special Analysis." Randi.org. http://archive.randi.org/site/jr/021805a.html.

rebelskum. 2017.

@rebelskum. "James Alefantis' once-public Instagram, Jimmycomet, now preserved on Steemit blockchain!" Steemit. https://steemit.com/pizzagate/@rebelskum/james-alefantis-once-public-instagram-jimmycomet-now-preserved-on-steemit-blockchain.

Redmond, P. (Writer). (2020, February 02). PPR episode 201 Jeffrey Epstein, Wackenhut, and mobbed up ninjas [Podcast]. In Porkins Policy Radio.

Reid, E. (1972). *The mistress and the mafia: The Virginia Hill story.* New York, New York: Bantam Books.

Reinhard, R. Beth (2019, August 10). Trump and EPSTEIN Partied together. then a Palm BEACH mansion came between them. https://www.sun-sentinel.com/news/politics/fl-ne-wp-epstein-trump-palm-beach-buddies-20190731-z4aj6xux2zb6jott4deqonla4m-story.html

Reinhold, Robert (January 24, 1990). "The Longest Trial – A Post-Mortem. Collapse of Child-Abuse Case: So Much Agony for So Little." *New York Times*.

Relman, Eliza (October 9, 2019). "The 25 women who have accused Trump of sexual misconduct." Business Insider.

Reporter, D. (2012, October 16). Oprah embraces 'MOTHER ROLE' as she watches first class graduate from school she founded in South Africa. https://www.dailymail.co.uk/femail/article-2218202/Oprah-embraces-mother-role-watches-class-graduate-school-founded-South-Africa.html

Reuters. Fact check-false QAnon claims that Oprah is wearing an ankle monitor during interview. (2021, March 10). https://www.reuters.com/article/factcheck-oprah-ankle-idUSL1N2L81CO

Rogers, Taylor N. 2019. "Here are all the famous people Jeffrey Epstein was connected to." Business Insider. https://www.businessinsider.com.au/famous-people-jeffery-epstein-money-manager-sexual-trafficking-connected-2019-7?r=US&IR=T.

Rosenberg, R., and B. Golding. 2016. "Anthony Weiner sexted Busty brunette while his son was in bed with him." *New York Post*, August 29, 2016.

Rosser, N. (2001, January 22). Andrew's Fixer: She's the Daughter of Robert Maxwell and She's Manipulating His Jetset Lifestyle. https://www.mintpressnews.com/wp-content/uploads/2019/10/ANDREW_S-FIXER_SHE_S-THE-DAUGHTER-OF-ROBERT-MAXWELL-AND-1.pdf

Sarkisian, J., & II, M. (2021, March 18). The LAPD is investigating a rape allegation against Armie Hammer. Here's a timeline of the ACTOR'S controversial fall from grace. https://www.insider.com/armie-hammer-cannibal-dms-controversy-explained

Saxe, David B. 1994. "Koons v. Koons," Custody Suit. casetext. https://casetext.com/case/koons-v-koons.

Saxon, Wolfgang (February 10, 2004). "Donald Barr, 82, Headmaster And Science Honors Educator." *New York Times*. p. A25.

Sgueglia, Kristina. 2019. "Top MIT official resigns in wake of explosive report on donations facilitated by Jeffrey Epstein." CNN. https://www.cnn.com/2019/09/08/us/jeffrey-epstein-mit-official-resigns/index.html.

Shakhnazarova, N. (2019, January 31). 'John of god' cult leader allegedly RAN child sex slave farm.

https://nypost.com/2019/01/31/john-of-god-cult-leader-allegedly-ran-child-sex-slave-farm/

Shalev, Z. (2020, January 22). Blackmail exclusive: Narativ: Blackmailing america. https://narativ.org/2019/09/26/blackmailing-america/

Sharlet, Jeff (March 2015). "Are You Man Enough for the Men's Rights Movement?" *GQ*.

Shaw, David. "Media Skepticism Grew as McMartin Case Lingered : News Analysis." *Los Angeles Times*, January 21, 1990. https://www.latimes.com/archives/la-xpm-1990-01-21-mn-980-story.html.

Sherman, Gabriel (August 9, 2019). "Powerful Men, Disturbing New Details in Unsealed Epstein Documents." *Vanity Fair*.

Shewan, Dan. "CONVICTION OF THINGS NOT SEEN: THE UNIQUELY AMERICAN MYTH OF SATANIC CULTS." Pacific Standard. SEP 8, 2015

Silverman, Craig. 2016. "How A Completely False Claim About Hillary Clinton Went From A Conspiracy Message Board To Big Right Wing Blogs." BuzzFeed. https://www.buzzfeed.com/craigsilverman/fever-swamp-election.

Silverstein, K. (2016, January 29). The salacious Ammo Even Donald Trump won't use in a fight AGAINST Hillary Clinton. https://www.vice.com/en/article/j59vm8/the-salacious-ammo-even-donald-trump-wont-use-in-a-fight-against-hillary-clinton-bill-clinton

Sisak, Michael R.; Balsamo, Michael; Neumeister, Larry (August 17, 2019). "Medical examiner rules Epstein death a suicide by hanging." AP NEWS. Archived from the original on September 4, 2019.

Skolnik, Fred and Berenbaum, Michael. *Encyclopaedia Judaica*. 1945– (2nd ed.). Detroit: Macmillan Reference USA in association with the Keter Pub. House. 2007. pp. 32–34. ISBN 9780028659282.

Skvarla, Robert. "CONSPIRACY USA: JEREMIAH FILMS, BILL CLINTON, AND THE SATANIC PANIC." *Diabolique Magazine*, May 17, 2021. https://diaboliquemagazine.com/jeremiah-films-bill-clinton-and-the-satanic-panic/.

Sky News. "Jimmy Savile Inquiry Now Criminal Investigation." Sky News. 19 October 2012.

Smith, T. (2000, February 20). Society Snapshots. https://www.newspapers.com/clip/33687080/trump-epstein-pro-am-tennis-tourney/

Spargo, Chris. 2019. "Jeffrey Epstein was allowed to travel to NYC unsupervised on overnight trips for the final seven months of probation and stay at his mansion near Central Park playgrounds and a victim's school." DailyMail.com. https://www.dailymail.co.uk/news/article-7290777/Jeffrey-Epstein-allowed-travel-NYC-unsupervised-overnight-trips-probation.html.

Stanglin, Doug (July 10, 2019). "Inside Jeffrey Epstein's New York mansion: 'Vast trove' of lewd photos, a life-size doll and other oddities." *USA Today*.

Steel, E., Eder, S., Maheshwari, S., and Goldstein, M. (2019, July 26). How Jeffrey Epstein used the BILLIONAIRE behind Victoria's secret for wealth and women. https://www.nytimes.com/2019/07/25/business/jeffrey-epstein-wexner-victorias-secret.html

Stein, Jeff. 2016. "What 20,000 pages of hacked WikiLeaks emails teach us about Hillary Clinton." Vox.com. https://www.vox.com/policy-and-politics/2016/10/20/13308108/wikileaks-podesta-hillary-clinton.

Stewart, James B. 2020. "These Are the Deutsche Bank Executives Responsible for Serving Jeffrey Epstein." *New York Times*. https://www.nytimes.com/2020/07/13/business/deutsche-bank-jeffrey-epstein.html.

Stickel, E. G. (1990). *Archaeological Investigations of the McMartin Preschool site*, Manhattan Beach, California (Rep.).

Stockler, Asher (August 10, 2019). "Top HUD Official Promotes Clinton Conspiracy Theory in Wake of Epstein's Apparent Suicide." Newsweek.

Stone, J. (2015, January 30). Westminster 'paedophile ring': EX-MI6 SPY Sir PETER HAYMAN named in. https://www.independent.co.uk/news/uk/politics/westminster-paedophile-ring-investigation-mi6-spy-sir-peter-hayman-named-dossier-10014295.html

Stuart, T. (2020, September 17). A timeline of Donald Trump's Creepiness while he OWNED Miss Universe. https://www.rollingstone.com/politics/politics-features/a-timeline-of-donald-trumps-creepiness-while-he-owned-miss-universe-191860/

Summers, A. (2012, January 01). The secret life of j edgar hoover. https://www.theguardian.com/film/2012/jan/01/j-edgar-hoover-secret-fbi

Summers, A. (2013). *Official and Confidential: The Secret Life of J. Edgar Hoover*. New York, New York: Open Road Media.

Talbot, D. (2016). *The devil's chessboard: Allen Dulles, the CIA, and the rise of America's secret government*. London, United Kingdom: William Collins.

TFPP Wire. 2019. "Actor Who Accused Spielberg, Colbert Of Pedophilia Found Dead." The Federalist Papers. https://thefederalistpapers.org/opinion/actor-accused-spielberg-colbert-pedophilia-found-dead.

thejazzcat. 2018. "Pizzagate: How it all Started." steemit. https://steemit.com/politics/@thejazzcat/pizzagate-how-it-all-started.

Thompson, P., & Delano, A. (1991). *Maxwell a portrait of power.* London: Corgi Books.

Thomas, G., & Dillon, M. (2003). *Robert Maxwell, Israel's superspy: The life and murder of a media mogul.* New York, New York: Carroll and Graf.

tidus8922. 2016. "Todd d. STERN dreams about John Podesta's "Hotdog stand in Hawaii … "" reddit.com. https://www.reddit.com/r/ImagesOfHawaii/comments/59pd6a/todd_d_stern_dreams_about_john_podestas_hotdog/.

Tlee1641 (Reddit user). R/Conspiracy – artwork from the home OF GHISLAINE Maxwell. notice the symbol on the cloth. (n.d.). https://www.reddit.com/r/conspiracy/comments/hmmh6a/artwork_from_the_home_of_ghislaine_maxwell_notice/?utm_source=amp&utm_medium=&utm_content=post_title user Tlee1641

Trebay, G. (2011, November 18). A career provocateur. https://www.nytimes.com/2011/11/20/fashion/marina-abramovics-crossover-moment.html

Tron, G. (2021, April 23). Was notorious child sex ring Leader John NORMAN connected to John wayne gacy? https://www.oxygen.com/true-crime-buzz/was-john-norman-connected-to-serial-killer-john-wayne-gacy

TruthStamps. 2020. "LIST OF 50+ CELEBRITIES ASSOCIATED WITH JEFFERY EPSTEIN." Truth Stamps. https://truthstamps.com/all-the-celebrities-associated-with-jeffery-epstein/.

Tychsen, Anders, Michael Hitchens, Thea Brolund, and Manolya Kavakli. "Live Action Role-Playing Games." Games and Culture 1, no. 3 (July 2006): 252–75. https://doi.org/10.1177/1555412006290445.

Unger, C. (2021, January 21). "He's a lot of fun to Be With": Inside Jeffrey Epstein and Donald Trump's Epic Bromance. https://www.vanityfair.com/news/2021/01/jeffrey-epstein-and-donald-trump-epic-bromance

U.S. DOJ. Louisiana Man Pleads Guilty to Federal Charge For Threatening Pizza Shop in Northwest Washington Archived (press release), U.S. Department of Justice (January 13, 2017).

U.S. Department of Justice. "Grand Jury Charges Ed Buck with Four Additional Felonies, Including that He Enticed Victims to Travel Interstate to Engage in Prostitution." United States Department of Justice. August 4, 2020

Valentine, Douglas. *The Phoenix program.* (2016). New York, NY: Distributed by Open Road Integrated Media.

van der Reijden, Joël. 2017. "Pizzagate: Disinfo, Truth, New Dutroux X-Dossiers Ties." Institute for the Study of Globalization and Covert Politics. https://isgp-studies.com/pizzagate.

Verkaik, Robert. "The mystery of Maxwell's death," *The Independent,* 10 March 2006

Viera, Mark (November 5, 2011). "Former Coach at Penn State Is Charged With Abuse." *New York Times.*

Wainman, L. 2015. "Inside Homes: Private Viewing." *Washington Magazine.* https://washingtonlife.com/2015/06/05/inside-homes-private-viewing.

Ward, Vicky (June 27, 2011). "The Talented Mr. Epstein." *Vanity Fair.* New York City.

Ward, V. (2019, July 09). Jeffrey Epstein's sick story played out for years in plain sight. https://www.thedailybeast.com/jeffrey-epsteins-sick-story-played-out-for-years-in-plain-sight

Washington Post. "2 Acquitted of Trying to Sell Military Cargo Planes to Iran." The Washington Post. ISSN 0190-8286.

Watson, P. J. (2016, November 04). "Spirit Cooking": Clinton campaign Chairman invited to Bizarre Satanic Performance. https://web.archive.org/web/20161104130805/http://www.infowars.com/

spirit-cooking-clinton-campaign-chairman-invited-to-bizarre-satanic-performance/

Webb, W. (2019, July 18). Hidden in plain sight: The Shocking origins of the Jeffrey Epstein case. https://www.mintpressnews.com/shocking-origins-jeffrey-epstein-blackmail-roy-cohn/260621/

Webb, W. (2019, August 21). Government by Blackmail: Jeffrey Epstein, Trump's mentor and the dark secrets of the Reagan era. https://www.mintpressnews.com/blackmail-jeffrey-epstein-trump-mentor-reagan-era/260760/

Webb, W. (2019, August 26). Mega group, maxwells AND Mossad: The spy story at the heart of the Jeffrey EPSTEIN SCANDAL. https://mintpressnews.cn/mega-group-maxwells-mossad-spy-story-jeffrey-epstein-scandal/261172/

Webb, W. (Writer). (2020, April 24). Epstein victim Maria Farmer speaks With Whitney Webb, full phone call – Part 1 [Video file]. https://youtu.be/MGtDj8drWvE

Webb, W. (2020, June 24). Former Israeli Intel official Claims Jeffrey Epstein, Ghislaine Maxwell worked for Israel. https://www.mintpressnews.com/ari-ben-menashe-jeffrey-epstein-ghislaine-maxwell-israel-intelligence/262162/

West, J. (2016, August 30). Former models for Donald TRUMP'S agency say they violated immigration rules and worked illegally. https://www.motherjones.com/politics/2016/08/donald-trump-model-management-illegal-immigration/

Whatley, S. (2017, December 07). Oprah's South Africa School plagued by Second sex scandal. https://www.huffpost.com/entry/oprahs-south-africa-schoo_n_181161

Wieder, B. and Hall, K. (2020, November 14). FBI wanted to arrest Epstein while he was judging a beauty pageant. The plan was overruled. https://www.miamiherald.com/news/state/florida/article247183924.html

WikiLeaks. 2012. "The Global Intelligence Files," Emails leaked from the global intelligence firm Stratfor. WikiLeaks. https://wikileaks.org/gifiles.

WikiLeaks. 2016. "Fw: Tax breaking news." Email to John Podesta from Jake Siewert re Dennis Hastert. WikiLeaks. https://wikileaks.org/podesta-emails/emailid/11508.

WikiLeaks. 2016. "NEW LIFE CHILDREN'S REFUGE – HAITIAN ORPHAN RESCUE MISSION," Emails leaked from the Hillary Clinton Email Archive. WikiLeaks. https://wikileaks.org/clinton-emails/emailid/3776.

WikiLeaks. 2016. "Pizza.jpg," Email from Doug Band to John Podesta. WikiLeaks. https://wikileaks.org/podesta-emails/emailid/10037.

WikiLeaks. 2016. "Re: Did you leave a handkerchief," Email to John Podesta, leaked by WikiLeaks. https://wikileaks.org/podesta-emails/emailid/55433.

WikiLeaks. 2016. "Re: Farmers L update and welcome mat," Email to John Podesta from Tamera Luzzatto. WikiLeaks. https://wikileaks.org/podesta-emails/emailid/46736.

WikiLeaks. 2016. "Various emails," Emails leaked from the account of John Podesta. WikiLeaks. https://wikileaks.org/podesta-emails/.

WikiLeaks. 2016. "Fwd: Dinner." Emails leaked from Tony to John Podesta about Marina Abramović dinner. https://wikileaks.org/podesta-emails/emailid/15893

Wikipedia. Moloch. (2021, May 17). https://en.m.wikipedia.org/wiki/Moloch

Wilkinson, T., & Rainey, J. (1990, January 19). Tapes of Children Decided the Case for Most Jurors. *Los Angeles Times*. https://www.latimes.com/archives/la-xpm-1990-01-19-mn-224-story.html.

Wyatt, W. J. (2002). What was under the mcmartin preschool? A review and behavioral analysis of the "tunnels" find. Behavior and Social Issues, 12(1), 29-39. doi:10.5210/bsi.v12i1.77

Yarhi Published Online February 13, E. (n.d.). Seagram. https://www.thecanadianencyclopedia.ca/en/article/seagram-company-limited

Zadrozny, Brandy; Collins, Ben (August 8, 2018). "How three conspiracy theorists took 'Q' and sparked Qanon." NBC News.

Zimmerman, Malia. 2016. "Billionaire sex offender Epstein once claimed he co-founded Clinton Foundation." Fox News. https://www.foxnews.com/us/billionaire-sex-offender-epstein-once-claimed-he-co-founded-clinton-foundation.

PART 2

Belgian Senate. "Belgian parliamentary report concerning the stay-behind network," named "Enquête parlementaire sur l'existence en Belgique d'un réseau de renseignements clandestin international" or "Parlementair onderzoek met betrekking tot het bestaan in België van een clandestien internationaal inlichtingenetwerk" pp. 17–22. 1991.

Bilderberg Group. Where and When will the BILDERBERG MEETING 2020 take place? (n.d.). https://www.bilderbergmeetings.org/frequently-asked-questions

Bilderberg Group. "Bilderberg Meetings 1954 Conference Report." Bilderberg Group, May 31, 1954. https://publicintelligence.net/bilderberg-conference-1954/.

Bilderberg Group. "Bilderberg Meetings 1966 Conference Report." Bilderberg Group, March 27, 1966. https://publicintelligence.net/bilderberg-conference-1966/.

Bridge, R. (2017, June 4). Bilderberg 2017: Should we be worried yet? https://www.rt.com/op-edge/390852-bilderberg-2017-chantilly-virginia-secrecy/

Bromberger, D. (Writer). (1977). Actualités [Television series episode]. In Actualités. TF1.

Council on Foreign Relations Website. (n.d.), from https://www.cfr.org

Council on Foreign Relations Annual Report (Vol. 2005-2006, Rep.). (2006). New York, NY: Council on Foreign Relations.

Cuttlefish_btc. (2016, February 20). Column he edited, asking for Playboy to investigate: POLICE spying, Secret Nazis in high places, POPE / mafia / army collusion etc. Wilson's. https://twitter.com/cuttlefish_btc/status/701179653831184384?s=21

D'Angelo, Filippo. (December 18, 2015). "Gelli, Renzi e la P2 – Interviste a Claudio Martelli e Rino Formica." L'Avanti (in Italian). Archived from the original on May 14, 2020.

Engdahl, William, A Century of War: Anglo-American Oil Politics and the New World Order. (London: Pluto Press, 2004), pp. 130-132

Flamigni, Sergio (2003). La tela del ragno (2nd ed.). Edizioni Caos

Francovich, A. (Writer). (1992). Gladio [Television broadcast]. In Timewatch. BBC.

Freeman, X. (2019, June 14). Famous freemasons list. https://www.ranker.com/list/famous-freemasons/user-x

Ganser, Daniele (2004). NATO's Secret Armies: Operation GLADIO and Terrorism in Western Europe (PDF). ISBN 9780714685007

Ganser, Daniele. "Terrorism in Western Europe: An Approach to NATO's Secret Stay-Behind Armies" (PDF). ISN. Whitehead Journal of Diplomacy and International Relations, South Orange NJ, Winter/Spring 2005, Vol. 6, No. 1.

Haberman, Clyde; Times, Special to The New York (Nov 16, 1990). "EVOLUTION IN EUROPE; Italy Discloses Its Web Of Cold War Guerrillas." New York Times.

Hayden, B. (2020). Power of Ritual in Prehistory: Secret societies and origins of social complexity. S.l., UK: CAMBRIDGE UNIV PRESS US.

Head, J. (2010, January 18). Bizarre story of Pope's FAILED ASSASSIN. http://news.bbc.co.uk/2/hi/europe/8465527.stm

Heimbichner, C. (2020). Ritual America: Secret brotherhoods and their influence on american society. Port Townshend, WA: FERAL House.

Icke, D. (2001). Biggest secret: The book that will change the world. Bredbury, Stockport, UK: National Library for the Blind.

Johnston John, J. (2019, July 22). EXCL top Tories face questions over links to secretive foreign affairs group. https://www.politicshome.com/news/uk/political-parties/conservative-party/news/105448/excl-top-tories-face-questions-over-links

Len Scott, R. Gerald Hughes *Intelligence, Crises and Security: Prospects and Retrospects*, Routledge, 2008, p. 123

McCormack, Richard T. The Association for Diplomatic Studies and Training Foreign Affairs Oral History Project. Interviewed by: Charles Stuart Kennedy Initial interview date: January 2, 2002 Copyright 2007 ADST

McEnery, T. (2011, February 20). The 15 most powerful members OF 'SKULL And Bones'. https://www.businessinsider.com/skull-and-bones-alumni-2011-2

Midgley, R. (2018, June 06). Bilderberg group: The secret meeting of minds with OSBORNE, Rudd and Kissinger on this YEAR'S guest list. http://www.telegraph.co.uk/news/politics/7804197/The-Bilderberg-Group-fact-and-fantasy.html

Molitch-Hou, M. (2020, May 12). Paramilitary panda: Wwf land grabs rooted in covert apartheid history. http://therealityinstitute.net/2019/09/paramilitary-panda-wwf-land-grabs-rooted-in-covert-apartheid-history/

Neon Revolt. (2020, October 10). [P] – the Unseen masters of All #QAnon #GREATAWAKENING #WHOISP #Illuminati #13Bloodlines #payseur #springmeier. https://www.neonrevolt.com/2018/08/16/p-the-unseen-masters-of-all-qanon-greatawakening-whoisp-illuminati-13bloodlines-payseur-springmeier/

Parliamentary Commission. "P2 List, Report of the Parliamentary Commission, July 12, 1984, in "Elenco Delgi L'scritti alla Loggia," Archivo '900, February 2, 2006, http://www.archivio900.it/it/documenti/doc.aspx?id=42."

Reinvestigate 911. Bilderberg behind terrorism In Europe SAYS Italian supreme court judge. (n.d.). http://www.reinvestigate911.org/content/bilderberg-behind-terrorism-europe-says-italian-supreme-court-judge

Rettman, A. (2009, March 16). 'Jury's out' on future of Europe, EU Doyen says. https://euobserver.com/political/27778

Rockefeller Archives. The Trilateral Commission (North America) Records". Rockefeller Archives. rockarch.org

Ronson, J. (2001, March 10). Who pulls the STRINGS? (part 3). https://www.theguardian.com/books/2001/mar/10/extract1

Rosenbaum, R. (1977, September 1). The last secrets of skull And Bones: Esquire: September 1977. https://classic.esquire.com/the-last-secrets-of-skull-and-bones/

Shoup, L. (2004, October). Bush, Kerry, and the Council on Foreign Relations. https://thirdworldtraveler.com/Foreign_Policy_Institutions/Council_Foreign_Relations.html

Shoup, Lawrence H. & Minter, William (1977). *Imperial Brain Trust: The Council on Foreign Relations and United States Foreign Policy*. Monthly Review Press. ISBN 0-85345-393-4.

Skelton, C. (2010, June 09). Bilderberg 2010: Don't call it A POW-WOW! https://www.theguardian.com/world/blog/2010/jun/09/bilderberg-charlie-skelton-2010

Spence, R. (Writer). (2019). "The Freemasons." The Real History of Secret Societies, The Great Courses.

Spence, R. (2020, August 12). A history of the knights templar. https://www.thegreatcoursesdaily.com/a-history-of-the-knights-templar/

Spence, R. (2020, September 28). The origins of modern freemasonry. https://www.thegreatcoursesdaily.com/the-origins-of-modern-freemasonry/

Spence, R. (2020, September 28). Freemasonry: Symbolism and features. https://www.thegreatcoursesdaily.com/freemasonry-symbolism-and-features/

Sutton, A. (1995). *Trilaterals over America*. Boring, OR: CPA Book.

419

Teacher, D. (2015). *ROGUE AGENTS: The Cercle and the 6I in the Private Cold War 1951-1991* (Fifth ed.). Hastings, UK: ChristieBooks.

U.S. Dept of State. Misinformation about 'Gladio/Stay Behind' Networks Resurfaces." United States Department of State.

Vulliamy, Ed (December 5, 1990). "Secret agents, freemasons, fascists … and a top-level campaign

Wallis, J., &; Duguid, B. (n.d.). Robert Anton WILSON INTERVIEW. http://media.hyperreal.org/zines/est/intervs/raw.html

Willan, Phillip (June 24, 2000). "U.S. 'supported anti-left terror in Italy'." *The Guardian.*

Wood, P. (2013, July 03). 22. Obama's Trilateral COMMISSION team – top 25 of 2010. https://www.projectcensored.org/22-obamas-trilateral-commission-team/

PART 3

Albarelli, H. P. (2011). *A terrible mistake: The murder of Frank Olson & the CIA's secret Cold War experiments.* Springfield, OR: Trine Day.

Baddeley, Gavin (2010). *Lucifer Rising: Sin, Devil Worship & Rock n' Roll* (third ed.). London: Plexus. ISBN 978-0-85965-455-5.

Best, M. (2016, July 06). Ted GUNDERSON: From COINTELPRO planner to criminal and conspiracy theorist. https://glomardisclosure.wordpress.com/2016/07/06/ted-gunderson-from-cointelpro-planner-to-criminal-and-conspiracy-theorist/

Blanco, Juan. "Stanley Dean Baker: Murderpedia, the *Encyclopedia of Murderers.*" Stanley Dean Baker | Murderpedia, the encyclopedia of murderers. Accessed June 9, 2021. https://murderpedia.org/male.B/b/baker-stanley-dean.htm.

Constantine, A. (2007, August 21). Michael Aquino Revisited. http://aconstantineblacklist.blogspot.com/2007/08/michael-aquino-revisited-was-he-guilty.html?m=1

Cooper, Paulette. "The Scandal Behind the "Scandal of Scientology."" www.cs.cmu.edu.

Day, D., & Hotchner, A. E. (2006). *Doris Day: Her own story.* London, UK: Royal National Institute of the Blind.

DeCamp, J. W. (2005). *The Franklin cover-up: Child abuse, Satanism, and murder in Nebraska.* Lincoln, Nebraska: AWT.

Dyrendal, A. (2012). *Satan and the Beast: The Influence of Aleister Crowley on Modern Satanism.* In 1383351065 1010411719 H. Bogdan & 1383351066 1010411719 M. P. Starr (Eds.), Aleister Crowley and Western esotericism: An anthology of critical studies. New York, NY: Oxford University Press.

Ehrensaft, D. (1992, April). Preschool child SEX abuse: The aftermath of the Presidio case. https://pubmed.ncbi.nlm.nih.gov/1580341/

Goldston, Linda. "CHILD ABUSE AT THE PRESIDIO THE PARENTS' AGONY, THE ARMY'S COVERUP, THE PROSECUTION'S FAILURE." *San Jose Mercury News,* JULY 24, 1988

Gorightly, A. (2009). *The shadow over Santa Susana: Black magic, mind control, and the Manson family mythos.* London, UK: Creation Books.

Horsley, J. (2019). *The vice of kings: How socialism, occultism, and the sexual revolution engineered a culture of abuse.* London, UK: Aeon Books.

Kurtis, Bill. Investigative Reports with Bill Kurtis, *The Son of Sam Speaks: The Untold Stories* (1997); 29:35 – 29:42

La Fontaine, Jean (1999). "Satanism and Satanic Mythology." In Bengt Ankarloo; Stuart Clark (eds.). *The Athlone History of Witchcraft and Magic in Europe* Volume 6: The Twentieth Century. London: Athlone. pp. 94–140. ISBN 0-485-89006-2.

Levenda, P. (2011). *Sinister forces: A grimoire of American political witchcraft* (Vol. 2). Walterville, OR:

Trine Day.

Lewis, James L. (2001). *Satanism Today: An Encyclopedia of Religion, Folklore, and Popular Culture.* Santa Barbara: ABC-Clio. ISBN 978-1576072929.

Lyons, Arthur. *Satan Wants You.* London: Mayflower, 1972.

Maclay, K. (1987, August 10). FBI investigates PRESIDIO CHILD molest case. https://apnews.com/article/b6377fb5aceb98a9b0fe99ab978213cc

New York Times. ARMY will CLOSE Child-care center. (1987, November 16). *New York Times.*

Newton, Michael. *Raising Hell: an Encyclopedia of Devil Worship and Satanic Crime.* London, UK: Warner, 1994., p. 18.

O'Neill, T., & Piepenbring, D. (2020). *Chaos: Charles Manson, the CIA, and the secret history of the sixties.* New York, NY: Back Bay Books/ Little, Brown and Company.

Opperman, Ed. Guest: James M Rothstein NYPD [Radio broadcast]. (2013, October 17). In The Opperman Report. Las Vegas, NV: Stitcher.

Opperman, Ed. My Personal Experience With Ted Gunderson [Radio broadcast]. (2020). In The Opperman Report. Las Vegas, Nevada: Spreaker.com.

Raschke, Carl. *Painted Black: from Drug Killings to Heavy Metal – the Alarming True Story of How Satanism Is Terrorizing Our Communities.* New York, NY: Harper & Row Publishers, 1990. p. 149.

Sanders, E. (1971). *The family.* New York, NY: Thunder's Mouth Press.

Sanders, E., & Veitch, R. (2016). *Sharon Tate: A life.* Boston, MA: Da Capo Press.

Spence, R. B. (2008). *Secret agent 666: Aleister Crowley, British intelligence and the occult.* Los Angeles, California: Feral House.

Taylor, Yuval (March 23, 2008). "Funk's Death Trip." PopMatters.

Terry, M. (1989). *The ultimate evil: An investigation into a dangerous satanic cult.* New York, NY: Bantam Books.

Terry, M. (1993). *Inside Edition.* New York, NY: WNYW.

Urban, H. B. (2008). *Magia sexualis: Sex, magic, and liberation in modern Western esotericism.* Berkeley, California: University of California Press.

Urban, H. B. (2012). *Aleister Crowley and Western esotericism: An anthology of critical studies.* In 1381853429 1009426733 H. Bogdan & 1381853430 1009426733 M. Starr (Eds.), Aleister Crowley and Western esotericism: An anthology of critical studies. New York, NY: Oxford University Press.

U.S. Court of Appeals for the Fourth Circuit. Michael A. Aquino, Plaintiff-appellant, v. Michael P.w. Stone, Secretary of the Army, Defendant-appellee, 957 F.2d 139 (4th Cir. 1992), Justia.com (U.S. Court of Appeals for the Fourth Circuit – 957 F.2d 139 (4th Cir. 1992) December 2, 1991).

United States District Court For the Eastern District of Virginia – Alexandria division – Michael A. Aquino – plaintiff, civil action v. no 90-1547-a the honorable Michael P. W. Stone – Secretary of the Army, Department of the Army, Washington, D.C., defendant.

van Luijk, Ruben (2016). *Children of Lucifer: The Origins of Modern Religious Satanism.* Oxford: Oxford University Press. ISBN 978-0-19-027510-5

Woolfolk, John. Restraining Order Against Cult Founder Granted. *San Francisco Chronicle,* June 24, 1994, p. D7.

Wyllie, T. R., & Parfrey, A. (2009). *Love, sex, fear, death: The untold story of the Process Church of the Final Judgement.* Los Angeles, CA: Feral House.

PART 4

Advisory Committee on Human Radiation Experiments. "Chapter 3, part 4: Supreme Court Dissents Invoke the Nuremberg Code: CIA and DOD Human Subjects Research Scandals," Advisory Committee on Human Radiation Experiments Final Report. Archived from the original on March 31, 2013.

Albarelli, H. P., Jr., & Kaye, J. S. (2010, August 11). The hidden tragedy of the CIA's experiments on children. https://truthout.org/articles/the-hidden-tragedy-of-the-cias-experiments-on-children/

Albarelli, H. P. (2011). *A terrible mistake: The murder of Frank Olson & the CIA's secret Cold War experiments*. Springfield, OR: Trine Day.

Associated Press. (2020-02-07). "Harvey Weinstein trial hears from expert on unreliable memories." *The Guardian*.

Apter, C. (2019, January 14). The traumatic origin of dissociative identity disorder. https://www.mentalhealthtoday.co.uk/blog/teach-me-well/denying-the-traumatic-origin-of-dissociative-identity-disorder-denies-those-who-live-with-it-a-recovery

Aviv, R. (2021, March 29). How Elizabeth loftus changed the meaning of memory. https://www.newyorker.com/magazine/2021/04/05/how-elizabeth-loftus-changed-the-meaning-of-memory

Bain, Donald. (1976)The Control of Candy Jones, Chicago: Playboy Press

Beilinson, David; Galinsky, Michael and Suki Hawley. *Who Took Johnny*. USA: RumuR Inc, 2016.

Belli, R. F. (2012). True and false recovered memories: Toward a reconciliation of the debate. New York, NY: Springer.

Bellows, A. (2019, July 27). Technology and the pursuit of happiness. https://www.damninteresting.com/technology-and-the-pursuit-of-happiness/

Bhandari, S. (Ed.). (2020, January 22). Dissociative identity disorder (multiple personality disorder): Signs, symptoms, treatment. https://www.webmd.com/mental-health/dissociative-identity-disorder-multiple-personality-disorder

Blihar, D., Delgado, E., Buryak, M., Gonzalez, M., & Waechter, R. (2020). A systematic review of the neuroanatomy of dissociative identity disorder. *European Journal of Trauma & Dissociation, 4*(3), 100148. doi:10.1016/j.ejtd.2020.100148

Blumenthal, Max (August 24, 2009). "Behind the Obama-Hitler Slur." The Daily Beast.

Bowart, W. H. (1979). *Opération mind control*. Paris, France: B. Grasset.

Brand, B. L., Sar, V., Stavropoulos, P., Krüger, C., Korzekwa, M., Martínez-Taboas, A., & Middleton, W. (2016). Separating fact from fiction: An empirical examination of six myths about dissociative identity disorder. Harvard Review of Psychiatry, 24(4), 257-270. doi:10.1097/hrp.0000000000000100

Brand, B. L., Webermann, A. R., & Frankel, A. S. (2016). Assessment of complex dissociative disorder patients and simulated dissociation in forensic contexts. *International Journal of Law and Psychiatry, 49*, 197-204. doi:10.1016/j.ijlp.2016.10.006

Brandt, Daniel (1996-01-03). "Mind Control and the Secret State." NameBase NewsLine. Archived from the original on 2012-08-04.

Brown, D., Frischholz, E. J., & Scheflin, A. W. (1999). Iatrogenic dissociative identity disorder – an evaluation of the scientific evidence. The Journal of Psychiatry & Law, 27(3-4), 549-637. doi:10.1177/009318539902700308

Carlton, Jim. Of Microbes and Mock Attacks: Years Ago, The Military Sprayed Germs on U.S. Cities, *Wall Street Journal*, (October 22, 2001).

Cannon, M. (1996). Project monarch: The tangled web – (Cathy O'Brien & mark Phillips) – By Martin Cannon 1996. https://mcawareness.livejournal.com/7369.html

Church Committee. "The Select Committee to Study Governmental Operations with Respect to Intelligence Activities, Foreign and Military Intelligence." Church Committee report, no. 94-755, 94th Cong., 2d Sess. Washington, D.C.: United States Congress. 1976. p. 392.

CIA. (1954, February 10). Document 190691: Hypnotic Experimentation and ReSearch [CIA subject was hypnotized to shoot another subject with an unloaded pistol].

CIA. (1951, September 25). Document 190527: SI and H Experimentation [CIA subject was hypnotized into placing an incendiary device in an office desk drawer].

CIA. (1951, July 9). Document 140393 [CIA-contracted hypnotist boasts his ability to hypnotize women and have sex with them].

CIA. (1951, July 9). Document 17395 [CIA study of dissociative states].

Constantine, A. (1996, May 12). Ethics complaints filed Against ELIZABETH LOFTUS (FMSF). http://www.astraeasweb.net/politics/loftus.html

DeCamp, J. W. (2005). *The Franklin cover-up: Child abuse, Satanism, and murder in Nebraska*. Lincoln, Nebraska: AWT.

Delgado, J. M. (1959). Division of instrumentation: Electronic command of movement and behavior*. Transactions of the New York Academy of Sciences, 21(8 Series II), 689-699. doi:10.1111/j.2164-0947.1959.tb01715.x

DePrince, A. P., Brown, L. S., Cheit, R. E., Freyd, J. J., Gold, S. N., Pezdek, K., & Quina, K. (2011). Motivated forgetting AND Misremembering: Perspectives from Betrayal trauma theory. True and False Recovered Memories, 193-242. doi:10.1007/978-1-4614-1195-6_7

DiMeo, Sarah. "Faded Out – Ep 21 Extended Episode: John Gosch Sr." Episode. Faded Out 1, no. 21. Connecticut , April 12, 2018.

Drozdiak, William. "U.S. Held Mengele After War." *Washington Post*. WP Company, June 27, 1985. https://www.washingtonpost.com/archive/politics/1985/06/27/us-held-mengele-after-war/db2d487b-dfd0-47ae-b8a5-987de28e8b89/.

Estabrooks, G. H. (april 1971). Hypnosis Comes of Age. Science Digest.

Gale Encyclopedia of Medicine. Bender-Gestalt Test." Gale Encyclopedia of Medicine (3rd ed.)

Goodman, G. S., Gonzalves, L., & Wolpe, S. (2018). False memories and true memories of Childhood trauma: Balancing the risks. *Clinical Psychological Science*, 7(1), 29-31. doi:10.1177/2167702618797106

Gray Faction. Who are the conspiracy therapists? (2021, January 26). https://greyfaction.org/resources/proponents/who/

Hajjar, L. (2012, August 06). Opinion: Kubark's very long shadow. https://www.aljazeera.com/opinions/2012/8/6/cia-kubarks-very-long-shadow

Hammond, C. (1992, June 25). Hypnosis in MPD: Ritual Abuse. Speech presented at Fourth Annual Eastern Regional Conference on Abuse and Multiple Personality in Virginia, Alexandria.

Hanson, C. (1998, June 1). Dangerous therapy: The story of Patricia Burgus and multiple personality disorder. https://www.chicagomag.com/Chicago-Magazine/June-1998/Dangerous-Therapy-The-Story-of-Patricia-Burgus-and-Multiple-Personality-Disorder/

Heaney, K. (2021, January 06). The memory War. https://www.thecut.com/article/false-memory-syndrome-controversy.html

Hersh, Seymour M. (1974-12-22). "Huge C.i.a. Operation Reported in U.s. Against Antiwar Forces, Other Dissidents in Nixon Years." The New York Times. ISSN 0362-4331.

Horgan, J. (2017, October 13). Bizarre brain-implant experiment sought to "cure" homosexuality. https://blogs.scientificamerican.com/cross-check/bizarre-brain-implant-experiment-sought-to-cure-homosexuality/

Horrock, Nicholas M. "Private Institutions Used In C.I.A Effort To Control Behavior. 25-Year, $25 Million Program. New Information About Funding and Operations Disclosed by Documents and Interviews Private Institutions Used in C.I.A. Plan." New York Times. August 2, 1977.

Horrock, Nicholas M. (4 Aug 1977). "80 Institutions Used in CIA Mind Studies: Admiral Turner Tells Senators of Behavior Control Research Bars Drug Testing Now." New York Times. Archived from the original on 30 March 2021.

Jacobsen, Annie (2014). *Operation Paperclip: The Secret Intelligence Program to Bring Nazi Scientists to America*. New York: Little, Brown and Company. p. Prologue, ix

Kaye, J. (2015, April 07). New book: Antimalarial drugs part of secret program to torture detainees at guantanamo. New Book: Antimalarial Drugs Part of Secret Program to Torture Detainees at Guantanamo

Lacter, E. P. (2011). Ritual abuse and mind control: The manipulation of attachment needs. In *RITUAL ABUSE AND MIND CONTROL: The manipulation of attachment needs*. London, UK: Karnac Books.

Lovern, J. D. (1993). Spin Programming: A Newly Uncovered Technique of Systematic Mind Control. Lecture presented at The Sixth Western Clinical Conference on Multiple Personality and Dissociation in California, Irvine.

Mark, V. H., & Ervin, F. R. (1976). *Violence and the brain*. New York, NY: Medical Dept., Harper & Row.

Marks, John (1979). *The Search for the Manchurian Candidate*. New York: Times Books. chapters 3 and 7. ISBN 0812907736.

Martin A. Lee; Bruce Shlain (2007). *Acid Dreams: The Complete Social History of LSD: The CIA, the Sixties, and Beyond*. Grove/Atlantic. pp. 373–. ISBN 978-080219606

McGowan, D. (2004). *Programmed To Kill*. Bloomington, Indiana: IUniverse.

McMaugh, K. (2020, January 21). ISSTD news. https://news.isst-d.org/the-rise-and-fall-of-the-false-memory-syndrome-foundation/

Mullen, C. (1996). *Final report of the Advisory Committee on human radiation experiments. In Final report of the Advisory Committee on Human Radiation Experiments*. New York, NY: Oxford University Press.

Nagourney, E. (2000, February 17). Martin orne, 72, psychiatrist and expert on HYPNOSIS, DIES. https://www.nytimes.com/2000/02/17/us/martin-orne-72-psychiatrist-and-expert-on-hypnosis-dies.html

National Public Radio (NPR), 9 Sept. 2019, *"The CIA's Secret Quest For Mind Control: Torture, LSD And A 'Poisoner In Chief"*

Neimark, Jill (1996). *"The diva of disclosure, memory researcher Elizabeth Loftus." Psychology Today*. 29 (1): 48–53.

Newswald, D. W., Gould, C., & Graham-Costain, V. (1991). Common Programs Observed in Survivors of Satanic Ritualistic Abuse. The California Therapist.

Nickson, Elizabeth (October 16, 1994). "Mind Control: My Mother, the CIA and LSD." *The Observer*

O'Brien, C., & Phillips, M. (2001). T*rance formation of America: The true life story of a CIA mind control slave*. Reality Marketing.

Ofgang, E. (2017, March 06). Yale's forgotten master of mind control. https://www.connecti-cutmag.com/health-and-science/yale-s-forgotten-master-of-mind-control/article_0fe-ceb10-d499-593d-b438-b89c00378bfb.html

O'Neill, T., & Piepenbring, D. (2020). *Chaos: Charles Manson, the CIA, and the secret history of the sixties*. New York, NY: Back Bay Books/ Little, Brown and Company.

Paris J (2012). "The rise and fall of dissociative identity disorder." *Journal of Nervous and Mental Disease*. 200 (12): 1076–9. doi:10.1097/NMD.0b013e318275d285. PMID 23197123. S2CID 32336795.

Rockefeller Commission. *"Rockefeller Commission Report." Michigan State University Libraries* – Electronic Resources.

Sachs, A., & Galton, G. (2008). *Forensic aspects of dissociative identity disorder*. London, UK: Karnac Books.

Savoy, R. L., Frederick, B. B., Keuroghlian, A. S., & Wolk, P. C. (2012). Voluntary switching between identities in dissociative identity disorder: A functional mri case study. Cognitive Neuroscience, 3(2), 112-119. doi:10.1080/17588928.2012.669750

Schlumpf, Y. R., Reinders, A. A., Nijenhuis, E. R., Luechinger, R., Van Osch, M. J., & Jäncke, L. (2014). Dissociative part-dependent resting-state activity in dissociative identity disorder: A controlled fmri perfusion study. PLoS ONE, 9(6). doi:10.1371/journal.pone.0098795

Select Committee on Intelligence and the Subcommittee on Health and Scientific Research of the Committee on Human Resources. Project MKUltra, the Central Intelligence Agency's Program of Research into Behavioral Modification. Joint Hearing before the Select Committee on Intelligence and the Subcommittee on Health and Scientific Research of the Committee on Human Resources, United States Senate, Ninety-Fifth Congress, First Session" (PDF). U.S. Government Printing Office (copy hosted at the New York Times website). August 8, 1977.

Senate Select Committee on Intelligence and Committee on Human Resources. "Senate MKUltra Hearing: Appendix C – Documents Referring to Subprojects, (p. 167, in PDF document page numbering)" (PDF). Senate Select Committee on Intelligence and Committee on Human Resources. August 3, 1977. Archived from the original (PDF) on 2007-11-28.

Springmeier, F., & Wheeler, C. (1996). *The Illuminati formula used to create an undetectable total mind controlled slave*. Clackamas, OR: Springmeier & Wheeler.

Sydney Morning Herald. Killers 'Trained by U.S. Navy'. (1975, July 7). The Sydney Morning Herald.

Talbot, David. *The Devil's Chessboard: Allen Dulles, the CIA, and the Rise of America's*, London, UK: Harper Collins UK, 2016.

U.S. Congress. (1974). Individual rights and the Federal role in behavior modification: A study. Washington, D.C.: U.S. G.P.O.

Van der Reijden, J. (n.d.). False memory Syndrome Foundation: QUESTIONABLE board MEMBERS tied to the CIA's MKULTRA program and child abuse. https://isgp-studies.com/false-memory-syndrome-foundation-fmsf

Waldvogel, B., Ullrich, A., & Strasburger, H. (2007). Blind und sehend in einer person. Der Nervenarzt, 78(11), 1303-1309. doi:10.1007/s00115-007-2309-x

Whalen, Andrew. 12/7/18 at 7:24 PM (2018-12-07). "How the CIA used brain surgery to make six remote control dogs." *Newsweek*.

Wilson, A (2002-11-03). "War & remembrance: Controversy is a constant for memory researcher Elizabeth Loftus, newly installed at UCI." The Orange County Register.

PART 5

Bates, Stephan. "Police admit Dutroux video bungle." guardian.co.uk. The Guardian. June 16, 1999

BBC. 'Crazy Brabant Killers': Brussels murder mystery 'clue." BBC News. 2017-10-24.

Bulté, Annemie, Douglas de Coninck, and Marie-Jeanne van Heeswyck. Les Dossiers X: Ce Que La Belgique Ne Devait Pas Savoir Sur L'affaire Dutroux. Bruxelles, Belgium: EPO, 1999.

La Dernière Heure. "Le pédophile Dutroux raconté par Sabine!." *La Dernière Heure* (in French).

France 3. "Passé sous Silence: Témoin X1 Régina Louf - SILENCE ON TUE DES ENFANTS" - France3." youtube. France 3. Jan 3 2017

Frenkiel, Olenka. "Belgium's silent heart of darkness." guardian.co.uk. *The Guardian*. May 5, 2002

La Libre. "Procès Dutroux-bis: Michel Nihoul inculpé, non lieu en vue" (in French). La Libre. 3 May 2010.

Reuters. "275,000 in Belgium Protest Handling of Child Sex Scandal." *New York Times*. October 21, 1996

Trouw. "Steeds Vond Vader Marchal Een Woord." Trouw, September 3, 1996. https://www.trouw.nl/nieuws/steeds-vond-vader-marchal-een-woord~b1a22a15/.

van der Reijden, Joël. "Beyond the Dutroux Affair: The Reality of Protected Child Abuse and Snuff Networks." Beyond the Dutroux Affair: The Reality of Protected Child Abuse and Snuff Networks, July 25, 2007. https://isgp-studies.com/belgian-x-dossiers-of-the-dutroux-affair#Dutroux.

Waterfield, Bruno. "Charleroi: the most depressing city in Europe becomes more depressing by the day." *The Telegraph*. 29 March 2009.

Zembla (March 18, 2003) "De X-dossiers"

PART 6

Anglesey, Anders. "QAnon Followers Targeted by New Messianic Mythology Sabmyk." *Newsweek*, March 5, 2021. https://www.newsweek.com/sabmyk-qanon-followers-new-messianic-mythology-1573971.

Anglesey, Anders. "Sabmyk Creator Says QAnon-Style Conspiracy Is Just a Game." Newsweek. Newsweek, April 15, 2021. https://www.newsweek.com/sabmyk-creator-says-qanon-style-conspiracy-just-game-1583531.

Ankel, Sophia. How Tucker Carlson went from a CIA reject to the most-watched person on cable news, accused of peddling prejudice to millions, August 27, 2020. https://www.msn.com/en-us/news/us/how-tucker-carlson-went-from-a-cia-reject-to-the-most-watched-person-on-cable-news-accused-of-peddling-prejudice-to-millions/ss-BB16VUWK.

The Associated Press. "Army Investigates Psyops Officer for Role in Washington on Day of Capitol Riot." *The Guardian*. Guardian News and Media, January 11, 2021. https://www.theguardian.com/us-news/2021/jan/11/army-investigates-psyops-officer-officer-emily-rainey-capitol-riot.

Associated Press. "Trump goes after Obama on US citizenship, says citizenship questions remain unanswered." Associated Press. April 7, 2011.

Bale, Jeffrey M. (1989) Right-wing Terrorists and the Extraparliamentary Left in Post-World War 2 Europe: Collusion or Manipulation? *Lobster* No. 18. In *Lobster* 19

Beckhusen, Robert. "U.S. Spies Want to Play Alternate-Reality Games (For Work, They Swear)." Wired. Conde Nast, March 13, 2013. https://www.wired.com/2013/03/iarpa-alternate-reality-games/.

Benner, Katie, Alan Feuer, and Adam Goldman. "F.B.I. Finds Contact Between Proud Boys Member and Trump Associate Before Riot." *New York Times*, March 6, 2021. https://www.nytimes.com/2021/03/05/us/politics/trump-proud-boys-capitol-riot.html.

Bicks, Emily. "Is Thomas Schoenberger the Mastermind Behind QAnon?" Heavy.com, January 26, 2021. https://heavy.com/news/thomas-schoenberger-qanon/.

Blake, Aaron. "Analysis | Tucker Carlson's Wild, Baseless Theory Blaming the FBI for Organizing the Jan. 6 Capitol Riot." *Washington Post*. WP Company, June 16, 2021. https://www.washingtonpost.com/politics/2021/06/16/tucker-carlsons-tinfoil-hat-theory-blaming-fbi-jan-6/.

Browne, Ryan. "Pentagon Shake-up Continues as Another Top Official Departs." CNN. Cable News Network, December 1, 2020. https://www.cnn.com/2020/11/30/politics/pentagon-official-departs/index.html.

Bump, Philip (October 15, 2020). "Rather than condemn the QAnon conspiracy theory, Trump elevates its dangerous central assertion." *Washington Post*.

Cadwalladr, Carole. "The Great British Brexit Robbery: How Our Democracy Was Hijacked." *The Guardian*. Guardian News and Media, May 7, 2017. https://www.theguardian.com/technology/2017/may/07/the-great-british-brexit-robbery-hijacked-democracy?fbclid=IwAR1vFi0g5q-sy8rNlvcsglO3kbt201FqFnnbiwNpT2usL_C7LFfQSUAAkvzA.

Chappell, Bill. "Train Engineer Says He Crashed In Attempt To Attack Navy Hospital Ship In L.A." NPR. NPR, April 2, 2020. https://www.npr.org/sections/coronavirus-live-updates/2020/04/02/825897966/train-engineer-says-he-crashed-in-attempt-to-attack-navy-hospital-ship-in-l-a.

Connolly, Griffin (July 5, 2020). "Former Trump aide Flynn appears to make pledge to QAnon in July 4 video." *The Independent*.

De Brosse, Sherman (April 14, 2007). "MICHAEL RICONOSCIUTO: The Math/Science Wizard Who Said TOO Much, Part 1." ForwardAmerica.

Emery, David (September 17, 2016). "Did Clinton Supporters Start the 'Birther' Movement?." Snopes. Archived from the original on March 30, 2018.

Evelyn, Kenya (January 9, 2021). "Capitol attack: the five people who died." The Guardian.

Fenton, Justin (2009-09-11). "Video prompts ACORN firings." The Baltimore Sun.

Friedman, Dan; Breland, Ali (August 13, 2019). "Michael Flynn and George Papadopoulos are scheduled to speak at a conference organized by a QAnon supporter." Mother Jones.

Gaudiano, Nicole, and Michael Stratford. "Education Secretary Betsy DeVos Resigns, Citing Violence at the Capitol." POLITICO. POLITICO, January 8, 2021. https://www.politico.com/news/2021/01/07/education-secretary-betsy-devos-resigns-456294.

Gerstein, Josh. 'Are you QAnon?': One Trump official's brush with an Internet cult gone horribly wrong. POLITICO, January 20, 2021. https://www.politico.com/amp/news/2021/01/19/qanon-trump-ezra-cohen-watnick-460520.

Goldman, Adam (April 11, 2018). "Trump National Security Aide Ousted From White House Re-emerges at Justice Dept." The New York Times. ISSN 0362-4331.

Gray, Rosie (July 23, 2017). "The Man McMaster Couldn't Fire." The Atlantic. Archived from the original on July 24, 2017.

Guffey, Robert. "What Are the True Goals of QAnon? It's the 21st Century's Ultimate Catfish Scheme." Salon. Salon.com, October 16, 2020. https://www.salon.com/2020/09/13/what-are-the-true-goals-of-qanon-its-the-21st-centurys-ultimate-catfish-scheme/.

Halper, Evan. "'Uncharted Waters.' Judges Are Banning Some Capitol Riot Suspects from the Internet." Los Angeles Times, March 25, 2021. https://www.latimes.com/politics/story/2021-03-25/judges-weigh-whether-to-ban-capitol-riot-suspects-from-Internet.

Hamburger, Tom, and Matea Gold. "Flynn Files Amended Disclosure Report Showing Additional Payments." Washington Post. WP Company, August 3, 2017. https://www.washingtonpost.com/politics/flynn-files-amended-disclosure-report-showing-additional-payments/2017/08/03/c76180c8-78a4-11e7-9eac-d56bd5568db8_story.html.

Harkins, Gina. "In Unprecedented Joint Letter, Top Military Brass Denounces U.S. Capitol Riot." Military.com, January 12, 2021. https://www.military.com/daily-news/2021/01/12/unprecedented-joint-letter-top-generals-denounce-us-capitol-riot.html.

Hartigan, Matt. "Meet The Man Who Solved The Mysterious Cicada 3301 Puzzle." Fast Company. Fast Company, April 1, 2015. https://www.fastcompany.com/3025785/meet-the-man-who-solved-the-mysterious-cicada-3301-puzzle.

Hayes, T. B., A. Collins, M. Lee, M. Mendoza, N. Noriega, A. A. Stuart, and A. Vonk. "Hermaphroditic, Demasculinized Frogs after Exposure to the Herbicide Atrazine at Low Ecologically Relevant Doses." Proceedings of the National Academy of Sciences 99, no. 8 (2002): 5476–80. https://doi.org/10.1073/pnas.082121499.

HenryKrinkle. "FBI Agent Accidentally Reveals Own 8chan Posts; Attempts to Redirect White Supremacist Rage against Russia." Current Events Inquiry, August 4, 2019. https://ceinquiry.wordpress.com/2019/06/17/fbi-8chan/.

Hinkelman, Michael (October 25, 2008). "Judge rejects Montco lawyer's bid to have Obama removed from ballot." Philadelphia Daily News. Archived from the original on October 28, 2008

Hoback, Cullen. "Do You Believe In Coincidences?" Episode. Q: Into the Storm, Episode No. 2. HBO, March 21, 2021.

Hoback, Cullen. "Game Over" Episode. Q: Into the Storm, Episode No. 5. HBO, March 21, 2021.

Hoback, Cullen. "The Storm." Episode. Q: Into the Storm, Epsidoe No 6. HBO, April 4, 2021.

Honegger, Barbara. October Surprise. New York, NY: Tudor Pub. Co., 1989.

Hopsicker, Daniel. "Jeffrey Epstein, the CIA, Dyncorps, & N-Number N474AW." MadCow, July 12, 2019. https://www.madcowprod.com/2019/07/12/jeffrey-epstein-the-cia-dyncorps-n-number-n474aw/.

Hosenball, M. (2021, June 14). FBI warns that QAnon followers could engage in 'real-world violence'. Reuters. https://www.reuters.com/world/us/fbi-warns-that-qanon-followers-could-engage-real-world-violence-2021-06-14/?utm_source=twitter&utm_medium=Social.

House Select Committee on Assassinations. January 2, 1979. Oswald, David Ferrie and the Civil Air Patrol, House Select Committee on Assassinations, Volume 9, 4, p. 110.

Hsu, Spencer. "U.S., South Korea Dismantle Secret Online Network That Shared Thousands of Videos of Child Sexual Abuse." *Washington Post*. WP Company, October 16, 2019. https://www.washington-post.com/local/legal-issues/us-south-korea-dismantle-secret-online-network-that-shared-thou-sands-of-videos-of-child-sexual-abuse/2019/10/16/cdae13c2-eb63-11e9-9c6d-436a0df4f31d_story.html.

Itkowitz, Colby; Stanley-Becker, Isaac; Rozsa, Lori; Bade, Rachael (August 20, 2020). "Trump praises baseless QAnon conspiracy theory, says he appreciates support of its followers." *Washington Post*.

Jarvis, Jacob (July 6, 2020). "Michael Flynn's Lawyer Denies Ex-Trump Aide Intentionally Used QA-non Slogan." *Newsweek*.

Kaminska, Izabella. "The 'Game Theory' in the Qanon Conspiracy Theory." *Financial Times*, October 16, 2020. https://www.ft.com/content/74f9d20f-9ff9-4fad-808f-c7e4245a1725.

Kaplan, Alex (August 1, 2019). "Trump has repeatedly amplified QAnon Twitter accounts. The FBI has linked the conspiracy theory to domestic terror." Media Matters for America.

Klippenstein, Ken. "Inside Wikistrat, the Mysterious Intelligence Firm Now in Mueller's Sights." *The Daily Beast*. The Daily Beast Company, June 4, 2018. https://www.thedailybeast.com/in-side-the-mysterious-intelligence-firm-now-in-muellers-sights.

Lamothe, Dan; Sonne, Paul; Leonnig, Carol D.; Davis, Aaron C. (January 20, 2021). "Army falsely de-nied Flynn's brother was involved in key part of military response to Capitol riot." The Washington Post.

Landis, Fred 'Georgetown's Ivory Tower for Old Spooks', Inquiry, 30 September 1979

Lenz, Liz (September 5, 2018). "The mystery of Tucker Carlson." *Columbia Journalism Review*.

Leonnig, Carol D.; Davis, Aaron C.; Hermann, Peter; Demirjian, Karoun (January 10, 2021). "Outgoing Capitol Police chief: House, Senate security officials hamstrung efforts to call in National Guard." *Washington Post*.

MacLeod, Alan "Facebook's New Propaganda Partners." FAIR, September 25, 2018. https://fair.org/home/facebooks-new-propaganda-partners/.

Mantyla, Kyle. "Jerome Corsi Has Uncovered Irrefutable Proof Of The Authenticity Of 'QAnon'." Right Wing Watch, January 11, 2018. https://www.rightwingwatch.org/post/jerome-corsi-has-uncov-ered-irrefutable-proof-of-the-authenticity-of-qanon/.

Marchetti, Victor (August 14, 1978) *The Spotlight*

Marr, Kendra (March 17, 2011). "Donald Trump, birther?." Politico. Archived from the original on March 20, 2011.

Marsh, Heather. "Wikileaks, Data Justice and a New Internet." Heather Marsh, July 11, 2019. https://georgiebc.wordpress.com/2019/06/18/wikileaks-data-justice-and-a-new-Internet/.

Martin, Robbie. 2020. "The Origins of #QAnon, Follow the White Rabbit Into a Deeper Layer of the MAGA Cult Pt 1 of 2," Podcast. Soundcloud. https://soundcloud.com/media-roots/the-origins-of-qanon-follow-the-white-rabbit-into-a-deeper-layer-of-the-maga-cult-pt-1-of-2.

Mazzetti, Mark, Ronen Bergman, David Kirkpatrick, and Maggie Haberman. "Rick Gates Sought On-line Manipulation Plans From Israeli Intelligence Firm for Trump Campaign." *New York Times*., Octo-ber 8, 2018. https://www.nytimes.com/2018/10/08/us/politics/rick-gates-psy-group-trump.html.

mi5terp. "Q PROOFS! You Want Some Proof It Is Real?" Steemit. Accessed June 11, 2021. https://steemit.com/q/@mi5terp/q-proofs-you-want-some-proof-it-is-real.

Michael, J G. "ARG Pioneer Joseph Matheny on the Counterculture's Hijacking from Corporatization to QAnon." Episode. Parallax Views, August 5, 2019.

Miller, Greg; DeYoung, Karen (March 30, 2017). "Three White House officials tied to files shared with

House intelligence chairman." *Washington Post.* Archived from the original on March 31,

Miller, Richard. "Redacted Doc." TwitLonger, November 14, 2020. https://www.twitlonger.com/show/n_1srfire.

Miller, Zeke; Colvin, Jill; Seitz, Amanda (August 20, 2020). "Trump praises QAnon conspiracists, who 'like me very much." Associated Press.

Monzat, René. Enquêtes sur la droite extrême, *Le Monde*-éditions, 1992, p. 89

Moore, Jim. "JFK's Assassination Greased the Wheels for QAnon and Covid-Deniers | James Moore." The Independent. Independent Digital News and Media, February 13, 2021. https://www.independent.co.uk/voices/qanon-conspiracy-origin-jfk-covid-denier-anti-vaxx-b1801838.html.

Moore, Robert. "Lucky 17 and Q? How Conspiracy Theories Are Turbo-Charging in Trump's America." ITV News. ITV News, November 22, 2018. https://www.itv.com/news/2018-11-22/lucky-17-q-and-the-tippy-top-president-how-conspiracy-theories-are-being-turbo-charged-into-donald-trumps-america.

Morlin, Bill (July 20, 2018). "Terrorism suspect makes reference to extremist conspiracies." Southern Poverty Law Center.

Moyer, Matthew. "Stephanie Murphy Announces New Legislation barring QAnon Adherents from Holding Federal Security Clearances." Orlando Weekly. Orlando Weekly, February 8, 2021. https://www.orlandoweekly.com/Blogs/archives/2021/01/22/stephanie-murphy-announces-new-legislation-barring-qanon-adherents-from-holding-federal-security-clearances.

Nakashima, Ellen, and Dan Lamothe. "Christopher Miller, Trump's Surprise Acting Defense Secretary, Has a Thin Resume for the Job but Deep Experience in Counterterrorism." The Washington Post. WP Company, November 10, 2020. https://www.washingtonpost.com/national-security/acting-defense-secretary-chris-miller/2020/11/09/43a4296e-22d0-11eb-8599-406466ad1b8e_story.html.

Neumeister, Larry (2010-04-20). "ACORN CEO outside court: 'We're on life support." Associated Press

Nieuwsuur (August 9, 2016). "Assange belooft nieuwe onthullingen over Clinton" (in Dutch). Nieuwsuur. Archived from the original on March 19, 2018.

Nixon Library. MARCH 22, 1973, "Transcript of a recording of a meeting among the president, John Dean, John Erlichman, H. R. Haldeman, and John Mitchell on March 22, 1973 from 1:57 to 3:43 p.m."

Norris, Jesse J. "Accounting for the (Almost Complete) Failure of the Entrapment Defense in Post-9/11 U.S. Terrorism Cases." Law & Social Inquiry 45, no. 1 (2015): 194–225. https://doi.org/10.1017/lsi.2019.61.

Novet, Jordan. "U.S. Trade Group Asks VP Pence to 'Seriously Consider' Invoking 25th Amendment to Remove Trump." CNBC. CNBC, January 7, 2021. https://www.cnbc.com/2021/01/06/national-association-of-manufacturers-calls-dc-protests-sedition.html.

O'Keefe, James. Complete ACORN Baltimore Child Prostitution Investigation Transcript BigGovernment.com; September 10, 2009

Opperman, Ed. "JAMES M ROTHSTEIN NYPD Ret. – Process Church, Son of Sam, Manson, and More." Spreaker, 2015. https://www.spreaker.com/user/oppermanreport/james-m-rothstein-nypd-process-church.

Pasternack, Alex. "Before Trump, Cambridge Analytica Quietly Built 'Psyops' for Militaries." Fast Company. Fast Company, September 25, 2019. https://www.fastcompany.com/90235437/before-trump-cambridge-analytica-parent-built-weapons-for-war.

Pieczenik, Steve. 2016. "The Hillary Clinton Takeover of the United States." YouTube. https://www.youtube.com/watch?v=ov5kvWSz5LM.

Pilkington, Mark. *Mirage Men: an Adventure into Paranoia, Espionage, Psychological Warfare, and UFOs.* New York, NY: Skyhorse, 2010.

Sommerland, Joe. "Alex Jones's Craziest Conspiracy Theories, from the New World Order to Gay Frogs." The Independent. Independent Digital News and Media, August 9, 2018. https://www.independent.co.uk/news/world/americas/us-politics/alex-jones-radio-show-us-alt-right-conspiracy-theories-youtube-infowars-illuminati-frogs-a8483986.html.

Quist-Arctom, Ofeibea, Trial and Triumph: Stories Out Of Africa, NPR, October 9, 2008.

Reinstein, Julia (March 18, 2019). "The Suspected Gambino Mob Boss Killer Had Apparent QAnon Messages Scrawled On His Hands In Court." BuzzFeed News.

Rosenberg, Matthew; Haberman, Maggie (August 20, 2020). "The Republican Embrace of QAnon Goes Far Beyond Trump." New York Times. ISSN 0362-4331.

Ruelas, Richard (January 4, 2021). "QAnon follower sentenced to nearly 8 years in prison for standoff near Hoover Dam." The Arizona Republic.

Russell, Dick. "Spook Wars in Cyberspace." Dick Russell. High Times, July 1, 1997. https://dickrussell.org/1997/06/01/spook-wars-in-cyberspace/.

Schmidle, Nicholas. "Michael Flynn, General Chaos." The New Yorker, February 18, 2017. https://www.newyorker.com/magazine/2017/02/27/michael-flynn-general-chaos.

Schwellenbach, Nick, and Carol D. Leonnig. "Despite Allegations, No Prosecutions for War Zone Sex Trafficking." Center for Public Integrity, July 17, 2010. https://publicintegrity.org/national-security/despite-allegations-no-prosecutions-for-war-zone-sex-trafficking/.

Slevin, Colleen. "Woman accused in QAnon kidnapping plot pleads not guilty." Associated Press.

Snider, Steven. Le Cercle: Fratelli Neri, May 21, 2016. http://visupview.blogspot.com/2016/05/le-cercle-fratelli-neri.html.

Snider, Steven. The Postmodern King of the World, March 7, 2021. http://visupview.blogspot.com/2021/03/the-postmodern-king-of-world.html?m=1.

So, Linda. "Oath Keeper Claims She Met with Secret Service before Capitol Riot." Reuters. Thomson Reuters, February 21, 2021. https://www.reuters.com/article/us-usa-trump-capitol-arrests-idUSKB-N2AL0L5.

Sommer, Will (June 19, 2018). "QAnon, the Crazy Pro-Trump Conspiracy, Melts Down Over OIG Report." The Daily Beast.

Sommer, Will (October 17, 2019). "Rudy Giuliani's Twitter Feed Is a Boomer Conspiracy-Theory Sh*tshow." The Daily Beast.

Stanley-Becker, Isaac (August 2, 2020). "How the Trump campaign came to court QAnon, the online conspiracy movement identified by the FBI as a violent threat." Washington Post.

Sumner, Mark (January 30, 2021). "Miller Disarmed National Guard." The National Memo.

Tau, Byron, and Rebecca Ballhaus. "Israeli Intelligence Company Formed Venture With Trump Campaign Firm Cambridge Analytica." The Wall Street Journal. Dow Jones & Company, May 23, 2018. https://www.wsj.com/articles/israeli-intelligence-company-formed-venture-with-trump-campaign-firm-cambridge-analytica-1527030765.

Trickey, Erick. "Fact-Checking QAnon Conspiracy Theories: Did J.P. Morgan Sink the Titanic?" Washington Post. WP Company, August 4, 2018. https://www.washingtonpost.com/news/retropolis/wp/2018/08/04/how-j-p-morgan-didnt-sink-the-titanic-and-other-qanon-conspiracy-theories-debunked/.

Tumulty, Karen (June 12, 2008). "Will Obama's Anti-Rumor Plan Work." Time. Archived from the original on November 2, 2008.

Unger, Craig. The War They Wanted, The Lies They Needed, Vanity Fair, July 2006

UNIRockTV. "CBTS_STREAM BAKER INSIDER EMAIL EVIDENCE REVEAL." Pastebin, May 17, 2018. https://pastebin.com/dZbP9hCt.

U.S. Congress "PN2368 – Lt. Gen. Charles A. Flynn – Army." U.S. Congress. December 20, 2020.

U.S. Department of Defense. "Acting SECDEF Announces OSD Changes at Fort Bragg, NC." U.S. DEPARTMENT OF DEFENSE, November 18, 2020. https://www.defense.gov/Newsroom/Transcripts/Transcript/Article/2419853/acting-secdef-announces-osd-changes-at-fort-bragg-nc/.

Valentine, Douglas. *The CIA as Organized Crime: How Illegal Operations Corrupt America and the World*. Atlanta, George: Clarity Press, Inc., 2017.

Watson, Ben. "Today's D Brief: SOLIC, Elevated; CISA Chief, Fired; 1,560 More Die of COVID; DoD's Rare-Earths Move; And a Bit More." Defense One. Defense One, November 18, 2020. https://www.defenseone.com/threats/2020/11/the-d-brief-november-18-2020/170145/.

WeRemembers. "Visit Tracy Twyman's Page on We Remember." Free online memorials for sharing memories. We Remember. Accessed June 11, 2021. https://www.weremember.com/tracy-twyman/1n4u/memories.

Winter, Jana. "Exclusive: FBI Document Warns Conspiracy Theories Are a New Domestic Terrorism Threat." Yahoo! News. Yahoo!, August 1, 2019. https://news.yahoo.com/news/fbi-documents-conspiracy-theories-terrorism-160000507.html.

WSJ Staff. "Donald Trump, Whoopi Goldberg, Spar Over Obama on 'The View.'" *Wall Street Journal*. March 24, 2011. Archived from the original on April 27, 2011.

Index

Barbour, Mary Ann 105
Barr, Donald 41, 414
Barton, Gloria 98, 99
Barton, Sara 98, 99
Baudouin (king) 320
Baughman, Ann-Marie 269
Beanz, Tracy 375
Bear Stearns 33
Beatles, The 165
Beatrix (queen) 140
Beausoleil, Robert 175
Beavers, William 249
Beck, Aaron T. 88, 107, 274, 407
Belfast Telegraph 56, 407
Belli, Melvin 248, 278, 422
Bender, Lauretta 235-238, 399, 423
Benediktsson, Bjarni 57
Ben-Menashe, Ari 33, 34, 36, 40, 50-53, 407, 411, 413
Bennewitz, Paul 342-347, 349, 356
Benny, Jack 264
Berger, Rainer 91
Berg, Jerry 57, 192, 407
Berg, Philip J. 357
Berkowitz, David 181, 183-194, 197
Berlusconi, Silvio 137
Bernhard (prince) 140
Bewakings-en opsporingsbrigade (BOB) 299-301, 305, 315, 316, 318, 321, 323, 324, 328, 329
Bezos, Jeff 27
Bibee, Bruce 219
Biden, Joe 1, 398, 399, 403
Bieniek, Sebastian 404
Bilderberg Group 139-142, 319, 418, 419
Bill & Hillary Clinton's Circle of Power 109
bin Laden, Osama 356, 392
Binney, Bill 367, 368, 377
Bisignano, Gina 403
Bittencourt, Sabrina 22
Black, Conrad 46
Black, Leon 27
Blair, Tony 27, 141
Blake, William 377, 405, 426

Blauer, Harold 235
B'nai B'rith 32
Boas, Roger 129-131, 329
Boeynants, Vanden 307, 322, 323, 327-329, 337
Bohemian Rhapsody 56
Bolan, Tom 41
Bolton, John 385, 386
Bonaparte, Napoleon 403
Bonacci, Paul 61, 66-68, 72, 76, 113, 115, 265, 266, 286-292
Boner, Troy 63-66, 68, 71, 75
Book of the Law, The 156, 163, 167, 409
Boone, Donny 187, 192
Borge, Kamel Nacif 56
Bougerol, Jean-Marie 323, 324
Bouhouche, Madani 329, 330
Boullan, Abbé 152
Bourgeois, Louise 18
Bourlet, Michel 299, 315, 336
Braisted, Frank A 167
Braun, Bennett 268-273
Breitbart, Andrew 15, 357-359, 365, 411
Breslin, Jim 181, 182, 183
Brethren of the Free Spirit (cult) 151
Brin, Sergey 46
British Journal of Psychiatry 282
Broadbent, Steven 349
Brock, David 18, 362, 408
Bromberger, Dominique 140, 418
Bronfman, Charles 32
Bronfman, Samuel 29, 31, 32, 41, 410
Browning, Willie 219
Brown, Julie 25
Brunel, Jean-Luc 45
Bryant, Nick 58, 60, 61, 64-68, 70, 72, 74, 114, 115, 408
Brzezinski, Zbigniew 140
"bU74pXJK" 14
Buchan, Donald J. 96
Buck, Ed 115, 116, 416
Buckey, Peggy 88, 103
Buckey, Ray 88-90, 98, 99-101, 103
Buckley, William F. Jr. 137
Buckman, John 238, 239, 241

National Review Online 357
National Security Agency (NSA) 40, 52, 344, 351, 352, 354, 367, 377, 398
Nebel, John 262
Nelson, Rusty 59, 66, 68, 70, 71, 139
New Clinton Chronicles, The 110
New Federalist, The 291
New Republic 368
Newsweek 51, 74, 415, 425, 426, 428
New York (magazine) 44
New York Daily News 41, 178, 181, 183, 413
New York Post 15, 48, 183, 410, 414
New York Times 22, 67, 96, 139, 216, 275, 386, 407, 409, 410, 412, 414-416, 418, 421, 423, 425-428, 430
Nichols, Louis 29
Nihoul, Michel 55, 302-304, 306, 307, 309, 311, 314, 315, 318, 320-322, 329, 330, 335, 425
Nixon, Richard 67, 413, 423, 429
Noe, Nick 392
Noriega, Manuel 354, 427
Norman, James 354
Norman, John 56
Norris, Chuck 91, 389, 429
North Fox Island 55, 56
North, Oliver 50, 68, 276, 355
Northrop, Sara "Betty" 166
Nouvel Europe Magazine (NEM) 322, 323, 324
Nunes, Devin 367
NXIVMNXIVM (cult) 29

O

Obama, Barack 17, 43, 140, 291, 357, 361, 364, 367, 369, 375, 398, 401, 413, 420, 422, 426, 427, 430, 431
O'Brien, Cathy 255, 257, 264-266, 285, 286, 338, 422, 424
October Surprise 13, 51, 368, 427
Office of Naval Intelligence (ONI) 167
Office of Strategic Services (OSS) 32, 37, 41, 123

Ofshe, Richard 278
O'Hara, Nick 70, 73
O'Keefe, James 357, 358, 359, 429
Oklahoma City Bombing 225
Olson, Frank 105, 129, 131, 235, 242, 420, 422
Omaha World-Herald 63, 66, 68, 70-72, 74, 288
O'Neal, Shaquille 136
O'Neill, Tom 179, 199, 200, 202-211, 246, 248-250, 421, 424
Ong's Hat 383
Operation Babylift 73
Operation Bluebird 230
Operation Gladio 5, 137-139, 141, 212, 222, 293, 321, 322, 325, 327, 342, 365-368, 389, 418, 420
Operation Mockingbird 402
Operation Paperclip 39, 254, 294, 423
Operation Seaspray 232
Operation Sunrise 293
Operation Underworld 29
Opperman, Ed 196, 225, 405, 421, 429
Oprah Winfrey Show, The 21, 88
Opus Dei 328, 336
Ordo Mysteria Mystica Maxima (MMM) 156
Ordo Templi Orientis (OTO) 156, 157, 160, 165, 166, 167, 169, 192
Ormiston, Karen 63, 65, 67
Orne, Martin 264, 275
Orr, Robert 74
Osmond, Humphry F. 85, 411
Oswald, Lee Harvey 248, 405, 428
Owen, Alisha 63-69, 71, 72

P

Paine, Thomas 135
Paley, William 139
Palm Beach Post 45
Palmieri, Jennifer 16
Papadopoulos, George 392, 427
Parry, Robert 51, 52, 413
Parsons, John Whiteside "Jack" 165, 166
Patrón, Emilio Gamboa 56

Violet, Jean 97, 141, 328
Vogelsong, Joshua Ryan 19
von Steuben, Baron 134
Vuchetich, Pamela 71

W

Wackenhut Corporation 40, 324, 329, 350, 356, 408, 414
Waco, the Big Lie 110
Wadman, Robert 63, 64, 70, 73, 291
Wahl, Albert 201, 291
Wakefield, Hollida 274
Wallace, Mike 40
Wallis, Roy 124, 169, 420
Wall Street Journal 368, 422, 430, 431
Ward, Vicky 33
Warren, Earl 136
Warren, Nancy 136, 177
Washington, Eulice 59-62, 66, 69-71, 287
Washington Examiner 68, 408
Washington, George 134
Washington Post 17, 383, 402, 404, 409, 411, 413, 416, 423, 426-430
Washington, Tasha 59
Washington Times 68
Washington, Tracy 59, 60, 61, 70
Wathelet, Melchior 337
Watkins, Jim 380
Watkins, Ron 380-382, 389
Watson, Paul Joseph 80, 81, 398
Watson, Tex 202, 208
Wayne, John 136
Weaver, Randy 110
Webb, Barbara 59, 60
Webb, Don 217
Webb, Jarrett 59, 60, 61
Webb, Whitney 28, 29, 30, 32, 33, 41, 47, 52, 68, 82, 83, 84, 417
Webster, William 224
Wehner, John 90
Weinberger, Caspar 354, 355
Weiner, Anthony 15, 84, 363, 365, 410-412, 414
Weinstein, Harvey 22, 23, 276, 336, 422
Weiss, Howard 192
Welch, Edgar Maddison 22

Wells, Sheilah 179
West, Louis Jolyon "Jolly" 208, 209, 210, 246-250, 273, 275
Wexner, Leslie 3, 25, 26, 31, 32, 34, 41, 46, 48, 83, 84
Wheatland, Julian 386
Wheeler, Cisco 229, 425
White, George 264
Whiteley, Paul 177
Whitlock, John 38
Whitson, Reeve 210-212
WikiLeaks 13-17, 21, 80, 110, 359, 360, 363, 415, 417
Wikileaks Media 360
Wilbur, Cornelia 268
Wilcox, Kathy 99
Wilde, Oscar 136
Willems, Pascal 309, 337
Williams, Brian 139
Williams, William 263
Willson, Laurel Rose 88
Wilson, Dennis 179, 202
Wilson, Edwin 30, 31, 124, 125, 202, 203, 263, 276, 418, 425
Wilson, Robert Anton 87, 124, 152, 196, 213, 218, 420
Winfrey, Oprah 2, 21, 22, 88
Wired 383, 410, 426
Wolff, Karl 293
Wolfowitz, Paul 141
Woodling, Bruce 102, 106
Woodward, Bob 353
World Anti-Communist League (WACL) 5, 328
World Jewish Congress 32
Wright, Matthew 119, 396
Wyatt, W. Joseph 92, 93, 417
Wylie, Tim 171, 172, 176, 193-195, 197

X

X-Dossiers, The 309, 310, 313, 330, 336, 416
X-Men 56

Y

Yarborough, Don 355

449